D0066159

Britain

Yesterday and Today

1830 to the Present

A History of England

GENERAL EDITOR: *Lacey Baldwin Smith*

I

The Making of England 55 B.C.–1399

C. WARREN HOLLISTER

UNIVERSITY OF CALIFORNIA, SANTA BARBARA

II

This Realm of England 1399–1688

LACEY BALDWIN SMITH

NORTHWESTERN UNIVERSITY

III

The Age of Aristocracy 1688–1830

WILLIAM B. WILLCOX

UNIVERSITY OF MICHIGAN

IV

Britain Yesterday and Today: 1830 TO THE PRESENT

WALTER L. ARNSTEIN

ROOSEVELT UNIVERSITY

Britain

YESTERDAY AND TODAY

1830

TO THE PRESENT

WALTER L. ARNSTEIN
Roosevelt University

D. C. Heath *and Company:* Boston

TO

CHARLOTTE

DA
30
.H65
V.4

Preface

CARL BECKER ONCE COMPLAINED that everybody knows the job of the historian is "to discover and set forth the 'facts' of history." The facts, it is often said, speak for themselves. The businessman talks about hard facts, the statistician refers to cold facts, the lawyer is eloquent about the facts of the case, and the historian, who deals with the incontrovertible facts of life and death, is called a very lucky fellow. Those who speak so confidently about the historian's craft are generally not historians themselves; they are readers of textbooks which more often than not are mere recordings of vital information and listings of dull generalizations. It is not surprising that the historian's reputation has suffered; he has become a peddler of facts and a chronicler who says "this is what happened." The shorter the historical survey, the more likely it is for the textbook writer to assume godlike detachment, spurning the minor tragedies and daily comedies of men, and immortalizing the rise and fall of civilizations, the clash of economic and social forces, and the deeds of titans. Nimbly he moves from the indisputable fact that Henry VIII divorced Catherine of Aragon and married Anne Boleyn to the confident assertion that this helped to produce the Reformation in England. The result is sublime but emasculated history. Men wept when Good Queen Bess died, but historians merely comment that she had lived her allotted three score years and ten. Anglo-Saxon warriors were sick with fear when Viking "swift sea-kings" swept down on England to plunder, rape and kill, but historians dispassionately note that the Norse invasions were a good thing; they allowed the kingdom of Wessex to unite and "liberate" the island in the name of Saxon and Christian defense against heathen marauders. British soldiers rotted by the thousands in the trenches of the First World War, but the terror and agony of that holocaust are lost in the dehumanized statistic that 750,000 British troops died in the four years of war.

In a brief history of even one "tight little island," the chronology of events must of necessity predominate, but if these four volumes are in any way fresh and new, it is because their authors have tried by artistry to step beyond the usual confines of a textbook and to conjure up something of the drama of politics, of the wealth of personalities, and even of the pettiness, as well as the greatness, of human motivation. The price paid will be obvious to anyone seeking total coverage. There is little in these pages on literature, the fine arts or philosophy, except as they throw light upon the uniqueness of English history. On the other hand, the complexities, the uncertainties, the endless variations, and above all the accidents that bedevil the design of human events – these are the very stuff of which history is made, and these are the "truths" which this series seeks to elucidate and preserve. Moreover, the flavor of each volume varies according to the tastes of its author. Sometimes the emphasis is political, sometimes economic or social; but always the presentation is impressionistic – shading, underscoring or highlighting to achieve an image which will be more than a bare outline and will recapture something of the smell and temper of the past.

Each book was conceived and executed as an entity capable of standing by itself, but at the same time the four volumes were designed as a unit. They tell the story of how a small and insignificant outpost of the Roman Empire hesitantly and not always very heroically evolved into the nation which has probably produced and disseminated more ideas and institutions, both good and bad, than any state since Athens. The hope is that these volumes will appeal both to those interested in a balanced portrait of the more discernible segments of English history – *The Making of England* (55 B.C.–1399), *This Realm of England* (1399–1688), *The Age of Aristocracy* (1688–1830) and *Britain Yesterday and Today* (1830 to the present) – and to those who seek the majestic sweep of history in the story of a people whose activities have been wonderfully rich, exciting and varied. Erasmus once wrote, "The important thing for you is not how much you know, but the quality of what you know." In this spirit these volumes have been written.

Lacey Baldwin Smith

Contents

MAPS

Acknowledgment is made for the use of illustrations to the Boston Public Library (p. 71); Culver Pictures (pp. 1, 30, 51, 58, 69, 111, 147, 160, 192, 222, 238, 255, 276, 294, 329); the Cunard Steamship Company, Ltd. (p. 249); the Imperial War Museum (p. 249); from *London Echoing*, by James Bone: Johnathan Cape, Ltd. (p. 321); the London *Daily Express* (p. 314); the Mansell Collection (p. 24); and the Radio Times Hulton Picture Library (p. 178). Maps by Aldren A. Watson.

Chapter 1

𝕽𝖊𝖋𝖔𝖗𝖒 or Revolution?

CHANGE and continuity are the contrasting shades of the historian's spectrum, and any society at any time contains some elements of each. The Britain of 1830 was the product of a heritage receding into the mists of early Anglo-Saxon times and of the often harsh and immediate impact of industrial and political change. The era of the periwig, the gilt-handled sword, and the silk breeches was only yesterday. The century of the top hat and the iron horse, of the umbrella and the blast furnace was new and strange and exciting to a realm that was moving into an unprecedented revolution of mass production, mass housing, mass transportation, and mass destruction.[1]

Alexis de Tocqueville and the Britain of 1830

Most Englishmen were too close to the momentous forces of their age, which were subtly transforming eighteenth-century

---

[1] The two most reliable general accounts of Britain in the first half of the 19th century are E. L. Woodward, *The Age of Reform, 1815–1870* (Oxford, 1938), and Asa Briggs, *The Age of Improvement, 1783–1867* (London, 1958). The most detailed account of the topics discussed in this chapter may be found in Volumes II and III of Elie Halevy's *History of the English People in the Nineteenth Century* (Paperback Edition: London & New York, 1961). Relevant biographical studies include G. M. Trevelyan's *Lord Grey of the Reform Bill* (London, 1920) and Graham Wallas, *Francis Place* (London, 1908).

oligarchs into nineteenth-century plutocrats, to perceive the full import of the change or to evaluate the settled balance between what was old and what was new in 1830. That job was reserved for a shrewd and perceptive Frenchman, Alexis de Tocqueville, who was soon to immortalize his name with his classic description and interpretation of the United States of Andrew Jackson's day, *Democracy in America.* Tocqueville never wrote a similar study of the British Isles, but the notes he took on two trips to Britain during the early 1830s provide a revealing if partial account of how British society impressed a non-British but well read and well traveled contemporary.[2]

Tocqueville surveyed an England still largely rural and unaccustomed to the roar and clatter of the steam locomotive, but he sensed that the future was being molded by the extraordinary changes taking place in commerce and industry—not by the apparently sluggish growth in farm production. Consequently he concentrated his attention on London and a number of provincial cities. He was fascinated by the forces which continued to attract the rural populace to the cities and the factories and by the boundless energy manifested by industrialists and workers alike in growing cities like Birmingham. "These folk never have a minute to themselves," he reported. "They work as if they must get rich by the evening and die the next day." Though appalled by the housing conditions in some of the growing industrial towns and impressed by the number of English people dependent in whole or part on poor relief, Tocqueville appraised the average standard of living in England as superior to that of his native France.

Though England was for Tocqueville a bustling commercial country, it remained equally an intensely aristocratic and class-conscious land. Yet it was clear to the Frenchman that the English aristocracy differed markedly from that of prerevolutionary France. It was smaller; it was more highly respected; and it was far more open to accession from below. Respect, saw Tocqueville, was the result of accessibility: it was because a wealthy merchant had the hope one day of becoming a peer himself that he did not distrust the aristocracy *en masse.* Similarly, the law of primogeniture, in accordance with which only the eldest son inherited his father's titles and estates, resulted in a continual seeping down of the aristocracy into the middle classes, bringing to English upper-class society a cohesion which did not exist in France. Certain professions had become the traditional preserve of the younger sons of the aristocracy. In the case of Tocqueville's friend, Lord Radnor,

---

[2] Alexis de Tocqueville, *Journeys to England and Ireland.* Trans. by George Lawrence and K. P. Mayer. Ed. by J. P. Mayer. (New Haven, 1958).

the eldest son inherited title and fortune, the second son became canon of Salisbury Cathedral, the third a captain in the navy, and the fourth a banker in London. Had there been additional sons, they might well have found comparable openings in the law, by buying commissions in the army, or by becoming administrators in India. Significantly, Tocqueville was less struck by the distinctions between classes based on heredity or law than by the differences based on wealth. Material gain seemed to him to be a primary motive among all classes.

While Englishmen remained a "naturally religious" people, Tocqueville branded the established Church of England as apathetic and unenthusiastic, the staunch defender of the old order which advocated government of and by the well-off and well-connected. The aristocracy and wealthy people generally felt comfortably at home amidst the carpets, upholstered pews, and splendor displayed by many Anglican churches. They also observed family prayers at home, and Tocqueville describes one such service in the home of a titled friend. The family having assembled, some twenty male and female servants all entered in hierarchic order of precedence and took their places about the room, kneeling and facing the wall. The master of the house then read the prayer while the others gave the appropriate responses.

Certain Englishmen may have been accustomed to receive spiritual truths from their social betters, but even more would have nothing to do with an established Church that was silent about the suffering and degradation of humanity found in the slums of Manchester or Leeds. The dissenting denominations — Presbyterians, Congregationalists, and Baptists — had recovered from their eighteenth-century doldrums and were growing in number more quickly than the established church. So was Methodism, that eighteenth-century evangelical offshoot from the Church of England. Yet the nonreligious were growing at a similar rate, and in a city of 300,000 like Manchester, only one inhabitant in four attended church on Sunday. Many a workman who had labored for twelve hours each weekday preferred to spend Sunday in bed or in a neighboring pub.

Tocqueville realized that for all of Britain's monarchical trappings, the center of British politics and the very soul of the kingdom resided in Parliament, that most exclusive and aristocratic club in all of Europe. Membership in the House of Commons was restricted to a minority of the propertied classes: the process of getting into the House could be incredibly expensive, and once there an M.P. received no salary. Although the size of the electorate was limited by a bewildering variety of property qualifications in many boroughs, it remained a costly proposition to canvass a constituency, fetch the voters to the polls, and in some cases feed and house them. Outright bribery was not uncommon in many an old borough whose poorer voters looked upon the bribe as a kind of income. The fact that the ballot was an open one made indirect pressure an obvious possibility, but Tocqueville was impressed at one election he attended by the fearlessness with which voters announced their choice. He was equally struck by the intense interest which such a "saturnalia of English liberty" aroused even among those poorer classes in the community who lacked any direct voice in determining the outcome.

Although Parliament gave direction to the kingdom and created law, most of its inhabitants experienced the full impact of government only on the local level, where the United Kingdom's more than 100 counties and 15,000 parishes remained worlds of their own. A justice of the peace in his county was far more imposing than a distant M.P. sitting at Westminster. Britain was less centralized than contemporary France, for ever since 1689 the unpaid justice of the peace had been a local sovereign, typical of the oligarchical government of the eighteenth century. The new factory towns were often in the grip of similarly oligarchical rulers; but extragovernmental turnpike trusts and local improvement commissions were attempting to cope with the problems created by rapid industrialization. They, rather than the country gentlemen J.P.s, foreshadowed the future pattern of local government.[3]

While some provincial cities were viewed by Tocqueville as harbingers of the future, others were seen as relics of the past. The university towns of Oxford and Cambridge, for example, seemed both architecturally and scholastically back in the Middle Ages. Latin and Greek were the chief subjects taught there, and the exact sciences had gained only indifferent entry into the curriculum. England's two universities were surprisingly small. Oxford had only 1500 students in attendance, and these were on vacation half the year. Many of the fellows who administered Oxford's constituent colleges did almost no work. Their liberty was limited only by the ancient tradition that (in emulation, perhaps, of their monastic predecessors) they not marry. The Oxford and Cambridge of the 1830s had long ceased to serve as refuges for impecunious scholars; tuition was high, and for the most part, it was the wealthy governing class which received its training there. The lower levels of England's education were as diverse and uncentralized as its local government. The efforts of private grammar schools, charity schools, and Sunday schools did result in a majority of adult English men

---

[3] K. B. Smellie, *A History of Local Government*, 3rd ed. (London, 1957).

and women who could read and write. By 1841, two thirds of all bridegrooms and one half of all brides could sign their names rather than their "X's" on the marriage register.

The other provincial cities visited by Tocqueville reflected the staggering industrial changes that were transforming Britain into the workshop of the world. Manchester was the center of the cotton textile industry. It had been built haphazardly, and the workers' hovels seemed carelessly scattered amidst "the huge palaces of industry," the cotton mills which converted ever larger quantities of American cotton into fabrics and thread. Women and children made up three quarters of Manchester's working force, which included some 60,000 Irish immigrants, many of whom lived in damp unsanitary cellars. Paved streets and an efficient sewage system were still largely on the drawing boards. It was Manchester, more than any other city, which was to inspire Marx and Engels with their ideas on class conflict in a capitalistic society. Tocqueville's reactions, however, were ambivalent. "From this foul drain," he wrote, "the greatest stream of human industry flows out to fertilize the whole world." Birmingham, the great center for the manufacture of iron, steel, and copper, seemed healthier, if only because the gulf between workmen and their masters was much less noticeable. And Liverpool, the little fishing village which had grown into a great port on the profits of the slave trade and the cotton trade, was positively "beautiful." What deeply impressed Tocqueville was that Liverpool's highly efficient shipbuilders were able to underbid French competitors in France itself despite the thirty-three percent tariff advantage possessed by the French builders. The city's leaders had the imagination to plan a mile-and-a-half-long railway tunnel under the town so that the port area might be connected more directly with manufacturing cities such as Birmingham and Manchester.

Ultimately, Tocqueville found much to admire in the England of the 1830s, although he discovered numerous paradoxes as well. Despite a closed political system, there *was* liberty of religion, speech, and press (though cheap newspapers remained handicapped by expensive stamp duties). In theory there was even equality before the law, though in actuality it tended to be vitiated by distinctions in wealth. A strong central government paradoxically coexisted with an unsystematic hodgepodge of local governments; yet both were restrained by judicial checks and balances. While Englishmen justly prided themselves on their individuality, Tocqueville was quick to note that they (like Americans) were far more likely than Continentals to found clubs and associations to further scientific, political, and business interests, or simply for recreation. For all its apparent complacency, political stagnation, and oligarchical rule, moreover, England was boiling with intellectual excitement. "In olden times," noted one of Tocqueville's hosts, "the English thought that everything about their constitution was perfect, both advantages and abuses. Today everybody is looking for what needs mending. Sometimes it is one thing, sometimes another but the process never stops." Perhaps this spirit of innovation, Tocqueville concluded, would enable the British so to amend their political structure that they would adjust peacefully to the democratic wave which (sometimes fearfully and sometimes hopefully) he foresaw sweeping the world and would escape the revolutionary violence which had already swept his own country. Tocqueville's prognosis was to prove accurate, but in 1830 the future looked cloudy at best.

The Demand for Reform

The year 1830 witnessed changes on both sides of the Channel: in France another revolution, a relatively bloodless one replacing Charles X, the last of the Bourbons, with Louis-Philippe of the House of Orleans, the "bourgeois king"; in England the succession of King William IV after the death of his brother, George IV. By law, the royal death was followed by a dissolution of Parliament and the holding of a new general election. In this election the subject of "reform" received a great deal of attention.

For a century and a half the mechanisms of the British constitutional structure had remained unaltered. The counties and boroughs of England, Wales, Scotland, and Ireland, despite demographic change, were represented in the House of Commons by the same number of members as at the time of William and Mary, and each borough retained its own particular tradition as to how its representatives were to be chosen. "Pocket" boroughs voted at the beck and call of their wealthy patrons; corporation boroughs were in the careful hands of a coterie of town fathers; and democratic boroughs such as Preston experienced rowdy electioneering, since the entire adult male population possessed the vote. The borough franchise was a matter of local "liberty" and local custom, rather than of Parliamentary statute. The county franchise on the other hand was somewhat more uniform; since 1432 each forty shilling freeholder (the owner of land worth that much in annual rental) had had the vote. By the early nineteenth century this provision would have created virtual universal manhood suffrage in the counties if the vast majority of countrymen had been freeholders. But most of them were leaseholders or tenants or day laborers and thus excluded from the franchise.

This diverse system had come under repeated attack during the later years of the eighteenth century. Some men argued simply that the democratic element of the "mixed" British Constitution, the House of Commons, ought to be made more democratic and more obviously and justly representative of the population, while the aristocratic and monarchical elements embodied in the House of Lords and the King should be allowed to retain their due influence on the government. A reform bill embodying appropriate changes in borough representation and franchise requirements came fairly close to success during the 1780s. The outbreak of the French Revolution in 1789 led to more extreme proposals; and men like Thomas Paine, Joseph Priestley, and William Godwin demanded not only that the House of Commons should be democratized but that the House of Lords and the crown should ultimately be abolished. As Thomas Paine put it, "as there is but one species of man, there can be but one element of human power; and that element is man himself. Monarchy, aristocracy, and democracy, are but creatures of the imagination; and a thousand such may be contrived as well as three. . . ."

The French Revolution briefly inflamed the British reform spirit, only to extinguish it in the end. All reform became associated with the guillotine and the reign of terror, and once Britain and France went to war in 1793, reaction set in. An embattled island, standing at times alone against the Napoleonic colossus, seemed to require political stability rather than change. Thus the social consequences of the industrial inventions and processes which were literally altering the English landscape and which contributed greatly to the ultimate military triumph of 1815 remained unreflected in the country's political structure. By the 1820s, however, reform was once again in the air, and political radicals, conservative Whigs, and aggressive industrialists all clamored in diverse ways for a fundamental change in the political system.

The practical political problem was, of course, that if a far-reaching political shift was to come about, it had to take place (barring revolution) inside Parliament itself. This meant, in a large number of cases, that M.P.s had to vote themselves out of power. This practical dilemma helps explain as readily as any appeal to abstract principle why men who were willing to reform the criminal code, alter ancient tariffs, and ease the political lot of religious minorities like Roman Catholics were far more reluctant to tackle a measure of general political reform. Yet if nothing was done, there was the haunting fear that the patience of the unenfranchised (especially of the new industrial classes) might become exhausted, and that the nineteenth century, like the seventeenth, would prove to be a revolutionary century in British history.

Tories and Whigs

One of the factors which helps to account for the ultimate timing of the Great Reform Bill was the breakup during the later 1820s of the ruling Tory party. It is an historical commonplace to point out that political parties in the eighteenth century did not mean what they do today; that government then was not party government, and that the situation in Parliament was complicated by the existence of family connections, of true independents, and of men who for reasons of patronage or habit always supported the Cabinet nominated by the king. Yet the terms "Whig" and "Tory" were used by eighteenth-century politicians and can be traced as far back as the 1670s. There were Whig and Tory tendencies on particular political issues, such as those dealing with the civil rights of Protestant dissenters and the practical power of the king; and during the long prime ministership of William Pitt the Younger (1784–1801; 1804–1806), a revived Tory party became dominant in Parliament. Opposition to the French Revolution and resistance to any tampering with time-honored English institutions became the Tory *raison d'etre*. During the prime ministership of Lord Liverpool (1812–27), the party first basked in the reflected triumph of Waterloo but later had to face the problem of dealing with the symptoms, if not the causes, of postwar economic distress. The "Peterloo Massacre" and the Six Acts of 1819 demonstrated that the Tory Government was better at silencing dissent than in curing its causes.

During the 1820s the party became enlivened with fresh faces in the Cabinet, and a shift in policy took place. Lord Liverpool remained Prime Minister, but in 1822 George Canning replaced Viscount Castlereagh as Tory leader of the House of Commons. Canning held no brief for parliamentary reform, but he was convinced that it could be avoided only if his party could win a reputation for being just a little less repressive and a little more willing to see merit in change. Under Canning, Toryism began to give up its intransigent stand against reform. The Combination Acts preventing the organization of trade unions were partially repealed. That harsh and capricious relic of the past, the criminal code which had demanded capital punishment even for the theft of two shillings, was softened and partially modernized. The first steps were taken to rationalize and lower the hodgepodge of the tariff system.

Not even the death of both Liverpool and Canning in 1827 and the selection in 1828 of that old warrior and Tory diehard, the Duke of Wellington, as the country's Prime Minister would stem the tide of reform. The Duke acquiesced in the repeal of those pillars of the ancient order — the Stuart Test and Corporation Acts, barring Catholics and dissenters from holding public office. Emancipating Protestant dissenters proved relatively easy, but opening the doors of Parliament to Catholics caused a furor and became one of the issues which eventually broke up the Tory party. Faced with the threat of civil war in Ireland unless Catholic Emancipation was granted, Wellington finally gave way. He feared that civil war in Ireland might restore the Whigs to power in England, a prospect he apparently viewed with even less favor than the presence of a few Catholic M.P.s at Westminster. The only stumbling block that remained was King George IV who, as his father before him, was convinced that a concession on Catholic Emancipation meant the violation of his coronation oath to uphold the privileges of the Church of England. By March 1829, the king was at last won over, and a Catholic Emancipation Bill was passed. It was coupled with a political "reform" bill raising Irish franchise requirements in order to assure the election of upper-class Catholics only.

In retrospect the repeal of the Test and Corporation Acts and Catholic Emancipation appear as milestones along the road to complete religious toleration in England. Yet from the point of view of the Tory party of 1829, they were most unfortunate, for the party was now split three ways. One wing was represented by the Canningites, many of whom had been excluded from Wellington's Cabinet in 1828. At the other extreme were the ultra-Tories who felt certain that in his treatment of the Catholic Question, the Duke had betrayed the principles of his party. In the middle now were Wellington and Sir Robert Peel, who had won his political reputation as a politically orthodox Chief Secretary for Ireland and as a cautiously reform-minded Home Secretary. In a sense the ultra-Tories were right. Their principles had been betrayed, for one of these principles had long involved the support of the Anglican Church as the one true church and therefore as the sole church whose members possessed full political privileges. Another principle of the party had been resistance to revolution, resistance to change. The underlying assumption of the party was that the time-tested fabric of the state was inviolable. Yet now that the need for change had been recognized in Ireland, the whole logic of resisting change — fundamental change — in England as well was going bankrupt. Wellington refused to see the logic of this position and remained in office, refusing to heed all demands for further reform, while his party was disintegrating around him.

Complementing the breakup of the Tory party in Parliament during the later 1820s was a revival of the Whigs. The role of the Whigs in Parliament during the previous half century is reflected in a capsule biography of Lord Grey, in many respects not the person one would expect to find as leader at one of the most significant turning points in British history. By 1830, Lord Grey had been a Member of Parliament, first in the Commons and then the Lords, for 44 years. He had entered the lower house as a precocious young man of 22 and had participated in the debates on parliamentary reform during the 1780s and early 1790s as a Foxite Whig. But then had come the French Revolution and, tarred by the brush of Jacobinism, reform ceased to be an issue of practical politics. Grey, like many another Whig magnate, retired to his country estate and visited Parliament only on occasion. He continued to pay lip service to a program featuring parliamentary reform, financial retrenchment, relief for Protestant dissenters, and the abolition of slavery in the British Empire; but for thirty years the cause of parliamentary reform — like that of world government in our time — remained a principle but not a policy.

During the 1820s, political reform became an issue again. M.P.s were introducing reform bills into Parliament, and radicals both inside and outside Parliament were suggesting much more extreme changes in the British constitutional structure. Lord Grey was no extremist. He agreed with the eighteenth-century viewpoint that a voice in politics belonged primarily to men of property, but in defining property, he became the champion of the men of new wealth by his willingness to include businessmen as well as landowners, London bankers and Manchester manufacturers as well as landed aristocrats. Then, too, Whigs like Lord Grey could never completely forget that the beginnings of their party had been based upon change, upon a revolution indeed, even if it was the relatively bloodless and respectable Revolution of 1688. The comparably bloodless and respectable French Revolution of 1830 provided Lord Grey and other advocates of reform with an additional incentive to seek political change in Britain.

The Great Reform Bill

The death of George IV and the new general election were to give Lord Grey his chance, even though the results of the election of 1830 were far from conclusive. Only in a minority of seats was there any real electoral contest, and it was by no means immediately clear that the Duke of Wellington and

Toryism had been repudiated. The cry for reform was more often heard, however, in the new Parliament than in the old, and when early in November 1830 the Duke made a bristling speech declaring that no possible change in the British constitution could improve upon the system that already existed, Whigs and Radicals were aroused, and even some moderate Tories were upset. When two weeks later the Cabinet was defeated on an important policy question in the House of Commons, Wellington handed in his resignation as Prime Minister. King William thereupon called upon Lord Grey to form a ministry. Thus at the age of 66, Grey found himself Prime Minister. The Whigs were back in power (though the new ministry contained a minority of moderate Tories as well). Radicals outside Parliament were clamoring for reform. Reform was ceasing to be a theory; it had become an opportunity to find new and lasting strength for a party which had spent the greater part of fifty years in the political wilderness.

In March 1831 Lord John Russell [4] introduced into the House of Commons a reform bill to disenfranchise dozens of small boroughs and to enfranchise numerous large ones and to make uniform the property qualifications of borough voters. Four important forces were now to become involved: the radicals outside Parliament for whom the bill might not go far enough; the House of Commons, for which it might be too much; the House of Lords, for which it was certain to seem to be a dangerous revolution; and King William IV, who was not opposed to a degree of reform on principle, but who would have much preferred that nobody become agitated about anything.

Grey was confronted with the problem of convincing the politically active groups outside Parliament that the bill went far enough to suit them. At first they were unsure. They sought universal manhood suffrage and a secret ballot and the bill obviously provided neither. But once the Tories began to attack the bill as a dangerously radical measure which, by depriving old boroughs of their right to representation, would confiscate private property without compensation, would transfer political power to the urban population, and would lead to the destruction of the monarchy, the radicals became convinced that the measure was worth fighting for. While for Lord Grey and his Whig colleagues the measure was a final one which would "remove at once, and for ever, all rational grounds for complaint from

---

[4] Grey's Cabinet consisted of ten peers and only three commoners. Russell's title was an honorary one which meant that his father was a member of the Lords though Russell himself had been elected to the Commons.

the minds of the intelligent and independent portion of the community," for the radicals it was merely a first step, a necessary prerequisite for the reforms they championed concerning the currency, the tariff, and local government.

The Whigs and the radicals thus had little in common, but for the moment this was forgotten as groups like Thomas Atwood's Birmingham "Political Union of the Lower and Middle Classes of the People" and Francis Place's London-centered "National Political Union" began to agitate in favor of the bill. "Nothing [is] talked of, thought of, dreamt of," wrote a contemporary diarist, "but Reform. Every creature one meets asks, What is said Now? How will it go? What is the last news? What do you think? and so it is from morning till night, in the streets, in the clubs, and in the private houses." On the night of March 22, the bill came to its second reading, and with the House of Commons crowded with more members than had ever before crammed themselves within its walls, the crucial vote came at 3 A.M. the next morning. The bill passed by a majority of one (302–301).

A one-vote majority was hardly sufficient for a bill which, though approved in principle, had still to be taken up clause by clause in the House of Commons and to be pushed through the House of Lords. A Commons defeat of one such clause a week later caused Lord Grey to advise the king to dissolve Parliament and ask for new elections. The election of 1831 was, in contrast to previous general elections, a referendum on a single issue, whether "the bill, the whole bill, and nothing but the bill" should be approved. By no means all constituencies had electoral contests, but wherever more than one candidate stood for election the victory went to the reformers. This became apparent in July, when a new reform bill introduced by Lord John Russell passed its second reading in the House of Commons by a vote of 367–231. It was subject to delays in committee — where it was voted on clause by clause — but in October it did reach the House of Lords. After a five-day debate, the Lords defeated the bill, 199–158. The result was to bring the nation to the very edge of revolution. Two London newspapers came out with black borders as a sign of mourning. The council of the Birmingham Union discussed the formation of a national guard as a prelude to possible violence. Birmingham armament manufacturers were prepared to supply their workers with guns and munitions should such a step ultimately seem necessary.

In December 1831 Lord Grey's ministry tried again. For a third time it introduced a reform bill with provisions substantially as before. Again it passed the House of Commons, and in April 1832 the principle of the bill was with the help of Tory "waverers" also approved, 184–175, by the House of Lords.

When the upper chamber began, however, to hack the details of the bill to pieces in committee, Lord Grey, basing himself on the precedent of Queen Anne's action in 1712, requested that the king either create fifty additional peers to provide a Whig majority or else accept the Government's resignation. William suggested that the creation of twenty peers might be satisfactory but that fifty were too many. He therefore accepted Grey's resignation and again called upon the Duke of Wellington to form a ministry. Once more the country seemed on the verge of revolution. Radical leaders urged their followers to stage a run on the banks and to refuse to pay taxes until Wellington resigned. After a week Wellington did resign, for by 1832 it had become impossible to be Prime Minister of England in the face of an obviously hostile House of Commons and an even more hostile public outside its doors.

With great reluctance William IV asked Grey to resume his office, and with even greater reluctance he agreed to appoint the fifty Whig peers Grey deemed necessary. The moment the king agreed, the battle was over. The Lords did not wish to be swamped, and they went on to approve the bill with little further ado. Wellington himself, out of a sense of duty to his monarch, abstained. On June 7, 1832, the bill received the royal assent and became the law of the land. The crisis had passed, but bitter recriminations were exchanged by both sides. While the Tories blamed the Whigs for arousing the public outside Parliament, the Whigs with justice retorted that they had saved the country from the revolution toward which Tory obstinacy was heading it. The country's political structure had been strengthened rather than weakened, for concession to sustained popular demand was the wisest policy for a governing aristocracy. Lord Grey, who continued to distrust radicals and who remained in every sense an aristocrat, found to his own surprise that he had become a popular hero in the bargain. The passing of the bill was everywhere greeted with the ringing of church bells, with illuminations and banquets, and Lord Grey, on a journey to the north of England, found his carriage repeatedly stopped and himself acclaimed. He could not understand it, he confided to an acquaintance. "My speeches were uniformly and strongly conservative in the true sense of the word."

Significance and Aftermath

The significance of the Reform Bill of 1832 lies only partly in its provisions. Indeed the student who reads its clauses today is unlikely to look upon it as particularly radical and more likely to concur with Lord Grey's assessment of its conservative nature. There was a redistribution of seats, so that each of 56 boroughs, including one uninhabited cow pasture, was deprived of its two M.P.s. Thirty additional small boroughs were deprived of one of their two members. Twenty-two new two-member boroughs and twenty new one-member boroughs were created, and sixty-five additional seats were distributed among the English counties. While metropolitan London and the industrializing Midlands and North were to be less underrepresented than before, numerous anomalies remained and the "pocket borough," the seat under the virtual control of a particular landed magnate, did not disappear completely.

In the boroughs the right to vote was uniformly granted to all urban householders who either owned a house worth £10 a year or paid rent of £10 a year or more. About one fourth to one third of the houses in an average borough fell into this category, and rents in London were so high that almost all genuine householders were enfranchised. In the counties the vote was extended to men who held property on lease as well as to freeholders. This was a step toward universal suffrage which at the same time tended to increase the electoral influence of landlords over their tenants, since all voting continued to be by public declaration.

One of the most important innovations made by the act was the substitution of a uniform regulation for local diversity in governing the borough franchise. The result was the disenfranchisement of voters in a few of the more democratic boroughs, but it is estimated that the total electorate increased by some 50 percent. One Englishman in five was now eligible to vote, and some 620,000 voters in England (and 814,000 in the British Isles as a whole) were registered at the general election of 1834. Moreover, as the population rose and as prosperity increased, the number of £10 householders in the electorate would grow accordingly even without further legislative change. From the Duke of Wellington's point of view, the harm had been done. "The revolution is made," he declared in 1833; "that is to say power is transferred from one class of society, the gentlemen of England professing the faith of the Church of England, to another class of society, the shopkeepers being dissenters from the church, many of them being Socinians [i.e. Unitarians], others atheists." Such a judgment was premature to say the least. The majority of Members of Parliament continued to be aristocratic in background during the generation that followed.

Although the Reform Act had in no sense established democracy in Britain, the measure may yet be described as a major step toward democracy because it led directly and inevitably to an overhauling of English local government, because it materially weakened the position of both the monarch and the

House of Lords, and because of the manner in which it became law. The newly reformed House of Commons decisively re-organized town government in the Municipal Corporation Act of 1835. This "postscript to the Reform Bills" dissolved 200 old corporations and set up in their place 179 municipal boroughs, each with a mayor and a fixed number of popularly elected town councillors who in turn chose a third of their number to be alder-men. Many a self-perpetuating small oligarchy, whose chief interest may well have been to choose two members of Parlia-ment rather than to govern a town, was thus replaced by a council chosen by and responsible to all the ratepayers of the community. The mandatory jurisdiction of the new municipal councils extended primarily over police and gaslight service, while sewers, street paving, and the water supply often remained in private hands or under the jurisdiction of independent im-provement commissioners. Yet, as in the case of the Reform Bill itself, uniformity of procedure replaced an often less equitable diversity, and in the course of the century the new municipal corporations tended to absorb functions still remaining in pri-vate hands.

The Reform Bill's effect upon the monarchy was even more immediate. It proved once again that in case of crisis, the crown could no longer hold out against the wishes of a Cabinet repre-senting the majority of the House of Commons. King William IV was not powerless, and on the question of the creation of peers he had resisted, but eventually he gave in just as his brother George IV had given in on Catholic Emancipation three years before. Step by step over the previous fifty years, the Hanoverian monarchs had been deprived, not of their theoretical authority, but of their practical ability to interfere with the political life of the realm. The Economic Reform Act of 1782 had limited the number of patronage positions, and between 1815 and 1822 over two thousand sinecures and comparable government positions were abolished.

The very character of the Hanoverians contributed to their decline. The intermittent and then permanent insanity of George III had necessarily limited that monarch's active role in politics during his later years. He had been succeeded first as regent and then as king by his son George IV. George IV had certain amiable qualities as a human being and as a patron of art and architecture, but in matters of personal morality and administrative diligence, he retains an unsavory reputation.[5] His relations with his wife were so bad that when in 1821 a royal messenger reported Napoleon's death to him with the words:

---

[5] J. H. Plumb, *The First Four Georges* (London, 1956).

"Your Majesty's greatest enemy is dead," the king expostulated: "Is *she*, by God!"

George IV had numerous mistresses, spent lavish sums of money, and was constantly in debt. Parliament was repeatedly asked to bail him out by appropriating extra sums. He did not endear himself to that body when, in the midst of the Napoleonic wars, with every Englishman expected to support the war effort and to give up peacetime luxuries and with food in often dangerously short supply, George not only boasted the best French chef of the day as personal cook but invited guests to everyday meals in which they had a choice of 116 different dishes served in nine different courses together with a multitude of wines. On special occasions the dinners would be even more complex. In an age in which the doings of crown prince, regent, and king were reported in great detail and often accompanied by hostile caricatures, it is understandable that George IV should come to be positively loathed by many middle-class Englishmen whose attitudes toward private morality and businesslike efficiency were beginning to assume the mantle we call Victorian. To such people, the King seemed to be a wasteful, immoral nonentity. No wonder then that *The Times* of London, that pillar, then as now, of respectability, monarchy, and history, should have published the most scathing of obituaries upon the King's demise in 1830: "There never was an individual less regretted by his fellow countrymen than this deceased king. What eye has wept for him? What heart has heaved one sob of unmercenary sorrow?"

William IV rated only slightly higher in the eyes of many of his subjects. He had lived for many years with a Mrs. Jordan, who had borne him ten illegitimate children before he had married his legal queen Adelaide at the age of 57. The *Spectator* took his death in 1837 very much in stride: "His late Majesty, though at times a jovial and, for a king, an honest man, was a weak, ignorant, commonplace sort of person." Quite obviously the British monarchy had reached a low point of prestige by the 1820s and 1830s. It had survived as an institution, but the widespread feeling of contempt toward George IV and William IV played a significant role in the decline of political influence on the part of the monarch.

An even greater role was played by the recrystallization of a fairly strong parliamentary two-party system by 1830 over the issue of reform. The stronger the party organization the more obvious was the leader of each party and the smaller was the choice for the king. In a parliament made up of numerous small factions with no deep ideological issues dividing them, and of numerous members who owed their jobs to royal favor, the monarch had much room to maneuver. The Reform Bill of

1832, in enlarging the electorate and making franchise requirements more uniform, encouraged not only the strengthening of the parliamentary party but helped bring about the beginnings of a national party organization as well. The more clearly the House of Commons could be said to reflect the will of the British people, the less plausibly could a monarch oppose it in the name of the "true" interests of his subjects. Thus the Reform Bill clearly weakened the political influence of the monarch.

The bill had a comparable effect upon the House of Lords. Not only had the course of the struggle demonstrated that in a showdown the House of Commons was the more powerful of the two chambers, but the act had weakened the chamber in another way. The significance of the House of Commons as the center of the more important debates and often the more vital personalities in politics had been clear as far back as the seventeenth century, but before 1832 the influence of the peerage had been felt less through the House of Lords itself than through the electoral influence its members exercised in the House of Commons. The peers were after all the very "borough-mongers" who had controlled so many seats in the Commons. Many if not all of these pocket boroughs had been abolished by the bill.

Yet it would be an error to dismiss the Lords after 1832 as a dying breed. Numerically, indeed, they were still increasing. In the mid-eighteenth century there had been less than two hundred peers; by 1830 there were more than five hundred. As many traditional eighteenth-century sinecures were abolished, both the monarchs and Prime Ministers had increasingly come to look upon the peerage as a suitable reward for political or other distinction. As a consequence the House of Lords, which had feared swamping in 1832, had, in another sense, already been swamped during the previous half century. Yet if the scarcity value of the peerage had declined, the social importance of peers remained very great during the mid-Victorian years; and, despite Wellington's fears, criticism of the House of Lords tended to abate for more than a generation.

At the same time that the Reform Bill had weakened the interest of king, peers, and landed gentlemen, it had notably strengthened the position of the new custodians of industrial wealth who now shared with old-line oligarchs the rule of the kingdom. The fundamental political imbalance caused by industrialization had been largely rectified, and it was no coincidence that within fourteen years of political reform, that bastion of Tory economic policy, the Corn Laws, should have been repealed or that within another generation liberal ideas, both in politics and trade, should have completely revamped Great Britain's economic and governmental systems.

Finally, it was the peaceful manner in which the bill was pushed through Parliament by the force of public opinion and extraparliamentary agitation which made the Reform Bill a landmark along the road to democracy. Perhaps the ultimate significance of the bill lies in the fact that it passed at all and without revolution. It proved, as Peel and Wellington had rightly predicted, the first act of the play rather than the last, yet within a very short time it was accepted even by diehard Tories who had dreaded its passage. Radicals, Whigs, and Tories had all learned one crucial lesson which they were to apply repeatedly during the succeeding century. When the object was reform, it was possible in the last resort to gain fundamental change peacefully. Henceforth, whatever the grievance, political agitation was not merely a legitimate but a practical way to achieve reform. The battle might be long and the opposition obdurate, but provided the grievance was real and enough people truly wanted change, a remedy by means of legislation rather than revolution was possible.

Chapter 2

The 𝕽𝖆𝖎𝖑𝖜𝖆𝖕 Age

IF WE WISH to understand the economic foundations of the Britain which had successfully weathered the Reform Bill crisis and comprehend the forces that had persuaded eighteenth-century oligarchs to share the good things of political life with nineteenth-century plutocrats, a few statistics are in order.[1]

The People

The population of England, Wales, and Scotland in 1831 was 16,161,183 — more than twice as many people as had lived in those areas seventy years earlier. Late in the eighteenth century, authorities had still debated whether the population of the country was increasing or decreasing, but the first official census of 1801 had helped make clear what every successive census confirmed, that despite considerable emigration the total population was on the rise. The average birthrate remained

---

[1] Still the most important single source of information for the subjects treated in this chapter is J. H. Clapham, *An Economic History of Modern Britain,* Vol. I (*The Early Railway Age, 1820–1850*), 2nd ed. (Cambridge, 1930). Much pertinent information is found in D. C. Douglas (General Editor), *English Historical Documents,* Vol. XII (Part I), which deals with the period 1833–1874 (London, 1956). Highly informative but somewhat technical is W. W. Rostow, *British Economy of the Nineteenth Century* (Oxford, 1948).

high, approximately 32 per 1000, while the death rate was substantially less, approximately 22 per 1000; and by 1851, the
population of England, Wales, and Scotland had swelled to
20,816,351. By 1851 something else had happened as well.
For the first time in the history of any large country, a majority
of the population lived in towns and cities. Not until 1920 did
the same situation prevail in the United States. The census of
1851 revealed a type of migration even more startling than that
across the Atlantic, the migration from farm to city. Of every
thirty-three city dwellers in the Britain of 1851 only thirteen
were city born. The towns and cities, for the most part, were
very new, very shoddy, and very crowded.

Earlier in the century Napoleon had taunted the English
with being "a nation of shopkeepers," and many of them still
were precisely that in the 1830s and 1840s. For a generation the
large-scale cotton mill, the huge iron foundry, and the deep coal
mine had been the portents of the future, but much manufacturing remained in the hands of small merchants or craftsmen with
only a handful of employees. Agriculture also continued to
play a highly significant role. For not only was one family in
five still engaged almost solely in farming, but the rural scene
included thousands of cobblers, blacksmiths, bricklayers, customer weavers, shopkeepers, and peddlers, who were part of a
traditional rural life rather than representatives of an industrializing urban society.

More people lived in the countryside in 1851 than had lived
on the entire island a century before. Much of the land was
divided into large estates owned by wealthy and socially significant landlords but not farmed directly by the men who
legally owned it. More than half the land was divided into farms
200 acres or larger, considerably larger than the average French
or German farm of the nineteenth century. Such estates were
especially common in southeastern England, but in Wales, Yorkshire, and Scotland, the family farm (held on long lease and
farmed without the help of regular outside labor) was widely
known. For every family which owned or occupied land on long
lease, there were two and a half families of hired laborers who
lived in small cottages with rarely more than two rooms and
often without a fireplace.

The process of enclosure had by the 1830s prevailed over
the common field system of earlier centuries, but though every
farm owner or occupier was now his own master in deciding
what crops to plant, this did not mean that all the improvement
brought by the eighteenth-century "agricultural revolution" had
borne fruit. Root crops were now a common substitute for the
practice of leaving land fallow, but while turnips were good
for the soil, they had a limited appeal as a diet staple. Agricul-

tural chemistry was still in its infancy, and few machines had eased the traditional farm toil. A steam-operated tractor proved to be an impractical luxury for most farmers. A mechanical thresher came into somewhat wider use during the 1830s, but its introduction had provoked widespread riots during a period of depression in 1829–1830. A practical reaper still lay in the future. The 1830s and 1840s were years of anxiety for the average farmer. The prosperous Napoleonic War years had been followed by intermittent depression ever since. Prices for wheat and most other grains tended in a downward direction, and even though the urban market was constantly increasing, prices received for beef and dairy products were tending downward also. The specter of overseas competition was drawing closer, and few individuals during these years regarded farming as the road to easy riches. As a result the wages and working conditions of agricultural laborers remained pretty much the same. The custom of giving each laborer his own garden or "allotment" was on the increase, but otherwise there was no apparent advance in his standard of living.

Industry and Banking

If Britain's "agricultural revolution" was a spotty and unsystematic development, can the same be said also of her much-vaunted "industrial revolution"? Certainly the term requires precise definition, for while there had been changes aplenty, no single British industry had undergone a complete technical revolution by 1830. The factory system had become the accepted method of organization in the cotton industry; the more than fifty cotton mills of Manchester employed on the average more than 400 workers apiece, and a few employed over a thousand. Yet the cotton mills were still in many ways uncharacteristic. They employed at most one person in thirty, and at the very time that 60,000 steam-powered looms had been installed, there still remained 240,000 handloom weavers. There were a few large iron foundries, shipyards, and pottery manufacturers as well, but the small workshop remained commonplace. The small retail shop remained even more commonplace as the primary method of distribution, and Campbell's in Glasgow with its 64 employees was the closest approach to a city department store. Open-air market stalls remained popular and survive even in the Britain of the 1960s.

One reason why small-scale manufacture continued to be widespread was that ever since the economic crash of 1720 known as the South Sea Bubble, the creation of joint-stock corporations had been made very difficult; they required either a Royal Charter or a separate Act of Parliament. The individual ownership or the partnership was thus the customary mode of organization, and it remained difficult for concerns under such auspices to raise large sums of capital because the law did not extend to them the legal privilege of limited liability. (Limited liability meant that an investor in a company which had gone bankrupt stood to lose only the sum of his investment; his other holdings were legally inviolate in the payment of creditors.) While the "Bubble Act" was repealed in 1825 and joint-stock companies were generally legalized in 1844, there remained widespread doubts about the ethics of limited liability, and not until Lowe's Act of 1856 was the right of limited liability generally accepted.

It is necessarily fallacious to speak of the process of industrialization as if it took place in a vacuum. A sizable urban population requires a sufficient food supply. A growing industrial society requires a sound currency and banking system. By the early nineteenth century, Britain had both. The Bank of England, founded in 1694, had come to seem to many Englishmen a financial Rock of Gibraltar. It had successfully weathered the financial crises of the Napoleonic wars. From 1797 until 1819 it had suspended the automatic exchange of its currency for gold on demand, but with the resumption of specie payment in the latter year, the British pound had become increasingly wedded to the gold standard. Peel's Bank Charter Act of 1844 indeed strengthened both the adherence of the Bank of England to the gold standard and its dominance in the issuing of currency. Hitherto, the expanding number of country banks had had the privilege of issuing currency outside the London metropolitan area. The Act of 1844 forbade newly chartered banks to issue their own currency, but it was not until the early twentieth century that the country had a single currency system. By this time, to be sure, the system of writing "cheques" had come to be substituted for many of the transactions which had been settled by the transfer of currency a hundred years before. The banking system was accompanied by a growing number of insurance companies, and by a variety of stock and commodity exchanges, most of which clustered near the Bank of England in the original borough of London.

Transportation

As important an adjunct to the process of industrialization as any other was transportation, for mass production is clearly unprofitable if the reduction in cost is eaten up by the expenses of moving the product to its potential customers. The traditional English modes of transportation, the navigable rivers, the coastal seas, and the network of usually badly kept roads and footpaths had come to seem less than satisfactory to many eighteenth-century Englishmen. In the latter part of that century the traditional system was supplemented by the building of turnpikes and canals. Good roads made it possible to travel by coach from London to Edinburgh in 43½ hours, but coaches and horses were ill adapted to moving bulky merchandise. The fact that this almost invariably went by water served as an incentive for the construction of canals to supplement the navigable river system. In the course of some eighty-five years, beginning in 1761 with the Duke of Bridgewater's canal from Manchester to Liverpool, a network of 2,500 miles of canals was built. Transportation costs on canals were only one quarter to one half as high as the cost of road carriage, but canal boats remained narrow and the traffic was slow. The boats were pulled by horses at an average speed of only 2½ miles an hour.

In the course of two decades, this relatively slow evolution of means of transportation was to undergo a drastic shift in favor of what Englishmen came to call the railway. The early history of the railway shows it to be, like Watt's steam engine of the 1770s, a by-product of the coal industry. Numerous short stretches of track were built to enable coal carts to be pulled along railed tracks by men or horses from colliery to riverside dock. During the Napoleonic wars, the increasing expense of horses and their fodder provided a new incentive for the development of alternate means of pulling the carts. Permanent steam engines which pulled the carts by means of cables were one possibility. Another was a mobile steam engine or locomotive which could pull a train of carts. In 1821 Thomas Gray published his *Observations on a General Iron Railway or Land Steam Conveyance; to supersede the Necessity of Horses in all Public Vehicles; showing its vast Superiority in every respect, over all the present Pitiful Methods of Conveyance by Turnpike Roads, Canals, and Coasting-Traders,* but before Gray's wordy prediction could be realized, a dependable iron rail and a reliable steam locomotive had to be invented. George Stephenson (1781–1848) played a highly significant role in the development of both. In 1825 the Stockton & Darlington line opened, the world's first public railway to carry goods other than coal with the aid of a steam locomotive. In 1830, with even greater fanfare, there was inaugurated the Liverpool & Manchester Railway. Stephenson's *Rocket* pulled a passenger train at speeds as high as thirty-five miles an hour. "You can't imagine," wrote one lyrical passenger, "how strange it seemed to be

First- and third-class coaches on the Manchester-Liverpool Railway in the 1830's. From a contemporary print.

journeying on thus, without any visible cause of progress other than the magical machine, with its flying white breath and rhythmical unvarying pace...." That the "magical machine" was a potential monster as well was made clear on the same occasion when in a freak accident a locomotive killed William Huskisson, the former President of the Board of Trade, while he was strolling with friends along a parallel track.

With the popular and financial success of the Liverpool & Manchester Railway established, a "sordid, selfish, and eventually ruinous saturnalia of railway speculation" began. Initially railway companies resembled turnpike trusts, and only in the late 1830s did it become clear that the companies would monopolize transportation on the tracks they built rather than open the roads to every individual carriage as turnpikes did. Nor did an alternate form of transportation, individual steam omnibuses using ordinary roads, catch on with the public. Whatever the cost in human lives, business reputations, and personal fortunes, by 1850 the "railway mania" had brought about a revolution in transportation:

YEAR	MILES OF LINE	NUMBER OF PASSENGERS	TOTAL CAPITAL INVESTED
1842	1,857	18,453,504	(1843)£ 65,530,792
1846	3,036	43,790,983	126,296,369
1850	6,621	72,854,422	240,270,745

By 1844 even Parliament had come to realize that what was taking shape was not a series of local improvements but a new national transportation system. And, indeed, this was the very thing which men like George Hudson, onetime linendraper and mayor of York, were seeking. During the 1840s Hudson succeeded in negotiating dozens of amalgamations and creating the London & Midlands railways system, a model for other big systems to follow. Unlike other major countries (including the United States, in which Congress subsidized railroads with huge land grants), the initial British railway system was built almost solely with private capital; but as early as 1844 Parliament began the process of regulation. Laws required that there should be at least one train a day on each line in both directions. It should travel on the average (stops included) at least twelve miles an hour. The maximum charge for passengers was to be a penny a mile. Children under three should be carried free and under twelve at half fare.

The basic English railway network was complete by 1850, although branch lines were to increase the total mileage considerably. The economic consequences were monumental. The turnpike and canal building booms stopped. Coaches ceased to ply the English roads and posthouses decayed. Many of the turnpike trusts were dissolved, and road building did not again become a national concern until the coming of the automobile in the twentieth century. The canals remained and some continued to serve as useful subsidiary means of transportation for bulky goods like coal, but no new ones were built. The railroads helped bring a vast expansion in the production of iron: 650,000 tons were manufactured in 1830 and 2,000,000 tons in 1848. A comparable expansion of coal production, from 21 million tons in 1826 to 44 million tons in 1846, was similarly stimulated by the railway. Accompanying the lengthening lines of track from the late 1840s on were the soon familiar telegraph poles and wires which by 1852 connected all major British cities.

The cost of transportation of many goods came to be a fraction of what it had been before. Railway construction, moreover, provided a new source of employment. During the 1840s as many as 200,000 village lads and Irish immigrants worked on rail construction gangs. Cattle drovers who since medieval times had driven their cattle from Devon, Hereford, and Scotland to East Anglia for fattening and then to London for market now shipped the animals direct by rail. Milk for the metropolitan areas could now be sent by morning milk train from thirty or forty miles away. The railways aided the post office, made possible the national distribution of London newspapers, and stimulated architects to design enormous Victorian gothic palaces to serve as the major terminuses of the railway lines. Even provincial stations could boast their ornate waiting rooms.

The social effects of the coming of the railway were equally significant. The average middle-class resident of eighteenth-century Birmingham had not visited London in an entire lifetime even though it was only a hundred miles away. By 1850 rail travel for almost all classes of Englishmen had ceased to be a novelty. Railway travel tended to bring Englishmen from various regions and various ranks of society into temporary communion, even if it gave new support to the notion that mid-nineteenth-century Englishmen, like the inhabitants of Plato's *Republic*, were divided into precisely three classes. Initially third class passengers simply rode in open trucks (see illustration) but the act of 1844 suggested that even such persons be protected from the rain. Evangelical moralists were inspired to compare life's pilgrimage to a railway journey:

The line to Heaven by us is made,
With heavenly truth the rails are laid;

From Earth to Heaven the line extends
And in eternal life it ends. . . .

The railway affected the everyday language of Englishmen as well, as men began to speak of "getting up steam" and "blowing off steam" and to reckon distances in hours and minutes rather than in miles. Finally, the railway came to represent the most obvious example of human progress, and Alfred Lord Tennyson urged:

Let the great world spin forever down the ringing grooves
   of change.

The poet laureate had not apparently taken a close look at the T-shaped rails on which his railway carriage sped.

Working Conditions

In many a history book, the 1820s, 1830s, and 1840s of British history have gone down not as years of dynamic progress—when the economy grew at a faster rate than ever before or since—but as years of suffering and deprivation, as that "bleak age" in which the "evils of the industrial revolution" made themselves manifest.[2] It has become almost a twentieth-century truism that the early nineteenth-century factory owner ground the faces of his workers in the dust, and evidence substantiating the pitiful conditions under which many an English worker labored during these years is indeed plentiful. Parliamentary blue books, those huge ponderous volumes which record in stenographic detail the hearings held and the conclusions reached by Royal Commissions and Select Committees investigating mines and factories, bear witness that hours were long and times often hard. Samuel Coulson told one Parliamentary Committee in 1832 about how in "brisk time" his children were expected to be in the cotton mills by 3 A.M. and to work until 10 P.M. with no more than an hour in all for mealtime breaks. In ordinary times they worked from 6 A.M. to 8:30 P.M. six days a week for a total wage of three shillings. Other women and

---

[2] The more pessimistic point of view is presented in such works as *The Age of the Chartists, 1832–1854* by J. L. and Barbara Hammond (London, 1930), the more optimistic by T. S. Ashton in *The Industrial Revolution, 1760–1830* (London, 1948), and elsewhere. The divergent approaches which historians have taken to this question are excellently represented in P. A. M. Taylor (ed.), *The Industrial Revolution in Britain: Triumph or Disaster?* (Boston, 1957), a volume in D. C. Heath's "Problems in European Civilization" series.

children were reported as having to crawl half naked through the narrow shafts of ill-ventilated mines. Apprentice brick-layers might have fourteen-hour days and expect punishment with the strap if they tarried. Chimney sweeps were expected to climb up and down narrow chimneys even though their el-bows and knees were bloodied; not only did they lack all educa-tional training, but they might not wash for six months at a time. Sir Edwin Chadwick's Commission on the Sanitary Con-dition of the Labouring Population (1842) found that thousands of workers in Liverpool and Manchester lived in airless cellars, and although the row houses which had been built on every neighboring hillside provided a modicum of shelter, they were often unaccompanied by paved streets, sewers, or garbage col-lectors. The average diet was often limited to rye bread, cheese, and beer, supplemented by potatoes, turnips, beans, and cabbage. Meat in the form of pork or bacon was often a once-a-week lux-ury among the lower classes while beef was virtually unknown. Every few years would come a period of "distress," and large numbers of workers were thrown out upon the streets without a job and without even a garden plot to call their own.

The reports make harrowing reading, but it may well be questioned whether the evils were necessarily the products of industrialization. It is clear that the process of economic change necessitated a severe readjustment for many a rural family, and that the move to the big city meant a breakup of old social ties and sometimes an end to the security of status which a rural village provided. Whether it meant actual impoverishment, a fall in real wages, has been seriously questioned by most twen-tieth-century economic historians.[3] It is demonstrable, more-over, that the classes most adversely affected by industrialization were not the workers in the factory towns but groups such as the 240,000 handloom weavers, victims of "automation" during the 1830s and 1840s who found it difficult to change occupations in their mature years. It was not the population of industrialized England which experienced famine in the 1840s but the people of neighboring, almost wholly agricultural, Ireland. An unin-dustrialized England could hardly have coped with a population that had almost doubled itself in half a century. Even at their worst, the slums of Manchester never approached the squalor of the slums of Bombay or Calcutta in unindustrialized India.

Long hours, low wages, the apprenticeship of children at the age of seven, and the insecurity brought by poor harvests

---

[3] A useful summary may be found in A. J. Taylor, "Progress and Poverty in Britain, 1780–1850: a Reappraisal," *History*, XLV (Feb., 1960), pp. 16–31. The debate continues, however, especially in the pages of *The Economic History Review*.

and disease were hardly nineteenth-century novelties. Indeed the very parliamentary reports which provide so much grist for the modern social historian's mill stressed the most extreme examples of misery and cruelty and may themselves be interpreted less as evidence of new evils than of a quickening of social conscience very much lacking a hundred years before. "Whatever the merits of the preindustrial world may have been," concludes one present-day scholar, "they were enjoyed by a deplorably small proportion of those born into it."

The advantages of industrialization were not immediately passed on to workers in part because of the expenses of the Napoleonic wars and also because the profits of industry were being plowed back into business. Such profits were a major source of capital, and the high degree of capital investment helps account for the exceptional rate of economic growth in the early nineteenth century, for English manufacturers did not permit wage levels (and their own private incomes) to rise as rapidly as productivity. The same type of regimen of sacrifice which British captains of industry imposed upon their workers and sometimes on themselves on an individual basis, the Soviet government has, on a state directed basis, imposed upon its people during the past forty years.

For all its manifold imperfections, the process of industrialization which got underway in Britain held within it the hope of the future. Industrialization created the prospect for the first time in human history that the mass of mankind—rather than a favored few—might spend its days at activities other than menial toil and live at a material level far above mere subsistence. Even by the 1830s and 1840s it had become clear that a solution to city sewage problems lay less in a state of mind than in the mass production of inexpensive iron pipes, and that the problems of disease could be met, in part, by the use of cheap washable cotton shirts and underwear and the widespread use of soap. Only an industrialized nation could afford the luxury of sending its children to school rather than to the farm or the factory. The self-confident nineteenth-century merchant breaking into new markets, the millowner adding to his factory, the ironmaster sending down his shafts and putting up his foundries where before had stood a bleak hillside, was in his own estimation not only seeking a fortune for himself but doing his share in developing his country and pushing back the threat of destitution. At least as much as the Whig politicians who had revamped the eighteenth-century constitution, they felt themselves to be the heralds of an age of improvement. On such grounds, as well as on their obvious economic strength, they had demanded and partially won a place in society and a share in molding their country's future.

Chapter 3

The Curious Years of 𝕷𝖆𝖎𝖘𝖘𝖊𝖟=𝕱𝖆𝖎𝖗𝖊

ALTHOUGH the 1830s and 1840s may justly be described as years of dynamic expansion symbolized by the coming of the railway, this growth was intermittent, and the age included years of "distress," of falling profits, of falling wages, of mass unemployment — and concomitantly — of political unrest. Depending upon which aspect of the age we emphasize we may look upon these years as the worldly and surprisingly complacent "age of Melbourne" or as an era of virulent social discontent — as manifested by Chartists and Corn Law Reformers — or as "the years of laissez-faire"; and since public professions and political actualities did not always coincide, we may justifiably call them "the curious years of laissez-faire." All these overlapping aspects will be touched upon in this chapter.

In the course of the 1830s both middle-class reformers and working-class reformers became increasingly disillusioned with the Whig Ministries headed in turn by Lord Grey (1830–34) and by Lord Melbourne (1834; 1835–1841). The Whig Government had been responsible for or had acquiesced in a number of important measures immediately after 1832 — the abolition of slavery and the Factory Act in 1833, the new Poor Law Act of 1834, and the Municipal Corporations Act of 1835 — but under the somewhat languid guidance of Lord Melbourne the Whig Government tended thereafter to rest on its laurels and to do little but perpetuate itself in office. Melbourne himself was a worldly and tolerant Whig aristocrat for whom the ultimate end of government was "to prevent crime and preserve contracts." Like most Whigs he was distrustful in equal measure of despotism and democracy, and although he occasionally supported particular reforms he was too conscious of the frailties of human nature to have much confidence in their efficacy.

The overwhelming parliamentary majority which the Whigs had amassed in 1832 had been eroded by the general elections of 1835 and 1837. Thereafter Melbourne could command a majority of only 24 in a House of Commons of 615 members. Even that majority rested upon a de facto alliance with Daniel O'Connell (1775–1847), the hero of the Catholic Emancipation struggle of 1829, and his Irish followers. The weaknesses of the Melbourne administration were scathingly satirized by a Tory rhymster:

> To promise, pause, prepare, postpone
> And end by letting things alone
> In short to earn the people's pay
> By doing nothing every day

If Melbourne gradually lost the support of middle-class voters, he successfully won the affection of the young Queen Victoria who, as the nearest heir to William IV, ascended to the throne at the age of eighteen upon her uncle's death in 1837. Melbourne served her as a political mentor and as the father she had lost years before. By 1839 she had become a confirmed Whig. When Melbourne resigned that year after a defeat in the House of Commons, Sir Robert Peel, the Tory leader, demanded that as prospective Prime Minister he be permitted to choose new ladies of the bedchamber for Victoria. The Queen was still too influential politically, Peel felt, for her confidantes to be all from the opposition party. Victoria refused; Peel thereupon declined to form a Government and Melbourne returned for two additional years as Prime Minister.[1]

It was during the age of Melbourne that there arose in England two of the most significant protest movements of the nineteenth century: the Chartists and the Anti-Corn Law League. Although historians have rightly seen the development of political and economic working-class organizations as a response to the challenge of industrialization, the size and power of such organizations have usually been influenced far more by short-range trends in the economy than by long-range trans-

---

[1] David Cecil's *Melbourne* (London, 1955) provides an illuminating portrait of the man and his world.

formations in society. Both the Chartist movement and the
Anti-Corn Law League—the latter a specifically middle-class
organization—were most immediately a response to the economic depression of 1837–39, although they continued to play
a significant role in British history for a decade thereafter.

The Chartists

The roots of Chartism go back to the world of London trade
unions, some of which began long before the nineteenth century as trade clubs for skilled artisans. Such organizations were
almost invariably small and localized, and although some of
these clubs became politically active during the 1832 Reform
Bill crisis, they had not attempted to join forces as a single national labor federation.[2]

Indeed the men who publicly sought to advance the interests of the workingman looked to the past as much as to the
future. William Cobbett (1763–1835), a prolific pamphleteer,
saw the factory system as the arch-enemy, as the means of
"commanding the common people to stoop in abject submission
to the few." He was a radical in his opposition to pensions and
sinecures for the rich, tithes for the Anglican clergy, and taxes
for a standing army. In his detestation of the growth of cities
and in his lament for the apparent decay of rural life he was
a Tory.

Robert Owen (1771–1858), generally regarded as the father
of English socialism, was almost as conservative. By temperament he was more an egalitarian aristocrat than a democrat.
His early years were spent as cotton manufacturer in Scotland.
Owen, who was more interested in education than in profits,
made an industrial showplace of his mills at New Lanark. He
provided his workers with schools and houses and presided over
his model community as a benevolent despot. He became convinced that the solution for the problem of intermittent unemployment and for the evils of industrial competition generally
was the creation in rural areas of model communities in which
all members would labor in concord at those tasks which best
suited them. In contrast to later Marxist socialists, Owen
preached class cooperation rather than class struggle between

---

[2] The Chartists are discussed in detail by Mark Hovell, *The Chartist Movement*
(London, 1918).   Asa Briggs (ed.), *Chartist Studies* (London, 1959) stresses regional variations.   Relevant biographies include G. D. H. Cole, *Life of Robert
Owen* (London, 1925), Donald Read and Evie Glasgow, *Feargus O'Connor* (London, 1961), and A. R. Schoyen, *The Chartist Challenge* (London, 1958).

employer and employee. Idle landlords, soldiers, and priests, on the other hand, were dismissed as nonproductive parasites who had no place in the ideal society.

In the course of a long life, Owen became involved in a variety of schemes such as the abortive utopian community in the United States, New Harmony, Indiana. It was upon his return to England in the early 1830s that he became involved in the formation of a national trade union movement, the Grand National Consolidated Trades Union (1834) whose objective it was to unite the working classes in a decisive but peaceful struggle to inaugurate the Owenite millenium. The union's purpose was not simply "to obtain some paltry rise or prevent some paltry reduction in wages" but by means of cooperative production and sales to establish "for the productive classes a complete dominion over the fruits of their own industry." The Grand National began to collapse in the very year it was first organized. Major trade unions such as the builders, potters, spinners, and clothiers refused to join, and new factory workers tended to hold aloof. Employers, moreover, resisted its objectives with lockouts and the breaking of strikes. The Government showed its opposition to all unions when it supported the prosecution of the leaders of the Friendly Society of Agricultural Laborers at Tolpuddle in Dorset on the technical ground that they had administered unlawful oaths. Six of "the Tolpuddle martyrs" were exiled to Australia.

Although most of Owen's specific projects failed, the spirit behind them did not. The cooperative ideal, at least on the retail level, bore new fruit in Rochdale in 1844. There 28 Lancashire weavers began a successful cooperative grocery store and later a cooperative shoe factory and textile mill. The Rochdale Society, like Robert Owen, aimed at once at moral elevation and material comfort. "The objects of this Society," ran the Rochdale prospectus, "are the moral and intellectual advancement of its members. It provides them with groceries, butcher's meat, drapery goods, clothes, and clogs." The Rochdale cooperatives were widely emulated so that by 1862 there were 450 such societies with 90,000 members. Equally important was the founding of numerous Friendly Societies such as the Odd Fellows and Foresters whose purpose it was to gather small weekly savings in order to protect workers, and potentially their widows and orphans, against the contingencies of sickness and death. By 1847 such societies had a million and a half members.

Owen had never been particularly interested in political action, but the failure of the Grand National Consolidated Trades Union and the onset of the depression of 1837 revived the interest of many working-class leaders in a political solution to their problems. By the summer of 1837, 50,000 workers were either out of work or on short time in Manchester alone. The poor harvests and business failures of the late 1830s affected human emotions and imaginations as well and brought to the fore what came to be called the "Condition of England" question. Friedrich Engels (1820–95), the German-born Manchester manufacturer, wrote about it. So did Thomas Carlyle (1795–1881) and Benjamin Disraeli (1804–81), who in his novel *Sybil* popularized the concept that England was divided into "two nations," the rich and the poor.

Convinced that economic salvation could come only by political means and convinced equally that neither the aristocrat nor the factory owner was a suitable representative for the unenfranchised workingman, the London Workingman's Association, headed by William Lovett (1800–77), in consultation with Francis Place and a number of radical M.P.s drew up in 1837 a People's Charter. It consisted of six points: (1) universal manhood suffrage, (2) annual parliaments, (3) voting by secret ballot, (4) equal electoral districts, (5) abolition of property qualifications for Members of Parliament, and (6) payment of Members of Parliament. Most Chartists were confirmed believers in Parliament, but they demanded a completely democratized Commons, and declared that: "The House of Commons is the People's House, and *there* our opinions should be stated, *there* our rights ought to be advocated, *there* we ought to be represented or we are SERFS."

At an enormous meeting in Birmingham in August 1838, the Charter was officially adopted by workingmen representatives from all parts of the country. It was at Birmingham also that the voice of Feargus O'Connor (1796–1855) began to dominate Chartist proceedings. O'Connor had a paradoxical background for an English working-class leader. He was a Protestant Irish landlord whose family claimed descent from the eleventh century "high king of Ireland." In his 30s O'Connor set out to establish himself as a political Radical and as a supporter of Irish nationalism. He served in Parliament from 1832 to 1835, when he was unseated for lacking a sufficient amount of property. He then turned to English reform movements and sought in Chartism an alliance of Irish peasants and English workers against what seemed to be their joint oppressors. His bombastic manner and eloquent oratory appealed to large groups of overworked, uneducated, and hungry people, and in his newspaper, the *Northern Star*, which boasted the then astonishing circulation of 50,000 copies a week, he called for a "holy and irresistible crusade" against the government in power. O'Connor represented the militant side of Chartism as did George Julian Harney, who habitually wore a red "cap of liberty" and who in 1839 sent thrills of horror up aristocratic spines by predicting that: "Before the end of the year the people shall have universal suffrage or death."

More moderate Chartists were put off by the tactics of O'Connor and Harney, but the militants clearly won converts and during the winter of 1838–39 the movement gained momentum. Torchlight meetings were held throughout England for the purpose of electing representatives to a giant London convention in 1839 which was to prepare a petition to Parliament. While agreed on the Charter itself, the London convention soon split on the question of what to do if the Charter was rejected. Some delegates wanted the Chartist convention to become a permanent "anti-Parliament"; others suggested a "national holiday" (i.e. a general strike); still others hinted at the use of physical force.

The Charter petition was introduced to the House of Commons in June 1839. It bore 1,280,000 signatures, but after a cursory debate the House, in effect, rejected the Charter by a vote of 235 to 46. As a consequence the London convention broke up in confusion, and a number of riots during the following winter led to the arrest of at least 500 Chartist leaders, including Lovett and O'Connor. O'Connor, dubbed "The Lion of Freedom" by his more ardent followers, continued to edit the *Northern Star* from jail, but for the moment the movement lacked centralized direction, and an upturn in the economy weakened its hold upon many workers. When, however, depression returned with a vengeance in 1841 and 1842, Chartism revived. A permanent National Charter Association with centralized leadership and machinery for collecting a regular subscription of a penny a week was set up. In May 1842 another monster petition bearing this time more than 3,300,000 signatures was presented to the House of Commons. It too was resoundingly rejected, 287–59.

Chartism, like so many workingmen's movements, was a child of bad times, and when the sun of prosperity returned in 1843, social protest began to subside. Moreover, it had little or no upper-class support, and Parliament never really took the Charter seriously. As Thomas Babington Macaulay (1800–59), the Whig historian and M.P., put it in 1842, universal suffrage would be "fatal to the purposes for which government exists" and was "utterly incompatible with the existence of civilization." The purpose of constitutional government was to provide a legal framework within which public issues might be reasonably discussed and resolved. An illiterate or ill-educated populace which gained political domination, he declared, would necessarily fall prey to demagogues. The result would be either anarchy or the mass confiscation of property and the consequence would be not the alleviation but the deterioration of the lot of the poor.

The Chartists' only hope was to win in a time of crisis sufficient working-class support to intimidate if not to convince the government. Yet even at the height of Chartist agitation, many workers remained aloof. The movement was strongest in Birmingham and the midlands, but a working class which included such disparate elements as factory operatives, handloom weavers, domestic nail-makers, and self-educated artisans tended to show far greater loyalty to occupation and locality than to the abstract concept of class. Chartism was weakened not merely by its failure to gain upper-class support or to solidify its ranks, but by a persistent vagueness about the economic means by which the weak were to become powerful and the poor to become rich. One Chartist orator exemplified this woolliness of thought when he assured his listeners: "If a man ask what I mean by universal suffrage, I mean to say that every working man in the land has a right to a good coat on his back, a good hat on his head, a good roof for the shelter of his household." Somehow political democracy was to produce fair shares for all, yet few Chartists were socialists in the sense that they wished to overturn the capitalist organization of industry. It is true that O'Connor, who once compared the unfortunate effects of machinery on workingmen's lives to the effects of the coming of the railway on the lives of horses, seemed to dream at times of a return to a rural utopia, but most Chartists remained incipient capitalists. As one critic told a gathering of workingmen: "Denounce the middle classes as you may, there is not a man among you worth a half-penny a week that is not anxious to elevate himself among them. . . ."

The last gasp of Chartism came in 1848. Inspired by political revolution in France, Italy, and Germany, and galvanized into action by another downturn in the economy, a new convention gathered signatures for a third monster petition and decided to form itself into a National Assembly on the French model if the Charter was rejected. The government took formidable precautions. Almost every London gentleman was created a special constable in order to handle the crowd which was expected to march upon the houses of Parliament. The gathering was not as large as predicted, if only because of the steady rain, a familiar handicap for all outdoor demonstrations in England. Feargus O'Connor, who had resumed leadership in the movement, was ordered to stop the march, and he did so. Instead the petitions were transported to Parliament in three hansom cabs while everyone else went home.

The third Charter, which did no better in the House of Commons than the previous two, came to be looked upon as something of a fiasco. The almost two million valid signatures would have seemed to show impressive popular support, but because O'Connor had extravagantly claimed five million signatures, the smaller number was deemed insignificant. Renewed prosperity caused the Chartist movement to peter out permanently during the next three years. In retrospect, to be sure, the Chartist movement cannot be dismissed outright. As the Populist movement was to do in the late nineteenth-century United States, so Chartism frightened the respectable middle and upper classes, and like its American equivalent it was killed by prosperity; but the essential reforms advocated by each were to be enacted at different times under different auspices. Within only three quarters of a century, five of the Charter's six points — annual parliaments being the sole exception — were to be enacted into law in Britain.

The Corn Law Reformers

The other big protest movement occasioned by the depression of 1837–39 was the Anti-Corn Law League. To understand the significance of the Corn Laws in nineteenth-century English history it is important first of all to realize that "corn" in British usage refers to all grains, i.e. wheat, oats, barley, etc., and not particularly to American corn (or maize). During the Napoleonic wars, English landlords and farmers had been encouraged to raise all the grain they could. Once the war was over they were faced with the problem of a grain surplus. The government, sympathetic to their interests, sought to protect them against foreign competition with the Corn Laws of 1815, which barred foreign imports until the domestic price was so high as to threaten famine at home. The Corn Laws did not and could not prevent sharp ups and downs in the domestic price of grain. When an abundant harvest provided a supply greater than the effective public demand, the price would go down, Corn Laws or no. Yet the Corn Laws became the rock on which Tory economic policy rested. They were justified as a necessary protection for English agriculture and also, as food imports slowly increased, as a necessary source of revenue for the national exchequer.

The Britain of the early nineteenth century had been left by the Napoleonic wars with what contemporaries justly regarded as a major financial problem. Americans in the mid-1960s tend to be concerned about the size of their national debt, but it hardly approximates in impact that of early nineteenth-century England. Whereas the national debt of the United States government today is a little over half the total annual national income, the national debt of Britain in 1827 was over two and a half times as great. Whereas interest payments on the national debt absorb slightly more than 10 percent of the annual national budget in the United States in the 1960s, they absorbed 52 percent of the British budget for 1827. Since the major part of the government's income was derived from customs and excise taxes, the Corn Laws seemed an important source of revenue as well as of agricultural protection.

Beset by the economic depression of 1837–39 and disillusioned with a Whig government that was proving just as aristocratic and almost as Tory as that of the Duke of Wellington, a group of Manchester industrialists headed by George Wilson (1808–70) and Richard Cobden (1804–65) came to the conclusion that their own economic salvation and also the political salvation of middle-class radicals lay in the abolition of the Corn Laws. "The English people cannot be made to take up more than one question at a time with enthusiasm," confided Cobden, and the new League decided to concentrate upon the "total and immediate" repeal of the Corn Laws as that issue. They hoped to attract the support of all those who resented the privileges and entrenched influence in national life enjoyed by the aristocracy—even after 1832—for the Corn Laws had come increasingly to seem "the symbol of aristocratic misrule."

The Anti-Corn Law League was in one sense the outcome of the teachings of the classical economists. Adam Smith, in his *Wealth of Nations* had concluded that the economic prosperity of men and nations was best advanced if each worked at that task for which he was best suited. It seemed clear by the 1830s that England was designed by God for the role of an industrial power which exported its surplus manufactures in exchange for the raw materials (and food stuffs) of other lands. In hindering this role the Corn Laws appeared to contradict the will of nature itself.

It would be a mistake to see the work of the League as that of a group of detached economists. It was rather the best organized pressure group Britain had ever known, and it broke precedent by seeking to persuade not merely the traditional governing class but also the unenfranchised masses. It was a highly effective lobby which appealed as much to human emotions as to material interests and whose speakers cited the Bible as often as they quoted economic statistics. The League appealed to the manufacturer: Repeal the Corn Laws and your workers will have cheaper food and will therefore put less pressure on you for higher wages. Moreover, the lands from which the food will be imported will then have the means to buy English manufactured goods. The League appealed to the workers: Repeal the Corn Laws and the price of bread will go down. The day of "the Big Loaf" will be at hand, and you will be assured of more regular employment. The League even attempted, if not very successfully, to appeal to the farmer: The Corn Laws keep the rents you pay your landlords at artificially high levels. Repeal the Corn Laws and your rents will fall. The League appealed to the humanitarian: The age of mercantilism has brought wars as nations squabble over trade advantage. The Corn Laws are the last great bastion of mercantilism. Repeal the Corn Laws and the result will be free trade for Englishmen. As other nations follow England's lead, the economic causes of war will disappear. An era of international fellowship will be at hand. Or to phrase it even more simply: Repeal the Corn Laws and the result will be international peace.

Although the League was increasingly successful in raising money from wealthy manufacturers, its campaign proved for the moment insufficient, even though it included tracts and lectures, as well as tea parties and bazaars at which free trade handkerchiefs, bread plates, and teapots were sold. The Chartists obviously resented the rivalry of the League, but its arguments made some impression upon workingmen. Yet for the moment its influence upon the country was more widespread than its influence upon Parliament. As late as 1840 an anti-Corn Law resolution was defeated 300–177 in the House of Commons; and by 1841 the League became convinced that if it were to achieve economic reform it would have to participate actively in politics. It organized registration drives to see that all eligible free traders were on the pollbooks, and on occasion it ran its own candidates. When the Whigs came out in support of a lower fixed rate on corn imports in 1841, the League threw its support toward the Whigs rather than the Tories in the general election of that year. The results were, for the moment, disappointing. Individual Free Traders, Richard Cobden most importantly, gained a seat in the House of Commons; but a revived Tory Party under Robert Peel's leadership took over with an apparently solid 78-vote majority. The League's drive continued and Cobden's disciple, John Bright (1811–89), a Quaker manufacturer from Rochdale, added his eloquent voice to Cobden's own; but the parliamentary repeal of the Corn Laws seemed just as far away as ever.[3]

Peel and Repeal

Peel's ministry (1841–46) proved more helpful to the free traders than had been expected. Sir Robert Peel, who had

---

[3] Norman McCord, *The Anti-Corn Law League, 1838–1846* (London, 1958).

gained stature during his years in opposition after the debacle of 1832 as an exponent of responsible and restrained criticism, had clearly molded a potent political force in his revived Tory Party. Peel himself was not a "popular" leader. He was reserved and kept his own counsel, "an iceberg with a slight thaw on the surface." He was, moreover, not nearly so satisfied with a policy of simply preserving the status quo as many of his party would have preferred. He was by background the son of a successful textile printer and the type of hard-working administrator the Manchester industrialists appreciated. As Prime Minister, Peel felt it his duty to read all foreign dispatches, to keep up a steady correspondence with Queen Victoria and Prince Albert, to hold numerous private interviews, to superintend all patronage both in the civil service and the Anglican Church, to prepare for debates, to spend eight hours a day for 118 days a year in the House of Commons, and to "write with his own hand to every person of note who chooses to write to him." Peel embodied what came to be known as the Victorian "gospel of work."[4]

In the Budget of 1842 Sir Robert introduced certain far-reaching reforms which were ultimately to make the repeal of the Corn Laws easier. Hoping to overcome a succession of Whig deficits, he reintroduced the income tax as a significant source of government revenue. This Napoleonic war expedient had been abolished in 1817. Peel reintroduced it at a fixed rate of 7d in the £1 (slightly less than 3 percent) and at the same time sponsored a general reduction in protective duties for 750 of some 1,200 itemized articles. With the assistance of his equally hard-working colleague, William Ewart Gladstone, who served first as Vice-President and then as President of the Board of Trade, some 430 articles, including imported raw cotton, were struck off the customs altogether, and in 1845 all remaining taxes on exports were ended. The English fiscal system was being streamlined in a way suitable to a highly industrialized nation.

As the years of Peel's ministry went on, the Prime Minister became increasingly equivocal on the subject of the Corn Laws. Although the country had recovered from the economic depression of the early 40s, the defenders of the Corn Laws always found it difficult to answer the argument that their stand favored high food prices. Many free traders began to pin their hopes on Peel's public conversion to their cause, for they admired him far more as a statesman than they did Lord John Russell, who had taken over the leadership of the Whigs from

---

[4] G. R. Kitson Clark, *Peel and the Conservative Party*, London, 1929.

Lord Melbourne and who announced his conversion to complete free trade in 1845.

The Irish Famine

The industrialists were not disappointed, for Sir Robert's own conversion to free trade came during the winter of 1845–46 when famine struck Ireland. For almost a century the greater part of the Irish population had become accustomed to a diet consisting of a single staple, the potato. Meat might be a once-a-month treat, but day after day, three times a day, most Irishmen ate salted, boiled potatoes. The potato had been introduced into Ireland by 1600 from its South American home, but it was not until the eighteenth century that it came to predominate over the dairy and grain products which had hitherto provided Ireland's staple foods. As a food the potato had a number of advantages. It could be stored easily and it could be made edible simply by being boiled. It was easy to grow and less subject to being stolen, burned, or trampled on than wheat or rye. It grew in the hills as well as the plains. Most significantly it fed a family on less than half as much land as wheat required. Until the 1820s the monotony of the potato was offset by its abundance. An average laborer was expected to consume ten to twenty pounds of potatoes a day, and together with milk this provided him, even by twentieth-century dietetic standards, with more than sufficient calories and vitamins.

The potato may well have been a major cause for the rapid growth in the Irish population which began during the eighteenth century. From approximately four million people in 1780 it increased to over eight million by 1840, not counting the hundreds of thousands who had already emigrated to England or across the Atlantic. A potato diet apparently increased the fertility rate, while the landholding system did nothing to encourage thrift or late marriage. Irish tenants lacked any incentive to improve their property, so as soon as sons reached manhood they would receive a portion of their father's holding on which to start a potato patch of their own. The great danger for a population so completely dependent upon a single crop was that, for reasons of weather or disease, the crop might fail, and there was no substitute source of food. Potatoes could not be stored for more than a year so that the surplus of one year could not make up for the scarcity of the next. Since Ireland was a largely rural society, many parts of it lacked an organized food trade or even the custom of using money.

By 1830, regional failures of the potato crop in Ireland had become dangerously frequent, but it was not until 1845–47 that a potato blight ruined almost the entire crop. It was, as Lord John Russell said, "a famine of the thirteenth century acting upon a population of the nineteenth." At least half a million people died either directly or indirectly of starvation. At least a million more fled the land as refugees. Many went to England; more than ever before sought material salvation in the New World.

The British Government of the day sought in vain to cope adequately with the famine, but the potato failure convinced Peel that, at the very least, all barriers to the importation of food should be ended. In November 1845 he proposed that the Corn Laws be suspended. In May of 1846 he convinced the House of Commons that it should end them completely, and with the aid of the Duke of Wellington, he obtained the concurrence of the House of Lords. In the process he split his party, for while the opposition Whigs voted almost solidly for repeal, the Tory Party was shattered. 112 of his party voted with Peel, but 231 voted against him. Within a month of repeal, his ministry was defeated and Lord John Russell replaced him as Prime Minister.

Although Peel had sacrificed his party and his career to repeal the Corn Laws, his actions did little to save Ireland. A generation of Irish nationalists became convinced, indeed, that the Irish famine had been a deliberate plot on the part of the English government to rid the world of Irishmen. "The Almighty . . . sent the potato blight," declared John Mitchel, "but the English created the Famine." Not until the mid-twentieth century did a group of revisionist Irish historians conclude that the truth, as so often, was not so simple.[5]

The half million Irishmen who died in the Great Famine were not the victims of a plot but of a government that lacked both the experience and the administrative machinery to handle such a crisis and of a political theory that did not consider relief to be one of the proper functions of government. "A government," wrote *The Economist,* "may remove all impediments which interfere to prevent the people from providing for themselves, but beyond that they can do little." Peel did arrange for an emergency shipment of American maize, or "Indian corn," but Russell preferred to rely almost solely on the operations of the Poor Law. If people were out of work and hungry, the local poor law guardians were expected to supply them with relief money from the poor rates for their labor on public works or in the poorhouse. The lack of food would serve as an incentive for

---

[5] R. D. Edwards & T. D. Williams (eds.), *The Great Famine: Studies in Irish History, 1845–1852* (Dublin, 1956). See also Cecil Woodham-Smith, *The Great Hunger* (New York, 1963).

local storekeepers and merchants to import food from abroad which the starving could purchase with their relief funds. According to the assumptions of classical economists, the system should have worked. What Russell and other Englishmen overlooked was that rural Ireland almost totally lacked the highly sophisticated network of merchants and shops which they took for granted in England. Even the emergency shipments of wheat did little for people who did not know how to grind the grain and bake the bread.

If the repeal of the Corn Laws did not prevent the Irish famine, it did leave a lasting mark upon the economic, political, and social scene of nineteenth-century England. Some modern experts have their doubts whether the repeal of the Corn Laws produced the decades of prosperity into which the country moved, but contemporaries were by and large willing to give the credit to the Anti-Corn Law League. Even British agriculture did not suffer greatly, at least for a generation; and the doctrine of Free Trade came to be defined by a nineteenth-century professor of economics as "a truth like those of physical science, [resting] on the solid basis of established fact."

Politically, the repeal of the Corn Laws determined the shape, or shapelessness, of British politics for the next two decades. The anti-Repeal Tories were condemned to minority status, and for a time the Peelite Tories became a separate third party. The Whigs, with no clear issue to hold them together, tended to disintegrate into factions; and the relatively stable two-party system that had emerged from the crisis of the Reform Bill of 1832 was broken. The consequences, however, of Peel's actions were not all bad. One of his chief motives in repealing the Corn Laws had been to heal the class conflict that seemed to be growing between the two ruling elements of the kingdom — the landowners and the factory owners. Though Sir Robert left behind him a shattered Tory Party, he bequeathed when he died in 1850 a far more important legacy — a united land. At the close of the year of his death the *Annual Register* could report that "the domestic affairs of the British nation presented a tranquil and, with partial exceptions, a cheering aspect."

The Trend Toward Laissez-Faire

The obvious success of the Anti-Corn Law League in 1846, in contrast to the dismal failure of the Chartists, has helped contribute to one of the more persistent of historical oversimplifications, that the middle years of the nineteenth century marked the high-water mark of laissez-faire capitalism. In capsule form the thesis goes something like this:

During the sixteenth, seventeenth, and early eighteenth centuries the nations of Europe were under the sway of the doctrine of mercantilism. This doctrine induced national governments to take a very considerable interest in economic affairs; it encouraged them to regulate imports and exports, to aid the development and undertake the government of colonies, to regulate the quality of manufactured goods and supervise the conditions under which these goods were made, all in order to further the economic interests of the nation and its people as a whole. Then in the eighteenth century came a group of "enlightened thinkers," the Physiocrats in France and Adam Smith in Britain, to argue that mercantilism was mistaken and to suggest that a nation would prosper most not by enacting a mass of restrictive legislation regulating the procedures of manufacture and the terms of trade but by leaving economic affairs alone. Do away with restrictions; allow the government to confine itself essentially to the role of policeman; let it keep order at home and defend the nation against enemies abroad; and permit the law of supply and demand to operate freely. If every man were allowed to follow his own self-interest then, as if by an invisible hand, in the very act of following his own self-interest, he would promote the interests of his country as well. Let every nation engage in those economic activities for which its climate, its natural resources, and the skills of its people best fit it. This was Adam Smith's prescription for the economic ills of his age: laissez-faire. As far as possible, leave things alone.

According to the thesis, men did not immediately begin to heed the wisdom of Adam Smith—it was especially difficult to do so in the midst of the Napoleonic wars—but in the course of half a century his ideas, and those of like-minded "classical economists," came to be widely accepted, so that at the very time that the Great Reform Bill was overhauling the political structure of the realm, economic reformers were abolishing the old remnants of mercantilistic legislation and promoting the adoption of laissez-faire. The great triumph of laissez-faire came with the repeal of the Corn Laws in 1846. The final part of the thesis is that England continued to be guided by laissez-faire until the twentieth century, when, as a result of socialist ideas and other factors, it developed into the welfare state of the 1950s and 1960s.

Though it remains a vast oversimplification, the thesis summarized above has a degree of validity. The phrase laissez-faire, it must be remembered, tends to be used interchangeably for government policy toward at least two distinct concerns: the commercial relationship between one country and another; the relationship between workers and employers within the same country. Adam Smith was primarily interested in doing away with, or at least in reducing, the numerous unreasonable—and therefore, to him, unnatural—restrictions of his day upon international commerce. He was less concerned with the relationship between capital and labor, if for no other reason than that in eighteenth-century Britain a good deal of practical laissez-faire already existed in this area, even if it had not yet received theoretical justification. The Elizabethan apprenticeship laws were still in the statute book, and the local Justices of the Peace retained the power to set wage limits and price limits, but such laws were enforced only sporadically and were not always applicable to conditions in the new factory towns.

Two economists of the late eighteenth and early nineteenth centuries gave added sanction to the belief that the government ought not to interfere in the relationship between capital and labor. Thomas Malthus reached the pessimistic conclusion that the human population had an inherent tendency to outrun the food supply and that government intervention in the form, say, of setting minimum wages would simply result in workers having more children. State interference might, he admitted, relieve poverty for the time being, but in the long run the standard of living would not improve substantially above subsistence level. David Ricardo with his so-called "Iron Law of Wages" reached a similarly dreary conclusion. There was, he saw, only so much money to go around. If one group of workers, either by unionization or by means of government aid, were granted more, the result would merely be that some other group would end up with less. Once again laissez-faire appeared to be the best answer. It may seem surprising that the economic "models" constructed by the classical economists were essentially static in nature at a time when the economy, empirically observed, was so obviously expanding dynamically, but such paradoxes would appear to be not infrequent in human history.

In any event, by 1813 the remnants of the Elizabethan apprenticeship laws had been repealed and one barrier, if a largely theoretical one, to workers and employers making their own employment arrangements was removed. The question of whether labor unions did or did not meet the test of laissez-faire remained open. On the one hand, it was argued that a group of men acting together to force wages up was violating natural economic law—that was the logic of the Combination Acts of 1799 which prohibited labor unions. Yet one could equally argue that true laissez-faire consisted in letting both men and their employers do what came naturally, and if organizing labor unions came naturally, then perhaps true laissez-faire implied that the government ought not to interfere. On that basis the Combination Acts were partially repealed in 1824 and 1825, though for half a century the question remained unsettled whether or not a labor union was a conspiracy under English common law.

If there were some indications of a trend toward laissez-faire in domestic labor relations, that trend was far more marked in the field of foreign commerce. The actions of Pitt in the 1780s and of Huskisson in the 1820s were continued by Peel and Gladstone in the 1840s, and the great triumph of the Anti-Corn Law League in 1846 was succeeded by the repeal of the last of the Navigation Acts in 1849. It was, to be sure, not theory alone which destroyed those remnants of seventeenth-century mercantilism, but the fact that in the 1840s British manufacturers and shippers were more efficient than their rivals.

To this extent the thesis that laissez-faire triumphed in nineteenth-century Britain is accurate. It is accurate in another way as well. Almost every organized political group in Britain in the first half of the century believed in it. Certainly all parties denounced the evils of big government, though by continental standards Britain's central government in 1830 was absurdly small. Whereas France's Minister of the Interior had direct authority over 200,000 employees scattered throughout his country, Britain's ministers had rule over scarcely 21,000 government officials. Nine thousand of these, however, were the hated customs officials, who swarmed the land inspecting every tea seller and tobacconist eight times a year and laid down exacting regulations for everything from the brewing of spirits to the manufacture of glass and paper.

Most Whigs by this time had been sufficiently "enlightened" by the classical economists to regard government intervention in the economy as intrinsically wrong. The radicals from the start had been suspicious of the central government as the entrenched home of the aristocracy; and they regarded state control as simply an excuse for paying lazy aristocrats to do nothing and the Home Office as a den of police spies. The Tories by tradition were less ready to accept the ideas of the classical economists, and Samuel Taylor Coleridge, the romantic poet, observed with disdain that the laissez-faire economists were prepared to dig up the charcoal foundations of the Greek temple at Ephesus in order to provide fuel for their steam engine. The Tories boasted of their greater concern with matters spiritual and their more paternal interest in the welfare of the factory worker, but in practice they too were opposed to the expansion of the central government. They expected to maintain their paternalism through voluntary associations or through those pillars of Tory control, the parish vestry, the local magistrate, and the town council. It would seem therefore that in theory, as well as in practice, laissez-faire characterized the mood of the time. ". . . The course of modern legislation," concluded a parliamentary committee in 1851, "seems to have been gradually to remove restrictions on the power which everyone has in the disposal of his property, and to remove those fetters on commercial freedom which long prevailed in this country."

The Trend Toward State Intervention

Despite all the evidence to support the thesis that the Britain of the second quarter of the nineteenth century was a land of laissez-faire, the fact remains that the powers of the central government were on the increase between 1833 and 1854. A central government which had rarely touched the life of the ordinary individual and which had shown little concern for his well-being became directly involved with his working conditions, his health, and to some extent, his education. This curious development in the teeth of the most sacred professions of the major political parties must be sought in the growing conviction among well-to-do families that the filth, disease, and human suffering to be found in Britain's towns was a man-made evil which could be and should be controlled and reformed by the only agency strong enough to act—the central government.

The two groups which did most during the first half of the nineteenth century to influence government to intervene in social conditions were the Evangelicals and the Utilitarians. The Evangelicals were those elements within the eighteenth-century English Church which came to believe that the forms of worship and the theological interests of their church had lost touch with the daily life of the common people. Christianity ought to mean, they felt, a personal involvement in religious worship and also a personal involvement in the way men lived. John Wesley's Methodists had in time broken off from the Anglican Church but some evangelically minded men remained within the fold, and it was their efforts, allied with those of members of the nonconformist denominations, which had spearheaded the antislavery crusade of the early nineteenth century and which had succeeded in freeing some 700,000 Negro slaves (at a cost of £20,000,000 to the English taxpayer) by means of parliamentary statute in 1833.

It was this antislavery movement which helped forge a new instrument in British domestic politics—the weapon of organized moral indignation. It was this spirit that drove such men as Lord Ashley (1801–85)[6] to insist, despite all economic

---

[6] After 1851, the 7th Earl of Shaftesbury.

theories, that Parliament legislate protection for children who worked in factories and mines, for chimney sweeps, and for the insane. It was this appeal to evangelical morality, to faith expressed through good works, which may well have been the single most potent force behind nineteenth-century social reform.[7]

What was needed, however, was not only moral indignation, which tended to peter out in ineffective sermons and newspaper editorials, but a comprehensive theory of government responsibility and a systematic awareness of the problems of public administration. This was provided by the Utilitarians, a small group of well-educated men who followed the ideas of Jeremy Bentham (1748–1832), that "most celebrated and influential teacher of the age." Bentham was an extraordinary man with an astonishing variety of interests. He tried to simplify the English language; he proposed a League of Nations; and he coined the word "international" as well as words like "maximize" and "minimize." He was one of the chief founders of the University of London, a completely secular institution which in the 1820s broke the centuries-old monopoly upon English university education held by Oxford and Cambridge. When Bentham died he was one of the first men deliberately to leave his body to science, and his mummified form resides to this day in the basement of University College, London.

Bentham, like Adam Smith, was a man of the age of reason, and the object of his lifetime was to put the institutions of his day to a simple test: are they useful? Bentham cared little whether institutions were traditional; he cared even less whether they had ancient religious sanction; he did not believe in "natural rights" any more than in natural duties. The only test was the utilitarian test: how useful is it? And for Bentham those institutions were "useful" which promoted the greatest happiness of the greatest number of people. He was not concerned with the happiness of nations because he did not believe in nations except insofar as they were aggregations of individuals—in that sense Bentham was like Adam Smith, an individualist.

In one very important respect, however, Bentham differed from Adam Smith. Smith had argued for a *natural* identity of

---

[7] The best book-length treatment of the subject of this subchapter is David Roberts' *Victorian Origins of the British Welfare State* (New Haven, 1960). G. Kitson Clark provides illuminating insights in *The Making of Victorian England* (London, 1962). Elie Halevy explores the intellectual origins of utilitarianism in *The Rise of Philosophical Radicalism* (London, 1928). Relevant biographies include J. L. & Barbara Hammond's *Life of Lord Shaftesbury* (London, 4th ed., 1936) and Samuel Finer's *Life and Times of Edwin Chadwick* (London, 1952).

interests; he had contended that if individuals are allowed to follow their own economic interests they will naturally promote the interests of their society. Bentham argued instead for an *artificial* identity of interests. Men, in following their own interests, he maintained, promote the interests of their fellows only if the laws of their society are so arranged that their own self-interest will be channeled in the direction of the common good. A pickpocket may decide that his own self-interest lies in seeking out people in the marketplace and picking their pockets. He will thereby be following his own self-interest, but he will hardly promote the greatest happiness of the greatest number. If, however, society has set up a well-enforced law against pickpocketing and the pickpocket feels almost certain that he will be caught and sent to jail for a year, then he will hardly be following his own self-interest in picking pockets. His self-interest may dictate entering a different profession, one which will more readily promote the greatest happiness of the greatest number.

Bentham used the same criterion in determining types of punishment. The only object of legal punishment, he contended, is to deter, not to exert vengeance. Therefore the ideal punishment is the sentence just harsh enough to deter the pickpocket. A harsher punishment – the death penalty, for example – might in fact have the opposite effect, for a jury, regarding the legal penalty as too severe for a mere pickpocket, might decide to acquit him altogether, and the criminal counting on such an attitude would not be deterred from his crime.

Although Bentham had no love for bureaucracy for its own sake, it is clear that his doctrine of "the artificial identity of interests" might require a great deal of government intervention. Bentham was a writer, not a lecturer or a parliamentary reformer, but he built up a circle of associates, men like Sir Edwin Chadwick (1800–90) and John Stuart Mill (1806–73) who applied his criteria of reasonableness to a great many institutions. The Benthamite method, as employed by Chadwick, was to discover a problem and to bring pressure upon Parliament or the ministry to appoint a Select Committee or a Royal Commission to explore it. The Committee or Commission then would hold hearings and draft a statute to reform the abuses found. The statute would often require the creation of a new department of government which had authority to lay down uniform regulations and to appoint a force of inspectors to see to it that local authorities carried out the provisions of the law.

Although their underlying motivations might differ widely, Evangelicals and Utilitarians joined forces on numerous occasions in the 1830s and 1840s in the interests of social reform. The process got under way in 1832 when a parliamentary Select

Committee headed by Michael Sadler, a Tory Radical, first pub-
licized the appalling extent of child labor in unhealthy cotton
mills. This led to a more thorough investigation the following
year headed by two good Benthamites, Edwin Chadwick and
Southwood Smith. The Royal Commission report confirmed
the existence of the long hours worked by factory children, the
physical fatigue engendered, and the lack of education from
which such children suffered. The Factory Act of 1833, based
on the Commission's report, provided that no child under nine
should be allowed to work in textile factories (eighteenth-century pauper children had usually been put to work by the time
they were seven), that children between 9 and 13 work no more
than eight hours a day and receive a minimum of three hours
of schooling, and that adolescents between 13 and 18 work no
more than twelve hours a day. Most important of all, four factory inspectors were to be appointed to enforce the law. Thus
the all-important precedent was set up. Unlike the Factory Acts
of 1802 and 1819, which had virtually remained dead letters,
the enforcement of the statute was not to be left in the hands
of the local magistrates.

If there was to be supervision of the textile mills, then
government regulation of the mining industry could not be far
behind, and years of agitation by Lord Ashley led to the appointment of a Royal Commission on Mines in 1840. The Commission
compiled a three-volume indictment of the horrors of the mines
– foul air, the danger of explosions, long hours, and immorality.
More successful in arousing public opinion than the statistics
were the pictures of seminude women and bedraggled children
pulling coal carts on their hands and knees along three-foot-
high mine shafts. The Mines Act of 1842, which passed the
House of Commons with only sixteen dissenting votes, prohibited the employment in mines of all women and of all boys
under thirteen and, at Chadwick's suggestion, made provision
for government inspectors. The pressure of coal-mine owners
in the House of Lords reduced the minimum age for boys to ten
and did little for adult miners. However, the large number of
accidents in the mines – 765 of 200,000 active miners lost their
lives in 1849 – led to the Mine Inspection Act of 1850, which
brought conditions underground for all miners under some
degree of central government supervision.

So far government control had been limited to specific industries, but as early as 1830 Lord Ashley began to fight for a
general ten-hour bill, a law which would limit the work of all
women and young people in factories to no more than ten hours
a day. Though Ashley was himself a Tory, the bill received more
support from Whigs than Tories, but it was repeatedly defeated.
Only in 1847 at a time of depression in which manufacturers

Coal mining in Staffordshire in the 1840's. Wood engraving by J. W. Whimper.

found it difficult to argue that the machines had to be kept busy continually did the bill pass. Although the bill did not apply to adult male workers, it affected them as well, because in many factories it was impractical to have different shifts for the different sexes. By the late 1840s, indeed, the sixty-hour week had become commonplace in English factories. Men worked Mondays through Fridays from 7 A.M. to 7 P.M., with an hour and a half off for meals, and on Saturdays from 7 A.M. to 2 P.M., with half an hour off for meals.

A far more difficult problem to which the Benthamites sought to find a solution was the Poor Law. The problem of rural pauperism had been endemic in England, and ever since Elizabethan times it had been the responsibility of each parish to provide a refuge of last resort to the paupers, the ill, aged, and insane of the community. The success with which this task was accomplished varied greatly among Britain's thousands of parishes, for in the eighteenth century there was no central supervision of their efforts. A fateful change in the Poor Law administration had begun in 1795 when the Berkshire magistrates at Speenhamland had ordered the overseers of the poor not only to provide "outdoor relief" (outside the poorhouse) to the unemployed but to supplement the wages of employed rural laborers whenever the price of the standard loaf of bread exceeded a shilling. The "Speenhamland system" seemed superficially beneficial, but it had unhappy results. Generally adopted throughout Southern England by the 1830s, it kept agricultural wages low and forced many a hitherto independent worker upon poor relief. Landlords had no incentive to raise wages because they knew that the wages of their workers would be supplemented from the poor rates. Rural pauperism clearly demoralized the farm laborer while the steadily increasing poor rates seemed to many a taxpayer an insufferable burden.

Successive parliamentary committees found the Poor Law wanting, but until 1833 no one in Westminster could figure out a way of persuading the parishes to carry out a uniform, enlightened policy of poor relief. The Royal Commission of that year, dominated by Chadwick and by Nassau Senior, the economist, came up with a solution in the spirit of Utilitarian economics. The parishes of a particular area were to be amalgamated into district boards managed by elected poor-law guardians, who were to establish workhouses, forbid "outdoor relief" to all able-bodied workers, expand provision for pauper education, and provide improved care for the aged and the ill. The district boards were to be under the supervision of a central board of three Poor Law Commissioners who would issue uniform regulations and supervise their enforcement. The recommendation received a mixed reception in 1834; but in the hope that the new program would prove less costly than the old relief system, the report was translated into law.

Of all the social reforms of the 1830s and 1840s, the Poor Law of 1834 remains historically the most controversial. It was only three years after its passage that Charles Dickens first wrote about little Oliver Twist, who was sent by the poor law guardians to a dismal workhouse to subsist on "three meals of gruel a day, with an onion twice a week, and half a roll on Sundays." The *Times* of London, a Tory journal, printed this fictional tale as it did many supposedly true stories of floggings, filth, and squalor in workhouses. The *Times* especially denounced the workhouse test, according to which no able-bodied man could gain relief except in the workhouse. In keeping with the doctrine of the classical economists, workhouse life was deliberately to be made less attractive than any private employment. Thus the laborer would have every incentive to seek the latter. The *Times* conceded that the monetary cost of the poor law operations had been reduced from an average of £6,700,000 a year (1825–34) to about £4,500,000 a year (1834–43), but it judged appalling the resulting human suffering. While the verdict of the *Times* has been echoed by many historians, recent scholars have become more judicious in placing the act in its historical setting. It is clear that the workhouses established by the act were at least as clean and comfortable as the homes of the average English laborers of the day. The Poor Law Commissioners provided a sufficiently nutritious diet and authorized no corporal punishment for adults. Nor were they overly rigid in enforcing the workhouse test in periods of depression; in 1839–40, 86 percent of all relief recipients, including the ill and the aged, received aid outside the workhouse.

The Commissioners were doubtless somewhat rigid in insisting on certain psychological discomforts, such as silence at mealtimes. They were unduly fearful that workhouse conditions would be superior to, rather than worse than, those outside. Whatever its disadvantages, however, the Poor Law Act did ensure central supervision for local poor relief; and, under the energetic administration of Sir Edwin Chadwick, a general upgrading of institutions caring for the poorest groups in British society was accomplished. Moreover, the machinery of the Poor Law became the means by which the central government became involved in such matters as the health and sanitation in the new industrial towns where local borough government was being overwhelmed by the magnitude of filth and disease.

Medical men in Liverpool and Manchester had long connected the spread of cholera with the lack of proper sewage facilities; but it was only when Chadwick, using his authority as one of the Poor Law Commissioners, investigated the situation in detail that widespread public attention was directed to the problem.   In his classic *Report on the Sanitary Condition of the Labouring Population of Great Britain* (1842), Chadwick compiled a grim record of undrained streets, impure water, and airless and crowded tenements, all of which he saw closely related to the prevalence of crime, disease, and immorality. The report led to a fullfledged Royal Commission and to the creation of a Health of Towns Association which rivaled the Anti-Corn Law League as a pressure group.   The establishment of local boards of health supervised by a national Board of Health seemed to many the only appropriate solution; but numerous municipal corporations, private water companies, and similar vested interests feared that their powers would be curtailed.   Local taxpayers were concerned that a national Board of Health would order expensive improvements for which they would have to pay.   The controversy over the issue of centralization caused the question to hang fire for several years, but the threat of a new cholera epidemic induced Parliament in 1848 to establish a national Board of Health with the power to confirm the appointment and dismissal of local surveyors and health officers.

Other examples of the unwitting "administrative revolution" of the 1830s and 1840s may be cited: a commissioner was appointed to confirm the constitutions of savings banks and friendly societies (1833); a central inspectorate for prisons was created in 1835; the same was done for lunatic asylums in 1842; a Merchant Marine Commission to regulate conditions on merchant vessels was established in 1854; and a Charity Commission to supervise private philanthropy was created in the same year.   As the *Times* observed in 1850, "the solicitude of the public and the government for the physical and moral wellbeing of every class of the labouring population ... is one of the most humane and distinguishing characteristics of the present time."

The Church and Education

A related question on which Utilitarians and Evangelicals could see eye to eye was the condition of the Church of England. It seemed obvious to both groups that the old church was in dire need of reform.   There were enormous, and irrational, differences between the incomes received by ecclesiastical peers and the pittances paid to many a parish vicar.   Moreover, all Englishmen were still legally required to pay tithes (literally one tenth of income paid in money or goods) to support clerical salaries and they were similarly subject to church rates for the repair of parish churches. Such obligations were only sporadically enforced, however, and the precise financial practice tended to vary as greatly from parish to parish as had the franchise requirements before the Great Reform Bill. Yet the archbishops of Canterbury and York still lived as feudal overlords, attended by a huge retinue and dispensing lavish hospitality. The bishops in the House of Lords had not endeared themselves to reform-minded Utilitarians by their almost unanimous opposition to political reform. The widespread practice of absenteeism and pluralism and the obvious failure of the church to adapt itself to the needs of the growing industrial towns were trenchantly criticized by the Evangelicals. The tradition-bound High Church seemed indeed to be the high-and-dry church.

In order to correct some of these irregularities, Lord Melbourne's Whig Ministry established an Ecclesiastical Commission in 1836 to end abuses in the church and to reduce the anomalies of wealth among the various bishoprics and parishes. A Tithe Commission was set up to work out a suitable pattern of taxes due the Church, and a secular Registrar General's Office was established to take over the traditional role of the parish in registering births, deaths, and marriages. In the name of utilitarianism and in the face of the protests of many of her leaders, the Church of England, that most ancient of the country's institutions, was to be reconditioned and modernized.

The Church of England responded far more willingly to another kind of reform—that of the spirit. There began at Oxford during the 1830s an intellectual revival of the High Church position along lines echoing the ideas advanced by Archbishop Laud in the seventeenth century. This so-called "Oxford Movement" engaged more fully the attention of many upper- and middle-class Englishmen than did many of the social reform movements of the era. The leading force in the movement was John Henry Newman (1801–90), a young Anglican divine at Oxford whose eloquent sermons and polished prose writings once again made High Church Anglicanism a vital creed. Newman stressed the independence of the Church and frowned upon the kind of toadying to the secular world demonstrated by one Bishop of London who apologized in the House of Lords for taking a stand on a particular issue at variance with that of the statesman who had recommended his appointment.

Newman stressed the idea that the Anglican Ecclesia was not just another Protestant church but was one whose faith and doctrine were rooted in the undivided church of medieval Catholicism and which differed from the Church of Rome only in denying obedience to the Pope. The leaders of the Oxford Movement emphasized vestments and ceremonials in the Catholic tradition and opposed steadfastly the philosophical assumptions of the eighteenth-century Enlightenment that the Kingdom of Heaven might be hoped for on earth. Newman and his colleagues attracted a number of able followers; but when in 1841 he went so far in tract #90 as to interpret the Anglican Thirty-Nine Articles in such a way as to seek to reconcile them completely with Roman Catholicism, he raised a furor. Most of the High Church party did not wish for an actual reunion with Rome, but Newman himself could find no halfway point between atheism and Roman Catholicism and was admitted to the Church of Rome in 1845. He spent the remaining forty-five years of an often difficult life within his adopted church, thereby adding intellectual distinction to a church which most Englishmen tended to identify with poor and often ignorant Irishmen. Despite Newman's loss, the revived High Church party within the Anglican Church remained a significant force which emphasized authority, tradition, and the duty of worship and which inspired the revival of religious orders within the church for the first time since Henry VIII had closed the monasteries in the 1530s.

Although religion was a significant factor in promoting many of the social reform movements of the age, its role in one particular field, that of education, was essentially divisive. Britain in the 1830s had no national system of education as did many continental nations. Most schools were under religious auspices, and attendance was voluntary. Utilitarians and other reformers agreed that Britain's schools were grossly deficient. About one third of the children between five and fifteen attended no school at all, while those who did might attend only Sunday school or highly inadequate day schools. Teachers were so poorly paid that generally only those applied for posts who had failed in all other occupations. Dr. James Kay (1804–77),[8] the Assistant Poor Law Commissioner who became the most eloquent advocate of educational reform during this period, cited as examples of incompetence the teacher who had ordered for his classroom two globes, one for each hemisphere, and the teacher who had refused to take the class roll because King David had gotten into trouble counting the Children of Israel. A national system of education with rate-supported district schools inspected by the central government and offering nondenominational religious education had been proposed to Parliament as early as 1820. The Church of England was up in arms at such a suggestion, and during the 1830s it showed itself equally averse to any attempt by the

---

[8] After 1849, Sir James Kay-Shuttlesworth.

government to supervise its role as national educator. The Church was willing to accept an annual subsidy from the national government, but the decision by the Whig ministry in 1839 to set up a Committee on Education within the government and appoint two inspectors to oversee government grants raised a new furor. On this issue the Church was supported by almost the entire Tory party, for the issue of religion remained a party issue in a manner in which the Factory and Mines Acts were not. The Ministry won out, however, and thus, by the late 1840s, with Kay as secretary to the Committee on Education and with two inspectors, the state had in a very tentative fashion assumed responsibility for educating its people; yet none of the reformers were satisfied with the manner in which the question had been resolved.

What is clear is that by 1850 two important precedents had been established in Britain: (1) that the government might interfere in economic affairs in order to protect the individual citizen, (2) that the national government might supervise local government in order to assure administrative efficiency. These precedents had been established in the face of a prevalent government philosophy which accepted most of the dictates of laissez-faire. The paradox is explicable on the basis that the politically influential public opinion of the times did recognize a need for social reform and was aware of the inadequacies of local government. All parties were fearful of centralization, and only the Utilitarians viewed a national bureaucracy with any degree of favor. But by working partly on the basis of Benthamite ideas and partly on the basis of what one critic called "presumptuous empiricism," a somewhat ramshackle Victorian administrative state had in fact been set up. All social ills had scarcely been remedied, but the Benthamite *Westminster Review* could take comfort in 1853 in the fact that "We are receding fast from the barbarism of former times and as a community we are awakening to a far stronger and more general sense of the claims and dues of all classes. We are beginning to estimate our objects and possessions more according to rational principles." At the very time that Britain was proclaiming the decisive victory of laissez-faire in international commerce, it had taken a series of giant strides in the direction of state intervention at home.

Chapter 4

The 𝕻𝖆𝖝 Britannica

THE BRITAIN which occupied itself during the second
quarter of the nineteenth century with railway building and
political and social reform was often equally involved with
affairs on the other side of the English channel and beyond
the seas. Britain was one of the five members of the "Concert
of Europe" which had emerged from the Congress of Vienna
of 1815. Although that Congress was often to be criticized for
the manner in which it reaffirmed monarchical government
on the Continent and quashed the nationalistic aspirations
of various European peoples, it did prove the prelude to ninety-
nine years without a conflict comparable to the Napoleonic
wars. It provided a pattern for avoiding war by leaving none
of the great powers (Britain, France, Russia, Prussia, and
Austria) with a sense of overriding grievance and by giving new
sanction to the "balance of power" concept. No single power
was to be allowed to dominate the Continent, and no power was
to annex territory or strengthen its military influence without
gaining the approval or acquiescence of its fellows. Treaties
were not to be broken lightly, and whenever a threat to the
general peace arose, the "Concert" powers were to participate
in negotiations to settle disputes peacefully. The relative success of the resulting "balance of power" during the half century

after 1815 rested not least of all in the fact that no permanent or rigid system of alliances divided the great powers.[1]

Britain's Place in the World

To the extent that Britain was preeminent in preserving the European peace during the century that followed the Congress of Vienna, it is justifiable to refer to that century as the *Pax Britannica*. The *Pax Britannica* was never identical to the *Pax Romana* of eighteen hundred years before, for unlike the Romans of that time, the British of the nineteenth century had neither the strength nor the will to impose peace by force of arms. The role of Britain as the significant, and often decisive, mediator, depended on other factors. There was Britain's unique sense of security within an island bastion which even Napoleon had failed to storm. There was Britain's ability, demonstrated repeatedly during the early decades of the nineteenth century, to combine domestic liberty with order and to achieve reform without revolution. Britain's constitutional monarchy was the idol of Continental liberals, and her economic successes caused even the most reactionary of European powers to sit up and take notice. The total tonnage of British shipping increased from two and a half million to four million tons between 1827 and 1848. By 1850, some 60 percent of the tonnage of the world's ocean-going vessels was British and perhaps one third of the world's international trade involved British interests. London was the world's financial center. England had served as "the paymaster of Europe" during the Napoleonic wars, and during the postwar years even major powers like Austria and Russia habitually floated loans in London.

Britain's preeminence depended also upon the fact that it held the world's largest overseas colonial empire, though during the 1830s and 1840s this empire seemed at times a dubious advantage. At a time when tariff barriers were falling, when navigation acts were being abolished, when the principle

---

[1] Two comprehensive surveys of British foreign policy are Lord (William) Strang, *Britain in World Affairs* (New York, 1961) and R. W. Seton-Watson, *Britain in Europe, 1789–1914* (Cambridge, 1937). More specialized works include Albert H. Imlah, *Economic Elements in the Pax Britannica* (Cambridge, Mass., 1958), *The Cambridge History of British Foreign Policy,* Vol. II (Cambridge, 1923), and C. K. Webster, *The Foreign Policy of Palmerston, 1830–1841* (London, 1951). Also worth noting are the various essays in J. P. T. Bury (ed.), *The Zenith of European Power, 1830–1870* (Cambridge, 1960), which constitutes Vol. X of the *New Cambridge Modern History*.

of "free trade" was triumphing, the eighteenth century mercantilistic justifications for colonies had largely ceased to exist.
If foreigners could trade with Canada, Australia, or India on
the same terms as English merchants, what were colonies but
expensive encumbrances?   Money had to be spent to govern,
police, and protect them, but what did they provide in return?
Such at least was the classical liberal argument.

It was not in the colonies that Britain invested most funds.
Until 1850 almost two thirds of British overseas capital investment flowed to Continental Europe and almost one third to the
United States and to South America.   Many more British (and
Irish) emigrants went to the United States than to all the colonies put together.   Of over 2,200,000 emigrants between 1830
and 1850, some 1,346,000 went to the United States.   Thus most
English statesmen of the day became more involved with what
has been called "the empire of free trade" than with territorial
empire building.   They sought the acquisition of new trading
outlets for British industries, not the expensive political control
of subject territories.

At the same time that the classical, laissez-faire, economists advocated a policy whereby Britain would divest itself,
both for moral and financial reasons, of all her colonies except
those vital to military and commercial enterprises, a group of
"colonial reformers" looked forward to an empire transformed
into an association of autonomous self-governing nations.
Unlike the more pessimistic classical economists, colonial
reformers like Lord Durham (1792–1840) did not expect Canada,
Australia, and New Zealand—where Englishmen had settled
and English nations were being created in the wilderness—to
sever all ties with the mother country.   Once self-government
had been granted to these lands, they expected ties of sentiment
to prove more powerful than bonds of force in providing a community of interest between such settlement colonies and the
mother country.

When a rebellion occurred in Canada in 1837, it was not
surprising then that the Melbourne ministry should have
appointed as High Commissioner of British North America a
"colonial reformer," Lord Durham, to survey the situation.
The rebellion itself was soon crushed, but the subsequent report, published in 1839, provided a pattern for "dominion"
status and self-government within the British sphere.   Durham
suggested that Canadian ministers be made responsible to the
colonial legislature rather than to the royal governor for all
domestic affairs.   The recommendation was not immediately
adopted, but it was put into practice during the governorship
(1847–54) of Lord Elgin, Durham's son-in-law.   From Canada
the idea spread, so that by 1872 most of the English-speaking

areas of the empire had achieved a form of responsible self-government.

Ultimately the *Pax Britannica* rested not only on Britain's adherence to liberal economic and political policies but also on Britain's military strength. Although Britain's army was reduced to minimal size after the Napoleonic wars and although Britain ranked fourth among the great powers in population, the British navy remained unchallenged "mistress of the seas." It stood unrivaled not because it was kept up to strength–only 17 of 95 capital ships were in commission in 1827–but because the other powers had laid up even more of their vessels. The British navy was not only a force to be reckoned with by every Continental power but also acted as a kind of international police force to suppress pirates and to control the illegal international slave trade. It served merchant vessels of all lands by preparing and publishing charts and maintaining order throughout the world.

The Foreign Policy of Palmerston

At first Great Britain assumed her post-Napoleonic responsibilities grudgingly and often ineptly, and Sydney Smith probably summed up the average Englishman's isolationist inclinations when he wrote in 1823:

> ... For God's sake, do not drag me into another war! I am worn down, and worn out, with crusading and defending Europe, and protecting mankind; I *must* think a little of myself. I am sorry for the Spaniards – I am sorry for the Greeks–I deplore the fate of the Jews; the people of the Sandwich Islands are groaning under the most detestable tyranny; Bagdad is oppressed; I do not like the present state of the Delta; Tibet is not comfortable. Am I to fight for all these people? The world is bursting with sin and sorrow. Am I to be champion of the Decalogue, and to be eternally raising fleets and armies to make all men good and happy? We have just done saving Europe, and I am afraid that the consequence will be, that we shall cut each other's throats.... If there is another war, life will not be worth having.[2]

---

[2] W. H. Auden (ed.), *The Selected Writings of Sydney Smith* (New York, 1956).

By 1832, however, Britain was over her war weariness, and the Whig political triumph of 1832, coinciding as it did with the growing recognition of Britain's role as "workshop of the world," created the domestic atmosphere necessary for a foreign policy more in accord with the term *Pax Britannica*. The minister most directly associated with the dynamic, self-righteous, and sometimes dangerous foreign policy that resulted was Lord Palmerston,[3] who became Foreign Secretary in 1830 and was to hold the post for the greater part of the twenty years that followed (1830–34; 1835–41; 1846–51). Initially a Tory, he had been converted to Whiggism and had come to champion liberal reform on the Continent. This penchant led him into policies which would be described in the mid-twentieth century as "brinkmanship," though Palmerston himself insisted that he was simply a friend "of free institutions," never a promoter of revolutions. Few people questioned Palmerston's superb qualifications for his post. He wrote and spoke French fluently; he knew Spanish, Italian, and Portuguese well. He was familiar with every person in his department. He personally read all dispatches from abroad, and he replied to a great many in his own hand.

Although Palmerston believed that Europe was hopelessly divided into two antagonistic camps – reactionary Russia, Prussia, and Austria versus liberal France and Britain – he was as concerned as had been his predecessor, Canning, to preserve the balance of power and to avoid permanent formal alignments. This was evident during the first major crisis of his administration when revolution broke out in Belgium. Belgium, ever since the Vienna peace settlement of 1815, had been attached to the Dutch monarchy as a bulwark against French expansion. A declaration of independence by a provisional Belgian government late in 1830 was a clear violation of the Vienna treaty. The king of the Netherlands would have welcomed Russian and Austrian intervention on his behalf, but the Belgian insurgents gave him no time; and Palmerston, in order to forestall foreign intervention, suggested instead a London conference to discuss the matter of an independent Belgium. The Eastern powers reluctantly acceded.

After a great deal of hard bargaining – Palmerston attended seventy meetings on the Belgian question – the five major states of Europe agreed upon a protocol establishing an independent Belgium as a permanently neutral state under

---

[3] Since Lord Palmerston held an Irish rather than an English peerage, he was eligible to sit in the House of Commons, and he had indeed served in that body since 1807. The best biography of Palmerston is the two-volume study by H. C. F. Bell (London, 1936).

an international guarantee. Palmerston had the satisfaction of installing upon the new Belgian throne Leopold of Saxe Coburg, a German prince and uncle of the young Victoria, heir apparent to the English throne. Although the protocol was ratified by the great powers in 1832, the Dutch king did not resign himself to the inevitable until Anglo-French forces had intervened militarily and had forced the Dutch out of Antwerp by a joint bombardment of the city. By wielding the big stick and even threatening war, Palmerston had maintained the peace and balance of Europe and installed a liberal constitutional monarch upon his throne.

The reconciliation between the Eastern and Western Powers which Palmerston's settlement of the Belgian question brought about lasted only a short time, for Western liberal opinion was angered by the harsh Russian repression of the Polish revolutionaries of 1830 and by the similar repression going on in various German states. In 1832 the situation was complicated by a new threat to the balance of power in the Near East, where, as the Greek revolution of the 1820s had demonstrated, Russia, Britain, and France all had potentially conflicting interests of commerce, strategy, and prestige. This time the Ottoman Empire, that proverbial "sick man of Europe," was faced with a revolt by one of its provinces. Mohammed Ali, a Balkan adventurer who had become Pasha of Egypt, was warring against the Sultan in Constantinople in order to gain complete control of the whole empire, which still included the eastern third of the Mediterranean Sea. The French were sympathetic to Mohammed Ali, while the Russians, who had long sought to defeat—and ultimately to partition—the Ottoman Empire, reversed their position and now came to the Sultan's aid. With Russian help, Mohammed Ali's territorial gains were confined to Syria. As Russian influence increased in Constantinople, so also did Palmerston's fears that Turkey would become a Russian satellite. "The Russian Ambassador becomes chief Cabinet Minister of the Sultan," Palmerston complained, but for the moment there was little he could do about the matter.

In 1839, however, the battle between Mohammed Ali and the Ottoman Sultan again erupted. Palmerston, who saw the Mediterranean as an increasingly important British trade route even before a Suez Canal seemed a likely engineering project, hoped to maintain the peace and to promote his country's interests by "neutralizing" the Near East, in much the same manner as he had done in Belgium. In order to forestall the French influence standing behind Mohammed Ali and in order to weaken Russian influence over the Ottoman Sultan, he proposed a joint guarantee of Turkish integrity by all the great powers on condition that Turkey close the Dardanelles to all warships in any conflict in which Turkey was a neutral.

Palmerston succeeded in winning the support of the Russian Czar, Nicholas I, by joining the Russians in aiding the Sultan against Mohammed Ali. The Austrians and the Prussians also concurred, but the French, angered by Britain's high-handed action, did not. Palmerston, however, held his ground, and war between the two countries seemed imminent in 1840 until the French backed down and accepted the general settlement. Palmerston's "big stick" tactics, based on British economic and naval strength, appeared again to have been justified, and the Czar was so pleased with the new Anglo-Russian diplomatic alignment that he proposed a permanent alliance between the two countries. His offer was politely turned down, but he did make a formal state visit to Britain in 1844.

Anglo-American and Anglo-Chinese Relations

In the meantime, the Whig ministry of Lord Melbourne had been replaced by the Tories under Peel in 1841, and Lord Palmerston had given way to Lord Aberdeen (1784–1860) as Foreign Secretary. The new Secretary lacked Palmerston's flair for diplomacy, but his own methods were probably more suited for settling a number of difficulties which had arisen between Britain and the United States. A period of friendly relations between the two nations after the War of 1812 had given way to a decade of discord. Overt American aid to the Canadian rebels of 1837 had led British troops to retaliate by seizing the American ship *Caroline* and sending it ablaze over the Niagara Falls. Canadians and Maine backwoodsmen carried on a form of undeclared guerrilla war over the un-settled Maine-Canadian border, and the two countries had also clashed over the British navy's right to search vessels suspected of carrying slaves.[4] Feelings between the two countries had been exacerbated by American resentment of British wealth and power, while British tourists like Charles Dickens found "a general lack of civilization" on the western side of the Atlantic. When several American states defaulted on their debts as a result of the depression of 1837, British investors were furious. The American eagle, observed *Punch*, was a predatory bird "extremely fatal to the large species of goose called the creditor."

---

[4] A sound brief summary is provided in Henry Kurtz, "The Undeclared War between Britain and America, 1837–1842," *History Today*, Nov. & Dec., 1961.

Concession, rather than Palmerstonian bellicosity, was the tone of Aberdeen's handling of the American crisis. In 1842, the border conflict between Maine and Canada was resolved by a treaty which awarded approximately three fifths of the disputed territory to Maine and two fifths to Canada. The British also provided what was interpreted in the United States as a belated apology for the *Caroline* incident; and the United States promised anew to cooperate with Britain's efforts to curb the illegal international slave trade.

Two years later Great Britain kept her patience when James K. Polk won his bid for the Presidency of the United States on the platform of "Fifty-Four Forty or Fight" and claimed all of Oregon as far as the Alaskan border as American territory. Although the British navy was put on a war footing, the London *Times* urged the policy that ultimately prevailed in Whitehall: "We are two peoples, but we are of one family. We have fought, but we have been reconciled." British commercial interests were opposed to war; and once President Polk had become involved in a comparable dispute with Mexico, he decided to give way. A treaty of 1846 provided that the 49th parallel, the boundary between Canada and the United States from the Great Lakes to the Rocky Mountains, should be extended to the Pacific Coast — except for Vancouver Island, which remained Canadian — and war between the two countries was once again averted.

At the same time that Lord Aberdeen had been calming the diplomatic storms which had agitated Anglo-American relations, he was involved in a somewhat different type of trouble with China. There he reverted to more Palmerstonian tactics. British merchants had for decades been eager for greater trading concessions from the empire of China, which had long looked with disdain upon the "western barbarians" from Europe. A disagreement between the Chinese authorities and a group of British merchants, some of whom had been importing opium into China, led in 1839 to the so-called "Opium War." The British fleet bombarded Canton, and British troops took Shanghai and entered the Yangtse Valley. By the Treaty of Nanking (1842), the Chinese were forced to open Shanghai and Canton to foreign merchants and to pay the claims of British traders whose goods had been seized. The then uninhabited island of Hong Kong was ceded outright to the British, to join Singapore, which had been acquired in 1824, as one of two chief British outposts in the Far East. The Chinese customs service was reorganized under British auspices. From the Chinese point of view, the Treaty of Nanking, which also ceded the legal privilege of "extraterritoriality" — exemption from Chinese legal jurisdiction — to most foreigners, marked the beginning of a century of humiliation for China. From the British point of view, it marked the widening of "the empire of free trade," the area in which British merchants and all others might trade without constraint.

Palmerston Again

In 1846, with the fall of the Peel ministry and Russell's assumption of the Prime Ministership, Palmerston returned to the foreign office. He had long sought to encourage peaceful internal reform within the Continental monarchies as an antidote to violence, and the revolutions which broke out all over Europe in 1848 lent weight to his admonitions. Palmerston's prime purpose in 1848, however, was as before to preserve the European balance of power and to avoid a general war. France had once again become a radical republic, and Palmerston was eager to prevent a Continental attack upon France as well as to stop any expansionist drive by the new republic eastward. Especially touchy was the situation in Italy. Here the Kingdom of Sardinia sought to take advantage of the apparent breakup of the Austrian Empire in order to wrest the Italian provinces of Lombardy and Venetia from Austrian rule and create a unified Italian state. Palmerston, like most Englishmen, was sympathetic to a unified Italy if it could be brought about peacefully; but he feared that French intervention on behalf of the Italians would touch off a general European war. British diplomatic intervention did help restore peace between Austria and Sardinia in 1849, at the price of antagonizing Austria.

The *Pax Britannica* involved not only the forwarding of British commercial interests throughout the world and the use of diplomatic pressure to preserve the balance of power. It also, especially as applied by Palmerston, involved more than a touch of bombast in idealistic dress. Palmerston's unquestioned belief in the moral righteousness of all Englishmen and in the self-evident superiority of the English constitutional system antagonized the great powers and relegated some of the less powerful states of Europe and Asia to an avowedly inferior status. "These half-civilized governments," declared Palmerston in 1850, "all require a dressing every eight or ten years to keep them in order. Their minds are too shallow to receive an impression that will last longer than some such period and warning is of little use. They care little for words, and they must not only see the stick but actually feel it on their shoulders before they yield to that only argument which to them brings conviction, the *argumentum baculinum*."

Palmerston's attitude is well illustrated by the Don Pacifico incident of 1850, which involved Greece, a country which had been set up under the protection of Britain, France, and Russia in the 1820s. During the decades that followed, foreign secretaries like Palmerston had taken a highly avuncular attitude toward Greece and had not hesitated to chide the new nation about many minor and not so minor matters: brigandage on the Greek roads; day to day police administration; Greek tardiness in paying the interest due on its national debt; the failure of the Greek king to make a sufficient apology to the Turkish ambassador after having insulted him at a court ball, etc. In 1847, the Athens home of Don Pacifico, a moneylender of Portuguese Jewish ancestry, was pillaged by a Greek mob. The Greek government eventually made partial compensation, but Don Pacifico was unsatisfied and appealed directly to Palmerston with a detailed list of his claims. He had been born on Gibraltar, Don Pacifico pointed out, and was therefore by law a British citizen. Palmerston saw the incident as another example of Greek skulduggery and endorsed every one of Don Pacifico's claims, including the £27,000 value he put on some Portuguese bonds which had been destroyed in the fire.

Palmerston asked the Greek government for appropriate compensation for Don Pacifico. When it hesitated, he ordered a British squadron of fourteen ships under Admiral Parker to proceed to Greek waters. On January 17, 1850, Parker and the English Minister to Greece sent an ultimatum to the Greek government. Receiving no reply within twenty-four hours, the British admiral proclaimed a blockade of Greece and seized several Greek ships. France and Russia complained about Britain's high-handed action. But since a British fleet held the command of the seas, the Greeks had no choice but to submit to Palmerston's demands.

The French government, which had sought to mediate the dispute, was furious and recalled its ambassador to London. Queen Victoria and Prince Albert were equally upset. The Queen had long been at odds with Palmerston over his policies and his method of conducting diplomacy. As she had become accustomed to the role of Queen, she increasingly resented the number of occasions on which the Foreign Secretary took action without her knowledge. Moreover, as her husband trained her to read the foreign dispatches assiduously, she became convinced that Palmerston was at heart a wild revolutionary hostile to her Continental fellow monarchs.[5] And this time, Palmerston did indeed appear to have gone too far. A Conservative motion

---

[5] See Brian Connell, *Regina vs. Palmerston* (New York, 1961).

of censure passed the House of Commons by a vote of 169 to 132 and Russell's ministry seemed on the verge of defeat.

One of Palmerston's supporters thereupon introduced a resolution supporting the Foreign Secretary's policies as "calculated to maintain the honour and dignity of this country" and the House was launched on a full-dress, five-day foreign policy debate in which every major public figure participated. Gladstone for one criticized Palmerston's foreign policy as one motivated by a "spirit of interference." It was preferable, he thought, for a British Foreign Secretary to heed "the general sentiment of the civilised world" rather than to challenge all comers like a medieval knight at a tournament.

Palmerston defended his handling of the Don Pacifico case and of foreign affairs generally in an eloquent five-hour oration. He denied that the British Goliath had bullied Greece: "Does the smallness of a country justify the magnitude of its evil acts?" When justice was denied, even to a Don Pacifico, it was Britain's duty to interfere. In a final flurry, he summed up the moral foundations of the *Pax Britannica*, its reason for being, and the foreign policies that sustained it:

> We have shown that liberty is compatible with order; that individual freedom is reconcilable with obedience to the law. . . . I contend that we have not in our foreign policy done anything to forfeit the confidence of the country. . . . I therefore fearlessly challenge the verdict which this House . . . is to give on the question now brought before it . . . whether, as the Roman, in days of old, held himself free from indignity, when he could say *Civis Romanus sum* [I am a Roman citizen]; so also a British subject, in whatever land he may be, shall feel confident that the watchful eye and the strong arm of England, will protect him against injustice and wrong.

It was Palmerston who carried the day, and the motion supporting his policies was approved by a vote of 310 to 264 in the House of Commons and by a less specific but perhaps even larger majority by the man in the street — or, as Palmerston liked to call him, "the man in the omnibus with the umbrella." For many such men, Palmerston seemed John Bull incarnate, and for such men British honor and universal justice were, after all, identical.

Chapter 5

𝕻rosperity, Propriety, and Progress

Like ancient Gaul, the reign of Queen Victoria can most conveniently be divided into three parts. And the mid-Victorian period, which commenced symbolically with the opening of the Great Exhibition of 1851 and ended with the onset of the "great depression" of 1873, can most readily be studied as a unit. For most Englishmen, these two decades were, in contrast with the previous age, years of prosperity. All things considered, it was a period of social harmony in which both talk and consciousness of class division subsided. It was an age when underlying assumptions about the necessity for a high degree of individualism at home, free trade abroad, and progress in the affairs of mankind were accepted by most with uncritical, almost religious, conviction. Many Englishmen, but never all, were therefore filled with a pleasing sense of self-confidence and complacency.

The Age of Prosperity

Terms such as "prosperity," "stability," and "complacency" are necessarily relative; but in contrast to the age that had gone before, they are appropriate enough. An Englishman of 1848, looking back upon the agitation of the Chartists, the triumph of the Corn Law Reformers, and the social legislation resulting from the Royal Commission reports on factories and mines, might well have predicted that an even more noteworthy age of political and social reform was in the immediate offing. Yet the mid-Victorian years were to see no such remarkable examples of political agitation, nor was the landed aristocracy, whose bell had presumably tolled in 1846, to disappear from the social or economic scene.

Thus at the same time that industrialization had come to be accepted as a way of life and the predominance of an urban civilization assured, it was becoming clear that the economic revolution would bring not social confusion and bloodshed, nor even an easily discernible "triumph of the middle classes," but instead a far more gradual and peaceful readjustment of social groups and a widespread survival of habits, occupations, and institutions from earlier centuries. In politics these mid-Victorian years were a lull, an "age of equipoise" between the political storms of the first half of the century and the yet more drastic changes still to come.[1]

A vivid symbol both of Victorian material progress and of the sense of self-satisfaction to which it gave rise was the Great Exhibition of the Works of Industry of all Nations which opened in London in May 1851. There had been a few similar exhibitions on a small scale in France, but this was the first true World's Fair; and Britain, as the workshop of the world, was clearly the appropriate host country. The central building of the exhibition was the Crystal Palace, in essence a gigantic greenhouse made of iron and glass, over 1800 feet long and more than 400 feet wide. [See illustration.] Its ceiling was high enough to enclose some of the tallest elm trees in Hyde Park, sparrows and all. The chief inspirer of the exhibition, the Queen's husband, Prince Albert, hopefully saw its purpose as a presentation of "a true test and a living picture of the point of development at which the whole of mankind has arrived . . . and a new starting point, from which all nations will be able to direct their further exertions." With this in mind, the exhibition displayed the wonders of the new industrial world. The United States exhibited a sewing machine. The French demonstrated a new medal-making machine which could produce fifty million medals in a single week. An electric telegraph office with direct connections to Edinburgh was set up by a British company. More than half of the 13,000 exhibitors were British, and they exhibited not only the latest textile machinery

---

[1] The period is well described and analyzed in such books as G. Kitson Clark, *The Making of Victorian England* (London, 1962), W. L. Burn, *The Age of Equipoise* (London, 1964), Asa Briggs, *Victorian People* (Chicago, 1955), and Vol. II of J. H. Clapham's *Economic History of Modern Britain* entitled *Free Trade and Steel, 1850–1886* (Cambridge, 1932).

Opening Day at the Crystal Palace Exhibition. Drawn on the spot (1851) by George Cruikshank.

but such ingenious contraptions as "an alarm bedstead, causing a person to arise [quite literally] at any given hour" and the British equivalent of an automatic baseball pitching machine, "a cricket catapulta, for propelling the ball in the absence of a first-rate bowler."

Perhaps the greatest tribute to mid-Victorian economic efficiency was the fact that the exhibition had been planned and the Crystal Palace erected within a single year and that on the opening day, May 1, all exhibitors but the Russians were ready. Hundreds of thousands of people were on hand to greet Queen Victoria and Prince Albert, who delivered the opening speech, and the Archbishop of Canterbury, who pronounced the opening prayer, and the Duke of Wellington, who delivered neither speech nor prayer but who was cheered by the people merely for having managed to survive to see it at all. The hero of Waterloo and the villain of 1832 had managed to retrieve a high measure of popular esteem by 1851, and he was able to render his country a final service on the occasion of the Great Exhibition. When Queen Victoria asked the Duke's advice as to how best to deal with the nuisance of sparrows within the great glass building, his reply was succinct: "Try sparrow hawks, Ma'am."

It was clearly a grand day for a great many Englishmen. One observer, the daughter of an aristocratic Whig landlord who had married the owner of one of Britain's largest iron foundries, marveled at how "all this pomp and panoply were called together to do honour to the industry of millions, whose toils, erst scorned upon, seemed suddenly ennobled." Industrialization had come of age and had at last brought to industrialist and factory worker alike the accolades of all groups, even the landed nobility. The purpose of the exhibition, to be sure, was not merely to exhibit British industrial superiority but to proclaim to all foreign visitors the gospel of free trade and universal peace and the glories of the British Constitution.

As the next two decades were to demonstrate, these lessons were not all learned, though in 1851 it certainly appeared as if countries like France and the United States were following the British along the road to free trade and sensible and stable constitutional government. Universal peace was soon to be broken by the Crimean War; and the French across the Channel, instead of adopting the British Constitution were about to proclaim another Napoleon as emperor. But the inept war against Russia was to end without unduly disrupting domestic prosperity and tranquillity, and Napoleon III was to prove to be a respectable bourgeois emperor and not a dangerous firebrand. Thus to some degree the hopes of 1851 were to pervade the whole era, and as Macauley wrote, "1851 would long be remembered as a singularly happy year of peace, plenty, good feeling, innocent pleasure and national glory."

There was certainly massive statistical evidence of progress and prosperity. Annual coal production figures rose from 65 million tons to 125 million between 1854 and 1874, while the production of pig iron kept pace. In 1856 Henry Bessemer announced the development of the first process for making steel inexpensively and a few years later William Siemens introduced the new "open hearth" method of producing high-tensile steel; by the 1870s the age of iron was rapidly giving way to the era of steel. Precision tool making had come to be a major British industry and the manufacture of interchangeable standard parts and the use of machine tools which could adjust measurements to a thousandth of an inch had become commonplace. The steam engines which Boulton and Watt had turned out by hand in the 1780s were being mass produced by 1860.

The railways continued to be a major user of metals both at home and abroad. A network of 6,621 miles of track in 1850 expanded to over 16,000 miles by 1873 and the number of passengers per year increased from 64 million to 455 million. Aside from the continued trend toward amalgamating small railway companies, however, there was relatively little technical innovation during these years. Third-class coaches open to the weather and to flying sparks from the locomotive had been replaced by enclosed carriages; but the English traveler continued to prefer his train cut into compartments like a succession of stagecoaches, rather than be exposed to his fellow passengers en masse as in an experimental American "coach" train imported from Detroit.

During the 1850s the Yankee Clippers and other American vessels rivaled British merchant vessels in speed and number; but the American Civil War ended American competition. The result was a shipbuilding boom in Britain. Despite conservative doubts about the ability of iron to float, the iron ship powered by steam came into its own, though steamships made up only 5 percent of British merchant shipping in 1850. By 1874 the proportion was still only 33 percent; and only in 1900 did the total tonnage of steam- and motor-powered ships surpass that of sailing ships. British predominance on the seas, however, remained unchallenged. Sixty percent of the world's steamships flew the British flag.

A boom in shipbuilding and shipping industries went hand in hand with an expansion of trade. Whereas the market value of British exports had increased only 14 percent between 1817 and 1842, it jumped during the next twenty-five-year period by 282 percent. Ever increasing quantities of coal, iron, steel, machinery, and textiles were leaving British ports, while correspondingly larger quantities of raw cotton, raw wool, wheat, and timber were entering them. Britain exported not only the products of industry but also money. As recently as 1815 British investments abroad had been virtually balanced by foreign investments in Britain. By the 1850s, however, a net total of £264 million had been invested overseas, and two decades later the amount had jumped to £1058 million. British investors were helping to build railroads all over the world — in Russia, Spain, Switzerland, Denmark, Turkey, Brazil, and the United States as well as in India and other British colonies. In 1857, £80 million in American railroad securities were held by British investors and each of nineteen European railway companies had at least one British director. Very often it was British iron, steel, and locomotives and in some cases British contractors and even laborers who did the work.

Perhaps most surprising of all, the 1850s and 1860s remained prosperous years for British agriculture. For the moment at least the landowners who had steadfastly fought the repeal of the Corn Laws and who had freely predicted that repeal would spell disaster for British agriculture seemed to have been proved wrong. Not that imported grain did not play an increasingly significant role in the English diet; only 26 percent of the grain consumed in 1850 had been imported; but by 1870 the percentage had risen to 48 percent. With a growing population, however, this still left a large market for British farmers, and until 1872 the total acreage under cultivation continued to increase. There was a new emphasis upon scientific farming, upon better estate management and the use of new techniques such as steam-powered tractors. Life in rural England did not, however, alter appreciably. As of 1871, half of all England was still owned by 7,400 people. Although the powers of the local Justices of the Peace were beginning to be curtailed by the use of elective local bodies and by the establishment of a rural police network, there remained numerous villages owned by an individual landowner. Agricultural laborers fared better in those areas where industry competed for their services, but in most parts of the country their lot remained a bare and simple one, and the medieval duel between poacher and gamekeeper had not yet ended.

Agricultural prosperity should not be attributed exclusively to profits derived directly from the land. "All that can be said about land," explained Lady Bracknell in Oscar Wilde's *Importance of Being Earnest,* is that "it gives one position, and prevents one from keeping it up." Land gave an Englishman social status, but its financial value lay less in agriculture than in the coal or iron that might be found beneath it, the sale of rights-of-way to the railways that might traverse it, or the rentals of the houses that might be built on top of it. Never had such development opportunities been so plentiful as in the middle years of the 19th century.

This rosy picture of economic growth, which in statistical terms averaged 3.2 percent per year between 1850 and 1873, was in part the result of the continuing growth of the British population. The birthrate held fairly steady at 35 per 1,000 and the death rate at 22 per 1,000; and although hundreds of thousands continued to emigrate, the net population of England, Wales, and Scotland increased from 20,817,000 to 26,072,000 between 1851 and 1871. Only in Ireland did emigration and other social aftereffects of the Great Famine initiate a steady population decline. The rise in population was significantly accompanied by an improvement in the standard of living. Whatever the controversy about working-class living standards during the first half of the nineteenth century, there is no question that the third quarter of the century brought a marked rise of real wages. That historical myth but statistical necessity, the *average* workingman and the *average* lower middle-class man of 1873, whose numbers had doubled during the previous thirty years, had a third more purchasing power than his father before him. The per capita consumption of sugar and tea had more than doubled since the 1830s. Working-class activities were now more often inspired by the hope of improving conditions and less frequently by the fear of things getting worse. The middle-class shopkeeper could now afford a comfortable house (perhaps in the suburbs) with carpets in the living room, antimacassars on the solid upholstered furniture, an aspidistra in the front hall, paintings and engravings covering the walls, and a piano for the daughters of the house to play.

Averages are by definition misleading, and it would be as idle to dwell on the "prosperity" of most agricultural laborers as on the "rising standard of living" of the inhabitants of the London chronicled by David Mayhew, the tens of thousands of street-sellers, scavengers, street-sweepers, rat-killers, street musicians, unskilled laborers, beggars, and thieves who exemplified the poverty, as well as the variety and vitality, of the greatest metropolis on earth.[2] Even at the height of the mid-Victorian boom, unemployment did not disappear nor did the poor. Yet there was no gainsaying the relative economic improvement, the decrease of social tensions, and the air of confidence that underlay the argument that the proper cure for poverty was for the underprivileged to work hard and raise their status.

---

[2] See Peter Quennell (ed.), *Mayhew's London* (Spring Books, n.d.).

Englishmen of the time tended to attribute their prosperity to two doctrines stressed by the classical economists: free trade and the gold standard. The kingdom had both, and Great Britain, it appeared, was being suitably rewarded by Divine Providence for its economic orthodoxy. Modern economic historians tend to feel that the cause and effect relationship was not quite so simple, but it is manifest that the abolition of tariff barriers had reduced earlier drags on economic growth. There were other factors, however, contributing to prosperity: Britain's technological leadership, the willingness of her business leaders to take risks, and their confidence in a government being carried on in a similarly efficient and businesslike manner. In a significant sense, mid-Victorian Englishmen were reaping the harvest sowed by their forefathers — the suffering, the austerity, the self-imposed reinvestment that had made possible the earlier stages of industrialization. Many of them were imbued with a moral code and fervor which gave them not only a sense of achievement but also a sense of manifest destiny; God was on the side of the custodians of the machine and of the new impulses of the industrial world.

Victorian morality

It is always difficult to sum up the ethos or atmosphere of an age, especially if, like the mid-Victorian, it lies only a century in the past and is documented by an immense profusion of books and journals, pictures, buildings, and pieces of furniture. Clearly, not all Victorian Englishmen thought or acted alike. Yet it may be possible to postulate some reasonably valid generalizations about "Victorianism." It is perhaps easier for us to do this than for historians writing in the 1920s, when writers like Lytton Strachey and Philip Guedalla busily and wittily debunked what they regarded as Victorian prudery, hypocrisy, and stuffiness. "Victorian" remains for us a synonym for "old-fashioned" when referring to attitudes toward sex, but we have in the past forty years become appreciative (even slightly envious) of Victorian political ideals. We have come to regard pieces of Victorian furniture as valuable antiques (so long as they are small enough to fit into our houses) and, even in the United States, many a "Victorian" building has been designated and preserved as "an architectural landmark." [3]

---

[3] Mid-Victorian morality and much else are dealt with in books such as the volumes by Briggs and Clark referred to earlier. G. M. Young's *Victorian England: Portrait of an Age* (London, 1936; Paperback, 1961) is at once discursive and brilliant. The following books throw much light on Victorian intellectual history:

It is, in any event, wiser if more difficult to try to understand Victorianism than to ridicule it, especially if we view it less as a universally congenial or universally practiced moral and social code than as a set of ideals about efficiency and thrift, seriousness of character, respectability, and self-help to which the Victorians themselves often failed to adhere. Yet they tried. The maxim "honesty is the best policy" was to serve not merely as a slogan but as an accepted and demonstrable truth. In the business world, it was by the profession (and often practice) of such virtues that a merchant or an industrialist justified his role in society; and mid-century British businessmen did indeed establish more of a reputation for reliability than for sharp trading. Bankruptcy was regarded not merely as a financial but as a moral disgrace.

Morality in government was given similar, perhaps even greater stress, and it may well be that the institution of a non-political civil service was "the one great political invention in nineteenth-century England." The eighteenth-century political machine had been oiled with "influence" and patronage, but many sinecure positions had been abolished during the first third of the century; and under Benthamite influence there was much talk as to how the national government might be made yet more efficient and competent. It was at the request of Gladstone, then Chancellor of the Exchequer, that a report was prepared in 1853 which recommended the open competitive examination as the ideal route toward government service, a method first used to recruit officials serving the English East India Company.

Accordingly, the Civil Service was to be divided by 1870 into an "intellectual grade" of decision-making posts and a "mechanical grade" of copying clerks and others. Promotion was to be neither on the basis of political pressure nor seniority but only on merit. This did not mean the "democratization" of government service, though fears were expressed that the less quick-witted scions of aristocratic families might fare badly in the examinations. In practice, successful applicants for the "intellectual grade" positions were products either of those aristocratic strongholds, public schools like Eton and Harrow, or of the universities. The introduction by Gladstone of the independent auditing of exchequer accounts gave added support to a growing demand for governmental honesty which

---

D. C. Somervell, *English Thought in the 19th Century* (London, 1929); Crane Brinton, *English Political Thought in the 19th Century*, 2nd ed. (London, 1949); Walter Houghton, *The Victorian Frame of Mind* (New Haven, 1957), and the article by Noel Annan, "The Intellectual Aristocracy" in J. H. Plumb (ed.), *Studies in Social History* (London, 1955).

was being equally stressed in the conduct of elections and in municipal administration.

Emphasis upon morality was similarly, if less happily, characteristic of the Victorian taste in art, architecture, and music. The most popular paintings were large, realistic, and sentimental, and they were painted by artists whose personal morality was beyond cavil. Morality was given similar stress in music, with hymns and, to a lesser extent, religiously inspired oratorios being highly esteemed. This was not, to be sure, an age in which England could boast great composers. Continental Europeans tended to regard England as an "unmusical" country, though particular singers from abroad found it financially worthwhile to tour the British Isles.

In architecture it was A. W. N. Pugin (1812–52), a Roman Catholic by conversion, who quite deliberately introduced Victorian "Gothic" as a style more religiously inspired than the classical Georgian style. Victorians delighted in immense, heavy, and ornate railway stations and town halls, though the preponderant style was in truth less Gothic than eclectic. A typical structure displayed examples of almost every style known to architectural history, Byzantine, Romanesque, Gothic, Tudor, and Renaissance. The results were esthetically confusing and deliberately ill-proportioned from the eighteenth-century point of view. Oddly enough, while Victorian architecture was indulging in a riot of exotic styles and liberating itself from the rigid dictates of Georgian "good taste," it made little use of the new materials afforded by the industrial society. Except for the iron and glass used in the Crystal Palace, Victorian buildings remained immense monuments to the stonemason and the bricklayer.

Perhaps the most widely remembered element of Victorianism is its deliberate deemphasis of sex. Ideally sex was never to be referred to in conversation or in print, and one Victorian critic regarded Charles Dickens' greatest merit to lie in the fact that "in forty works or more you will not find a phrase which a mother need withhold from her grown daughter." Continence became the professed ideal for the gentleman, who in the sexual as in the business world was expected to postpone immediate gratification for his ultimate domestic and financial benefit. To be named in a divorce suit equaled bankruptcy as a source of social disgrace. The reproduction of the species became the only acceptable justification for sexual activity, and the praises of domestic family ties came to be sung more loudly than ever before in British history. The Victorian family was a patriarchal one in which a wife was in no sense her husband's legal equal but in which she was most obviously and significantly the mother of his children. Families were large,

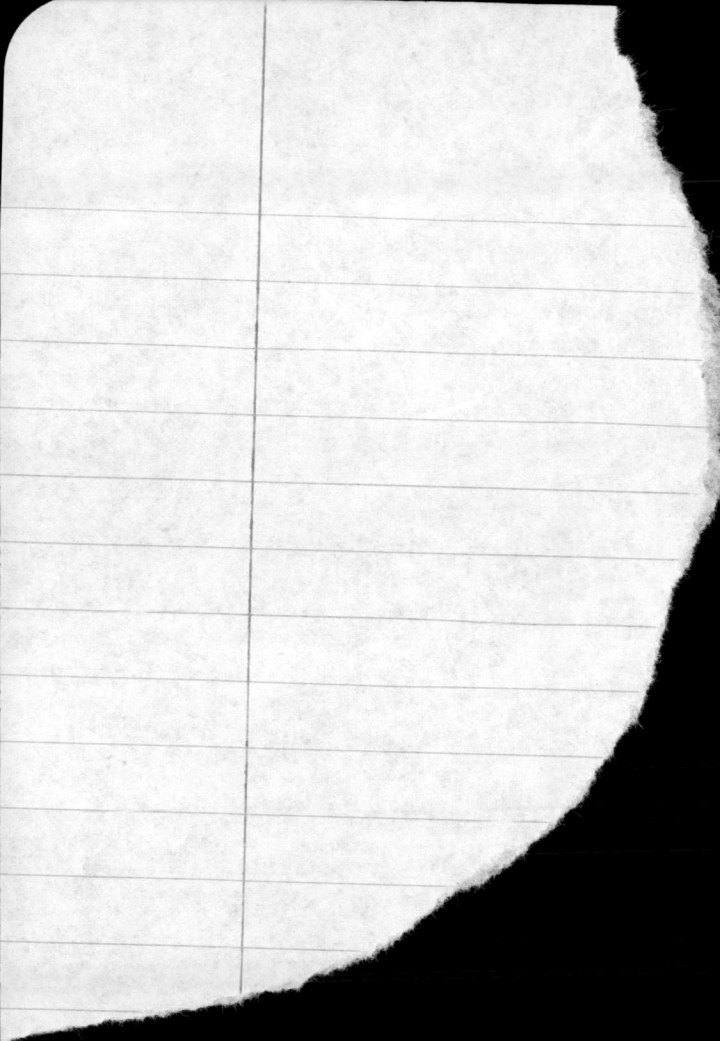

and the average wife spent "about fifteen years in a state of pregnancy and in nursing a child for the first year of its life." In such households it was almost a necessity that "little children should be seen and not heard," for the alternative was bedlam. It was the home, in any event, which was felt to be the center of moral virtue and a refuge against the barbarism of the outside world.

Victorian prudery could lead to such absurdities as the separation of the works of male and female authors on library shelves and the use of euphemisms such as "limbs" for "legs." "Horses sweat; gentlemen perspire; young ladies are all in a glow," went one Victorian conjugation. It was in the "Victorian" United States, to be sure, rather than in England that a British visitor discovered the "limbs" of a grand piano in a girls' school decently clad in little frilled trousers. Certainly it was "Victorianism" which helped give the word "immoral" the connotation it retains – that of opposing sexual convention rather than practicing fraudulent bookkeeping or telling lies or beating children. The price paid for a rigid sexual code was the prevalence of prostitution. One London street was described in the 1850s as "the Western counterpart of an Eastern slave market," and it was estimated that one house in sixty in London was a brothel. Similarly the increasingly strict legal and social control of what society judged to be obscene literature gave rise to a flourishing illicit trade in pornography.

The question of the origins of the admirable as well as the hypocritical elements in Victorian social code is a disputed one. Two factors must first be recalled: Victorian morality was not exclusively British (counterparts in attitude could obviously be found in the France of the Second Empire, in the United States of Lincoln's and Louisa May Alcott's day, and in Czarist Russia) and the roots of Victorian morality can be traced back at least half a century before the accession of Victoria in 1837. Some significant "Puritan" elements necessarily have an even longer history. It was in 1818 that Thomas Bowdler, a well-to-do physician and part-time social reformer, added a new verb to the language by bringing out the Family Shakespeare, "in which nothing is added to the original text; but those words and expressions are omitted which cannot with propriety be read aloud in a family." Shortly thereafter he submitted Gibbon's *Decline and Fall of the Roman Empire* to similar treatment so that the work would not "raise a blush on the cheek of modest innocence."

One highly significant root of "Victorianism" was the evangelical religious revival which continued unabated until the middle decades of the century. Until 1851, the growth of church membership increased more rapidly than did the population, and an enormous amount of enthusiasm and hard work went into the effort to bring the message of religion to those groups in society who had been overlooked in the rapidly growing cities or forgotten during an earlier century. Church and chapel building [4] went on at an unprecedented rate. The number of Congregationalist chapels increased three and a half times between 1801 and 1851; the number of Baptist meeting places multiplied fourfold; and the number of Methodist halls multiplied more than fourteen times during these same years. There was a comparable Roman Catholic revival, encouraged by Irish immigration and by such noted converts as Newman and Henry Edward Manning (1808–92); the latter headed the revived Roman Catholic hierarchy for a generation. The Anglican Church grew less rapidly, but invigorated in spirit by the Oxford Movement and reformed in administration by the Ecclesiastical Commission of 1836, it remained dominant in the countryside and by the 1850s even began to show signs of adjusting its parish system to the new industrial towns. Revival meetings on the American model were popular among many nonconformists, and the evangelically minded "Low Church" remained a prominent facet of Anglicanism.

The unique religious census of 1851 revealed that of almost 18 million people, over 7 million were regular churchgoers. Impressive as these figures are by twentieth-century standards, Victorians were appalled to learn that at least five million of their countrymen (who had neither the excuse of youth nor old age nor illness) turned their backs on both church and chapel. Anglicans were even more horrified to discover that almost half of the faithful were not members of the Established Church.

For many a Victorian, the Bible remained from first page to last the revealed word of God. Heaven and Hell were as certain as the sun in the sky and the Last Judgment as real as a businessman's weekly balance sheet. The Bible provided the most comprehensive system of thought and code of ethics available, and the church or chapel furnished the introduction to music, literature, philosophy, and history. In the words of G. M. Young:

> Evangelicalism had imposed on society, even on classes which were indifferent to its religious basis and unaffected by its economic appeal, its code of Sabbath observance, responsibility, and philanthropy; of discipline in the home, regularity in affairs; it had created

---

[4] The places of worship of the nonconformist denominations in Britain are usually referred to as "chapels."

a most effective technique of agitation, of private persuasion and social persecution."[5]

The evangelical revival was only one factor contributing to the creation of Victorianism. The Victorian unbeliever appears to have been possessed by as strong a sense of duty as were professed Christians, and his moral code was not readily distinguishable from that of the churchgoer. For a utilitarian like John Stuart Mill, being good for good's sake was obviously as powerful a motive as being good for God's sake. Thus "good behavior" was the result not only of church authority or of fear of the police on earth or punishment in the next world, but also of the pressures of social conformity and the hope, stemming from the Age of Enlightenment, that man, when left to his own devices, was fundamentally good. As David Copperfield put it, "We can all do some good if we will."

The Victorian code was obviously a response to the needs of an emerging industrial society and the consciousness that "civilization" provided a thin veneer at best for man's antisocial tendencies. It stressed the virtues of duty and industry because absenteeism and idleness were dangerous relics of the past, the preindustrial society of the eighteenth century. The emphasis on thrift was a reaction to the still popular attitude of "Eat, drink, and be merry," and take no heed for the morrow. The creed of self-help was a virtue preached most earnestly to those who were not necessarily in a position to practice it. "Character" was a highly acclaimed ideal because rowdyism and drunkenness, despite the efforts of a growing army of nonconformist temperance reformers, were still widespread. Seen as a set of ideals rather than as the attributes of a whole society, Victorianism becomes more understandable. Its snobbery reflected the impact of new classes wishing to secure a position in the traditional hierarchy. Its hypocrisy resulted from the attempt to lay claim to standards of conduct which proved too hard to maintain consistently. Its prudery was the by-product of a battle for decency by a people many of whom were just emerging into "civilized" society.

The Middle Class Ethos

One of the fascinating elements of "Victorianism" was the process whereby the "middle class" virtues of self-improvement,

---

[5] G. M. Young, *Victorian England: Portrait of an Age* (London, 1936).

perseverance, thrift, duty, and character came to influence the other classes in society. This transformation was most obvious in the royal family. The rakish sons of George III gave way to Queen Victoria and Prince Albert. Their marriage was based on love and mutual devotion as much as on convenience of state, and by the 1850s the royal family, with its nine children, had become the model family of the land. Mistresses, all-night gambling, and wild extravagance had given place to propriety and respectability. The story is told of the Victorian playgoer who went to see a performance of "Oedipus Rex" in which the hero murders his father, unwittingly marries his mother, and then blinds himself while his mother commits suicide. Murmured the playgoer as he emerged: "How different from the home life of our own dear Queen!"

Victoria's resolve on her accession at the age of eighteen "to be good" was in harmony with her age. The "Bedchamber Crisis" of 1839 in which the Queen and Sir Robert Peel clashed over who was to control the appointment of the ladies of the bedchamber was more a matter of morality than politics. Victoria was less intent on emphasizing the political power of the Crown than upon refusing to allow a Prime Minister to surround her with what (somewhat unreasonably) she feared might be dissolute and immoral political appointees. Prince Albert, who was not yet twenty-one at the time of his marriage to the Queen, shared her keen sense of propriety. He added a touch of "Germanic" thoroughness to the court, which did not always make him popular; but it at least coincided with the Victorian stress on the virtue of industry. Albert was also a vigorous advocate of scientific research and education and much preferred the company of authors, scientists, and social reformers to that of aristocrats whose main preoccupation was horse racing. He also had a sense of humor. When Alexis de Tocqueville wrote in 1856 that Prince Albert was the most remarkable prince he had ever encountered, the Prince Consort commented: "I apprehend his feelings are the same as those expressed by the King towards his Prime Minister in Blanche's 'White Cat':

> 'He is the cleverest man in our dominion
> For he is always of our opinion'."

Queen Victoria was less intellectual and (perhaps in consequence) more popular. She was also less easily amused.

Albert's death from typhoid fever in 1861 was a shock from which Victoria never completely recovered. Her state of mourning threatened to become permanent, and she refused to take part in any of the public ceremonies expected of monarchy, though she was ready enough to continue her conscientious concern with government business behind the scenes. Her decline in popularity helped give rise to a short-lived republican movement in the late 1860s; but her appropriateness as the prototype of Victorianism remained unquestioned.

The aristocracy as a whole was as much infected by "Victorian" morality as the monarchy itself. Lord Melbourne, who was named co-respondent in a divorce suit while Prime Minister (he was found innocent), and Lord Palmerston, who fathered several children by Lady Cowper (who later became Lady Palmerston) were relics of a passing age. "Publish and be damned," the Duke of Wellington had once exclaimed when threatened with the exposure of his indiscretions; but by the 1850s this Regency code of honor was in eclipse. People in high society had become far more responsible and sober. (At one time "even in the best society, one third of the gentlemen at least were always drunk"; by Victoria's reign, a gentleman was not expected to be seen intoxicated in public.) The change may well have benefited not merely their souls but also their pocketbooks and their life expectancy. "The aristocracy live in fear of the middle classes — of the grocer and the merchant," wrote Walter Bagehot in the 1860s. "They dare not frame a society of enjoyment as the French aristocracy once formed." G. K. Chesterton concluded, "The great lords yielded on prudery as they had yielded on free trade."

Not only had such "middle class" morality changed the tone of upper-class society, it was increasingly seeping down to the working classes as well. The 1850s, for example, saw the beginnings of respectable trade unionism in England. The Amalgamated Society of Engineers (1851) and the Amalgamated Society of Carpenters and Joiners were typical of the "New Model" Unionism. They did not seek to transform society, only to profit from it. They disliked strikes, and they believed in thrift, temperance, and steady habits and in building up large insurance funds. Their professed object was to do nothing "illegally or indiscreetly, but on all occasions to perform the greatest amount of benefit to ourselves, without injury to others." Such unions were essentially limited to "an aristocracy of skilled labor," but the boom of the mid-Victorian years encouraged the growth of respectable trade unionism among miners and, for a time, even agricultural laborers. In 1868 was held the first annual Trades Union Congress, a national confederation of British labor unions which foreshadowed both in scope and attitude the American Federation of Labor, organized in the 1880s.

The New Model Unions did much to disarm earlier middle-class distrust of trade unionism, and for a time trade union members were regarded as being under the protection of the

Friendly Societies Act of 1855. This act, by placing the mantle of government protection over the funds of voluntary societies did much to foster "self-help" among the lower middle-class groups and skilled workers. By 1874 there were 25,000 of these with over six million members, and the Registrar of the Friendly Societies, a Mr. Stephenson, had become a kind of universal Dutch uncle to the worthy laboring man.

> Mr. Stephenson, is [reported one official] as it were a minister of self-help to the whole of the industrious classes. The first penny deposited by a school child in a penny savings bank finds its way probably to a trustee savings bank, the rules of which are certified by Mr. Stephenson. When the boy begins to work for himself, if he has forethought and prudence, he very likely opens his own account, although still a minor, with a Savings Bank; toward the end of his apprenticeship he joins a benefit club or Odd Fellows lodge, certified by the same hand in a different capacity. If he desires to improve his mind he enters a Scientific or Literary institution, the rules of which have probably passed equally through the registrar's hand. If he becomes a member of a Trade Society, he learns that the only legal security for the funds is to be obtained by certification through the same hand. If he marry and have a family to provide for, he will seek to cheapen his living by entering a Co-operative Store, whose rules have received the same Registrar's sanction. As his capital accumulates, and he aspires to the possession of a house of his own, he subscribes to a Benefit Building Society, still certified by the same authority. On the other hand, if he has difficulties to pass through, the Loan Society, certified by the same person, will frequently have proved his first resource, perhaps a fatal one. And if he has remained satisfied with the low rate of interest of the Post Office Savings Bank [set up in 1861], he knows, or should know, that in case of dispute it is still Mr. Stephenson who will be the arbitrator. Thus, at every step in life, he will have been met by the authority of the same person, who has been for him, as it were, the embodiment of the goodwill and protection of the State, in all that goes beyond police, the poor law, justice, and the school.[6]

Perhaps a third of the population was more familiar with the possibility of entering the workhouse than with the prospect

---

[6] *English Historical Documents*, Vol. XII, Part I (1830–1874).

of investing funds in savings banks or borrowing from Building and Loan Societies; but for many Victorian artisans and shopkeepers, *Self-Help* was more than the title of a best-selling book by Samuel Smiles (1859); it was a reality as well as a credo.

Associated with the spread of "Victorianism" to the poorer classes of British society was a growing sense of law-mindedness. Genuine obedience to and deference for the law had not always been a notable English trait, but by the 1850s even working-class leaders had begun to take pride in their ability to assemble large crowds without disorder. When Queen Victoria visited Birmingham in 1858, self-satisfaction was expressed in the enormous crowds "who behaved as well in the streets as could any assemblage of the aristocracy at a Queen's Drawing Room."

The decrease in lawlessness was attributable not merely to a change in attitude but to the presence of an effective deterrent to crime in the form of city and rural police. The introduction of gas-lighting to cities was equally significant in adding to public security. By 1839 one observer found it possible to walk from one end of London to the other without molestation, a feat regarded impossible half a century before. The decline in crime was accompanied by a decrease in the severity of punishments. Flogging as an army punishment in peacetime was abolished in 1868, and during that same year the last public hanging took place at Tyburn. Thus ended one of the traditional, if dubious, sources of public amusement and edification. During the 1830s, cockfighting, bull baiting, and bearbaiting — the last-named sport actually subsidized by the government in the days of Queen Elizabeth I — were all made illegal.

Amateur and professional football and cricket were in due course to take the place of public spectacles like hangings, and the music hall was in the later years of the century to become a prime example of popular working and lower middle-class amusement. "The aim of the Music Hall," wrote Max Beerbohm in 1898, "is to cheer the lower classes up by showing them a life uglier and more sordid than their own." Its rough and tumble humor, its lusty singing, and its emphasis on audience participation did not make for the acme of decorousness. Yet it was a far cry from the brutality of its predecessors.

The social structure of mid-Victorian England is often described as one in which the middle classes had somehow conquered the upper classes. This view is far too simple. It may be more appropriate to see the change as one whereby the aristocrat was transformed into the gentleman. It might be difficult to define the word "gentleman," conceded Anthony Trollope (1815–82), the chronicler of that delightfully fanciful but true-to-life mid-Victorian county of Barsetshire, but he was certain

London in 1842.
St. Paul's Cathedral may be seen in the background.
Lithograph by T. Shotter Boys.

that "any one would know what it meant." To be a member of an old aristocratic family clearly gave one a head start. To lay claim to a coat of arms was an asset as was the prospective ownership of a large estate. But these attributes by themselves were no longer sufficient; character, education, and membership in a profession such as the law or the clergy (or medicine or architecture) had come to be almost as important.

It was not necessary to have gone to Oxford or Cambridge to be a gentleman, but it obviously helped. Both of the old universities increased in size during the middle years of the nineteenth century. But the increase of the combined entering class from 700 men a year in the early years of the century to 1600 men in 1880 was more a reflection of the increase in total population than of a growth in the ratio of those educated at a university. If one did not attend a university, it was most desirable that one went to a "public school." Eton, Harrow, Rugby, Winchester, and the rest were "public" only in the sense that education there was not by private tutor and involved training in the company of boys from other walks of life. A landowner's son might well encounter the son of an industrialist who had made good, but he was increasingly less likely to encounter the genuinely poor boy for whom a proportion of scholarships had been reserved in earlier centuries.

The public schools had long histories; but in the eighteenth century they had, according to Dr. Bowdler, been most noteworthy as "nurseries of vice." It was Dr. Thomas Arnold (1795–1842), who became headmaster of Rugby in 1828, who launched a nineteenth-century reform movement. "What we must look for," said Arnold, "is first, religious and moral principle; secondly, gentlemanly conduct; thirdly, intellectual ability." Organized athletics were also stressed. Rugby emphasized modern languages and the natural sciences as well as the classics, but to a surprising degree, Greek and Latin continued to dominate both the public school and university curriculum. Admittedly, they would not get you far (in a strictly utilitarian sense), but the assumption was that you were already somewhere when you took them up.

The public schools did teach self-discipline and independence from immediate family ties, for boys were enrolled at eight or nine. Their most important product was "the character of an English gentleman," but in a very real sense they trained the administrators of Victorian England and the Victorian Empire. It was public school gentlemen who were given the greatest encouragement to compete for the decision-making grades of the civil service. It was such gentlemen whom army reformers sought to fill the ranks of that service's commissioned officers. It was this same class of public school graduates —

comparable in training and outlook to the "guardians" of Plato's *Republic* – who went to India and Africa and elsewhere to take up posts in the imperial civil service. Schoolboy friendship influenced many a political appointment in later life, and old-school-tieism became one of the marks of the Established Victorian order.

Although even the reformed public schools were still tainted by brutality and often limited in intellectual scope, the genus "Victorian gentleman" did include intellectuals as well. Architects, civil and mechanical engineers, lawyers, and physicians elevated their professions by setting up permanent organizations to establish standards and gain prestige. The mid-Victorian world produced a considerable number of sober well-written journals of opinion such as the *Edinburgh Review* (1802), the *Westminster Review* (1828), and the *Saturday Review* (1858). Though not aristocrats by birth, men like Macaulay, the historian, John Stuart Mill, the economist and political scientist, and Walter Bagehot, the editor and social observer, all belonged to that privileged class of Victorian intellectuals who had the money and the leisure to read and write for such journals. They were gentlemen of good manners and good breeding, and they had the self-confidence and social prestige not only to reflect their age but to criticize it.

At the root of the mid-Victorian way of life lay a paradox. On the one hand, laissez-faire was implicit in the outlook of the age, not perhaps to the degree that the more dogmatic of the classical economists would have wished, but to a large degree nonetheless. Ultimately it was the law of supply and demand which was expected to promote the competition which in turn would produce the maximum number of goods and thus benefit society. The chief function of government was thus defined in negative terms, to see to it that the rules of the games were observed – to prevent frauds and enforce contracts – but not enter the game itself. The true progress of a business – and of a nation – was expected to be the result of individual initiative and individual self-help. This idea pervades not only Mill's *On Liberty* (1859) but that even more widely sold book published the same year, *Self-Help*. Its ebullient author, Samuel Smiles, assured his earnest reader:

> Englishmen feel that they are free, not merely because they live under those free institutions which they have laboriously built up, but because each member of the society has to a greater or less extent got the root of the matter within himself.

If, however, economic and social life was a scramble of individuals each out for his own good, then what bond held society together? It lay, Smiles believed, in a common set of moral standards, in "the unfettered energetic actions of persons, together with the uniform subjection of all to the national code of Duty."

In an age marked by a high degree of economic prosperity and social stability, in which the creed of progress was exemplified daily in the material world, numerous Englishmen came to view the world with a high degree of complacency; and the country's leaders showed little inclination toward tampering with its political institutions. Neither Lord Aberdeen (1784–1860), the Peelite who headed a coalition ministry, 1852–55, nor Lord Palmerston, the Whig who, with a brief interruption, served as Prime Minister during the decade that followed, was a domestic reformer by inclination. In some ways the period was retrogressive. Edwin Chadwick, the eager social reformer, was forced off the Board of Health in 1854, and four years later the entire office was abolished. "We prefer to take our chance of cholera and the rest, rather than to be bullied into health," declared the London *Times*. On the local level, sanitary improvement continued, however, and although Birmingham, whose corporation government was captured by extreme classical economists, became one of the sickliest cities during the mid-Victorian years, Manchester and Liverpool were spurred to set up voluntary boards of health. London also underwent improvements, for it was during the prosperous 1850s and 1860s that the "vast and shapeless city which Dickens knew — fog-bound and fever haunted, brooding over its dark, mysterious river" — was converted "into the imperial capital, of Whitehall, the Thames Embankment and South Kensington."

Observing the English people in the mid-1860s, Walter Bagehot found them "politically contented as well as politically deferential. . . . A man can hardly get an audience if he wishes to complain of anything." Lord Palmerston perfectly reflected this complacency about social and political reform legislation when he was asked at the opening of the 1864 Parliamentary session what his party's program was. He mused a moment and then answered, "Oh, there is really nothing to be done. We cannot go on adding to the Statute Book ad infinitum. Perhaps we may have a little law reform, or bankruptcy reform; but we cannot go on legislating forever."

The Critics of Victorianism

It would be a mistake to see complacency as the total atmosphere of the age, for Victorians could be as self-critical as they were self-confident. Thomas Carlyle (1795–1881) struck out against the "cash nexus" and "mammon worship" of his age, and he branded his society as one in which materialistic mediocrity dominated, a society lacking heroes. John Ruskin (1819–1900) shared Carlyle's distrust of a competitive industrial society, founded on free enterprise and machine production. He was repelled alike by the artistic shoddiness which he saw as the product of industrial civilization and by the continued prevalence of poverty. "The first duty of the state," he believed, "is to see that every child born therein shall be well housed, clothed, fed, and educated, till it attains years of discretion." Concern for the welfare of the lower classes was also expressed by such avowed "Christian Socialists" as Charles Kingsley (1819–75) and F. D. Maurice (1805–72).

Other critics accepted the basis of Victorian society while yet opposing some of its fruits. Walter Bagehot, for one, concluded that commercial civilization "begets a mind desirous of things." Matthew Arnold (1822–88) was still more biting in his criticisms and urged his contemporaries to seek for quality rather than quantity in life. He saw the English aristocracy as still "barbarians," the lower classes as still brutalized by the struggle for existence, and the middle classes as no more than "Philistines," narrow and prejudiced in outlook, handicapped by a "defective type of religion," "a stunted sense of beauty," and "a low standard of life."

> Your middle-class man [wrote Arnold scornfully] thinks it the highest pitch of development and civilization when his letters are carried twelve times a day from Islington to Camberwell . . . and if railway trains run to and from them every quarter of an hour. He thinks it is nothing that the trains only carry him from an illiberal, dismal life at Islington to an illiberal, dismal life at Camberwell; and the letters only tell him that such is the life there.

Matthew Arnold was a freethinker, unconvinced by religious dogmas but appreciative of religious moral teaching and of the literary splendor of the Bible. He was at the farthest end of the spectrum of a growing number of religious liberals or "Broad Churchmen" ready to embrace all varieties of Christian thought and willing to agree that the "higher criticism" of the Bible made popular by German scholars had cast great doubt upon many of its details. Their book, *Essays and Reviews*, published in 1860, was representative of such questioning of religious dogma. The authors, mostly Anglican clergymen, were criticized as heretics both by high churchmen like Bishop Samuel Wilberforce (1805–1873) and low churchmen like Lord Shaftesbury, the most eminent of Evangelical laymen.

It may seem curious to cite Charles Darwin (1809–82) as one of the critics of Victorianism, because in background and character – and perhaps even in bearded appearance – he seems so very Victorian himself. Yet his own work did as much as that of any other man to raise doubts about the religious and philosophical underpinnings of Victorian thought. Darwin, like Isaac Newton almost two centuries before, came not at the beginning of a process but toward the end – he was the man who summed things up. He confined himself primarily to a single science, biology; yet as Newton had influenced a great many men who were neither physicists nor mathematicians, so Darwin was to influence a great many people who were not biologists. In the case of Darwin as in that of Newton, some of the most far-reaching implications were drawn not by the authors themselves but by their more militant disciples.

Newton's key concept was that of a mechanical universe, a universe running year in, year out, in accordance with precise mathematical formulas which men had discovered or could discover. Darwin's significance lay in confirming the idea of evolution in the natural world – eternal change rather than eternal stability. Although the concept of biological evolution can be traced back to Anaximander among the ancient Greek philosophers, the prevailing doctrine until the early nineteenth century was the Aristotelian and scholastic belief in a fixed number of species, each fulfilling its appointed role in nature and each created in Biblical fashion at a precise point in time a few thousand years before.

During the early nineteenth century, the doctrine of evolution had, however, made headway in a variety of fields. In geology, Englishmen like Charles Lyell (1797–1875) were suggesting that earth had not been created in the beginning as it then existed but had been subjected to all kinds of evolutionary change. The discovery of fossils seemed to indicate that the age of the earth should be measured in terms of millions rather than thousands of years, and the accepted Biblical chronology was thereby overturned. Although Philip Gosse suggested that God had planted the fossils in the rocks to test man's faith, other Victorians rebelled at the idea of such a deception, dismissing it as decidedly unsporting on God's part. Lamarck, the French biologist, had put forward a theory of biological evolution; but the proposed method of its operation, the inheritance of acquired characteristics, had not won general acceptance.

The importance of Darwin's *Origin of Species* (1859) lay then less in the concept than in providing for the first time an immense accumulation of carefully collated data which supported the thesis. Geographical, geological, biological, and embryological evidence gathered over a period of twenty-five years he put together in such a fashion as to make the argument that the entire animal kingdom had evolved from an original one-celled organism no longer merely a possible hypothesis but the most plausible manner of accounting for the factual data assembled. Darwin not only demonstrated the case for evolution; he also suggested a method by which it had taken place: natural selection on the basis of chance variations. In effect, Darwin applied the Malthusian theory to the whole natural world. In any given generation, more organisms are born than can support themselves. No two organisms are identical. The organisms best fitted for their environment survive in the struggle for existence and become the parents of the next generation. Small changes can accumulate from generation to generation and thereby bring about changes of species including, ultimately, the development of an organism like man himself.

Upon the publication of the *Origin of Species* in 1859, Darwin found himself involved with two sets of critics: his fellow biologists, most of whom became converts to his notions, and the religious enthusiasts who received his ideas as being in direct opposition to God's Word as revealed in the Bible. The battle lines were drawn at the Metaphysical Society debate of 1860 at which Bishop Samuel Wilberforce criticized Darwin's theory as an absurdity. Turning to Thomas Henry Huxley (1825–95), who was to become Darwin's most cogent and forceful advocate, the bishop "begged to know, was it through his grandfather or his grandmother that he claimed his descent from a monkey?" Huxley quietly replied that he was present at the meeting in the interests of science and that thus far he had heard nothing to invalidate Darwin's ideas. He for one, he added, would not be ashamed to have a monkey for an ancestor; but he would be "ashamed to be connected with a man who used great gifts to obscure the truth." [7]

The Metaphysical Society debate was only the beginning of an intense controversy over the ultimate role of formal religion in Victorian life. Although the eighteenth century had known atheists and deists—usually among the upper class — the early nineteenth century had seen a reaction against deism and against attempts to remove the emotional and the miraculous from religion. Many nineteenth-century Englishmen read their Bible faithfully and believed in it literally. Some had been affected by the "higher criticism" of the Bible practiced on the

---

[7] William Irvine, *Apes, Angels, and Victorians* (New York, 1955).

Continent. Others had become aware of the conclusions of comparative anthropology on the variants of religious belief to be found throughout the world. But for most good Victorians, Darwin seemed to be by far the most severe threat to religion and the established order of things. The essential question was posed by Disraeli in 1864: "Is man an ape or an angel?" Like Disraeli, they also aligned themselves on the side of the angels.

Other mid-Victorians, however, felt less certain. Darwin seemed to indicate—and in *The Descent of Man* (1871) to demonstrate—that man was as much the product of natural evolution as any other plant or animal. Yet the Darwinian thesis was a hard one to stomach; what of the human soul? What place was there for a divine design in a world which was the result of the amoral and mechanical interplay of chance variations which had made some individual organisms more likely to survive than their rivals?

Some Victorians turned their back on science and sought refuge in religious fundamentalism. Others, as devoted to the pursuit of scientific truth as to their religious upbringing, sought a compromise which might harmonize Godless Darwinian evolution with Biblical revelation and orthodox Christianity. That some of the attempts to fashion such intellectual syntheses proved convincing is demonstrated by the fact that when Darwin died in 1882, he, like Isaac Newton, was buried in Westminster Abbey. For a good many Englishmen, the conflux of the higher criticism and Darwinism meant a spiritually painful adjustment to a world in which there was place for neither God nor dogma. Huxley himself coined the word "agnosticism" as the only appropriate solution.

Darwin's theories came to play an influential role not only in biology and religion but also in the social sciences. Men like Herbert Spencer (1820–1903) in England and Andrew Carnegie in the United States—thinkers often referred to as Social Darwinists—emphasized one particular part of Darwin's theory, that evolution was a struggle for survival in which only the fittest survived. As applied to economics, it meant the ceaseless struggle of the individual entrepreneur in which only the aggressive survived. For Herbert Spencer, Darwinism simply reinforced earlier predilections toward laissez-fairism in the economic world. Spencer was as doubtful as Malthus had been that human beings could do anything to interfere usefully with economic law. In the later years of the nineteenth century, other so-called Social Darwinists emphasized not so much individual as national or racial struggle. For such men, war provided the human analogy to the animal struggle for survival. Thus the Franco-Prussian War of 1870–71 seemed to demonstrate that the German "race" was superior to the

French "race," just as the Opium War of 1839–42 had demonstrated the white "race" superior to the yellow "race." The word "race" quite clearly came to be used in a less than precise manner, but it does seem evident that during the late nineteenth and early twentieth century the doctrine of "race" was given new meaning in the scramble for empire, and new pseudo-scientific support.

Not all social scientists drew the same implications from Darwinism. Some saw the logical inconsistency in interpreting the idea of struggle for survival so as to apply to individuals in one instance, to nations in another, and to "races" based on skin color in a third. Some biologists contended that natural history afforded numerous examples of animal species which survived by means of mutual aid rather than competition. Still others, such as Thomas Huxley himself, maintained that the pattern which the scientist had found in nature did not necessarily have to serve as a pattern for man's cultural development. If man's biological evolution was the product of millenia of variation and struggle for survival, then man's cultural development represented the triumph of his ability to use his mind over so-called "natural" processes. In Huxley's view, Social Darwinists like Spencer had mistaken the evolution of ethics for the ethics of evolution.

If Social Darwinism and its various tributaries merely illustrated anew the danger of making a discovery in one science the key to every other branch of knowledge, this does not undermine Darwin's long-range significance. The doctrine of biological evolution has come not merely to be accepted but to be taken for granted. The doctrine of natural selection has also largely stood the test of time, though twentieth-century geneticists have become much better informed on the causes and workings of the "chance variations" – or mutations – which play so important a role in the theory.

While in one sense Darwin was a critic of his age, in another he gave support to one of the chief credos of his times. If the implications of his ideas cast doubt upon Victorian religion and the static concept of the universe, at least they seemed to sustain the optimistic hope, in Darwin's own words, that "as natural selection works solely by and for the good of each being, all corporal and mental environments will tend to progress toward perfection." The thought contains an unacknowledged value judgment – for the success of an organism in adapting to a particular environment says nothing about the intrinsic value of that environment. But the conclusion helped reconcile the Victorians to Darwin. If the world was, indeed, in a constant state of flux, this was for most a sign that the present was better than the past and that the future would be better still.

Chapter 6

𝕎ar Drums Sound Afar

The Vienna settlement held firm for forty years, 1815–54. There were international squabbles, ideological tension, and domestic revolutions; but by and large, the great powers showed surprising restraint, respect for treaties, a reluctance to become tied down by inflexible alliances, and a willingness to cooperate against any threat to the balance of power. Lord Palmerston, though bellicose at times, had done his share to prevent events such as the Continental revolutions of 1848 from leading to international war.

During the third quarter of the nineteenth century as first France under Napoleon III and then Prussia under Bismarck sought a revision of earlier territorial boundaries, the Vienna system began to break down. Within less than two decades, six wars were fought: the Crimean War, the Austro-Sardinian War, the American Civil War, and the three wars of German unification. Britain was to be affected directly by the first and indirectly by the rest.[1] Although Palmerston was to survive

---

[1] The books cited in Chapter 4 are almost all relevant here. So are Kingsley Martin's *The Triumph of Lord Palmerston* (London, 1924), a study of the origins of the Crimean War, and Cecil Woodham-Smith's *The Reason Why* (New York, 1954) and *Florence Nightingale* (New York, 1951). Fundamental to an understanding of the nineteenth-century British Empire in India are Vols. V & VI of the *Cambridge History of British India* (Cambridge, 1929, 1932). Philip Woodruff's two-volume account, *The Men Who Ruled India* (New York, 1954) is more readable. A valuable book on the Sepoy Mutiny is T. R. Holmes, *History of the Mutiny,*

for the greater part of this turbulent period, his position was no longer that of Foreign Secretary. When in 1851 he rashly gave British approval to Napoleon's coup d'etat (making him President of France for life) without first consulting either Queen Victoria or his colleagues, he was asked to resign. His fall was hailed on the Continent as the triumph of counter-revolution, but in reality British foreign policy underwent little change. Lord John Russell, who assumed the post in 1852, defined that policy in words which would have received his predecessor's full endorsement:

> We are connected, and have been for more than a century, with the general system of Europe, and any territorial increase of one Power, any aggrandisement which disturbs the general balance of power in Europe, although it might not immediately lead to war, could not be a matter of indifference to this country and would, no doubt, be the subject of conference, and might ultimately, if that balance were seriously threatened, lead to war.

The Crimean War

The implied threat—that England might go to war in order to maintain the balance of power—was within two years put to the test. The Cabinet which became increasingly involved in the events which led up to the Crimean War was the Whig-Peelite Coalition of 1852, which had a Peelite, Lord Aberdeen, as Prime Minister, Russell as Foreign Secretary, and Palmerston in the unaccustomed role of Home Secretary. The war has been variously explained as the result of the ambitions of Napoleon III, of British economic interests in Turkey, and of the diplomatic machinations of either Lord Palmerston or Stratford de Redcliffe, the British ambassador in Constantinople. The conflict may more realistically be seen as part of a century-long rivalry between Russia and the Ottoman Empire. The Russians sought Constantinople and an outlet to the Mediterranean Sea and also the acknowledgment of their proprietory role as protectors of the Greek Orthodox subjects of the Moslem Sultan. Britain, France, and Austria, however, were equally

---

5th ed. (London, 1904). Martin D. Lewis' *The British in India: Imperialism or Trusteeship?* a volume in the Heath "Problems in European Civilization" series (Boston, 1962), introduces conflicting evaluations of the merits of British rule.

determined to keep Russian influence out of the Balkans and Near East and to maintain the neutrality of the Dardanelles, which had been accepted by the major powers in 1840 and which in effect blocked Russian expansion into the Mediterranean. Not unnaturally, the Turks soon learned that no matter how irresponsibly they acted, France and Britain would feel obliged to back them up. In May 1853, diplomatic relations between Turkey and Russia were broken. Part of the British navy was sent to the Black Sea as a peace-keeping force. Russian troops thereupon occupied the principalities of Moldavia and Wallachia (modern Romania). An attempt by the big powers to meet at Vienna and settle the issue by compromise was unsuccessful. The Turks refused to acknowledge Russia's special role as protector of Ottoman Christians, and the Russians were equally stubborn in their insistence. In October 1853, the Sultan announced that Turkey would go to war if the Russians did not evacuate the principalities within two weeks. The Czar refused, and war began. Late in November, the inept Russian Black Sea fleet sank an even more inefficient Turkish flotilla at Sinope.

The "massacre of Sinope" aroused British public opinion as no previous event had done. During the following months, latent Russophobia came to the surface. "Our statesmen," wrote the London *Globe* after Sinope, "have been too much in the habit of transacting business with Russia as if Russia were accessible to the ordinary motives of the rest of the European family." Added the London *Chronicle* shortly thereafter: "We shall draw the sword, if draw we must, not only to preserve the independence of an ally, but to humble the ambition and thwart the machinations of a despot whose intolerable pretensions have made him the enemy of all civilized nations!" Russia's domestic institutions were criticized—alone among Europe's great powers she retained the institution of serfdom—and her drive toward Constantinople was feared to be but the prelude to even vaster territorial ambitions. Urged on by jingoistic newspapers, Britain and France drifted into war against the Russian colossus. Their fleets entered the Black Sea, and both nations insisted that Russia confine her naval forces to the Crimean port of Sebastopol. The Russians refused, and war was declared in March 1854.

The war proved to be a limited one, partly because an expected Russian push upon Constantinople did not materialize. Indeed, in the fall of 1854 the Russian government decided to evacuate the disputed principalities. In the meantime, grandiose British and French speculations about a possible march on Moscow were quickly subordinated to the attainment of a more limited objective: the invasion of the Crimea and the capture of the Russian naval base at Sebastopol. In late summer a landing was accomplished by an expeditionary force of French and British troops—supplemented by Turkish and later by Sardinian contingents—but there was so much confusion that by the time they were ready to attack Sebastopol, the port had been reinforced. A long siege ensued, and as the winter and spring of 1855 wore on, with no sign of victory, the British public became notably less obsessed with fear of Russia and began to wonder why England had gotten into war in the first place. That the conflict never became "total" is demonstrated by the fact that in the midst of the war, a Russian loan was floated in the London money market. It was "in the ordinary way of business," wrote the Foreign Secretary, Lord Clarendon, and ought not to be interfered with.

As fear of Russia waned, dissatisfaction with the manner in which the British government was managing its part of the war increased. War correspondents pointed out in damning dispatches that the whole Crimean operation was being bungled. Individual British soldiers might show themselves to be as brave as ever, but as in the famous Charge of the Light Brigade at Balaclava, it was clear that the high command had blundered. Elderly and inexperienced generals were showing up the weaknesses of the system whereby commissioned officers purchased their positions, thus disbarring the abler soldier who lacked wealth and/or aristocratic connections. The system resulted in such incongruities as senior officers returning from the battlefield each evening to their wives (or mistresses) on private yachts. One young lieutenant, his squad pinned down by enemy gunfire, sought aid from the captain of a neighboring unit with the words: "You may recall that we were introduced last summer at Lady Parkington's!"

Equally serious were the lack of adequate food, supplies, and transportation and the failure to provide proper care for the sick or the wounded. Cholera was to prove a greater killer than gunfire. When the Aberdeen Cabinet ignored the growing demand for a full-scale investigation into the government's handling of the war, it was defeated by the overwhelming vote of 305 to 148, and Lord Palmerston replaced Lord Aberdeen as Prime Minister. "We turned out the Quaker and put in the pugilist," was a contemporary reaction to the event. Palmerston was clearly the more effective Prime Minister if only because, unlike most of his colleagues, he was a genuinely popular public figure. His appeal—like Canning's a generation before—transcended party lines, and he was probably the first English statesman deliberately to ingratiate himself with all shades of newspaper opinion.

While Parliament appointed a Select Committee to investi-

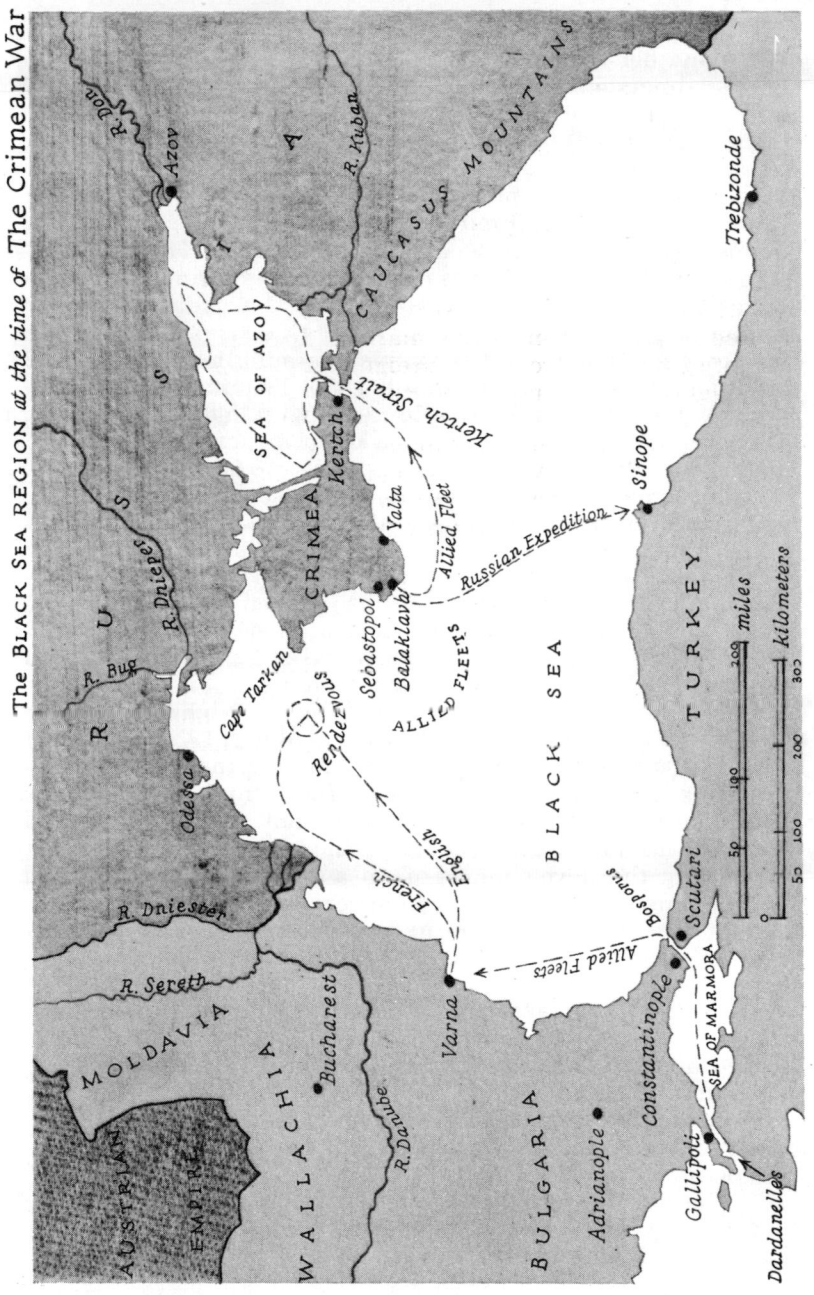

The BLACK SEA REGION *at the time of* The Crimean War

gate the conduct of the war and Florence Nightingale (1820–1910) and her volunteer nurses tended the sick in the Crimea, Lord Palmerston strengthened his position within the government. The fall of Sebastopol in September 1855 enhanced his reputation still further and made it possible to end the war. Once the port had surrendered, Napoleon III announced that he had no desire to continue the fighting, and since there were three times as many French troops in the Crimea as British troops, his attitude was necessarily influential. The new Russian Czar, Alexander II, was equally eager to bring the war to a close, and inasmuch as Russian troops had inflicted several resounding defeats on the Turks in the Caucasus, he could sue for peace without a sense of complete humiliation. By the time land operations ceased in March 1856, Britain had lost more than 32,000 of the 96,000 volunteers who had fought in the Crimea. Almost 3,000 had been killed in action; more than 11,800 had died of wounds, and almost 18,000 from disease.

Although the actual fighting had been inconclusive, the war produced a number of significant consequences, both at home and abroad. The temporary outcry in Britain against aristocratic incompetence (especially in the army) soon subsided, but a few permanent reforms resulted: the War Department was reorganized and at last separated from the Colonial Office. A new army medical school was begun which accepted the use of chloroform, new surgical techniques, and the modern nursing profession as fashioned by Florence Nightingale. The Treaty of Paris, which ended the war in March 1856, weakened Russian power in the Near East by forcing the Czar to withdraw his troops from the mouth of the Danube. Russia was similarly compelled to acknowledge that it had no special authority as protector of Greek Orthodox Christians, thereby permitting the development of an autonomous Romania and Serbia outside the immediate sphere of Russian influence. Russia agreed to neutralize the Black Sea by ceasing to maintain or establish along its coast "military-maritime arsenals." Russian power, which after 1848 had been at a nineteenth-century high, was never to be so great again until the twentieth century. In the meantime the Turkish Empire had been preserved and the Ottoman Sultan was admitted formally to the Concert of Europe, which was reconstituted in 1856 when Austria and Prussia, neither of which had participated militarily in the Crimean War, both took part in the peace conference.

Despite the fact that the concept of a Concert of Europe had been restored, the years that followed were to show less national self-restraint, respect for treaties, or cooperation than the previous forty years; and in Britain, once the war was over, there was great reluctance to become embroiled in Continental affairs. Despite his association with an aggressive foreign policy, Palmerston himself remained popular; but even Palmerston began to show an increasing hesitance to become overly involved in Europe. When asked to aid the advocates of a project to build a tunnel under the English Channel, his reply was to the point: "What! You pretend to ask us to contribute to a work the object of which is to shorten a distance which we find already too short."

A prominent exception to the tendency toward nonintervention in European affairs was the British concern with the struggle for the unification of Italy. Many prominent Englishmen were pro-Italians as they had been pro-Hellenes. Italian exiles like Mazzini had long carried on their political agitation from London; and Count Camilio Cavour, Prime Minister of the Kingdom of Sardinia after 1851, made Britain his parliamentary model. When the war of 1859, which pitted Sardinia and France against Austria, forced Austria to cede Lombardy (the central section of Northern Italy) to Sardinia, most Englishmen sympathized; and when Napoleon III decided to halt the war and to permit the Austrians to restore the unpopular despotic rulers of the central Italian duchies of Tuscany and Modena, the English press was horrified. English sentiment approved of Cavour's use of plebiscites demonstrating that the inhabitants of these duchies preferred to become part of a united Italy. At the same time, it opposed the acquisition by Napoleon III of Savoy and Nice (districts of the Kingdom of Sardinia adjoining the French frontier) as his pieces of silver for having helped Cavour. When Garibaldi launched his romantic expedition to bring Sicily and Southern Italy into a united Italian Kingdom, the British Foreign Secretary declared that the Italians had good reason to take up arms against their oppressor. Rather than censure Victor Emmanuel, the King of Sardinia and prospectively the proper constitutional monarch of a unified Italy, Lord Russell preferred to speak of "the gratifying prospect of a people building up the edifice of their liberties."

The statement was widely applauded in England and gained for Britain wide popularity in Italy, for none of the other big powers supported Italian unification so strongly. Nor did Queen Victoria, whose sympathies lay with the Austrian emperor at Vienna and who referred to Russell and Palmerston as "those two dreadful old men." The substantial unification of Italy nonetheless became an accomplished fact, and British diplomacy was not least among the factors which made it possible.

American Division and German Unification

The next major conflict which involved British interests was the American Civil War. British public opinion had long been hostile to slavery; but since President Lincoln indicated in the spring of 1861 that the purpose of the suppression of the rebellion of the Southern states was to restore the union rather than to abolish slavery, there was some public sympathy with the Southern position. The Confederacy seemed to have as much right to rebel against the United States as the Greeks had to revolt against Turkey, the Italians against Austria, or for that matter, the thirteen American colonies against England. The position of the British government remained formally neutral from start to finish. Although the British recognition of Southern belligerency in May 1861 was regarded by Northerners as an unfriendly act, it merely took cognizance of a state of affairs which Lincoln himself had previously acknowledged in proclaiming a blockade of the Southern ports.

The British government never did extend recognition to the Confederacy as an independent nation, although the "*Trent* Affair" in the autumn of 1861 brought Great Britain and the United States to the brink of war. The captain of a Northern vessel had stopped the *Trent,* a British ship enroute from Havana to England, and had kidnapped James M. Mason and John Slidell, two Confederate representatives on their way to London. The act was applauded in the North, but in Britain it was looked upon as a great affront to British neutrality and to the freedom of the seas. The British army in Canada was quickly reinforced, and Palmerston's government sent an ultimatum demanding an apology and the release of Mason and Slidell within seven days. In his last official act before his unexpected death from typhoid fever, Prince Albert modified the belligerent tone of this dispatch. In turn, President Lincoln ordered the release of the two Southerners. The crisis subsided, though Anglo-American relations were repeatedly strained by the Confederate use of blockade-runners and blockade-breakers such as the *Alabama*, which had been built in British shipyards. As long as such vessels were not armed in British waters, explained Russell, the government could not legally prevent their construction. The argument was somewhat specious, because once the United States had taken a firm stand against this laissez-faire position, the British government solved the problem (in 1863) by purchasing from British shipbuilders a number of the vessels ordered by the Confederates.

The hopes of the Confederacy long rested upon the prospect that a cotton famine would provide the economic lever which would force Britain and France to intervene on its behalf. By 1862 there was indeed great distress in Lancashire as numerous Manchester cotton mills shut down. The government arranged for subsidies to the local poor rates and for special public works projects. It never thought of entering the war, however, for the sake of cotton. Rather it encouraged the development of substitute sources of the raw material in Egypt and India. By 1863, Lincoln's Emancipation Proclamation had, in any event, turned the mass of the British public opinion against the Southern cause; and although Anglo-American relations continued to be shadowed by the "*Alabama* claims," the danger of war died down.

From the vantage point of twentieth-century Britain, the cardinal blunder committed by the makers of British foreign policy in the 1860s was to permit the unification of a Germany under Prussian leadership. Yet it must be remembered that Britain's ability to influence European affairs was necessarily always greater at the periphery—in Belgium, Portugal, Italy, Greece, and in the Black Sea—where sea power could be utilized. To intervene in the center of the Continent, a powerful ally was needed. The only ally who might have helped stop the war between Denmark and an Austro-Prussian coalition in 1864 was France, but the British were still far too suspicious of Napoleon III's own territorial ambitions in Belgium and the Rhineland to rely upon him. Thus Palmerston's somewhat hasty promise to aid the Danes remained unfulfilled. Flaunting the "big stick" in Northern Europe in 1864 was not so easy as it had been in Greece in 1850, if only because the British navy could not by itself halt the Prussian army.

Even after its lightninglike victory over Austria in 1866 had again demonstrated the military prowess of the Prussian army, most British statesmen remained more fearful of France than of Prussia. The fact that the Franco-Prussian War of 1870–71 was apparently begun by France caused much sympathy to go to Prussia. Bismarck himself might be distrusted, but even the realization that the war was transferring the role of dominant Continental power from France to the new German Empire did not raise undue British fears. As one prominent English editor put it, France was "a nation that always hated us," while Germany was "a nation that never hated us." Queen Victoria, whose eldest daughter had married the Prussian crown prince, saw the German cause as that "of civilization, of liberty, of order, and of unity." By the time the war ended, British sympathy had begun to shift to defeated France; but the British government was provided with at least one satisfaction. Both sides heeded its warning that if either power invaded neutral Belgium, Britain would aid the other. The

Belgian frontier remained unimpaired. A less pleasant consequence of the war was Russia's unilateral decision to abrogate the restrictions upon the use of its navy in the Black Sea which had been imposed at Paris in 1856. The British government made the best of a situation it could not rectify alone by refusing to recognize the change until an international conference in London had signed a protocol declaring that nations could not unilaterally denounce treaties without threatening the system of international law. Russian acknowledgment of the principle of international law was then followed by the international recognition of the political reality – Russian abrogation of the Black Sea clauses. British statesmen after 1870 had reason to look upon the world with considerably less confidence than Palmerston had done a generation before, and though the next forty years were for Western and Central Europe decades of peace, Britain's moral, economic, and international position in the world had materially changed – she now had to share predominance with a new, vigorous, and ambitious Germany.

The Sepoy Mutiny

During the 1850s and 1860s the war drums sounded not only in Europe and North America but also in distant India, where decade by decade the sphere of British influence had increased, although the number of British citizens involved remained, by any reckoning, extraordinarily small. The original focus of British trade with India had been the East India Company, which since the passage of Pitt's India Act in 1784 had shared power with a government-approved Board of Control in London whose president was after 1812 always a member of the Cabinet. For the time being the Company remained a body which "maintained armies and retailed tea"; but in 1813 it lost its chartered monopoly of British trade with India. For a time it retained its monopoly on the China trade, but in 1833 it was ordered to bring all its commercial business to an end. As compensation, the proprietors received an annuity of £630,000 charged on the territorial revenues of India.

During the 1830s and 1840s the sphere of direct British rule in India continued to expand until by 1850 it included almost two thirds of the subcontinent. The remainder was in the hands of independent princes who acknowledged Britain as the paramount power in India and were bound to her by treaties. Theoretically the Mogul emperor at Delhi still governed this vast realm, but his practical significance was nil. From the British point of view, these were years of reform in India; and indeed, at their best, the British governors-general and their lieutenants resembled the "guardians" of Plato's republic. They went to India less to make fiscal fortunes than to win reputations as bestowers of a benevolent despotism. Reform to them necessarily implied westernization, and westernization generally meant the introduction of English institutions. These institutions included English law and English forms of land ownership. Reform meant the destruction of criminal bands and the gradual establishment of an unprecedented degree of law and order over much of India. It also included a competitive civil service system which actually preceded the establishment of a similar system in Great Britain itself. Indians were eligible for appointment to the civil service, and if for the moment there was no emphasis upon self-government in India, there was at least great emphasis upon good government.

Westernization also implied the increasing use of English in what had always been a multilingual geographical area. Indian education was to be primarily in English on the sound Victorian premise that "a single shelf of a good European library was worth the whole native literature of India and Arabia." An English education, to be sure, enabled young Indians to read in the original the works of John Locke, Thomas Jefferson, and John Stuart Mill.

Reform meant also the abolition of a number of traditional Hindu customs such as female infanticide, *suttee*, and *thuggee*. *Suttee* provided that a faithful Hindu widow throw herself upon her husband's funeral pyre. The custom had not been universal, but as late as 1844, one chieftain's funeral led to the death of ten wives and three hundred concubines. *Thuggee*, the Hindu word from which our word "thug" is derived, involved professional robbers and highwaymen who justified their activities in religious terms but who made peaceful commerce along many Indian roads all but impossible.

Reform also increasingly came to mean great public works programs: the building of roads and harbors and telegraph lines—by 1870 the Bengal was directly linked to London by cable. It involved the introduction of a nationwide postal service, the beginnings of immense irrigation projects, and by the 1850s a huge network of railway lines. These improvements, paid for by revenue collected in India or through bond issues, helped make meaningful the vast new free trade area which the subcontinent represented. Not surprisingly, most Englishmen had come to take great pride in their Indian Empire. That Indian trade was valuable to Britain none would have denied, but the Indian trade was now open to the merchants of other lands as well, and the reforms seemed to benefit the Indians most of all.

It must be acknowledged that many a native Indian came to see these same reforms in a different light. Eighteenth-century British rule had been marked by outright exploitation in a way in which nineteenth-century rule was not, but it had involved much less foreign interference in Indian politics, social life, and religion. The British governing class made no secret of its assumption of cultural and intellectual superiority and preferred to remain aloof. The "guardians" as a class, while often highly respected and credited with a sense of justice, were little loved. Indians were admitted to the lower branches of the Indian civil service and permitted to dominate the lower ranks of the Indian army, but otherwise their influence in governing their own country steadily declined.

The reform of Hindu customs necessarily implied interference with Indian religion. While European missionaries, who trooped to India in increasing numbers in the early decades of the nineteenth century, looked forward to the gradual supplanting of Hinduism by Christianity, faithful Hindus – as well as Moslems and Sikhs – not unnaturally feared what they interpreted as forcible Christianization. Irrigation canals might bring a greater abundance of food, but they might equally damage the sacred Ganges; and the subordination of native languages might harm religious ritual. Similarly, the British reform of the Bengal land law might simplify and rationalize land ownership, but it clashed with a thousand years of history and custom. The supplanting of village custom by complex legal procedures did not necessarily benefit the average Indian villager any more than the commercialization of agriculture, with its emphasis upon cash crops for exports (such as cotton, jute, indigo, and grain), increased the general sense of economic security. Unhappily, as the nineteenth century proceeded, the Malthusian dilemma continually reasserted itself in India. The advantages of an increase in the efficiency of agriculture and the bringing of additional acres under cultivation were counterbalanced by a growing population, and the standard of living of the average Indian villager rose but little above subsistence level. Reform was obviously a two-edged sword, and differing judgments over the desirability of British reforms produced the Sepoy Mutiny of 1857.

The Indian army of the day was made up ordinarily of Sepoys (i.e. natives) who outnumbered the British soldiers by a ratio of almost six to one (230,000 to 40,000). Complaints among the Sepoys that Hindu caste privileges were being ignored and that sacred customs were being violated rose to fever pitch in January 1857 when the rumor swept numerous Sepoy regiments in the Bengal that the grease used for the cartridges of the newly introduced Enfield rifle was made of the fat of cows

INDIA *at the time of* THE Sepoy Mutiny: 1857

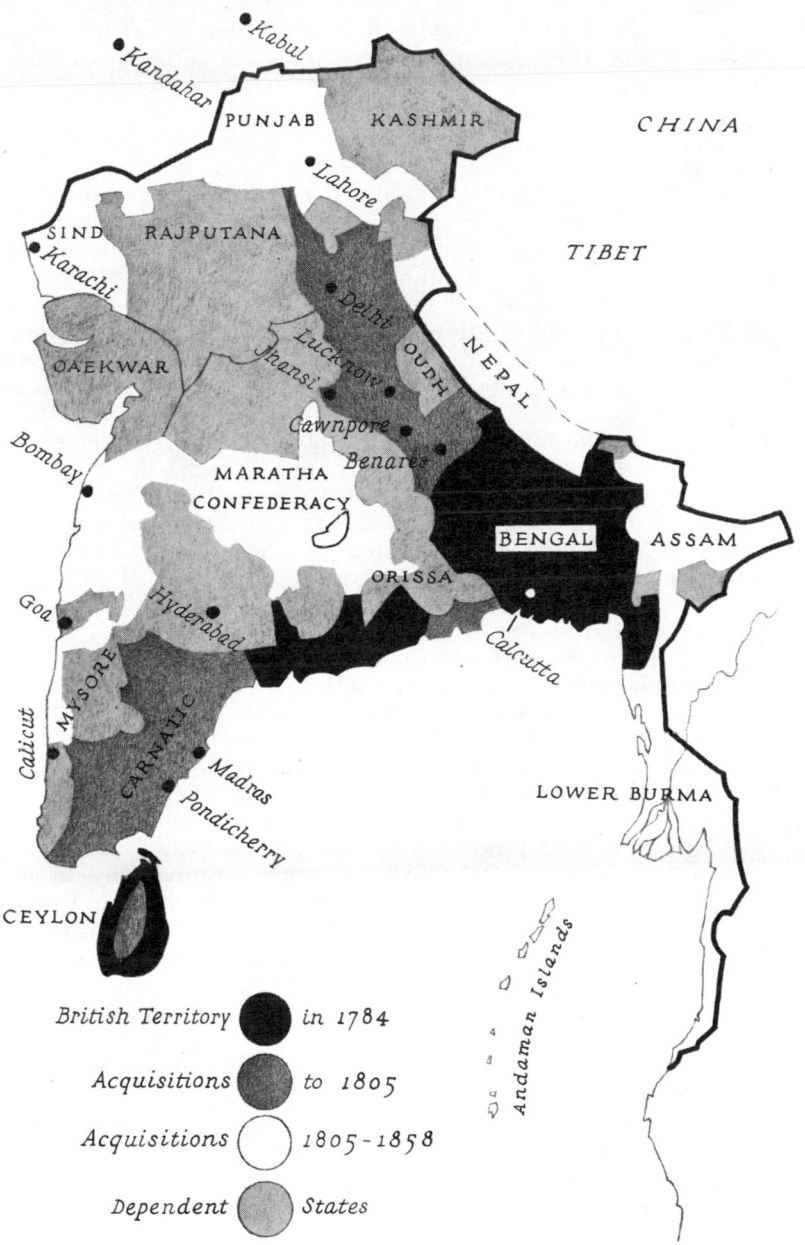

British Territory ⬤ in 1784

Acquisitions ⬤ to 1805

Acquisitions ◯ 1805-1858

Dependent ⬤ States

and pigs. Since every cartridge had to be bitten before insertion into the rifle, this meant that the religious scruples of both Hindus (in the use of cow fat) and Moslems (in the use of pig fat) were being disregarded. The rumors had some basis in fact, and the reassurances of British regimental officers were dismissed as lies. Rumbles of revolt and numerous court-martials of Sepoys led in May to a mutiny by three regiments, who shot their British officers and marched on Delhi where they killed all the English men, women, and children they could find and pledged their allegiance to the old Mogul emperor.

Although most British commanders were blindly confident in the loyalty of their native troops and refused to disarm them, a similar rebellion occurred at Jhansi. Cawnpore was captured and Lucknow was besieged. Then the tide turned. In the late months of 1857, the British at Lucknow were relieved and Delhi recaptured. The mutinous Sepoys found themselves unable to take advantage of their overwhelming numbers. As a British relief force advanced up the Ganges valley with reinforcements, it countered massacre with massacre as a fit punishment for rebellion; and although "Clemency" Canning, the new Governor-General, helped stop indiscriminate revenge, the mutiny stirred up a great deal of racial hatred. By early 1858 the mutiny as such was over, though sporadic fighting continued in parts of north-central India for two more years.

The British were to look upon the struggle as no more than an army revolt, but some modern Indian nationalists have seized upon the mutiny as the first significant example of armed Indian national rebellion against British rule. To see the mutiny purely in military terms ignores the complicity of numerous Indian civilians and the widespread distrust of British "reform" measures. It also ignores such symbolic gestures as the attempted restoration of the Delhi emperor. Conversely, to see the mutiny as national in scope is to ignore the fact that most of southern and western India remained unaffected by the rebellion. Many Indian princes and most Indian villagers remained untouched by modern notions of nationalism, and a majority either remained loyal to or acquiesced in British rule even when it seemed in grave danger.

The mutiny marked a turning point in a number of respects. In 1858 the power of the East India Company was brought to a final close, and the British crown took over direct command of both the Indian army and the Indian government. The President of the Board of Control became the Secretary of State for India (still with a seat in the Cabinet) and the Governor-General became the Viceroy. The ratio of British contingents in the Indian army was increased, and the artillery was confined to the control of British troops. Although an extensive revision of the penal code was introduced after 1860, postmutiny viceroys were less reform-minded than their predecessors. They continued to encourage public works such as railways, and British private investment in Indian industry became sizable for the first time. But the government hesitated to interfere further with social and religious customs. A revival of orthodox Hinduism provided new discouragement for those English reformers who hoped that the slow infiltration of western culture would cause Indians to give up their age-old "superstitions" and "prejudices." Standards of governmental efficiency remained as high as ever, but the gulf between the rulers and the ruled had, if anything, widened. Englishmen back home, temporarily much stirred by the mutiny, rapidly lost interest in Indian affairs, and parliamentary debates involving India rarely attracted much interest.

In this respect, India resembled the other parts of the midcentury British empire. Trade continued to matter more than political control, and the settlement colonies often seemed a bother, an expense, and even a bore. "These wretched colonies. They are a millstone around our necks," Disraeli confided to a colleague in 1853. As Charles Dilke put it in 1868, why should "Dorsetshire agricultural labourers pay the cost of defending New Zealand colonists in Maori Wars"? After all, he added, in what proved to be a curiously unprophetic analogy: "It is not likely nowadays that our colonies would, for any long stretch of time, engage to aid us in our purely European wars. Australia would scarcely feel herself deeply interested in the guarantee of Luxembourg, nor Canada in the affairs of Servia." The same attitude prevailed among Cabinet members. On one occasion when Lord Palmerston found it difficult to persuade a suitable colleague to become Colonial Secretary, he finally expostulated to one of the Colonial Office's career officials: "Well, I'll take the office myself. Just come upstairs and show me on the map where these damned places are."

It was in this atmosphere of studied negligence that Australia, New Zealand, and Canada achieved virtual domestic independence, and when the British North America Act, forming Quebec, Ontario, and the western provinces into the federal, self-governing Dominion of Canada, passed the House of Commons in 1867, it received as much notice "as if it were a private Bill uniting two or three English parishes."

In the long run, this relative lack of interest in formal political control, though combined with a continued insistence upon opening and keeping open a worldwide market for British goods, helps make explicable much that may otherwise remain mysterious both in the nineteenth-century growth and the twentieth-century decline — or transformation — of the British Empire.

Colonization was seen by most Englishmen as essentially temporary and justifiable ultimately only in moral terms. Anthony Trollope, the novelist, provided this typically mid-Victorian appraisal:

> We are called upon to rule them [the colonies] – as far as we do rule them, not for our glory, but for their happiness. If we keep them, we should keep them – not because they are gems in our diadem, not in order that we may boast that the sun never sets on our dependencies, but because by keeping them we may assist them in developing their own resources. And when we part with them, as part with them we shall, let us do so with neither smothered jealousy nor open hostility, but with a proud feeling that we are sending a son out into the world able to take his place among men.[2]

---

[2] Cited in *Ideas and Beliefs of the Victorians*, British Broadcasting Assoc. (London, 1949).

Chapter 7

The 𝕽𝖊𝖋𝖔𝖗𝖒 𝕭𝖎𝖑𝖑 of 1867:
Causes and Consequences

THE RELATIVE domestic and political complacency of the 1850s and the 1860s was brought to an end in 1867. The rumblings which led to the political reform act of 1867 had been discernible for a number of years, but so long as Lord Palmerston lived and remained Prime Minister, his prestige and his conviction that the Reform Bill of 1832 had achieved as near perfect a constitution as was humanly possible discouraged any tampering with the English political system.

Prelude to Reform

It was toward the very end of the period of apparent placidity that Walter Bagehot provided his classic account of the English constitution.[1]   While this witty guide to the practices

---

[1] Walter Bagehot, *The English Constitution* (Garden City: Doubleday Dolphin), first published, 1867.   More recent works relevant to an understanding of this chapter include the works by Briggs and Woodward referred to earlier.   Both Gladstone and Disraeli are the subjects of classic multivolume biographies: John Morley, *Life of Gladstone,* 3 vols. (London, 1903); W. F. Monypenny and G. E. Buckle, *Life of Disraeli,* 6 vols. (London, 1910–1920).   The best one-volume biography of Gladstone is that by Sir Philip Magnus (London, 1954).   There is no completely adequate one-volume biography of Disraeli, but that by Andre Maurois

and assumptions of the mid-Victorian politicians has become hallowed by tradition for the twentieth-century student, *The English Constitution* impressed many of its early readers as the work of an iconoclast. Bagehot's main theme was that the practice of national government in England had ceased to correspond to the widely held eighteenth-century theory, still often echoed, that Britain's constitution was a balanced combination of monarchy, aristocracy, and democracy in the form of the Crown, the House of Lords, and the House of Commons. This was no longer true, contended Bagehot, for "a republic has insinuated itself beneath the folds of a Monarchy." The Queen retained significant "dignified" functions, but her practical or "efficient" functions were now limited to "the right to be consulted, the right to encourage and the right to warn." The House of Lords similarly retained significant dignified functions and provided the alternative of a worship of nobility to a worship of money. In practice the Lords were now, however, a secondary chamber which could at most revise or suspend the actions of the House of Commons.

The House of Commons itself was seen by Bagehot less as a legislative chamber than as the public forum in which both sides of any issue could be presented and as the body which, in effect, chose the Prime Minister. In the period between 1846 and 1867, with no organized political party in the majority and the House of Commons divided into Whigs and Tories, Peelites and Radicals and, at times, an autonomous Irish party, the tenure of a Prime Minister and his ministry was indeed often at the mercy of a vote of no confidence on a relatively trivial issue. Even if the House of Commons could not directly select the Prime Minister, it could and did choose to dismiss him on numerous occasions — six times between 1850 and 1860. The relative weakness of party organization made this indeed the golden age of the private member of Parliament. In the eighteenth century, many such private members had been controlled by patronage exercised by the crown or by wealthy peers; later in the nineteenth century, they were increasingly to come under strong party discipline. For the moment, however, their independence was at its height.

The most important governmental institution, said Bagehot, was one for which eighteenth-century political theory left no room, the Cabinet. The key to mid-nineteenth-century government, in Bagehot's estimation, was not the separation but the unification of powers, manifest in the Cabinet, which repre-

---

(New York, 1927) is distinguished by its literary grace. The best biography of Queen Victoria is Elizabeth Longford, *Queen Victoria: Born to Succeed* (New York, 1965).

sented "a hyphen which joins, a buckle which fastens, the legislative part of the state to the executive part of the state." The Cabinet was responsible to the House of Commons, but it could at will, by asking the monarch to call a general election, appeal to the electorate against that House. Cabinet members headed the various departments of state and had to defend their departments against the criticism of a Parliament of which they themselves were members.

In the sense that they favored such government by discussion — as well as a high degree of freedom of speech, press, religion, and enterprise at home and abroad — most English politicians of the mid-century era were liberals; but few were democrats who looked forward to an age of universal manhood suffrage. The country seemed contented, and the mass of the unenfranchised populace appeared satisfied with its government. "Not only," wrote Bagehot, "does the nation endure a parliamentary government, which it would not do if Parliament were immoderate, but it likes parliamentary government. A sense of satisfaction permeates the country because most of the country feels it has got the precise thing that suits it."

At the very time that Bagehot was writing, evidence was beginning to accumulate that some groups in British society were no longer satisfied with the status quo. The collapse of Chartism had led to a gradual revival of the earlier "radical" alliance of employers and employees against the "establishment" of titled and proprietary classes who, in the popular mind, were identified with special privilege and what seemed to be the still excessive cost of government. While John Stuart Mill was the "philosopher" of this radical movement, John Bright was its more typical leader. Bright was a Quaker who looked forward to a new franchise reform bill which would give the vote to all urban householders. It was such a bill which was the hope of the Reform Union of 1864, a national association essentially middle class in origin.

Although an M.P. since 1845, Bright himself had yet to be asked to join a Cabinet. Thus far indeed, no nonconformist had ever been a member of any British Cabinet. The man to whom Bright turned as the politician most likely to spearhead another bout of political reform was William Ewart Gladstone, an ex-Peelite who in 1859 had joined Palmerston's Whig Ministry as Chancellor of the Exchequer. The new Chancellor had followed Peel out of the Tory Party over the Corn Law fight. His sympathy with Palmerston's pro-Italian policy proved a further bar to a reunion with his onetime colleagues. His Cabinet position also gave Gladstone the opportunity to complete the work he had begun in Peel's Ministry almost two decades before, the elimination not only of every protective tariff but, as far as possible, every revenue tariff as well. He inspired the reciprocal trade agreement negotiated by Richard Cobden with France in 1860. With the Budget of 1860, Gladstone eliminated all tariffs whatsoever on 371 articles, leaving only 48 items on which a revenue tariff was collected.

It was as Chancellor of the Exchequer that Gladstone for the first time became a popular hero, when his decision to end all tariffs on manufacturing paper was vetoed by the Lords in 1860. Gladstone protested that the peers were preventing the development of a cheap press because they feared it would cater to the working-class reader. The following year, he reintroduced his measure to end the paper tax. This time, however, the provision was part of a consolidated budget which passed the House of Commons as a single appropriation bill rather than as one of a series. The House of Lords reluctantly accepted the new consolidated budget bill and was thus precluded from exercising a veto on individual money bills thereafter. To veto the entire budget would necessarily produce a constitutional conflict. It was Gladstone's influence also which kept defense expenditures down — despite Palmerston's misgivings — and which enabled the Chancellor of the Exchequer to take advantage of growing national prosperity to cut the income tax from 5 percent to 2 percent in the course of five years.

With free trade confirmed and a high degree of financial responsibility assured, Gladstone slowly became converted to the cause of parliamentary reform; and in the course of a debate in 1864, he declared that "every man who is not presumably incapacitated by some consideration of personal unfitness or political danger, is morally entitled to come within the pale of the constitution." Though the suffrage was not a natural right, it was in Gladstone's estimation a privilege which responsible workingmen had earned by their "self-command, self-control, respect for order, patience under suffering, confidence in the law and respect for superiors." Palmerston cautioned his colleague that it was not the business of Cabinet members to invite agitation, and the University of Oxford decided, in the general election of 1865, that Gladstone's views on both the suffrage and the possibility of the disestablishment of the Anglican Church in Ireland were not to its liking. He was defeated at Oxford, only to contest successfully a seat in the "popular constituency" of South Lancashire. He had come to be a hero of the masses, and he in turn reciprocated their regard.

The general election of 1865 was yet another personal triumph for Lord Palmerston, but before the new Parliament assembled, that doughty statesman had died at the age of 80. Lord John Russell — now in the House of Lords — became Prime Minister and Gladstone the leader of the majority in the House of Commons. If the death of Palmerston provided new impetus for reformers, then so also did the victory of the Union forces in the American Civil War. The American Republic with its political democracy, its equality of opportunity, and its freedom from an established church had long appealed to British radicals. Now that it had survived its ordeal of battle and had, in the bargain, rid itself of the darkest blot upon its escutcheon, Negro slavery, it served as a renewed inspiration. "The great triumph of the Republic," wrote John Bright, "is the event of our age and future ages will confess it."

The Reform Bills

In the spring of 1866 Gladstone introduced a reform bill to give the franchise to borough residents who owned property worth more than £7 a year and thus to enfranchise some 300,000 town artisans. Opinion within Gladstone's own party was strongly divided. For conservatives — both Whigs and Tories — the great danger the bill posed was not that the aristocracy would lose its remaining influence but that educated Englishmen would be swamped by the ill-educated. The government since 1832 had satisfactorily reflected the various interests of the country. Why therefore change it? The way to elevate the working classes was not to grant them the franchise en masse but to reserve it as a prize to be attained by thrift and self-improvement. "Reform," it was argued, "threatened to grant political leadership only to the mediocre and to limit the independence of the M.P. by making him the delegate rather than the representative of his constituency." Ultimately, there stood the specter that any further franchise reform would lead to a war on property and advance the cause of socialism.

While conservative Whigs voiced their fears about democracy, Gladstone contended that the purpose of the measure was not to establish democracy but simply to enfranchise an element of the population which was as entitled to direct representation as the wealthy financiers and manufacturers. With the Whigs divided, the Bill barely squeaked through the House of Commons and almost immediately became bogged down in committee. In June of 1866 Lord Russell resigned, and the Queen asked the Tory Lord Derby (1799–1869) once again to form a Government. As they had briefly in 1852 and 1858–59, Derby became Prime Minister and Benjamin Disraeli became Chancellor of the Exchequer and leader of the House of Commons.

The continued existence of the Tory party since 1846 was itself something of a tour de force because as early as 1852 it had dropped from its platform the key issue of agricultural protection which had separated it from its erstwhile leader, Robert Peel, in 1846. The Tories were divided from Lord Palmerston less by doctrine than by their retention of a separate organization. Disraeli, the leader of this minority party in the House of Commons since the late 1840s, had been in his early political life both a Tory and a Radical, an unusual but not unknown combination. His "Young England" movement had looked back to an idealized patriarchal rural England in which paternalistic landlords had earned the faithful service of devoted farmers and servants, and in which only the money-grubbing middle class merchants or industrialists played the role of villain. In 1866, however, Disraeli approached the question of reform less as a Tory Radical than as a "flexible" conservative. Both Derby and Disraeli thought the opportunity to benefit the party too good to be lost. Reform was sure to come. Why not let the Tories gain the credit?

An economic downturn in the fall of 1866 and an exceptionally poor harvest had temporarily produced large-scale unemployment and high prices; and, as in 1832, they provided an immediate economic motive for political change. Important, too, was the legal decision of *Hornby v. Close* (1866) which declared that trade unions were unlawful societies in restraint of trade and that their funds were therefore not entitled to the protection of the Friendly Societies Act of 1855. This decision brought into the reform battle many skilled workers who had previously been lukewarm, and a vocal demonstration in London's Hyde Park indicated that popular feeling had been aroused.

In order to introduce in 1867 a bill more comprehensive than Gladstone's of the previous year, Disraeli and Derby had first to convince their colleagues. They eventually won the approval of most of the Cabinet but had to introduce an incredibly complex scheme in order to satisfy the conservatives, who were appalled at the idea of being engulfed by democracy. The bill which Disraeli finally evolved extended the franchise to all urban rate-payers but gave a second (or sometimes third or fourth) vote to all university graduates, to owners of government bonds or savings bank deposits of £50 or more, to members of learned professions, etc. Thus the concept of "household suffrage" was to be qualified by a series of "fancy franchises," designed to protect quality from the consequences of quantity.

Once the bill was subjected to clause-by-clause debate, it was changed almost beyond recognition. The bill that emerged in June 1867 was a composite which none of the participants would have envisaged two years or even one year before. Of the 61 clauses of the final statute, only four had been passed as first introduced by the Tory government and 18 had been taken straight from Gladstone's measure of the previous year. Though Disraeli denied to the last his intention of bringing about "democracy," the result was far more democratic than either Disraeli or his opponents had wanted. In the United Kingdom as a whole, the registered electorate increased from 1,359,000 to 2,455,000 voters. In England alone, the number of county voters increased by 44 percent, the number of borough voters by 124 percent. Only in Ireland, where the number of borough voters was small to begin with, did the act have little impact.

The immediate political implication of the enfranchisement of this host of workingmen, clerks, and shopkeepers proved to be smaller than might have been expected, one reason being that the redistribution of seats which accompanied the bill was much less far-reaching than the franchise reform. Many small boroughs remained, and even after 1867 at least forty seats continued under the immediate influence of landed aristocrats. Moreover, workingmen continued to vote representatives of the old line parties into office rather than organize their own political groups. Nonetheless, as Lord Derby conceded, the country had taken "a leap in the dark."

For Disraeli, the passage of the bill constituted a major parliamentary triumph, and when Lord Derby resigned the Prime Ministership for reasons of ill health early in 1868, Disraeli took his place. It was the summit of a lifelong ambition for the man who always impressed many of his colleagues as a maverick. He was born a Jew at a time (1804) when Jews did not yet possess the full rights of English citizenship; and though baptized an Anglican at the age of twelve and henceforth a faithful member of the Church of England, Disraeli retained great pride in his ethnic ancestry. His youthful dandyism, his flamboyance, his success as a novelist, and his caustic wit all set him apart from the average Tory M.P.; but sheer parliamentary ability at length won him the respect of his colleagues and so in 1868 he had at last "climbed to the top of the greasy pole" of politics.

The new Prime Minister was not destined to hold his office long, for the Tories were still a minority in the House of Commons; and with a new reform bill on the statute book, a new general election was clearly in the offing. At the moment when Disraeli first became undisputed leader of the Tory or Conservative party, William Ewart Gladstone succeeded Lord Russell as head of the coalition of Whigs, Radicals, and Peelites who were henceforth universally to be known as Liberals. Gladstone had not emerged too well from the confused debates on the Reform Bill of 1867, but his stature rose anew when in 1868 he made the disestablishment of the Irish Church a central issue of British politics. The general election of November 1868 saw both the Liberal and the Conservative parties better organized than their predecessors had been in previous contests. Each was headed by a dynamic new leader and each separated from the other by specific issues. The victory was a personal triumph for Gladstone and gave his Liberal Party a majority of 112 seats. John Stuart Mill summed up the results as a brief dialogue:

"Disraeli (to the working classes): I have given you the franchise.

"The Working Classes: Thank you Mr. Gladstone."

The new Prime Minister had himself had to overcome nearly as many obstacles on the road to the Prime Ministership as had Disraeli. Gladstone's father had been a Scottish businessman who had settled in the thriving port city of Liverpool; this was a family background far different from the landed aristocratic heritage of Melbourne, Palmerston, and Russell. Gladstone, born in 1809, and thus five years younger than Disraeli, had had an orthodox education at Eton and Oxford at a time when the central doctrine taught there was that "the world never moves, except in the wrong direction."

Gladstone's family was a devout Anglican one, and in his youth, William was deeply tempted to become a clergyman. He finally decided that he could serve his church better in Parliament than in the pulpit. The religious element in his personality can hardly be overestimated, for liberalism to Gladstone meant not so much the political recognition of the natural rights of man as preached by the advocates of the Enlightenment but the final acknowledgment by man of the common fatherhood of God. A year after Disraeli had briefly "climbed to the top of the greasy pole," Gladstone confided to his diary, "I ascend a steepening path with a burden ever gathering weight. The Almighty seems to sustain and spare me for some purpose of his own, deeply unworthy as I know myself to be. Glory be to his name."

Gladstone's path to the Prime Ministership was almost the antithesis of that followed by Disraeli — while Disraeli had started out a radical and moved steadily toward Toryism, Gladstone was first elected to Parliament as an unbending Tory and ended his political career a radical. It was his youthful eloquence at Oxford in opposing the Great Reform Bill which had led the Duke of Newcastle to offer him the seat for a small pocket borough which had escaped disfranchisement in that bill. Gladstone had been easily elected; and although his first impression had been that his election was a tribute to his oratorical prowess, he discovered later that his patron had supplied the electors with free drinks and other services at a cost of twenty-five shillings a head. It had been an election in the already vanishing eighteenth-century tradition. Gladstone's path along the road to liberalism has already been traced—as Peelite, as financial reformer, and as advocate of European liberal nationalism in Italy and elsewhere—and it was as a reformer that he began his own first ministry.

The First Gladstone Ministry

The Liberal Ministry of 1868–74 was at once one of the strongest and one of the most reform-minded of the nineteenth century. Yet the legislative and administrative reforms it sponsored were very much within the earlier Whig and radical traditions. The Whig tradition of religious liberty was closely involved with the first great issue which Gladstone tackled, that of the disestablishment of the Anglican Church within Ireland. For Gladstone, the question illustrated the two qualities which any reform should have. One, it must be ripe for solution and have substantial public pressure for change behind it. Two, it must be a matter of justice. For Gladstone all great political decisions were ultimately moral decisions; and although Gladstone was as staunch a churchman as ever, he had come to look upon the Anglican Church in Ireland not as a support for true religion but as a handicap. The fact that all Irishmen were legally compelled to contribute directly or indirectly to the financial support of a religious organization to which but one in ten adhered tended to sully the moral position of the church and to make yet more difficult the reconciliation of Irishmen to British rule. Gladstone candidly confessed that his stand was at variance with his views of the 1830s. Then he had firmly advocated the privileged legal position of the Established Church. Then, too, he had shared with many Englishmen the hope now proved vain that Irishmen would at length desert the Roman Catholicism of their fathers.

The struggle over disestablishment took up the greater part of the 1869 parliamentary session. The Conservatives objected that the step not only broke with a tradition centuries old but also represented in a very literal sense an attack upon the property rights of the Church. Gladstone, at the height of his parliamentary form, piloted the measure through the House of Commons and, less directly, through the House of Lords. The Anglican Church in Ireland was consequently deprived of a quarter of its revenues and was turned into a private self-governing corporation dependent for income upon its endowments rather than upon legally enforceable tithes.

Many of the reform measures of the Ministry were concerned with increasing the efficiency of the government itself.

The Civil Service system, whose beginnings in England Gladstone had encouraged sixteen years earlier as Chancellor of the Exchequer, was extended in 1870 to almost all government departments. Edward Cardwell (1813–86), Gladstone's Secretary for War and, like Gladstone, an ex-Peelite, occupied himself with the reform of the army. The lot of the common soldier was improved by eliminating flogging as a peacetime punishment and by permitting short-term enlistments (six years on active service and six years in the reserve). A degree of streamlining was also introduced into the upper echelons, where the commander in chief (at the time the Duke of Cambridge, a cousin of Queen Victoria) was subordinated to the Secretary for War. The most controversial proposal proved to be the abolition of the purchase of army commissions. It was the swift Prussian triumph over France in 1870–71 which gave weight to the views of egalitarian reformers who condemned bought commissions as barriers to the natural rise of talent; and when the Lords refused to pass a bill to end the practice, the Queen was prevailed upon to end commission purchase by royal warrant.

Similar reforms were introduced into the English judicial system which, of all nineteenth-century European legal systems, had descended with the smallest alteration from its medieval foundations. The prevailing structure was a highly confusing one involving overlapping of courts in which some administered common law and others equity law. Moreover, there was no system of appeal and each of three common law courts retained unlimited jurisdiction over all cases. The Judicature Act of 1873 fused the common law and equity courts and established a single national court system in which the Queen's Bench, the Common Pleas, and the Exchequer Courts were retained as separate divisions with specified jurisdictions. The court system, as in the United States, was to have three levels: a court of original jurisdiction, a court of appeal, and a supreme court (the Judicial Committee of the House of Lords).

The Secret Ballot Act of 1872 was in one sense also a measure of administrative reform. The open ballot had long been advocated in England as a standard of manly courage; a voter, it was felt, should proudly avow his political convictions. Reformers had long wondered, however, whether the open ballot did not do more to encourage bribery than to promote manliness, and the act of 1872 was patterned upon measures successfully applied in the Australian colonies. It was passed with little fanfare, and indeed it is difficult to discern any obvious effects of its passage in England, except further to curtail aristocratic influence on elections.

In one sense the most important act of the first Gladstone ministry was one with which the Prime Minister himself was only indirectly concerned, the Education Act of 1870, which was steered through Parliament by William Edward Forster (1818–86). It established in Britain for the first time a national system of education in place of the essentially voluntary system which, since the 1830s, had received government subsidies either on the basis of the reports of state inspectors or on the basis of the number of students who passed government-sponsored examinations. The motive for the Forster Education Act was clear enough. An increasingly democratic government required a literate electorate. The issue which had hamstrung educational reform in Britain for half a century was that of the role of organized religion. By 1870 most nonconformists wanted a national school system under secular auspices. The Anglican Church, however, hoped to retain its predominant control over the school system. Like most controversial statutes, the new Education Act satisfied neither side completely. It authorized the election of local school boards which were given the power to levy rates, build schools, and hire teachers, wherever there was an insufficient number of private schools, and to pay the fees of children who continued to go to private schools. Anglicans resented the fact that religious education in the new board schools was to be nondenominational. Nonconformists bitterly pointed out that the elected school boards could (and did in many instances) subsidize religious education in Anglican schools. While the act of 1870 obviously did not end the debate over the role of organized religion in education, it did at long last set up a national system of education in England. Within a decade, elementary school education was made compulsory, and by 1891, it was made free to all. In the meantime, an act of 1871 had ended all religious restrictions upon students attending the traditionally Anglican universities of Oxford and Cambridge.

No legislative solution could be found, unfortunately, for the most ticklish domestic question which faced Gladstone — the position of the monarchy in a democracy. Gladstone's ministry coincided with a marked republican movement in England. Retrenchment-minded M.P.s were growing restive under the steady stream of demands to vote funds to enable the Queen's children to set up housekeeping; and Sir Charles Dilke (1843–1911), a Liberal M.P., launched an inquiry into the Queen's own finances. Joseph Chamberlain (1836–1914), head of the National Education League for free secular schools and soon to be elected Radical mayor of Birmingham, was telling cheering crowds that in England as in France a republic was inevitable.

The trouble was, Gladstone privately admitted, that "the Queen is invisible, and the Prince of Wales is not respected."

Ever since the death of Prince Albert in 1861, the now middle-aged Victoria had been "the widow of Windsor." She was as assiduous as ever in perusing state documents and in discussing the merits of prospective Anglican bishops; but she had almost ceased to attend to her ceremonial duties, and she hardly ever set foot in London. Edward, the Prince of Wales, had become an idle if amiable young man who had just been named co-respondent in a divorce suit. (He was found not guilty.) Since Gladstone never became a republican by conviction and revered the Crown as an institution, he repeatedly tried to make Victoria understand that it was for her own good that he wanted her to undertake a minimum of ceremonial duties. In order to tie Ireland more closely to England and in order to give the Prince of Wales something useful to do, he wished to make him the Irish Viceroy.

The Queen either could not or would not understand. She had a typically Hanoverian dislike of entrusting her son and heir with even the most mild semblance of political power, and on at least one occasion she refused to delay her summer vacation by even two days in order to prorogue Parliament in person. "Do *pet* the Queen a little," Mrs. Gladstone had once advised her husband; but the art which Disraeli possessed in overabundant measure, Gladstone possessed not at all. Disraeli sought the company of women and gloried in it. It was part of his nature to heap on flattery with a trowel, an ability which Gladstone thought hypocritical. Gladstone was invariably polite to Victoria, as even the Queen conceded, but she added: "The trouble with Mr. Gladstone is that he always addresses me as if I were a public meeting."

Despite the failure of Gladstone's efforts to mollify Victoria, the monarchy survived. More important, by the time his first ministry was terminated by the Conservative victory in the election of 1874, a substantial program of domestic reforms had been enacted, and the two-party system was more vital than ever. Gladstone's resignation from the Liberal Party leadership a year later in order to devote himself to theology seemed to presage the end of his political career. But circumstance and an apparently inexhaustible fund of personal energy were soon to dictate a revival of the Gladstone-Disraeli duel which, first as rival Chancellors of the Exchequer and then as rival Prime Ministers, had increasingly caused the two men to dominate the political world.

Notable though the Gladstonian reforms had been, they had almost all remained within the nineteenth-century liberal tradition of gradually removing the religious, economic, and political barriers which prevented men of varied creeds and classes from exercising their individual talents in order to improve themselves and their society. As the third quarter of the century drew to a close, the essential bastions of Victorianism still held firm — respectability; a middle-class government now shared not only by aristocrats but by industrious workmen; a prosperity which seemed to rest largely on the tenets of laissez-faire economics; and the *Pax Britannica,* a little shopworn, perhaps, but still a significant element of the international scene. The last quarter of the century was to bring an end to the mid-Victorian boom in the form of the paradoxical late Victorian "Great Depression"; and some of the apparent certainties of the mid-Victorian world were to be subjected to searching inquiry during these same years.

Chapter 8

𝔇𝔦𝔰𝔯𝔞𝔢𝔩𝔦 AND 𝔊𝔩𝔞𝔡𝔰𝔱𝔬𝔫𝔢

FOR PURPOSES of convenience, the last three decades of the nineteenth century will be considered as a distinctive unit. Such a classification, like most historical subdivisions, is open to argument. It may be contended, with some justification, that the 1880s were in fact a notable decade of transition — especially in Anglo-Irish relations, in British attitudes toward empire, and in the transformation of political attitudes regarding the proper role of the government in the national economy. It may also be argued that the last decade and a half of the Queen's reign were not typically Victorian at all — that, for example, neither Oscar Wilde nor George Bernard Shaw was in a "literary," as opposed to the strictly chronological, sense a Victorian playwright. Yet aside from the feeling of unity provided by Queen Victoria's longevity and the influence which continued to be wielded by Disraeli and Gladstone until their deaths, the period does have a common economic background; it was the age of the "Great Depression."

The Curious "Great Depression"

When Americans encounter the term "Great Depression," they are most likely to think of the years following the stock market crash of 1929 when for a number of years all the indices of economic prosperity went wrong: the rate of unemployment soared; the number of bank failures climbed; the total production of goods and services fell; the average standard of living declined. It was not until the beginning of the Second World War that most of these indices returned to their 1929 levels; and some, such as stock market price averages, did not do so until many years thereafter.

The "Great Depression" of 1873–96 was only partially analogous to the economic collapse of the 1930s. Although only some of the late nineteenth-century economic indices went downward—prices fell, profit margins fell, interest rates fell, agriculture declined—there were enough of them to prompt grave disquiet among many influential Victorians. They began to write and publish such pamphlets as *Protection and Bad Times* (1879), and *The Trade Depression: Its Causes and Its Remedies* (1885), and they secured the appointment of Royal Commissions to inquire into the farm depression and the depression in trade and industry.[1]

The plight of the agriculturist is most often cited in support of this concept of a late Victorian "Great Depression." The 1870s were marked by a series of bad harvests, climaxed by that of 1879, the worst in a century. Bad harvests, as such, were hardly a novelty. What was unusual about the 1870s was that the farmer was not compensated for fewer crops by higher prices. Prices stayed low, primarily because cheap freight rates and a rapid expansion of grain production in the American Midwest and to a lesser extent in the Russian Ukraine now made it possible to ship wheat and barley to England more cheaply than they could be grown at home. Whereas in 1860 it had cost 25 cents to ship a bushel of grain from New York to Liverpool, by 1886 large steam-powered freighters charged only five cents. The result was the increasing dependence of Britain on imported food. The decision to rely on food imports had, of course, been implicit in the repeal of the Corn Laws in 1846. Though wheat imports had in fact grown steadily after 1846, a variety of European and American wars and the continuance, for a time, of high freight rates had kept up the cost of grain so that the English farmer could compete successfully with imported food. As late as 1868, 80 percent of all food consumed in the United Kingdom was produced at home. During

---

[1] The "Great Depression" is considered in Rostow's *British Economy of the 19th Century* (Oxford, 1948) and in the last two volumes of J. H. Clapham's *Economic History of Modern Britain*, 2nd ed. (Cambridge, 1930–1938). Also worth noting are W. Ashworth, *The Economic History of England, 1870–1939* (London, 1960), H. Ausubel, *The Late Victorians* (New York, 1957), and articles such as A. E. Musson, "The Great Depression in Britain, 1873–96: A Reappraisal," *Journal of Economic History*, XIX (1959).

the late nineteenth century, that percentage dropped steadily as fast, cheap freighters brought in American wheat and, after 1878, refrigerated meat, as well as tropical fruits from the Mediterranean and tea from India and China.

The result is often spoken of as "the collapse of British agriculture." The phrase, though vivid, is not altogether accurate. It does fit the wheat farmers of southern England, for wheat acreage declined by 50 percent during these thirty years, and land devoted to all cereals declined by at least 25 percent. It is also suitable insofar as it reflects a time when contracting income made it difficult for landlords to invest money in land, buildings, and drainage which would have enabled their tenants to farm more efficiently. And so long as the government was unwilling to protect the farmer against American wheat by tariff barriers — and the doctrine of free trade had taken root too strongly to permit it to do so — the agriculturalist had to adapt himself somehow. Many landlords did so by turning their crop lands into pasture lands; for the cattle raiser found himself in a much less precarious position than the wheat farmer. He too had to face foreign competition; but low grain prices reduced his own costs, and as the standard of living rose, he discovered a rising demand for fresh meat sufficient to support the domestic as well as the American, Argentinian, and Australian beef raiser. Still other landlords sought economic salvation by catering to the growing demand for vegetables, fruits, and dairy products from a population which by 1900 was three quarters urban.

Many farmers survived, but it cannot be denied that the "Great Depression" in agriculture destroyed the economic underpinnings of the nineteenth-century aristocrat at exactly the same time that changes in county government were depriving him of his traditional local political influence. Nor can it be denied that agriculture played an increasingly smaller role as a contributor to the total national income. The proportion declined from 17.4 percent in 1870 to 6.7 percent in 1913. Finally, it remains clear that while many a landlord and farmer did adapt to his new competition and that agricultural efficiency rose rather than declined, England by the early twentieth century had ceased to be the model of progressive farming it had been in the mid-nineteenth century. Countries like Denmark and Holland, where a healthy agriculture was a matter of national survival, had adapted themselves with greater success.

Many an English businessman also thought of the late nineteenth century in terms of economic depression because the prices he received for his products were falling at a fairly steady rate. His profit margins were also falling, and the rates of interest on his investments were similarly on the decline.

A prolonged period of deflation has not occurred among industrialized nations in the twentieth century; therefore we may find the phenomenon difficult to understand. It was, however, a development limited not to Britain, but equally evident in the United States and continental Europe. The world's shortage of gold was often blamed for producing this deflation; at a time when more and more nations were adhering to a gold standard, the supply of that metal was not keeping pace with the growing volume of commerce. Many twentieth-century economists, however, suspect that a gold shortage was not the culprit. Their explanation lies rather in a growing industrial productivity at a time when the firms in the industrialized nations were sufficiently competitive to be unable to "administer" prices so as to prevent them from falling. Whatever the causes, the deflation was a fact. However comforting to the man with large bankholdings, the deflation was looked upon as a monster by the investor in search of high earnings and the debtor in search of cheap money (as in the United States, where the "Greenbackers" of the 1870s and the "free silverites" of the 1890s urged their particular inflationary panaceas).

If the price deflation was in many ways a worldwide phenomenon, another late Victorian tendency was peculiarly British: Britain's years as the "workshop of the world" were drawing to a close. By 1900, both Germany and the United States had surpassed Great Britain as an industrial power in annual steel production and other areas. The causes of Britain's relative decline are manifold. For one thing, Britain, having been first in the industrial process, had too much money invested in older machinery. British cotton manufacturers, for example, found it less worthwhile to invest in automatic looms than American manufacturers who were first starting up. There was the fact, increasingly bemoaned in late Victorian Britain, that private companies were not establishing their own research laboratories and that technical education generally seemed to be neglected. The fruitful marriage of academic science and industrial technology which was characteristic of Germany seemed absent in Britain. It was not that individual Englishmen had ceased to be inventive. It was, after all, Englishmen like Faraday and Maxwell who had laid the theoretical foundations for the practical utilization of electricity. It was Sir Charles Parsons who invented the steam turbine in the 1880s and the unsung J. W. Swan who deserves as much as Edison to be called the inventor of the electric light bulb. Yet electric power stations spread far more rapidly in the United States than in Britain; and until World War I the chief use of electric power was for lighting. Similarly, two English cousins, Gilchrist Thomas and Percy Gilchrist, perfected the process of making steel out of phosphoric iron, but it was the mines of Germany and France which benefited thereby. It was the researches of William Perkin, an Englishman, which first revealed during the mid-century that chemical dyes made out of coal tar were potentially much more economical than dyes made from plants. Yet it was in Germany that the chemical dye industry took root.

Before we become too overwhelmed with the unhappy consequences of the Great Depression for Britain, we should note that Britain's decline as industrial leader was relative rather than absolute. During a generation in which Britain's annual production of pig iron increased by 23 percent, Germany's multiplied five times and that of the United States six times. The steel output figures speak for themselves.

STEEL PRODUCTION [2] (in thousands of tons)

YEARS	UNITED KINGDOM	GERMANY	FRANCE	U.S.A.
1890	3,579	2,195	670	4,275
1896	4,133	4,745	1,160	5,282
1900	4,901	6,260	1,540	10,188

During the years 1870–1913, Britain's total output of manufactures doubled; but whereas in 1870 this output had constituted one third of the world's manufactures, by 1913 it had fallen to only one seventh.

In one sense the relative decline was inevitable. Once other countries had entered upon full-scale industrialization, it was to be expected that those with a larger population and a greater number of natural resources would ultimately overtake Britain. By the late nineteenth century, Germany had twice the population of Britain, and the United States, with plentiful supplies of coal and far more iron and waterpower, had two and a half times as many people. As early as the 1840s, the *Economist* had warned that the "superiority of the United States to England is ultimately as certain as the next eclipse."

The fact remains, however, that Great Britain was, industrially speaking, becoming less flexible. Ernest E. Williams, in *Made in Germany,* a best seller of 1896, attributed Germany's growing industrial and commercial strength in part to the help its businessmen were receiving from the state in the form of protective tariffs, to the high standard of technical education at home, and to the aid given by the consular services abroad. Equally important, Williams believed, was the spirit of enterprise displayed by German businessmen. They were willing

---

[2] Ensor, p. 277.

salesmen, eager to please their customers and to adapt their products to fit their customers' needs. Germany's industrial growth, he concluded, ought to be looked upon by Englishmen less as a threat than as a bracing challenge.

Many British businessmen came to view their vanishing industrial supremacy more as a cause for uneasiness than as a reason for giving up tried and true ways, but in certain fields Britain did in fact meet that challenge. She was still the world's largest importer and exporter, even though textiles had ceased to be predominant among exports which now included increasing amounts of raw coal and machinery. Britain also maintained the world's largest merchant fleet; in 1913, as in 1870, about one third of all oceanic trade was done in British ships, thereby adding highly significant "invisible exports" to the visible exports which helped pay for food and raw materials. Financially, London's Lombard Street remained the acknowledged center of world finance, the site of the largest banks and insurance companies.

The Great Depression may well have spurred many individual entrepreneurs and partnerships to transform their concerns into limited liability companies. Such corporations had become commonplace in commerce and banking by the mid-Victorian years; but it was only in the late nineteenth century that the typical cotton factory or blast furnace became a limited liability company. A good many remained private corporations, whose stock was held largely by members of the same family, rather than public corporations whose shares were traded in the stock market. Even on the eve of the First World War, the family firm was still far more characteristic of Britain than it was of the United States or Germany. The family firm was yet more persistent in France.

Some of these concerns sought to meet the challenge of the Great Depression by amalgamating, both vertically and horizontally. Vertical amalgamation had as its aim, as in the case of the steel mills, the monopolistic control of the entire process of production from the mining of the ore to the processing and delivery of the manufactured product. There was a drive in this direction, from 1894 to 1902 especially, among steel manufacturers, shipbuilders, and armaments-makers. Horizontal amalgamation was the attempt to undercut or buy out all competing firms. The closest British counterpart in this respect to the Standard Oil Company of the late nineteenth century in the United States was the Salt Union, which by 1888 monopolized 90 percent of British salt production. In textile dyeing, cement making, tobacco manufacturing, and a few other industries, the late 1890s were, as in the United States, an era of horizontal amalgamation in which oligopoly, the control of a particular industry by a few great firms, became common-place. Yet the drive in this direction never went so far in England as in the United States, and consequently, "trust-busting" never became a vital political issue.

One reason why the Great Depression impresses some economists as an inadequate term for the economic trends of the late nineteenth century is that the index to prosperity and depression which serves as the most significant indicator of economic sickness in the twentieth century – the rate of unemployment – did not notably increase. In particular years, such as 1879, 1885, 1886, and 1893, the rate of unemployment did indeed rise to 10 percent or more; and it was in 1888 that the word "unemployment," defined as the inability of a man to find a job through no fault of his own, first entered the dictionary. Yet the average rate of unemployment for the fourth quarter of the century, approximately 5 percent, differs little from the average rate for the mid-Victorian decades of prosperity. As for the average employed worker, his standard of living was favorably affected by the years of the Great Depression. His money wages rose little, if at all, but he paid less for food, clothing, and shelter. Reduced prices brought the benefits of increased industrial productivity to the average workingman. His real wages rose on the average of 2 percent a year at a time when his leisure hours also increased. The 60-hour week had been normal in 1870; the 54-hour week was typical by 1900. The standard of living rose most obviously in respect to food. Wrote an observer in 1899, "the sort of man who had bread and cheese for his dinner forty years ago now demands a chop." As the cost of tea and sugar continued to fall, these staples became commonplaces in the British diet. The "average workingman" remains as hypothetical an entity in the late nineteenth century as at any other time, and talk of such an average conceals the existence of vast pockets of poverty to which late Victorian reformers were at pains to call attention. Nonetheless, the Great Depression proved to be a period of relative industrial peace and of social satisfaction for many workingmen. In assessing the political, social, and imperial changes of the late Victorian period, the paradoxical facets of the Great Depression should be kept in mind. They clarify much that may otherwise remain puzzling.

Liberals and Conservatives

"When I am ill," wrote Sir William Harcourt, "I am in bed. When I am not, I am in the House of Commons." Harcourt

(1827–1904), the late Victorian M.P., Cabinet member, and (for two years) leader of the Liberal Party, reflected an absorption with politics common to many Victorian English gentlemen.[3] It was, moreover, an attitude increasingly congenial to large numbers of British citizens who were not "gentlemen" in the generally accepted sense. The Reform Act of 1867 had officially recognized their right to have a direct interest in politics, and this interest was reflected in the newspapers of the day.

As Walter Bagehot put it in the 1860s, the newspapers "give a precedent and a dignity to the political world which they do not give to any other. The literary world, the scientific world, the philosophic world not only are not comparable in dignity to the political world, but in comparison are hardly worlds at all." The newspapers of the 1860s and 1870s had been freed from the stamp taxes which during the first half of the nineteenth century curtailed popular journalism; and the steam press had made possible their rapid duplication. Yet the large majority of lower-class Englishmen were not yet daily newspaper readers; and a daily circulation of 200,000 copies, which London's *Daily Telegraph* attained in the 1870s, was still regarded as an exception. The influential *Times* of London could boast of a reading public of only 50,000 a day, and the more important provincial papers like the *Yorkshire Post,* the *Birmingham Post,* the *Manchester Guardian,* and *The Scotsman* of Edinburgh were selling 25,000 to 40,000 copies a day.

All these papers were first and foremost concerned with politics; even a provincial journal devoted several closely printed pages a day to stenographic reports of parliamentary debates. It is understandable then that a seat in the House of Commons represented the summit of ambition to many a Victorian Englishman. Parliament, in the public estimation, not only brought status and provided the nation's preeminent public forum, but it also decided important things. Finally, Parliament provided excitement, and a parliamentary debater was judged not only by what he said but by how he said it. Enthusiasm for such professional games as football and cricket was still in its infancy, but the sport of politics was keenly followed and widely reported in the press.

The competitive character of politics was particularly no-

---

[3] Even after thirty years the most illuminating introduction to late Victorian England remains R. C. K. Ensor's *England, 1870–1914* (Oxford, 1936). H. J. Hanham's *Elections and Party Management: Politics in the Time of Disraeli and Gladstone* (London, 1959) is a penetrating pioneer study. Relevant also for this chapter are the biographies and foreign policy surveys referred to earlier, A. J. P. Taylor's *The Struggle for Mastery in Europe, 1848–1918* (Oxford, 1954) and such more specialized works as W. N. Medlicott, *The Congress of Berlin and After* (London, 1938).

ticeable at a time when the confusion of parties of the 1850s had come to an end. Not only did representatives of the two major parties confront each other day after day from opposite benches in the House of Commons, but from 1867 to 1875, the dynamic team captains themselves, Gladstone and Disraeli, sat barely twenty feet apart on opposite sides of the Speakers' Table. In American presidential campaigns it has often happened that the two candidates for election have never even met one another, much less listened to one another's opinions; but Gladstone and Disraeli could not escape each other's verbal shafts. When Disraeli on one occasion complained that Gladstone had become "intoxicated by the exuberance of his own verbosity," his description, however self-interested, was based on firsthand observation.

Both parties were of necessity coalitions; but after the Reform Bill of 1867 the political independence of an individual Member of Parliament began to be somewhat more greatly circumscribed by party organization. The dominance of Gladstone and Disraeli spurred a greater degree of party loyalty. A member who had been elected in 1868 on the basis of a pledge to support Gladstone's leadership was presumably impelled to support his chosen leader on most issues. Even more significant, the Reform Act of 1867 necessitated a greater degree of organization if only because of a greatly enlarged electorate. Party organization on the national level had previously been very weak, nor had it been looked upon as being in any sense desirable. Party organization in the past was expected to come after the election, not before; and M.P.s were expected to organize themselves in Parliament and elect their leaders. The Liberals might have their Reform Club and the Conservatives their Carlton Club, but these were as much social organizations as distinct political institutions. On the local level, individual patrons played a dominant role. Party machinery might in fact be nonexistent in certain areas; and where there were no patrons, there might at most be tiny self-perpetuating oligarchies who chose the local candidate and got out the vote.

The Reform Act of 1867 stimulated a certain degree of national organization if only for the purpose of fostering voter registration and providing a list of possible candidates for constituencies which lacked suitable local candidates. In Britain the custom that a Member of Parliament necessarily come from the constituency he represents has never become a commonplace. The national organization — usually headed at the time by the party's chief whip in the House of Commons — might encourage constituency organizations to name candidates wherever local party leaders had failed to do so or to attempt to arbitrate when the local party leaders were split. Any attempt by such national organizations to influence party policy was, however, deemed suspect.

It was the Reform Act of 1867 which also prompted the growth of constituency organizations in order to attract the new working-class voters. The first prominent example of this sort was the "Birmingham caucus" set up by Joseph Chamberlain and Francis Schnadhorst. The Liberals of Birmingham had a particular incentive for building a party machine because the Reform Bill gave the city a third member while leaving each voter with the right to vote for only two candidates. The purpose of this provision – added to the bill at the behest of the House of Lords – had been to permit the Conservatives to concentrate their votes so as to elect at least one member out of three. Careful organization on a ward-by-ward basis by the Birmingham Liberals enabled them to instruct their adherents in such a manner that they divided their votes almost equally among three Liberal candidates, thereby foiling the intent of the 1867 proviso. "The Birmingham caucus" came to have ambivalent connotations for all Englishmen who feared that democracy would mean American-style political-machine and political-boss control in England. (The word "caucus" illustrates the element of "Americanization." It is by origin an American Indian word which was taken over to describe particular types of Congressional meetings. Its pejorative use as a synonym for leadership of local mass political organizations is peculiarly English.)

As matters finally worked out, the individual Birmingham voter had the right to elect the caucus, or leadership, of his constituency party organization; but since the average voter often did not bother to attend party meetings, this leadership necessarily remained in the hands of those who were interested. Consequently, party workers tended to choose party nominees, and this became the standard procedure in most constituencies.

If the independence of an individual M.P. was restrained by the growth of a strong local organization, then it was similarly curbed by the increasing influence of particular pressure groups which required candidates to take a stand before they received the organization's verbal or monetary support. In the case of the Liberals, such organizations included the Liberation Society (whose purpose it was to disestablish the Church of England in England itself), the United Kingdom Alliance (the leading temperance organization whose aim was to limit pub hours and permit individual communities, by means of "local option," to bar the sale of intoxicating beverages), and the National Education League. Most of the adherents of these organizations were nonconformists, and the Liberal Party was much dependent upon the nonconformist vote. What was novel in the late nineteenth century was the increasing number of nonconformists who were themselves elected M.P.s. There had been only 23 in 1833, ten of whom were Unitarians. By 1868 their number had risen to 55 and in 1880 there were 85, all but one of whom were Liberals. Politically sophisticated Unitarians and Quakers continued to be elected at a ratio far higher than their number in the nation at large would warrant. In contrast, Methodists and Baptists, whose members ranked lower in wealth and social status, tended to lag behind.

The attraction of nonconformists to the Liberal banner implied that the enlarged post-1867 electorate in Wales and Scotland was drawn to the Liberals more often than to the Conservatives, if only because—in the case of Wales—the Liberals were more likely to bring about the disestablishment of the Anglican Church in Wales as they had done in Ireland. Moreover, the Liberal Party was more successful at attracting the workingman's vote than were the Conservatives. When two men of distinct working-class origin, Thomas Burt and Alexander MacDonald, were elected to Parliament in 1874, they both took their seats on the Liberal benches, the first of an increasing number of "Lib-Labs."

The Conservative Party, as the 1870s began, was still largely in the hands of a coalition of landed oligarchs. Although Disraeli, in preparation for the election of 1874, encouraged efforts to register voters and to strengthen constituency party organizations, he continued to rely primarily on the local influence of the party's traditional leaders. Those leaders had long felt that they represented not a class but the whole agricultural community of landlords, tenant farmers, and laborers. Disraeli once observed captiously that the English aristocracy most resembled "the old Hellenic race; excelling in athletic sports, speaking no other language than their own, and never reading." More typical, however, was his comment on another occasion:

> The proper leaders of the people are the gentlemen of England. If they are not the leaders of the people, I do not see why there should be gentlemen. . . . If it be true that we are on the eve of troublous times, if it indeed be necessary that changes should take place in this country, let them be effected by those who ought to be the leaders in all political and social changes.

The Conservatives had their pressure groups as well. As the nonconformists tended to vote Liberal, so the Church Defence Institution (an advocate of the traditional role and privileges of the Anglican Church) supported the Conservatives. As temperance advocates adhered to the Liberal ranks and succeeded in bringing about in 1871 the passage of a restrictive licensing bill, so the brewing industry and pubkeepers generally became Conservatives. In the early 1870s, the strength of the party still rested in the rural areas where the lord of the manor held sway, but before the end of the century, the Conservative hold upon the rural voter was to weaken and its attraction for the urban voter was to increase.

While an analysis of their makeup and organization helps clarify the role of political parties in late Victorian England, it does not by itself explain why the Conservatives were victorious in 1874 and why the Liberals returned in triumph in 1880. The Liberal victory in 1868 has already been accounted for. Their defeat in 1874 was a tribute to Disraeli's skill in revamping his party and in creating the impression of a positive program. His new conservatism, as outlined in a speech at London's Crystal Palace in 1872, rested on three bases: social reform, the monarchy, and the empire. The Conservative Party was, in his opinion, more suited than the Liberal for promoting such things as sanitary reform and campaigning for better housing for the working classes. Disraeli's program of paternalistic social reform – "Tory democracy" – harked back to his youthful Tory Radical insistence that the Tory aristocrat, not the liberal industrial plutocrat or doctrinaire classical economist, was the true friend of the workingman.

Secondly, Disraeli sought to focus upon the monarchy once again as the symbol of national unity. This was the revival of an old Tory tradition, and it seemed an appropriate countermove against the temporary flurry of republican sentiment. Finally, there was the empire. The Liberals, argued Disraeli, had looked upon the empire in a far too penny-pinching manner. They had discounted it as an unnecessary expense, ignoring the tics of sentiment which still united Canadians, Australians, New Zealanders, and South Africans of British descent with the mother country. They had failed to appreciate the significance of India for Britain's international power and influence.

Gladstone's Liberal Party suffered in 1874 not only from a rejuvenated Tory platform but also from its own success in introducing reform legislation. Disraeli not unjustly compared the Liberal front bench to a range of "exhausted volcanoes." One difficulty with a successful reform program is that it alienates as often as it satisfies. Many Englishmen resented the Liberals' pro-temperance legislation. "I have been borne down in a torrent of gin and beer," explained Gladstone, when news of his defeat came. The Conservatives had a majority of 83 in Great Britain alone and, counting the new separate Irish Home Rule Party, which sat with the opposition, had an overall majority of at least 48 in the United Kingdom. Perhaps as important as the gin and beer had been the disillusionment of many nonconformists with the Education Act of 1870, which they interpreted as a subsidy to Anglicanism. Their abstention in 1874 cost the Liberals numerous seats.

The Disraeli Ministry of 1874–1880

For Disraeli, the election of 1874 was the political climax of his career. For the first time since the early 1840s, the Conservatives had again become the majority party. The election was in a very real sense his personal victory. Yet victory had come in some ways too late. Disraeli was already seventy years old. His wife had died a year before, and for the aging M.P. the loss was a great one. He was increasingly crippled by gout, and he no longer possessed the energy of his earlier years.

In many ways the most constructive aspect of Disraeli's ministry of 1874–80 was his social reform program, piloted through the House of Commons by his able Home Secretary, Sir Richard Assheton Cross (1823–1914). A Trade Union Act of 1875 gave complete government sanction to such trade union activities as peaceful picketing; it went considerably further in this direction than Gladstone's Act of 1871 had done. An Artisans' Dwellings Act, also passed in 1875, for the first time empowered local authorities to condemn, demolish, and reconstruct whole areas of city slums. A Sale of Food and Drugs Act of the same year banned all ingredients "injurious to health" and remained the fundamental statute on the subject for half a century. Part of the same program was the Public Health Act of 1875, a consolidating measure which armed British municipalities with the authority to impose proper water, sewage, and drainage facilities.

Though other acts of social legislation passed during Disraeli's ministry, both the Prime Minister himself and his Cabinet became increasingly absorbed with foreign affairs during the years that followed. Disraeli deliberately set about to launch a more forward policy which would stress the fact that Britain could not be ignored by continental diplomats. His skillful coup in 1876 secured for England the shares in the Suez Canal which the bankrupt Khedive of Egypt felt compelled to sell. The Suez Canal had been completed by a French company in 1869 and had almost immediately become Britain's "lifeline to India." More British ships used the canal than those of any other nation; Britain had therefore particular concern for the canal's protection; but the timing of Disraeli's coup had less to do with British ambition than with the Khedive's mishandling of his own finances. Faced with bankruptcy, he needed money in a hurry; and the £4,000,000 purchase price had to be obtained so quickly that it was impossible to obtain immediate Parliamentary consent. Disraeli thereupon borrowed the money from his friends the Rothschilds until such time as Parliament could and did consent to purchase the shares and appropriate the required sum.

A comparable stroke—though a more controversial one—was the Prime Minister's Royal Title Bill which added to Victoria's titles that of Empress of India. The new Empress was highly flattered, and those Indians who until 1858 had been accustomed to the existence of an emperor at Delhi now had a visible substitute; but whatever value the new dignity may have had in asserting British prestige in India and throughout the world was mitigated by the controversy occasioned in England itself. Most Liberals and many Conservatives regarded the title of "Empress" as essentially un-English and as not quite proper.

While Britain's naval strength remained unchallenged in 1874, Disraeli considered his country's situation vis-à-vis the Continental powers as dangerously isolated. France was still in the process of recovering from the Franco-Prussian War, and its new government, the Third Republic, did not yet seem securely established. Spain was racked by civil war and played no role in European affairs commensurate with its population. The central and eastern part of Europe was, however, dominated by three great autocratic monarchies, the new German Empire (with Bismarck as Chancellor), the Austro-Hungarian Empire, and the Russian Empire. These three powers were joined in a Three Emperors' League which harked back to the post-Vienna Holy Alliance. A major theme underlying Disraeli's foreign policy was his attempt to disrupt this League.

Of the three great monarchies, it was Russia which once again seemed most antagonistic to British interests. When Disraeli came into power in 1874, Anglo-Russian relations, cemented as they were by a marriage between Victoria's second son and Czar Alexander's only daughter, were friendly; but the perennial "Eastern Question" was soon to bring the two countries once again close to war. The gradual, if sporadic, process of Turkish decline as a Balkan and Near Eastern power was still going on, and although Disraeli's absorption with Near Eastern affairs is sometimes attributed to his "oriental" background, less mystical explanations fit the facts more easily. The "non-oriental" Palmerston had, after all, been equally involved with Near Eastern affairs in the 1840s and the equally "non-oriental" Aberdeen had found his government implicated in the Crimean War in 1854.

It was a revolt in 1876 in Bosnia, one of Turkey's Slavic provinces, which touched off a series of wars and internal upheavals within the Turkish Empire which almost immediately involved the Great Powers. For a time, Disraeli's government, though fearful of the consequences of the disintegration of the Ottoman Empire, had no fixed policy. The Prime Minister's gratuitous dismissal as "coffee house babble" of the reports — afterwards confirmed — of the systematic murder of 12,000 Bulgarian men, women, and children by Turkish troops brought Gladstone back into politics. The former Prime Minister had resigned the Liberal leadership in 1875; and partly because his rival no longer occupied his traditional seat in the front benches in the House of Commons, Disraeli had thought it safe in 1876 to retire to the House of Lords as Earl of Beaconsfield. The "Bulgarian atrocities" and Disraeli's apparently cynical reaction were too much for a man who viewed foreign affairs as well as economic ones from a moral position; and Gladstone eloquently challenged the proposition that Britain's chief interest lay in the territorial preservation of an immoral and non-Christian Turkey rather than in the succor of fellow Christians oppressed by the Sultan.

Public sympathy veered toward Turkey in 1877, however, when a Turkish rejection of a Russian-sponsored protocol asking Turkey to institute internal reforms and grant a greater degree of autonomy to its subject nationalities in the Balkans led to a Russian declaration of war. All the traditional fears of Russian aggression were revived, as the Czar's troops advanced toward Constantinople. Victoria wanted immediate war against Russia and asked that the Government "be bold" and "rally round the Sovereign and country." In the music halls, they were singing:

> We don't want to fight
> But, by Jingo, if we do
> We've got the men
> We've got the arms
> We've got the money too!

Disraeli was clearly sympathetic, but his Cabinet was divided, and when he at last authorized the British fleet to enter the Dardanelles, it was Abdul Hamid, the new Ottoman Sultan, who urged the British to go slow. The arrival of a British squadron, he warned, might bring on the very event Disraeli most wished to prevent, the Russian seizure of Constantinople.

For in the meantime, Turkey had sued for peace. In the Treaty of San Stefano, Russia and Turkey agreed that Russia should obtain Bessarabia, that the autonomous states of Serbia,

Romania, and Montenegro should be completely independent of Turkey, and that a large new Bulgaria should be created under Russian protection. Both Britain and Austria were outraged. They had been ignored as Russia extended its influence deep into the Balkans, and the international tradition that major territorial boundary changes should involve all the great powers of Europe had been flagrantly breached. The result was the Congress of Berlin, the most significant diplomatic gathering since Vienna in 1815. For the first time a British Prime Minister attended an international diplomatic conference in person — as did his new Foreign Secretary, the Marquess of Salisbury (1830–1903) — and for the first time in over two centuries such a gathering was not conducted exclusively in the French language. Disraeli, who spoke French with a strong accent, preferred to use his native English.

Although Disraeli and Salisbury returned from Berlin claiming to have brought "Peace with Honour," the scope of their diplomatic achievement is open to question. The main provisions of the Treaty of San Stefano remained unaltered, so that Turkey's once much-vaunted territorial integrity had clearly not been preserved. The big Bulgaria was split into three small states with various degrees of autonomy, and Austria was granted the right to occupy but not to annex Bosnia-Herzegovina. As subsequent events proved, Disraeli had not succeeded in breaking up the Three Emperors' League, but he had succeeded in placing Britain once again in the center of the European diplomatic stage. Britain, in addition to influencing the ultimate settlement, obtained the Turkish island of Cyprus. As Sir William Harcourt, a Liberal M.P., put it: "It was necessary to bring back something, and that something was Cyprus." Whatever the substance of his diplomatic triumph, Disraeli was for the moment a national hero, and a general election in 1878 might well have returned an even more strongly Conservative House of Commons. The date of election was, however, put off, and by the time it came, the state of public opinion had markedly changed.

Events in South Africa and Afghanistan were largely responsible. In South Africa, Lord Carnarvon, who had supervised the creation of the autonomous Dominion of Canada in 1867, looked forward to creating under British auspices a similar union of South Africa, made up of the two English coastal colonies (Cape Colony and Natal) and the two inland republics (Transvaal and the Orange Free State) inhabited by Boers, the descendants of the original Dutch settlers of South Africa. It was Lord Carnarvon's hope that a greater degree of British control would ease the perpetually strained relations between the Boers and the neighboring Zulus. The Boers, although they had agreed in theory to outlaw slavery, continued to practice it, and they both feared and hated their Zulu neighbors. It was the Zulu threat which caused the Boers to acquiesce for the moment in the British annexation of the Transvaal in 1877. An ultimatum to the Zulus, sent by the British High Commissioner in South Africa in defiance of instructions from London, committed British troops to a full-fledged Zulu war.

The war proved the mettle of the 40,000 skilled spear-throwers who constituted the Zulu army. It also led to the massacre of the inhabitants of a British fort and a prolonged military campaign. By the summer of 1879, the Zulu army had been destroyed, but the war had proved costly both in men and in money and was extremely unpopular in England.

Equally disagreeable things were happening to the English in India. The British viceroy had long been fearful of the Russian advance into Central Asia which seemed to pose an eventual threat to India. In the 1870s, the focus of this threat was Afghanistan, whose Amir preferred a policy of neutrality in lieu of becoming the satellite of either Russia or Britain. In order to forestall the Russians, however, the British insisted on the Amir's acceptance of a British military mission. When the Amir refused, the British army invaded the country and dictated a treaty ceding military control over the Afghan passes to Britain and accepting British control over Afghan foreign policy. Just as the British were celebrating their military success, a group of Afghan army mutineers massacred the new British minister in Kabul and his entire entourage. The war then began all over again, and the British press began to question the price of imperial glory.

British international discomforts gave Gladstone the opportunity for a political return. He was far too emotionally involved not to speak out against Disraeli and his policies and far too energetic to stay in political retirement. As a young man he had thought nothing of walking thirty miles a day. Even at the age of seventy, which he attained in 1879, his favorite exercises were still walking and felling trees upon his estate at Hawarden near Liverpool. When Gladstone was invited to be the Liberal candidate for the Scottish county of Midlothian, he was provided with a welcome opportunity to attack six years of "Beaconsfieldism." The "Midlothian campaign" of the autumn of 1879 and the winter of 1880, a long series of formal public addresses punctuated by a score of brief "whistle stop" speeches, marked the final conversion of the Tory of the 1830s into the popular democrat of the 1880s, the G.O.M. ("Grand Old Man") of the late Victorian scene.

Gladstone lacked the tact to get along with the Queen or even with his colleagues as easily as Disraeli did. He could, however, impress his colleagues with his intellect, his energy, and his impassioned parliamentary orations, and, unlike his Tory rival, he could electrify a crowd. Canning had for a time been a popular hero, and so had Palmerston; but never in the nineteenth century did an English statesman manage to embody the aspirations and gain the respect and admiration of millions of his countrymen as did Gladstone at the time of the Midlothian campaign.

His opponents, who regarded the proper site for a public speech to be the floor of the House of Commons and not an open air arena, ridiculed him as a demagogue. Gladstone's public appeals were indeed unorthodox, but he never condescended to his audience, and he appealed not to the self-interest of the masses but to their self-respect. Both privately and publicly, he looked upon "the people" as a high tribunal to whom he was presenting a legal case. The voters were to him a great jury of intelligent men who were concerned with political issues and who looked upon the casting of a vote, as Gladstone himself did, as a profound moral act.

In the speeches that comprised the Midlothian campaign, Gladstone stressed many subjects, but time and again he harked back to his main theme: that in foreign relations, it was not desirable for Britain to act unilaterally or to attempt to dominate others — as Disraeli had done. Rather Britain should support international public law and thereby neutralize the selfish aims of immoral powers. The small nations of Europe would then look to Britain as a guide to orderly and constitutional freedom. Britain should support their aspirations, as it had in Belgium and Italy, and not treat them as pawns, as Disraeli had done in the Balkans. Disraeli saw his prime duty as that of advancing British interests and upholding British honor by whatever means were available. For Gladstone, words such as "interest" and "honor" were meaningless if they were not reconcilable with underlying moral principles, with the cause of humanity, justice, civilization, and religion.

Gladstone's eloquent indictment of Disraeli, combined with Chamberlain's organizing talents on the constituency level and the agricultural and industrial depression of the later 1870s, resulted in a Liberal landslide in the general election of 1880. In the new House of Commons, 347 Liberals overshadowed 240 Conservatives and 65 Irish Home Rulers. Disraeli retired from the Prime Ministership; a year later, having completed his last novel — *Endymion*, the story of a young man who grows up to be Prime Minister of England — he was dead.

At the time of the Liberal triumph, the leadership of the party was still formally in the hands of the Marquess of Hartington, and Victoria would have much preferred him to Gladstone. "I never could take Mr. Gladstone ... as my minister again," she had written in 1879, "for I never COULD have the slightest particle of confidence in Mr. Gladstone after his violent, mischievous, and dangerous conduct for the last three years." But as Hartington soon made plain to her, she had no choice. It was clearly Gladstone who embodied the Liberal Party and Gladstone who had won the election.

Gladstone's Second Ministry (1880–1885)

Gladstone's second ministry was to be so bogged down by frustrations abroad and at home that it is easy to miss its real accomplishments. Although the Liberal slogan continued to be "Peace, Retrenchment, and Reform," the Liberal Party in 1880 lacked any pressing or agreed-upon reform program. The election had, after all, been fought primarily on the issue of foreign policy. The Ministry did, nonetheless, produce a notable series of legislative reforms. The Corrupt Practices Act of 1883 proved more significant than any other single measure in curbing electoral dishonesty. A series of acts did much to improve the position of the English tenant farmer. Henceforth he had the right of compensation for improvements he made on his lands and the right to guard his crops against the hares which had hitherto been protected as a hunting preserve of aristocrats. The legal transfer of land, long subject to entail and to century-long leases, was made much easier.

The single most important legislative action of the second Gladstone ministry was the passage of the Reform Bill of 1884, the act which, in effect, extended to the county voter the franchise which the act of 1867 had extended to the urban voter. The total electorate was increased from 3,150,000 to 5,700,000; and in the counties alone the number of voters was almost tripled. Although the result was not in theory universal manhood suffrage, the vast majority of adult males now possessed the vote. The only significant exceptions were men without a regular home, bachelors who lived with their parents, and butlers (and laborers) who lived with their masters.

The Reform Bill of 1884 did not elicit the kind of ideological debate which the Reform Bill of 1867 had produced. Some Englishmen might still have doubts about the theoretical virtues of political democracy, but it had ceased to be practical politics to debate the issue. The fact that the bill was not accompanied by a Redistribution Bill caused it to be initially rejected in the House of Lords, and for a few weeks in 1884 it appeared as if a major battle with the House of Lords was in the offing. Then, partly as a result of Queen Victoria's influence, a bipartisan committee was set up to work out an acceptable reapportionment act. This act did much to bring about the Chartist ideal of equal electoral districts. Though a few exceptions remained, it was the single-member district which now became standard in place of the traditional two-member borough or county. The Act consequently altered the fundamental basis upon which the English theory of representation had rested for about a thousand years. It was no longer the community which was represented — it was now the individual.

The Reform Act of 1884 helped complete the transition in both party machinery and party appeal which the Reform Act of 1867 had begun. It increased the role of party political organizations outside Parliament. The growth of the Birmingham caucus has been noted above. It was from an association of such local constituency organizations that Joseph Chamberlain in 1877 fashioned the National Liberal Federation. Relations between that organization and the legal party leadership in Parliament were not always smooth, especially since the general attitude of the National Liberal Federation was more radical than that of the more Whiggish party leadership. Similarly, in the wake of the Conservative defeat of 1880, a youthful Tory, Lord Randolph Churchill (1849–95) succeeded in the "capture" of the National Union of Conservative Associations as a vehicle for uniting the various Conservative constituency organizations, thus giving the party rank and file a sense of participation they had formerly lacked.

Although Churchill claimed to have taken over the mantle of "Tory Democracy" from Disraeli, it was not to the workingman that the Conservatives of the 1880s appealed most strongly. "The Conservative party have done more for the working classes in five years than the Liberals have done in fifty," declared Alexander MacDonald, the working-class M.P., in 1879; but it is noteworthy that he remained a member of the Liberal Party. The new converts to Conservatism were generally the suburban householders and the inhabitants of the more prosperous city districts. They were white-collar workers — clerks, teachers, and shopkeepers — whose income might not be higher than that of the factory worker but whose status aspirations were.[4] For the alteration of the theoretical basis of representation from community to individual coincided with an actual alteration of the old communities. In the old-style borough, the community leaders had lived side by side with the people

---

[4] James Cornford, "The Transformation of Conservatism," *Victorian Studies* (Sept., 1963).

they influenced, and, as in the country districts, regarded the interests of employer and employee as essentially one. In the sprawling industrial city, on the other hand, there was a growing pattern of residential segregation by class and income. The more prosperous tended to become faithful Conservative supporters, while the less prosperous became for the time being rather less regular Liberal supporters.

During the same decade, the increase in the rural electorate as well as legislation favoring the tenant farmer caused a profound change in the country areas. The shires had been traditionally in the hands of Tory squires who exercised great influence over their tenants. This influence had much declined by 1885; and in the general election of that year in which many an industrial city first provided a Conservative majority, many a rural borough for the first time voted Liberal.

The reforms of the second Gladstone ministry, real as they were, tended to be overshadowed in the public press by a series of domestic and foreign frustrations. An especially plaguing problem for Gladstone was the case of Charles Bradlaugh (1833–91), notorious atheist and advocate of birth control, who was not permitted by the House of Commons to take the required parliamentary oath and who was thereby prevented from taking the seat for which the electors of the Borough of Northampton had chosen him in 1880. His case aroused a flood of emotional oratory and testified to the continued significance in the Britain of the 1880s of organized religion and of the Victorian canons of respectability. Gladstone found it distasteful to defend the constitutional rights of a man whose atheistic convictions he found abhorrent; but when it proved impossible to defer the matter to the courts, he supported, in one of his most eloquent speeches, the Affirmation Bill of 1883. The bill would have granted Bradlaugh, and all other M.P.s, the right to affirm, rather than to swear, their loyalty to the crown; but public opinion was too hostile at the time to permit the bill to pass. Bradlaugh, whose Northampton constituents repeatedly elected him, was finally admitted to the House of Commons in 1886, and he secured the passage of a permanent affirmation bill in 1888. Thus Parliament, which had been opened to Roman Catholics in the 1820s and to professing Jews in the 1850s, was thrown open to avowed atheists in the 1880s.[5]

Although issues of foreign policy had helped Gladstone win the election of 1880, the same issues were equally responsible for the decline of his popularity by 1885. In Afghanistan, it is true, the situation was satisfactorily resolved. British troops were evacuated, but in return for a subsidy and a guar-

---

[5] Walter L. Arnstein, *The Bradlaugh Case* (Oxford, 1965).

antee against foreign aggression, the reigning Amir permitted Britain to control Afghanistan's foreign relations. Things went less well in South Africa. There Gladstone had promised to end the annexation of the Transvaal if elected. When disagreement in the new Liberal government delayed a settlement, the Boers went on the offensive and defeated a small British contingent at Majuba Hill in February 1881. Gladstone had to choose between fighting for an annexation in which he did not believe and making peace, thereby conceding to force of arms what he seemingly had refused to concede to reason. He decided to make peace, despite the fact that his decision was interpreted as an affront to British honor and a justification of Boer arrogance.

It was at the other end of Africa, however, where Gladstone had his greatest trouble. Egypt, in which Disraeli's purchase of the Suez Canal shares had involved Britain, proved to be the location of the ministry's greatest military victory and its most stinging defeat. The Khedive's extravagance had led in 1878 to an Anglo-French condominium with supervisory powers over Egyptian finances. This led to an outburst of Egyptian nationalism under one Colonel Arabi, who resented not only the British and the French but also the Turkish advisers who dominated the Khedive's court (for Egypt was still nominally a part of the Ottoman Empire). Negotiations for a joint Anglo-French intervention collapsed; and when in 1882 Colonel Arabi's forces staged a coup d'etat which resulted in the death of fifty Europeans in Alexandria, the British government intervened alone. Its navy shelled Alexandria; and in a model of military maneuvering, it collected and landed a 16,000-troop British army which, after a long night march, completely defeated Colonel Arabi's forces. Against his better judgment, Gladstone decided upon the temporary occupation of Egypt. Clearly a good deal of governmental and economic rebuilding was in order there, and the Prime Minister did not believe he could leave that task in the hands either of the Egyptians or of another European power.

In order to simplify the administration of Egypt, the British government decided to relinquish for the time being all Egyptian territorial claims to the area south of Egypt, the Sudan. General Gordon, a Victorian soldier-adventurer, was summoned to superintend the evacuation of the scattered Egyptian forces in the Sudan. He decided, instead, to make a stand to keep Khartoum and the Nile Valley in Anglo-Egyptian hands in the face of the fanatical Sudanese Mahdi (or Messiah) and his followers. The British Cabinet opposed the step but delayed – against local advice – in authorizing a relief expedition up the Nile to bring back General Gordon. A force was finally authorized and sent, but it arrived at Khartoum only on January 28, 1885, two days after Khartoum had been stormed and General Gordon killed. No single event of his career made Gladstone more unpopular. He had tried in his fashion to adhere to the moral foreign policy he had outlined in the Midlothian campaign, but good intentions were not always sufficient and events did not always oblige.

The general election of 1885 was thus fought in the face of a foreign policy record about which Englishmen had at best mixed feelings. The greatest accomplishment of Gladstone's second ministry in foreign affairs, the occupation of Egypt, was paradoxically one Gladstone looked forward to terminating as soon as possible. The years had, however, brought some significant legislative changes at home, most notably the Reform Act of 1884 and the accompanying Redistribution Act. These same years, finally, had brought a revival of the perennial Irish question; and it was Ireland rather than political reform acts or military maneuvers in distant lands which dominated British politics in the 1880s. Disraeli's death had brought the long parliamentary duel of Disraeli and Gladstone to a close, but Ireland was to add one last chapter to Gladstone's long career.

Chapter 9

The 𝔍𝔯𝔦𝔰𝔥 Question

THE IRISH Question is almost as old as English history itself. It is rooted in geography and in the fact that ever since the days of Henry II the inhabitants of a larger and more populous England have tried to control the inhabitants of her smaller, more backward island neighbor.

The Nineteenth-Century Background

Many Victorian Englishmen recognized that the treatment which their forebears had meted out to the Irish had often been unjust and that the Irish had been dealt with in the past as a conquered people. But this they felt was no longer true in the nineteenth century. The Irish now had their proper share of representation in the Parliament of the United Kingdom. The religion of so many of them, Roman Catholicism, was no longer a bar to their economic or political advancement. Their merchants were no longer discriminated against economically as they admittedly had been in the eighteenth century. The Irish, many Englishmen concluded, had both the privilege and the glory of being part of the worldwide British Empire.[1]

---

[1] In addition to Ensor's *England, 1870–1914* and the biographies of Gladstone referred to earlier, the following volumes throw specific light into the subjects taken up in this chapter: Lawrence J. McCaffey, *Irish Federalism in the 1870's*

When therefore Irish nationalists compared their lot to that of Greeks under Turkish rule or Italians under Austrian rule, most Englishmen failed to grasp the analogy. Nationalism remains admittedly a concept very difficult to define: geography, a common religion, and a common language are often cited as significant attributes of nationalism; yet there are nations, like the Swiss, which defy all three. Ultimately, the most potent source of nationalism is simply a state of mind, a widespread feeling on the part of a group of people that they constitute a separate nationality and therefore deserve to be a separate nation. What a nineteenth-century Irishman defined as loyalty to his own nationality a nineteenth-century Englishman might, with equal consistency, regard as treason to that more comprehensive focus of loyalty, the British Empire. Most nineteenth-century Irishmen were too pragmatic – and usually too absorbed in the day-to-day tasks of earning a subsistence living – to expect the establishment of an independent Irish nation. A few revolutionary "Young Irelanders" had that hope in the 1840s; so did the revolutionary "Fenians" of the 1860s. Some of the Fenians were emigrants to the United States who fought on the Union side in the American Civil War in order to gain the military experience to fight the real enemy, England. But their "invasion" of Canada in 1866 proved abortive; and their attempt to establish an Irish Republic in 1867 failed to evoke any widespread support among the Irish peasantry.

Most Irish leaders, men like Daniel O'Connell in the 1830s and 1840s and men like Isaac Butt in the 1870s, sought not independence but the more attainable objective of amelioration of social and economic conditions by parliamentary pressure and autonomy within the British Empire. British political leaders, unfortunately, were more prone to deal with Irish problems when they were brought to their attention in violent form than when Irish claims were pressed more calmly. The 1850s, the decade after the Great Famine, thus proved a relatively peaceful period in Anglo-Irish relations, even if it was a "peace of exhaustion" and even if Irish prosperity was the result of the earlier starvation and mass emigration which had cut the population and increased the relative food supply. No attempt was made at the time to promote fundamental agrarian reform, and Gladstone's attention to the Irish question was characteris-

---

(Philadelphia, 1962); C. C. O'Brien, *Parnell and His Party, 1880–1890* (Oxford, 1957); and J. L. Hammond, *Gladstone and the Irish Question* (London, 1938). Also informative are R. Barry O'Brien's two-volume biography of Parnell (London, 1899) and the first two volumes of J. L. Garvin's controversial multi-volume biography of Joseph Chamberlain (London, 1932, 1934).

tically first attracted by the Fenian "outrages" which marred this peaceful era. Though Gladstone recognized more readily than his fellow politicians the reality of Irish nationalism, his purpose was not to encourage it but to reconcile Irishmen to English rule. It was his hope that the disestablishment of the Anglican Church in Ireland in 1869 and an Irish Land Act in 1870 to aid tenant farmers would complete his "mission to pacify Ireland."

Two events of the 1870s shattered this hope. One of these was the agricultural depression. Its effects upon an Ireland which was ninety percent agricultural was even more severe than in England. As in Britain, farm prices declined; tenants were unable to meet rent payments; landlords attempted to convert arable land to pasture. But unlike England, there was no relief in the form of industrialization. The second highly influential event of the decade was the Secret Ballot Act of 1872. The act had little observable effect upon the way the average Englishman voted, but insofar as it freed tenant farmers from the revenge of their landlords, it had a very noticeable effect upon the way Irishmen voted. Almost immediately the Irish electorate began to assert its independence. Of 103 M.P.s elected in Ireland in 1874, some 59 called themselves neither Liberals nor Conservatives but Home Rulers. The phrase had been coined by Isaac Butt, a Protestant Dublin lawyer who headed the group. His aim was to establish a parliament in Dublin in which Irishmen might control all domestic affairs while leaving imperial defense and foreign policy in the hands of the British Parliament in Westminster. Butt was aware how averse most Englishmen were to any idea of repealing the Act of Union of 1801; he hoped, however, that "Home Rule" would impress them as a more palatable alternative. He pointed out that "Home Rule" would be a genuinely conservative solution in that an Irish parliament would protect Ireland against revolutionary tendencies. Despite Butt's electoral success in 1874, he made little headway in converting either of the major parties to his program; nor did the mass of the Irish peasantry – most of them as yet ineligible to vote because they did not meet property requirements – see "Home Rule" as a solution to their fundamental economic needs.

The Rise of Parnell

A more immediate solution to the agricultural problem seemed to rest in the Irish Land League, an organization founded in 1879 by Michael Davitt, an ex-Fenian. Its slogan was "The

Land For the People" and its purpose was to protect the peasantry against eviction and exorbitant rents. In the meantime, the economic depression and the apparent failure of Butt's attempts at gentle persuasion brought to the forefront within the Home Rule ranks a young man named Charles Stewart Parnell, who decided that far more extreme measures were needed. Though he was himself an Irish landlord and he distrusted Davitt's more radical proposals, Parnell gave his blessings to the League and actually became its president. At the same time he displaced Butt, who died in 1879, as Home Rule leader at Westminster. The economic and political movements were thus joined and the Home Rulers received thereby a mass following in Ireland.

At Westminster the Irish "third party" was beginning to attract more attention by reason of Parnell's brilliance in the art of political obstructionism. Though brief earlier examples are known, it was not until the late 1870s that any group in the House of Commons had ever so deliberately taken advantage of parliamentary rules of order to obstruct parliamentary business. Obstructionism did not win the Irish Home Rulers popularity, but it made it impossible any longer to ignore them. Moreover, Parnell's third party had money; a highly significant factor in financing both the Land League and the Home Rule Party in Westminster was the generosity of the Irish-Americans in the United States. A generation had gone by since the Great Famine, and enough of them had made good in the New World to enable them to do much for their compatriots back home. Many an Irish M.P. in the early 1880s spent half his time in Parliament and the other half touring the United States to collect funds.

The Disraeli ministry of 1874–80 made no genuine attempt to deal with Irish grievances; but when Gladstone returned as Prime Minister in 1880, it appeared for a while as if the situation would improve. Gladstone did after all have a reputation as a friend of Irish causes, and he and the Home Rulers had sat together on the Opposition benches. The new Gladstone ministry let lapse the most recent of many temporary "coercion acts" – statutes which sought to deal with Irish violence by suspending the writ of habeas corpus in Ireland – and it sponsored a bill to have the government pay compensation to evicted Irish tenants. The bill passed the House of Commons only to be vetoed by the House of Lords. The result was renewed Land League agitation in Ireland on behalf of evicted tenants. While the League did not publicly advocate violence, the burning of hayricks, the maiming of cattle, and the firing of shotgun blasts at houses during the night often followed in the wake of its agitation. Moreover, the League advocated a system of social ostracism whereby anyone who purchased a farm from which the previous tenant had been unjustly evicted would be totally ignored by his neighbors. They would not talk to him, buy from him, or sell to him. He was to be treated, in Parnell's words, like "a leper of old." The first victim of this policy was the agent of a large landowner in County Mayo, one Captain Boycott, who thereby unintentionally added a new word to the English language. At Westminster, in the meantime, the Irish renewed their filibustering tactics, which reached their height one night in January 1881 when the Parnellites kept the House of Commons in session for an unprecedented forty-one hours. Only then did the Speaker take it upon himself to set aside the rules and end the session.

The Gladstone ministry met the problem of violence in Ireland and obstruction in Westminster by a characteristic combination of sticks and carrots. The sticks consisted of a new "coercion act" early in 1881 and a change of parliamentary regulations a year later which made it much easier to shut off debate in the face of deliberate filibustering. The major "carrot" was the Irish Land Act of 1881, an epic piece of legislation which was piloted through the House of Commons by Gladstone himself. The statute granted to the Irish tenant farmers the "three F's" they had long demanded: fair rent, free sale, and fixity of tenure. The Act of 1881, once the machinery for its enforcement could be set up, proved far more effective than any previous efforts by the government to control landlord-tenant relations. It set down the principle that tenants as well as landlords had important rights in the land, a break with laissez-faire doctrine which late Victorian Liberals were often more willing to make when dealing with troubled Ireland than with England.

As often happens when agitation arouses human passions, a particular act of legislation did not at once calm the storm. The autumn of 1881 brought new violence in Ireland; this in turn caused the government to pass still another coercion act, to outlaw the Land League, and to place Parnell and his leading lieutenants under arrest in Kilmainham jail. Just when matters looked worst, both sides began to compromise. In April 1882, Gladstone and Parnell reached an understanding whereby the Government would release the Irish leaders and appropriate money to pay the arrears in rent of 100,000 Irish tenants. Parnell in turn promised henceforth to cooperate with the Liberal Government to end crime and disorder. Many Englishmen were outraged by this so-called "Kilmainham Treaty" which seemed to represent the appeasement of an arch-revolutionary. But Gladstone had, despite his insistence on moral principle, a pragmatic ability to forgive and forget; while Parnell, though suspected of being the devil incarnate by many Englishmen, was ultimately more a constitutionalist than a revolutionary. Yet Parnell impressed even his own supporters as a somewhat aloof and mysterious man. The haziness of his ultimate aims and the enigmatic nature of his character enabled him to do what no other Irish leader since O'Connell had accomplished, temporarily to unite revolutionaries and moderates on behalf of the cause of "Home Rule."

It was by one of those quirks of irony which seem to bedevil Anglo-Irish history that only four days after Parnell's release, the new Chief Secretary for Ireland, Lord Frederick Cavendish, should have been murdered in Phoenix Park, Dublin. Parnell himself was outraged, and denounced the murder in a manifesto. The assassins were eventually identified as members of "The Invincibles," a secret Irish murder club which flourished on the extremes of the Irish nationalist movement. Although the murder, which led to still another coercion act, necessarily marred what may be termed "the Spirit of Kilmainham," the atmosphere of cooperation did not disappear altogether during the next three years. Occasional acts of violence continued and the Parnellites opposed the Liberal Government in a number of instances, but affairs did not again reach the fever pitch of 1879–82.

The Parnellites had not, of course, forgotten that their ultimate aim was "Home Rule." Thus far no major English political leader had been converted to the idea; but in 1882 Gladstone surprised the House of Commons by indicating that he was not opposed to Irish Home Rule in principle but thought the project impracticable. By the spring of 1885, the Second Gladstone ministry had been damaged by the death of General Gordon at Khartoum and its Cabinet was split on a growing number of issues. A House of Commons defeat on a minor budget provision was almost welcomed by Gladstone as an excuse to resign. Since, however, the new district lines and poll books required by the Reform Act and Redistribution Act of 1884–85 had not yet been prepared, no immediate general election could be held. The new Conservative leader, the Marquess of Salisbury, agreed to head a minority caretaker government for the time being.

During the previous years a number of Irish M.P.s had drawn closer to the Conservatives as fellow opponents of the Gladstone ministry, and rising Conservative leaders like Lord Randolph Churchill began to play with the idea of a genuine Irish-Tory alliance. The Salisbury Government permitted the most recent coercion act to lapse, and the new Conservative Viceroy in Ireland hinted that a Conservative Government might approve some form of Home Rule. Irish M.P.s began to hope that it might be 1867 all over again. The Conservatives would introduce a reform bill, the Liberals would broaden it, and the Irish would benefit. With this expectation in mind, two days before the general election, Parnell issued a manifesto asking all Irishmen in England to vote Conservative.

The results of the election of November 1885 were ironic: Liberals, 335; Conservatives, 249; Irish Home Rulers, 86. In one sense the election was a triumph for Gladstone. Although the Liberals had lost numerous urban seats, they had made gains in the rural areas which almost compensated for their losses. Gladstone at the end of his second ministry clearly retained far more popular support than he had at the end of his first ministry in 1874. In a still more obvious sense, the election was a triumph for Parnell. In the 1880 Parliament he had never been able to count on the full-fledged support of more than forty Irish M.P.s; now his party had 86 out of 103 Irish members all pledged personally to him. He was indeed "the uncrowned King of Ireland." There was, however, a further irony: while neither major party could now govern without Irish support, the Conservatives did not have enough M.P.s to have a working majority even with Irish support. The practical grounds for a Tory-Irish alliance had collapsed.

The First Home Rule Bill

Before the new Parliament assembled in January, an indiscreet revelation by one of Gladstone's sons made it clear that Gladstone had been definitely converted to Home Rule. Whatever temptations the Conservative Government had had to deal with the problem now disappeared, and the Parnellites flocked en masse to the Gladstone banner they had scorned only two months before. Late in January, the Liberals and Irish combined to defeat the Conservatives in the new Parliament. Salisbury resigned, and Gladstone at the age of 76 became Prime Minister for the third time. Some Englishmen at the time and some historians subsequently accused Gladstone of gross expediency, of allying himself with the Irish Home Rulers because he needed Irish votes to govern. This judgment fails to take into account the fact that no one was more aware than the new Prime Minister that, although his conversion to Home Rule might gain him Irish support, it might equally well split his own party in the process. Much more influential in the slow formation of Gladstonian opinion had been the election results in Ireland. The populace, a majority of whose adult males were for the first time enfranchised, had overwhelmingly demonstrated its desire for Home Rule. This popular pressure helped convince him that the Irish question was a moral issue which deserved his complete support.

In April, Gladstone introduced a bill to create in Dublin a separate parliament and executive to handle Irish domestic affairs. The Parliament at Westminster, in which Irishmen would no longer be directly represented, would continue to have control of foreign policy (including trade agreements), defense, and the coinage. The bill aroused in England the kind of popular and parliamentary excitement not known since 1832. In June of 1886, the decisive vote came: the proposed statute was defeated, 343–313. A number of factors help explain this result: Parnell was still in the minds of many Englishmen a criminal and hardly the man to be entrusted with the government of Ireland. The bill thus seemed to be a reward for criminal behavior. Secondly, the proposal was in some ways too sudden. Gladstone, despite a number of masterful orations, found himself unable to convince two of his most important colleagues, the Marquess of Hartington (the head of the Whig wing of the party) and Joseph Chamberlain (on all other subjects the leading Radical of his party and, in the minds of many Liberals, the logical successor to Gladstone). On the vital division, Gladstone managed to retain 227 of his Liberal followers; but 93, including Hartington and Chamberlain, voted against him.

There were still other reasons for the defeat of Home Rule. It went against what might be called the spirit of the age in England. Not only did the bill, which was tantamount to repealing the Act of Union of 1801, revive old military fears that Ireland might someday be used by a foreign power to threaten England; but it was totally opposed by the exponents of late Victorian imperialism. This was a time when the British Empire appeared to be expanding and strengthening its ties, and Home Rule implied the very opposite of this trend. Finally there was the question of Ulster. Though Parnell himself was a Protestant, and though the Irish Home Rule party was by no means exclusively Roman Catholic, the Presbyterians of Ulster were fearful of being swamped in an Irish Parliament, the vast majority of whose members would in all likelihood be Roman Catholics. Men who opposed Home Rule on other grounds tended to stir the religious issue for political reasons.

Gladstone appealed to the electorate to reverse the verdict of Parliament in a new general election. Unlike the election of the previous year, there were now four parties in the field: Conservatives, Irish Home Rulers, Gladstonian Liberals, and Liberal Unionists (the followers of Hartington and Chamberlain who opposed the repeal of "Union" with Ireland and who set up their own party organization). There was no doubt as to how the nation felt. The results were bleak for Gladstone: 316 Conservatives; 78 Liberal Unionists; 191 Liberals; 85 Irish Home Rulers. For the moment, clearly, Home Rule was dead and the Liberal party divided in much the same fashion as the Tories had been split over the repeal of the Corn Laws in 1846.

More, however, was involved in the breakup of the Liberal party than just the Irish issue. For the right-wing Whigs in the party, the Home Rule crisis was simply the occasion to cut a tie which they had found increasingly uncomfortable.[2] Their departure did not deprive the party of mass support, but it did end the party's traditional aristocratic landlord connection. More significantly, it removed from Parliament nine tenths of its genuinely wealthy members and a majority of its peers, thus transforming the House of Lords into a more or less permanent organ of the Conservative party. The Whiggish Liberal Unionists drifted increasingly toward a permanent alliance with the Conservatives, just as many Peelites of the 1850s had drifted toward Liberalism. Politically, Chamberlain's defection was even more important than Hartington's. As a Radical who supported a sweeping program of free secular education, of land reform, of the disestablishment of the Church of England, of universal manhood suffrage, and of the payment of salaries to Members of Parliament, he seemed to be part of the wave of the future and much more at home in a Liberal party shorn of Whig support than in Salisbury's Conservative party.

Clearly, this was at first Chamberlain's view as well. His own plans for Irish local government did not really differ quite so much from Gladstone's Home Rule proposal as he made out; but Chamberlain was both an ambitious and practical politician. He decided therefore to let the unpopular Home Rule issue blow itself out, to allow the G.O.M. to retire, and then to return to lead the Liberal party in a genuinely Radical direction. The one factor Chamberlain did not count on was the incredible longevity of William Ewart Gladstone.

To become leader of the Opposition at the age of 77 was at best a discouraging prospect, but Gladstone set himself to the task of remaining in politics until he could convince his countrymen that justice to Ireland was not treason to England but a moral obligation and that only by concession rather than force could the two peoples be reconciled. So long as the G.O.M. remained in politics and kept the Irish issue alive, Chamberlain found it impossible to return to the Liberal fold, and eventually Chamberlain found his guiding star in imperialism and drifted

---

[2] Gordon L. Goodman, "Liberal Unionism: The Revolt of the Whigs," *Victorian Studies* (Dec., 1959).

toward Conservatism himself. In the meantime, the party split continued to grow. Henry Labouchere, a Gladstonian Liberal, went so far as to compare Chamberlain's behavior to that of Judas Iscariot. Historical analogies, Labouchere conceded, were seldom exact, but "Judas had some good about him. It is true that he betrayed his Master, but he did not afterwards stump Judea and appear on platforms surrounded by scribes and Pharisees."

As the Liberal party disintegrated, Salisbury's Conservative Ministry (1886–92) ruled Ireland with a firm hand. It was willing to make concessions in some areas, but on Home Rule it was adamant. Salisbury looked with sympathy upon proposals to aid Irish peasants in purchasing their own land; the first act providing such assistance had been passed under Conservative auspices in 1885. His Government included Ireland in the County Councils Act of 1888, a significant part of the late Victorian democratization of Britain. The administrative and judicial duties and powers wielded for centuries by appointed Justices of the Peace were now taken over by elective bodies. Women, if unmarried and otherwise eligible, were given the right to vote both for county and borough councillors. The Act was particularly significant for London, which was created as a separate county (including both the original small borough of London and the many neighboring boroughs which by 1888 constituted a metropolitan area of over three million people). This democratization of local government undercut still further the squirarchical tradition of England's rural areas, though habits of deference sometimes lasted longer than the economic and political institutions which had given rise to them. While analogous to American practices, such democratization was much at variance with the prevailing continental practice, both in republican France and in imperial Germany.

For the Irish, however, local government was insufficient, especially since it came in the midst of a new period of unrest. Renewed evictions in Ireland in 1886 had been followed by a radical Irish Plan of Campaign which urged Irish tenants to unite in defiance of their landlords and to pay only those rents which they considered fair. The number of evictions increased, and violence was more widespread than at any time since 1882. The new Chief Secretary for Ireland, Salisbury's nephew, Arthur Balfour (1848–1930), forced through Parliament a drastic new Crimes Act. Though Balfour attempted to be fair in his dealings between landlords and tenants, he saw his first duty as that of ending disorder, and he proved in practice to be more favorable to the landlords. His rule won the hatred of most Irishmen.

The year 1889 brought a rift in the clouds for Gladstone and Parnell. Twenty-four months before, at the very time that

Balfour had been piloting his Crimes Act through the House of Commons, a series of articles had appeared in the *Times* entitled "Parnellism and Crime." One of these articles included a facsimile letter, apparently written by Parnell a few days after the Phoenix Park murders of 1882, which condoned those crimes. Parnell at once called the document a forgery; but since he failed to bring suit, he was not generally believed. When other so-called secret letters were produced in 1888, Parnell asked for an independent investigation, and the Government acceded to the appointment of a special commission of three judges. The commission investigated the matter in some detail and questioned at length Richard Pigott, an Irish journalist, who, through an intermediary, had sold the letters to the *Times*. While in the witness-box, Pigott broke down and confessed that he himself had forged the letters. He fled to Spain, posted a full confession, and before he could be arrested in Madrid, committed suicide. The revelation was a sensation; and Parnell, for so long a villain in the English press, suddenly became the underdog hero, the victim of deceit and trickery. Keeping in mind the unpopularity of Balfour's rule in Ireland and the Government's steady loss of seats at by-elections, there can be little doubt that a general election late in 1889 or early in 1890 would have resulted in an overwhelming pro-Home Rule majority.

The Irish Question was not to be solved so easily as that; as usual it was dogged with bad luck, tragedy, and the quirks of individual personalities. Before 1890 had ended, Captain O'Shea had won a divorce suit against his wife in which Parnell was named as co-respondent. There was no defense, and Parnell, it seemed, had for ten years deceived O'Shea by living illegally with his wife. The revelation was a terrible shock to nonconformist sentiment in England, and Parnell was in due course denounced by the Roman Catholic clergy of Ireland as well. The true story of the affair makes Parnell seem as much victim as villain. Mrs. O'Shea had lived apart from her husband for many years before she met Parnell, but she had kept the pretence of the married state to please her wealthy great-aunt who was her (and O'Shea's) main source of financial support. Thus there had been no divorce and no remarriage, and for ten years Parnell and Mrs. O'Shea had for practical purposes lived as man and wife (with O'Shea's full knowledge) and had had three children. This unusual arrangement lasted as long as the great-aunt lived. When she died in 1889 at the advanced age of 97, O'Shea offered his wife a private divorce for £20,000; and only when she could not produce the money (because the will was being legally contested) did O'Shea sue for a public divorce and name Parnell as his wife's lover.

Whatever judgment may be passed on of Parnell's private virtues, it was clearly in the public interest of his party that he should retire, at least for the time being, from the leadership of his party. This he refused to do; and when Gladstone indicated that he could not continue the Irish-Liberal alliance in such circumstances, the Parnellites split. A majority backed Gladstone; but Parnell fought stubbornly on, contesting by-election seats, in which anti-Parnell Home Rulers now defeated pro-Parnell Home Rulers. Not a robust man to begin with, Parnell wore himself out and died in October 1891, less than a year after the divorce case judgment.

The Second Home Rule Bill

The Liberal party, shorn of most of its Whig landlords and of its Birmingham Radicals and apparently permanently allied with the Irish Nationalists, was more than ever the party of "the Celtic Fringe." At Newcastle in 1891, it embraced a radical program including church disestablishment in Wales and Scotland, local veto on liquor sales, the end of the few remaining plural franchises, and extensive land-law reform. Many of these proposals were in line with the earlier Liberal tradition, though a new, if vague, promise to limit legally the hours of labor for workingmen was certainly not.

The Liberals, with their new, controversial, and faintly welfare state creed, in alliance with their Irish Nationalist allies, won a majority in the general election of 1892. They thereby not only reintroduced the Irish Question into English politics but advanced the transformation of the Liberal Party from a mid-Victorian, essentially laissez-faire, middle-class organization into the social-reform-minded democratic party of the early twentieth century. The election results (Liberals, 273; Irish Home Rulers, 81; Conservatives, 269; Liberal Unionists, 46; Independent Labourite, 1) were not overwhelming and not nearly so favorable as they might have been before the Parnell divorce case, but they were sufficient to make William Ewart Gladstone Prime Minister for the fourth time at the age of 82.

This time Gladstone actually pushed a Home Rule Bill through the House of Commons. Unlike 1886, it was accepted by the Commons not merely as a principle but as an involved scheme of government each clause of which had been debated in detail. The bill was in most respects similar to that of 1886, except that this time it retained Irish M.P.s at Westminster for the purpose of voting on matters of Irish or imperial concern. Though beset by increasing blindness and deafness, Gladstone still retained his keen mind and his passionate eloquence, and the final passage of the bill after 85 sittings was in every sense a personal triumph for him.

Yet it was a vain triumph, for the House of Lords (in which the Liberals since 1886 had been a small minority), vetoed the measure, 419–41, after a scornfully brief debate. His colleagues did not wish to fight a general election on the issue of the House of Lords — largely because they were dubious of victory — and in March 1894, after a stinging lecture to the Upper House warning it that its days were numbered, Gladstone retired from the Prime Ministership and soon afterwards from the House of Commons in which he had sat for sixty-two years.

Oddly enough, the man who was most closely to follow in the G.O.M.'s footsteps was not an Englishman at all; for in a strange fashion, the Gladstonian tradition jumped the Atlantic to reappear in the person of Woodrow Wilson, a longtime admirer of the English statesman. Although Wilson's public career was much shorter, the two men resembled one another in their moral approach to politics, in their attitude toward international affairs, and in their difficulties with personal relations. There is a close parallel also in the great disappointments that marked the close of their careers: Gladstone on Irish Home Rule, Wilson on American entry into the League of Nations, each battling vainly against what they could only look upon as the blindness of their people. For the defeat of the second Home Rule Bill, as Gladstone was aware, had not resolved the Irish question; it had merely, as so often before, postponed it.

Gladstone lived on for another four years. He even emerged from retirement in 1896 in his eighty-seventh year to denounce before a mass audience in Liverpool the massacre of Armenians in the Turkish Empire. He spoke with the same passionate eloquence with which he had opposed the Bulgarian Massacres of the 1870s, Neapolitan misgovernment in the 1850s, and, for that matter, the Great Reform Bill back at Oxford in 1831. In 1898 he died.

Gladstone was a born parliamentarian, and though particular measures he sponsored and actions he took are as open to criticism as those of any other statesmen, few now deny his role as the embodiment of Victorian morality and conscientious public service. Arthur Balfour, himself a future Prime Minister and long-time admiring opponent of the Grand Old Man, observed at the time of his death that of all the political leaders of the century, it had been Gladstone above all who had raised in the public estimation the whole level of British politics. He had helped turn an aristocratic debating society into a national forum which wrestled with great moral problems, problems which, as the next chapter will remind us, were not limited to Ireland and England but encompassed the entire world.

Chapter 10

The High Tide of **Empire**

JUDGING by its effect upon the British party structure and by the incredible number of hours of parliamentary time devoted to it, the single most important question in late Victorian British history was the Irish Question, with all its various ramifications. As Prime Minister Salisbury complained in 1887, "Torn in two by a controversy which almost threatens her existence," England "cannot . . . interfere with any decisive action abroad." Yet curiously enough, it was during these same thirty years, when public attention was so constantly focused on the 32,000 square mile island next door with its five million people, that Britain acquired as colonies or protectorates some 750,000 square miles with twenty million people in Asia and the South Pacific, and approximately 4,400,000 square miles with sixty million people in Africa.[1]

The Causes of Imperialism

These sweeping additions to the existing empire, made up largely of Canada, Australia, New Zealand, and India, have

---

[1] The single most useful source for the subject of this chapter is *The Empire-Commonwealth, 1870–1919* (Cambridge, 1959), Vol. III of *The Cambridge History of the British Empire*. It includes the most comprehensive bibliography. Vols. V, VI, VII, & VIII, published earlier, are also relevant. T. W. Walbank's *A Short His-*

caused some historians to speak of the lands acquired after 1870 as the Third British Empire in contrast to the first (pre-1783) and the second (1783–1870). The mid-Victorian years had witnessed a notable lack of interest in the empire. The eventual independence of the settlement colonies had been looked upon as inevitable; and though the value of India was acknowledged by most Englishmen, trade rather than territory was regarded as the *sine qua non* of foreign affairs. If trade could be had without administration, so much the better. The ideal colonial administrator was inevitably the one who cost the home government the least money, required the fewest troops, and involved Britain in the smallest number of diplomatic entanglements. To a large degree, these attitudes persisted well into the 1880s. Disraeli's "forward" policy had resulted in the electoral rebuff of 1880; and though few British citizens of the day were literally "Little Englanders" who wished to end all of Britain's imperial ties, a majority were clearly consolidationists, rather than expansionists, and preferred to develop the empire that already existed rather than acquire new responsibilities in Asia and Africa. As late as 1883 a British textbook on colonies took it for granted that "the policy of England discourages any increase of territory in tropical countries already occupied by native races."

Yet this attitude changed rapidly until for a time in the 1890s the leaders of both parties, Salisbury for the Conservatives and Rosebery (Gladstone's successor as Prime Minister) for the Liberals, had become expansionists in outlook. The customary explanation for this so-called "New Imperialism" is a trio of economic requirements: markets, raw materials, and areas in which surplus funds might be invested. Such an explanation for territorial aggrandizement on the part of the major European powers was first elaborated in 1902 by a British journalist, John A. Hobson. Hobson's economic explanation, with special emphasis upon the need of capitalists for investment opportunities overseas, was taken over by Lenin in 1916 in his *Imperialism: The Highest Stage of Capitalism*. The industrialized capitalist nations, according to Lenin, had been able artificially to prolong their existence and stave off revolution at home by investing surplus funds overseas and exploiting native labor.

The Hobson-Lenin thesis remains influential in convincing independent "underdeveloped nations" that private foreign investment is synonymous with colonialism; but modern research

---

tory of India and Pakistan (New York, 1958) provides a useful summary account of the origins of modern Indian nationalism. Rayne Kruger's *Good-bye Dollie Gray* (Philadelphia, 1960) retells the history of the Boer War.

has made clear its fallaciousness as an explanation for late nineteenth-century imperialism. Although a few individuals made fortunes in underdeveloped areas, these lands usually lacked the necessary "social overhead facilities"—roads, railways, harbors, docks, dams, power plants, and schools—to secure a high return on an original investment. For most investors, they were too risky. Not surprisingly, then, British capitalists preferred to put money into advanced industrialized or semi-industrialized countries such as the United States, Germany, and Argentina, even though such lands were not part of the Empire. Of that minority share of capital that did go to the Empire, more was invested before 1914 in Australia and New Zealand alone—with their tiny but hardly "exploited" population—than in all of India and Africa put together.[2]

This does not gainsay the fact that particular British merchants, shippers, and even bankers sought and occasionally found profits in Africa. Yet the hope for commercial gain is almost as old a motive as man himself. Why then should merchants seek territorial and political domination in the late nineteenth century when before they had been satisfied with an "open door" for trading opportunities? One explanation is that whereas in the middle years of the century, the great powers seemed to be following the British lead in the direction of international free trade, by the 1880s this process had been completely reversed. The United States led the way with the protectionist Morrill Tariff of 1861. Germany and Austria-Hungary followed suit in the 1870s and France in 1892. In a world divided by rising tariff barriers, colonies began to regain some of the value they had possessed in an age of mercantilism. It was now being argued that Britain should occupy territories whose current commercial value was small but which might otherwise become part of the protective tariff sphere of another power. As the Great Depression ground on, such arguments were more and more often heard. When H. M. Stanley, the man who presumed to find David Livingstone, the great missionary-explorer, suggested to the British Government in the 1870s that it undertake the economic development of the Congo, the Government declined. By 1895, however, that attitude had altered. It *was* the Government's business, declared Prime Minister Salisbury, "to make smooth the paths of British commerce . . . for the application of British capital, at a time when . . . other

---

[2] See, e.g., Mark Blaug, "Economic Imperialism Revisited," *Yale Review*, L (March 1961). Robin Winks (ed.) provides a good introduction to the historical debate concerning the causes of late nineteenth-century empire-building in *British Imperalism: Gold, God, Glory* (New York: Holt, Rinehart, & Winston European Problem Studies, 1963).

outlets for the commercial energies of our race are being gradually closed."

The levying of protective tariffs by the industrial powers
of Europe and by the United States was but one aspect of a more
fundamental political change which was highly instrumental
in bringing about the "New Imperialism" — the emergence of
the new and militant German Empire as economically and politically the most powerful nation on the Continent. As a result
of the Franco-Prussian War, the balance of power in Europe had
been decisively altered and Britain's relative position seriously
weakened. Germany's fear of French revenge after 1871 had
led to the development of a series of alliances with Austria-
Hungary and the newly united Italian Kingdom on the part
of Bismarck, as well as the aforementioned Three Emperors'
League which tied Germany to Russia. France had consequently been isolated and, although Anglo-German relations
remained for the most part friendly, so — in a sense — had Britain.
The very fact that international relations on the Continent had
become fixed in a relatively rigid pattern helps explain the new
quest for colonies on the part of the major powers. It was at
times the by-product of a sense of insecurity in a Europe in
which the great powers could no longer maneuver diplomatically
by seeking or gaining influence in some petty German or Italian
state. The only areas which remained for diplomatic maneuver
were now outside Europe; and France, Italy, Russia, and Germany all turned their eyes to Africa. But in each case the
mainspring of their imperial expansion rested in Europe. "My
map of Africa," Bismarck explained in 1888, "lies in Europe.
Here is Russia and here lies France. That is my map of Africa."
In other words, the "scramble for Africa" was judged by the
major powers in terms of whether it aided or injured their relative strategic and political position in Europe. Such diplomatic
considerations played at least as significant a role in bringing
on the "new imperialism" as specific economic interests.

Once the "scramble for Africa" had started in the early
1880s, the surprising thing is that though it caused occasional
war scares, it did not lead to a general war between the great
powers. The map of the "dark continent" was painted a hodgepodge of bright imperial colors within little more than a decade;
yet the powers abided by the ground rules for African aggrandizement laid down at the Conference of Berlin in 1884–85.

Although the thoughts of statesmen may have been primarily upon the European balance of power, a host of other
motives inspired individual imperialists. Not the least of these
was that of "civilizing" the native races. The Anglican Church
Missionary Society had been active in Africa since the beginning
of the century, and most nonconformist denominations had

established their missions as well. It was missionaries like Livingston who had long been urging the white man's duty to bring civilization and Christianity to Africa. They discovered to their horror in the 1850s that, while British example and the British naval patrol had virtually ended the slave trade in West Africa, this iniquitous practice still flourished in East Africa. There the Sultan of Zanzibar protected the Arab vendors of human flesh who dominated the East African coastal trade. It was as a result of British pressure that the Sultan reluctantly restricted the East African slave trade which ended altogether in 1876. But slavery remained, and it was not until shocked public opinion and missionary zeal pressured the British government into establishing a protectorate over Zanzibar in 1895 that the institution of slavery was finally abolished there.

Although H. M. Stanley once estimated that if Christianity were able to teach the natives of the Congo no more than to cover their nakedness with a single Sunday-go-to-meeting dress apiece, this alone would create a market for "320,000,000 yards of Manchester cotton cloth," missionary pressure alone was rarely sufficient to bring direct government intervention. When the state did intervene, however, the missionaries were a significant humanitarian group reminding the British government that native peoples deserved protection, that they should not be exploited through forced labor, that they should be considered as equal before the law, and that whenever possible their customary forms of landholding and tribal government (though not religion) should be preserved.

The missionaries often shared in the assumption, fortified by the scientific findings of Social Darwinists like Benjamin Kidd and C. H. Pearson, that the European peoples, and especially the Anglo-Saxons, were innately superior to men of all other colors. That sense of superiority gave rise to much that was arrogant, cruel, and unwarranted, and was to earn for the white man the undying hatred of men not blessed with the same color of skin. Yet, as Rudyard Kipling suggested in "The White Man's Burden" (1899), that conviction of superiority was the motive that sent thousands of Englishmen to toil and suffer in remote parts of the earth:

> Take up the White Man's burden —
> Send forth the best ye breed —
> Go bind your sons to exile
> To serve your captives' need;
> To wait in heavy harness,
> On fluttered folk and wild —
> Your new-caught, sullen peoples,
> Half-devil and half-child.

Although in the 1960s old-style imperialism or colonialism may be condemned in toto, the late nineteenth-century imperialistic spirit cannot be understood unless it is realized that it included a considerable element of "Peace Corps" idealism.

Still another element behind late nineteenth-century imperialism was its popularity with the newly enfranchised masses; and at least one historian has maintained that the electorate which emerged from the Reform Bills of 1867 and 1884 was less inclined to take a penny-pinching attitude toward colonies than the industrious middle-class voter of the previous generation. It is true that the high tide of imperialism coincided with the rise of the popular press, and that the daily papers often made imperialism a romantic subject. It was, after all, a newspaper which sponsored Stanley's hunt for Livingston. The empire-building urge was inspired also by the works of Sir Rider Haggard (like *King Solomon's Mines*), Kipling's tales of India, and the ninety novels addressed by G. A. Henty to the youthful English reader. Henty's hero was almost invariably a typical product of England's public schools:

> a good specimen of the class by which Britain has been built up, her colonies formed, and her battlefields won — a class in point of energy, fearlessness, the spirit of adventure, and a readiness to face and overcome all difficulties, unmatched in the world.

It was writings such as these which helped mold the popular attitude toward the glories of empire "played out against a gaudy backdrop of tropical forests, and great sluggish rivers, and empty plains, and sand, and terrible mountain passes." [3]

Clearly a great many late Victorian Englishmen took a vicarious satisfaction in painting the map red, even if they had no personal wealth to gain thereby and even if the particular aim achieved—such as planting a flag in the middle of the Sahara desert—was of no conceivable economic value to anyone. Yet it would be dangerous to overstress the point. Imperialism might win elections; but to the despair of politicians, the public proved all too fickle, and imperialism might equally well lose elections, as it did in 1880 and was again to do in 1906.

---

[3] D. G. Creighton, "The Victorian and the Empire" in Schuyler & Ausubel (eds.), *The Making of English History* (New York, 1950).

Imperialism in Action

While the conquest of nonwhite peoples implied an element of paternalism as well as the use of force, it did not indicate any attempt to build up systems of self-government along the lines employed in the older settlement-colonies. Wherever direct British rule was set up, it was generally benevolent but essentially despotic. An excellent example is Egypt, where a Khedive, his Egyptian ministers, and a legislature constituted the visible government. More important than any of them, however, was Sir Evelyn Baring (later Lord Cromer; 1841–1917), who served as British consul-general and high commissioner from 1883 to 1907. It was Cromer who insisted on such Western notions as balancing the budget, who encouraged the building of the first Aswan Dam, and who battled against "the three C's – the Courbash, the Corvee, and Corruption." The Courbash, the strip of hippopotamus hide with which peasants had been flogged for millenia in order to make them work, was outlawed. The Corvee, the unpaid compulsory labor by which peasants were forced to clear the mud from the irrigation canals, was largely replaced by a system of wages and free labor. Cromer does not assert that the third C, Corruption, was altogether eliminated, but it "was greatly diminished."

There is little doubt that Cromer's rule marked a kind of golden age for the Egyptian peasant. Benevolence did not, however, make the British popular in Egypt; they could be arrogant, they could be unjust; they were foreigners both in culture and religion, and their continued presence eventually excited among the former ruling classes a strong spirit of nationalism. Moreover, the advantages of economic progress were largely counterbalanced by a rapid growth of population. It doubled between 1882 and 1922.

It is important to note, however, that both in Egypt and in many other regions of the empire, British rule rested less on periodic displays of force than on the widespread acquiescence of the native population. Leonard Woolf (1880–   ), later to become a noted writer and professed antiimperialist, recalls his youthful tenure in the British civil service in Ceylon:

Ceylon in 1906 was the exact opposite of a "police state." There were very few police and outside Columbo and Kandy not a single soldier. From the point of law and order nothing could have been more dangerously precarious than the Pearl Fishery camp, a temporary town of 30,000 or 40,000 men many of whom were habitual criminals . . . but we four civil servants never even thought about the possibility of our not being able to maintain law and order. And we were quite right.[4]

In both Ceylon and India, the British Raj was looked upon almost in family terms: the English civil administrator was regarded as a "father" who might behave unaccountably but who was disinterested and not lining his pockets by commercial speculations. As Mr. Woolf confirms, the typical British civil servant regarded businessmen as social inferiors and would not even admit them to his clubs.

Paradoxically, during the very years in which the British Empire was growing to its largest size and being bound more closely by the wonders of technology—ocean liners, railroads, and the telegraph—an earlier process of loosening the ties of empire was proceeding apace. Responsible government had been granted to most of the Canadian and Australian provinces, and to New Zealand, in the 1850s and to Cape Colony in 1872. Although permanent garrisons had been withdrawn from Canada and Australasia by 1871, all of the settlement colonies remained conscious of their dependence upon the Royal Navy, and in 1887 some of the Australian states agreed to pay a small annual subsidy to help support the Imperial fleet in Australian waters. It was in part the potential threat of Germany (which occupied part of New Guinea in 1884) as well as a growing awareness of the advantages of dealing in common with such questions as intra-Australian tariff barriers and immigration policy which led the autonomous Austrialian states to emulate Canada and form a federal Dominion of Australia in 1900. The proposed constitution, an amalgam of the British form of Cabinet responsibility and the American form of two-chamber federalism, was prepared by a constitutional convention of Australians but made operative by Act of Parliament at Westminster. Although theoretically the Parliament in Westminster might still legislate for the dominions, in practice this power had fallen into disuse. Only "influence and advice" remained. Even in foreign affairs, dominion governments now expected representation on British delegations negotiating commercial treaties affecting their interests. The dominions "already stand to us," observed one Liberal M.P., "in the virtual relation of friendly allied states speaking our tongue."

The same years that saw a continued growth in the self-governing dominions also witnessed the first stirrings of nationalist revolt in India and the beginnings of Western-style repre-

---

[4] Leonard Woolf, *Growing: An Autobiography of the Years 1904–1911* (New York, 1962).

sentative institutions in that land. In the wake of the Mutiny
of 1857, the Indian Civil Service, while not antagonistic to economic growth, had become in some ways less liberal and reform-minded. Though the vast majority of Indians remained
agricultural villagers, a sizable commercial class did grow in
the late nineteenth century and certain Indian industries during
the 1880s were aided by a 10–15 percent tariff. By 1914 India
could boast one of the world's five largest cotton textile industries, one of the two largest jute industries, the third largest
railway network, and a sizable coal-mining industry. Foreign
trade figures went up accordingly.

EXPORTS (in millions of pounds)		IMPORTS (in millions of pounds)
1834	8	4.5
1870	53	33.5
1910	137	86.0

Commercial and agricultural expansion was accompanied by a
comparable growth of population which rose from 100 million
in 1700 to 150 million in 1850 to 283 million in 1901. Despite
a runaway population and the fact that occasional famines
took millions of lives, India probably did experience a period
of genuine economic improvement in the nineteenth century.
Agricultural output per man-hour and per acre were both up,
and – keeping in mind the fact that millions of Indians remained
at a point barely above subsistence level – there may have been
a small increase in the average standard of living as well.[5]

The Indian Civil Service continued to be highly efficient
and merited its reputation for incorruptibility. Public protesta-
tions notwithstanding, the upper branches of that service remained almost totally closed to native Indians; and, although
an act of 1861 provided the bare beginnings of advisory legislative councils for provincial governors, the theme of British rule
continued to be one of benevolent despotism. In the early 1880s,
Lord Ripon, the British Viceroy nominated by Gladstone, initiated a program of local elective bodies, not so much to improve
the administration as to provide "a measure of political and
popular education." In 1892, Indian representation in the provincial councils was expanded.

By 1892 some Indians had come to conclude, however, that
they had far too small a role in the government of their own
nation. The word "nation" is instructive, because India, though

---

[5] See, e.g., Morris D. Morris, "19th Century Indian Economic History," *Journal
of Economic History* (Dec. 1963).

a civilization and at various times "an empire," became a nation only as a result of British rule. The Indian nationalism exemplified after 1885 by the annual meetings of the National Indian Congress was essentially a product of the British Raj. It was the English who brought political unification and a common language for the increasing number of educated Indians. Indian nationalism necessarily was fostered by cheap postage rates, by printing presses, and by the railway that facilitated national assemblies. The nationalist leaders were members of a small but growing class of lawyers, businessmen, and teachers, many of whom found inspiration in the writings of John Locke and Thomas Jefferson and in the lives of Mazzini of Italy, Kossuth of Hungary, and Charles Stewart Parnell of Ireland. Most early Indian nationalists, though irritated by the caste arrogance and sense of racial superiority manifested by the British in India, were adherents of liberal parliamentary methods; and only slowly, in the face of specific insults, did they come to realize that they would have to unite in a militant Western-style pressure group in order to gain recognition. One such affront was a change in the rules for the Indian Civil Service examinations in 1877 which made Indian candidates even less likely to be successful. Another was the largely successful protest by Englishmen in India against a bill of 1883 which would have made it possible for Europeans to be tried before Indian judges.

Not all Indian nationalists were Western-oriented, for in the late nineteenth century there was a widespread revival of Hindu religious thought.

> Once more [said the Swami Vivekanada in 1897] the world must be conquered by India. This is the great ideal before us. Let them come and flood the land with their armies, never mind. Up, India, and conquer the world with your spirituality! Spirituality must conquer the West. Where are the men ready to go out to every country in the world with the messages of the great sages of India?

Whether Indian spirituality conquered the world or not, the apostles of this Hindu Renaissance gave Indian nationalism a heightened fervor and emotional strength. It had another effect as well: it increasingly caused Indian Moslems to desert the National Congress. The followers of Mohammed feared that, if India attained autonomy under outspoken Hindu auspices, they might become a maligned minority; the result was the establishment by 1906 of a separate Moslem League as a rival to the Indian National Congress. Thus were laid the foundations of the division which in 1947 led to the partition of the subcontinent into India and Pakistan.

While the late nineteenth century is important for the beginnings of Indian nationalism and of representative government on the local level, India remained in the minds of most Englishmen the most precious jewel of the British Empire, one which was constantly growing in size and luster. Although the autonomous Indian princely states were no longer subject to annexation, adjacent areas still were. The Northwest Frontier was secured by the Afghan War of 1879, and Baluchistan was annexed. Farther east the greater part of Burma was added to the coastal areas already under British rule and was henceforth governed as part of British India.

Although the high tide of late Victorian imperialism can be discussed in terms of impersonal forces, it must always be recalled that the initiative both in economic and political expansion was taken by individual men who were on the scene, men like Sir George Goldie (1846–1925) in West Africa, Sir Harry Johnston (1858–1927) in East Africa, and preeminently by Cecil John Rhodes (1853–1902) in South Africa. No person managed more successfully than Rhodes to combine the down-to-earth practicality and the starry-eyed idealism which constituted the late nineteenth-century imperialistic spirit. He was the younger son of an Anglican clergyman and came to South Africa from England in 1870 for reasons of health. Apparently the climate was satisfactory, for he thrived both physically and economically. 1870 was the year in which diamonds were first discovered in South Africa; Rhodes proved to be a shrewd businessman who, by buying up the claims of discouraged miners whose capital had been exhausted, succeeded by 1886 in making himself director of a ten million dollar mining company paying dividends of 25 percent a year. By 1888 he monopolized 90 percent of the world's diamond output. Then, gold having been discovered in the Transvaal, he went into the gold-mining business with similar success. By 1890, he had an income of five million dollars a year.

Rhodes was always interested in far more than money. In a document he wrote when only 24 years of age, he declared it to be his life's purpose to work "for the furtherance of the British Empire, for the bringing of the whole civilized world under British rule, for the recovery of the United States, for the making of the Anglo-Saxon race into an empire." By 1890 he had the wealth to make at least a part of that dream a reality. He entered politics and became the Prime Minister of Cape Colony, one of the two South African lands in British possession, though even there a majority of the white population consisted of Boers rather than Englishmen. To the north lay the two Boer Republics, Transvaal and the Orange Free State, again virtually independent since 1881, though Britain continued to claim a vague and disputed suzerainty. Beyond lay a vast area, still largely unexplored, in which Portuguese, Germans, and others seemed to be dangerously interested. Rhodes' ultimate dream was to bring under British control a strip of territory extending all the way from South Africa to Egypt, so that a Cape-to-Cairo railway might be built. Rhodes was influential in having Britain in 1885 declare a protectorate over Bechuanaland. He then inspired the creation of the South Africa Company to explore and develop the area beyond. It was this company which, on the basis of a very dubious treaty made with a local native chieftain, began the development and settlement of Rhodesia.

Rhodes' plans did not always meet with the full backing of the Government in London. Gladstone, whose fourth ministry had been dominated by his vain attempt to extend Home Rule to Ireland, never became converted to the exuberant empire building of the 1890s. "There is a wild and irrational spirit abroad," he lamented. Lord Rosebery, his successor as Liberal Prime Minister, was, however, a professed imperialist. His brief ministry (1894–95) is best remembered, to be sure, neither for its exploits abroad nor at home but for the fact that the Prime Minister's horse won the Derby two years in succession. The feat did not endear Rosebery to a nonconformist Liberal electorate which frowned both on horse racing and gambling.

The Role of Joseph Chamberlain

The general election of 1895 brought back into power a strong coalition of Conservatives and Liberal Unionists. The Liberal Unionists by this time had become almost completely swallowed up by the Conservatives, though the alliance tended to use the word "Unionist," and the word "Conservative" fell into disfavor for several decades. This amalgamation was symbolized by the entry of Joseph Chamberlain, the ex-Radical, into Salisbury's Cabinet as Colonial Secretary. Imperialism was the cry of the hour, and the new secretary became one of its staunchest champions. The British, he had become convinced, were "the greatest of the governing races the world has ever seen" and were "predestined" by their defects as well as their virtues "to spread over the habitable globe." To critics who accused him of forsaking his earlier cause of social reform,

Chamberlain replied that only a strong empire could provide prosperity for the English workingman.

In ·the new Colonial Secretary, the empire builders in Africa found a statesman who not only approved of their projects but advocated that the government should promote colonial development directly by building railroads and ports, setting up schools of tropical agriculture and medicine, guaranteeing loans, and stimulating capital investment in every corner of the Empire. Chamberlain immediately forwarded plans to acquire Uganda as a protectorate. All that this territory in east-central Africa needed, he said, was what his own city of Birmingham already had—"an improvement scheme." Late in 1895, however, both Rhodes and Chamberlain found their plans for African expansion thwarted by some very stubborn Dutchmen, the Boers of the Orange Free State and the Transvaal.

The struggle for South African supremacy was in a sense the result of geological accident, of the fact that the Boers, by occupation conservative patriarchal farmers, should, in their flight from British control, have happened to settle on top of some of the richest gold and diamond mines in the world. From the 1880s on, miners from all over the world swarmed into the Transvaal and soon made Johannesburg one of the world's great boom towns. There many of the newcomers prospered. Their taxes helped transform the Transvaal from a poverty-stricken, backward farming state into a rich and growing community. On one subject, however, the Boers under President Paul Kruger were adamant: they would admit the Uitlanders (foreigners), they would tax them, but they would not grant them rights of citizenship. Increasingly the Uitlanders complained, and by 1894–95 a revolt was brewing. Cecil Rhodes encouraged it, and his lieutenant, Dr. Leander Starr Jameson, prepared a force of soldiers in the employ of the South Africa Company to be ready to march to the assistance of the Johannesburg revolutionaries. Plans went awry and the revolt collapsed; but late in December 1895 Dr. Jameson marched anyway, only to have his tiny band defeated and captured by the Boers.

Although the British government immediately denied any responsibility for the raid, it appeared to the world as a gross violation of international law by Britain. Chamberlain, who was certainly aware of Jameson's plans beforehand, escaped immediate censure; but Cecil Rhodes was forced to resign as Prime Minister of Cape Colony. He had alienated the Boers, and they continued to be a highly important segment of the white population of Cape Colony, as well as the dominant group in the Transvaal. The Jameson Raid also had international repercussions. It emphasized anew Britain's diplomatic isolation in the world at large.

In the decade before the Jameson Raid, Great Britain had looked to Germany for friendship. With the French alienated by the British occupation of Egypt and with the Russians continuing their pressure in the Near East and on the Indian frontier, England had naturally drifted closer to the Triple Alliance of Germany, Austria-Hungary, and Italy. Salisbury's secret Mediterranean Agreements in 1887 with Austria and Italy constituted a virtual *entente* (understanding) with the Triple Alliance; and the treaty of 1890, in which the British granted to Germany the small but strategic island of Heligoland in the North Sea in exchange for German concessions in East Africa, was seen as solid proof of Anglo-German understanding. After the fall of Bismarck in 1890, however, Germany fell into the hands of men eager to demonstrate in the colonial and military field that Germany was the "great power" which her population and industrial might seemed to indicate. Nothing showed the ebbing of Anglo-German understanding more clearly nor evoked so strong a sense of resentment in England as the telegram which the German Emperor, William II, sent to President Kruger after the collapse of the Jameson Raid. He congratulated Kruger upon having preserved the independence of his country "without appealing to the help of friendly powers." The implication was clear: Germany was prepared to go to war against Britain in South Africa.

Inasmuch as the embarrassment of the Jameson Raid coincided with an acrimonious dispute between Britain and the United States over the boundary between Venezuela and British Guiana, Britain did seem, for the moment at least, to be diplomatically isolated. It was all the more desirable, therefore, thought Joseph Chamberlain, to emphasize the ties of empire. This was done in 1897 with the Diamond Jubilee, the imperial celebration of the sixtieth anniversary of Queen Victoria's accession to the throne. From all over the world came the prime ministers, sultans, and chieftains, black, white, and yellow, to pay homage to the great White Queen. A similar celebration, the Golden Jubilee, had taken place a decade before, but the Diamond Jubilee, at once romantic and bellicose, was if anything even more unrestrained. Chamberlain hoped to utilize the Jubilee to take the first steps toward imperial federation, a joint customs union and defense union of the colonies which would ultimately be followed by the creation of an imperial parliament. Few of the colonial leaders were interested; and as long as Britain adhered to a policy of free trade, it was impossible to create any practical plan of imperial tariff preference. Chamberlain had to be satisfied with a poor substitute: the meeting at intervals of the various colonial prime ministers. Out of these gatherings eventually evolved one element of the old Empire that has endured – the regular meetings of the Commonwealth Prime Ministers.

In the meantime Chamberlain committed his government to military expansion in two parts of Africa. British troops were sent into Northern Nigeria, where they defeated the Ashanti warriors, freed the land from the slave trade, and made it safe for commerce. Several thousand miles to the east, the British commander of the Egyptian army, Sir Herbert Kitchener, was encouraged to reverse Gladstone's policy and reenter the Sudan, an area long claimed by Egypt. There General Gordon had been killed a decade before and there the Mahdi and his dervishes still held sway. Kitchener's force slowly made its way southward along the Nile valley, building a railway as it went. At Omdurman, Kitchener's Anglo-Egyptian army of 20,000 men met a dervish army almost three times its size. Modern artillery and rifle fire, supplemented by one of military history's last great cavalry charges – in which a young subaltern named Winston Churchill took part – overwhelmed the dervishes, who had more spears than rifles. Kitchener's army went on to reoccupy Khartoum and thereby avenge Gordon. Still farther upstream the British encountered a small French-Sudanese force under Captain Marchand which had made an extraordinary three-thousand-mile journey through trackless jungles, endless deserts, and blackish swamps to plant the French tricolor at Fashoda. Such were imperial emotions that for several months it appeared as if the Fashoda affair would actually bring war between France and Britain. But eventually France conceded the British claims to the Sudan, claims which Britain technically shared with Egypt; both the Union Jack and the Egyptian flag were raised. In return Britain acknowledged all French claims to the Sahara and other disputed parts of equatorial Africa.

The Boer War

Kitchener's triumph at Khartoum brought the Cape-to-Cairo railroad another step closer, but the Boers still refused to realize the "manifest destiny" of English imperialism in Africa. Britons and Boers were in a state of cold war. The Boers began to arm feverishly; and after his triumphant reelection as President of the Transvaal in 1898, President Kruger assumed dictatorial powers which ended any possibility of a peaceful compromise between the Uitlanders and the Boers. "There is no way out of the political troubles of South Africa except reform in the Transvaal or war," wrote Sir Alfred Milner (1854–1925), the new British High Commissioner in South Africa. And reform, he went on, did not seem to be in the offing; British citizens in the Transvaal were being treated like helots. After the murder of an English workingman, 20,000 Uitlanders petitioned the British government for help. Milner was an excellent administrator, but he was no diplomat, and protracted negotiations about possible reforms in the Transvaal got nowhere. Curiously enough, the step which finally led to war was not a British ultimatum to the Boers but a Boer demand in October 1899 that the British withdraw their troops and stop interfering in Transvaal domestic affairs. The British rejected the ultimatum and war began.

The European world looked upon the Boer War as a fight between a pigmy (Kruger's Transvaal and the neighboring Orange Free State) and an imperial giant. The war was more than a defensive one for the Boers. Kruger himself clearly sought to lead a united South Africa under native Dutch auspices and throw the British out altogether. In England, the war made good copy, for the new reading public was in a jingoistic mood, a spirit more bellicose than that of Chamberlain or the rest of the Government.

The first months of the war did not follow the prescribed path to imperial glory expected by the readers of the yellow press. For it was the Boers who invaded Cape Colony and Natal, who inflicted ignominious defeats upon the British, and who besieged the towns of Kimberley, Ladysmith, and Mafeking. These initial victories should not have surprised anybody, since the Boer army was twice the size of the British force on hand and since it possessed a superior type of artillery, Krup guns imported from Germany.

Back in England, public opinion quickly began to sober. Calls for volunteers received a ready response, and the other self-governing colonies offered contingents of troops. They saw the Boer War as an example of the mother country's championship of her overseas nationals and responded accordingly. By late winter in 1900 the tide of war had turned. Ladysmith and Kimberley had been relieved, and General Roberts had begun an invasion of the Orange Free State and the Transvaal. On May 31 Roberts' forces triumphantly entered Johannesburg; and five days later they occupied Pretoria, the Transvaal capital, and freed 3,000 British prisoners of war. President Kruger fled into exile. In the meantime, the relief of Mafeking, which had been heroically defended for 217 days by a force under Colonel Robert Baden-Powell, led to wild rejoicing in London. The result was both a new word in the language – "mafficking" (meaning to celebrate boisterously) and the inspiration for the subsequent British and later worldwide boy-scout movement.

The war seemed to be over. The Orange Free State and then the Transvaal were formally annexed by Britain, and in November, Lord Salisbury's Conservative government and

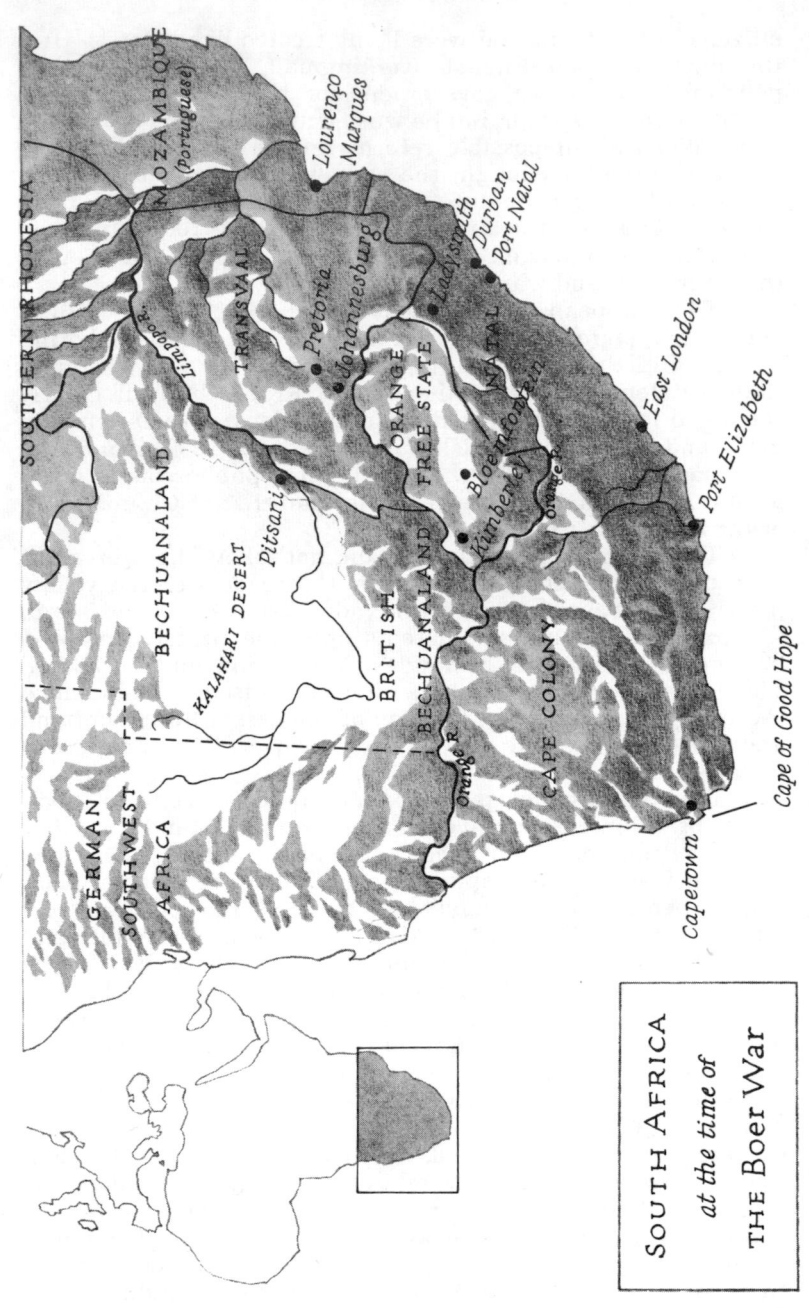

SOUTHERN RHODESIA

MOZAMBIQUE
(Portuguese)

Lourenço
Marques

Limpopo R.

TRANSVAL

Pretoria
Johannesburg

Durban
Port Natal

Ladysmith

NATAL

ORANGE
FREE STATE

BECHUANALAND

Pitsani

KALAHARI DESERT

BRITISH

BECHUANALAND

Bloemfontein

Kimberley

Orange R.

East London

Port Elizabeth

CAPE COLONY

Cape of Good Hope

GERMAN
SOUTH WEST
AFRICA

Orange R.

Capetown

SOUTH AFRICA
at the time of
THE BOER WAR

its imperialistic policies received a strong endorsement in the so-called Khaki election. The Liberal Party had been split by the war into Liberal Imperialists (like Rosebery, Herbert Asquith, and Sir Edward Grey) who supported the conflict, and "pro-Boers" (such as John Morley and the youthful David Lloyd George), who regarded it as morally insupportable. Not long after the general election and after General Roberts and many of the British had sailed for home, it became clear that the war was not in fact over at all. Small Boer contingents kept up a guerrilla war for another year and a half. Only by systematically denuding parts of the country of its farms and livestock and by gathering the inhabitants into concentration camps did Lord Kitchener, who had succeeded Roberts, finally bring the war to an end with the Peace of Vereeniging of May 1902.

By then the spirit of complacent self-righteousness and romantic glory with which the imperialism of the 1890s had imbued some Englishmen had passed its crest. The Boer War had been too bloody, too costly, and too cruel; 6,000 British troops had died in battle, 16,000 more of disease, and 23,000 had been wounded. The concentration camps and their appalling mortality rates, denounced in the House of Commons as "methods of barbarism" by Sir Henry Campbell-Bannerman, the new Liberal leader, had led to a new self-questioning mood in Britain. The high tide of imperialism had in some respects been an aberration which had not permanently halted the progress of Empire toward the form of Commonwealth foreshadowed by the older Liberal ideal.

By then, too, Queen Victoria was dead. In her old age she had become revered more as a symbol than as an active member of the British Constitution; but she had grown to welcome the public occasions she had long avoided. Nor had she lost all political power. As late as 1892 she successfully vetoed one of Gladstone's choices for a Cabinet post. To the last she remained conscientiously dutiful, if not always wise. She took great pride in her country and her Empire, and she supported the Government staunchly in its conduct of the Boer War. During Christmas of 1900 she had gone as usual to her palace at Osborne on the Isle of Wight. There she celebrated the advent of the twentieth century. Three weeks later, after a brief illness, she died in the presence of many members of her large family, including her eldest grandson, Emperor William II of Germany. The reign of almost 64 years, the longest in British history, was over. "We feel," said A. J. Balfour, the Conservative leader of the House of Commons, "that the end of a great epoch has come upon us." In fact, it had, for her death represented symbolically, at least, the conclusion to a century during which Great Britain's prestige and influence had reached their zenith.

Chapter 11

Society and Social **Reform**

At the same time that late Victorian Britain was being shaken by the struggle for Irish nationalism and alternately exhilarated and dismayed by the expansion of empire, it was experiencing a number of other changes. There were technical changes in industry and communications, a less noticeable transformation in the social structure, and a gradual but significant alteration in the attitude of the average Englishman as to the role which government should play in the affairs of the individual. There was an increasingly widespread acceptance of the idea that poverty, unemployment, and ignorance were neither crimes nor necessarily the personal fault of the victims but rather the evil products of an ill-educated society which demanded the attention of the leaders of government. These new impulses in late Victorian England must be examined with care if the more obvious political and social changes of the twentieth century are to be understood in their proper historical context.[1]

---

[1] Works relevant to this chapter, in addition to the books by Ensor, Ashworth, and Ausubel referred to before, include Helen Merrell Lynd, *England in the Eighteen-Eighties* (New York, 1945) and Herman Ausubel, *In Hard Times: Reformers Among the Late Victorians* (New York, 1961). The changing family structure is analyzed by J. A. Banks, *Prosperity and Parenthood* (London, 1954). Henry Pelling discusses English socialist groups and trade unions in *The Origins of the Labour Party, 1880–1900* (London, 1954). Two illuminating articles are J. H. Perkins, "The Origin of the Popular Press," *History Today* (July 1957) and Col.

The most easily observable changes were technological. As the railway and the telegraph had revolutionized the first two thirds of the nineteenth century, so the telephone helped transform the last third. It began a communications revolution which was soon to make letter writing seem unnecessarily time-consuming, while at the same time the typewriter was beginning to revolutionize business office methods, mark an end to the age-old occupation of copyist, and downgrade the virtue of good penmanship. The 1880s brought the tricycle — then an adult vehicle rather than a children's toy — and the next decade introduced the even speedier if more unstable bicycle. The wealthy had long had horses and carriages, but never before had members of the lower classes been able to afford their own means of conveyance. The 1880s also began the age of electricity. By the end of the century, most cities had their own central power stations. Gas-lighting both in the streets and in the wealthier private homes was gradually giving way to the incandescent bulb. Similarly, the electric streetcar was replacing the horse-drawn tram as the chief mode of municipal transportation. By 1900 the hand-wound gramophone was becoming known and the first successful experiments with motion pictures had taken place. The automobile run by a gasoline-driven internal combustion engine had been invented, but its possibilities were not yet foreseen. Until 1896 an automobile in Britain had to be preceded on the street by a man waving a red flag and was forbidden to exceed a speed of four miles an hour.

The Social Structure

Although such technological changes were obvious to the generation which experienced them, certain equally significant changes in the social structure were less immediately visible. For one thing, more people lived longer. The death rate, which had remained fairly steady during the first three quarters of the century, began to decline dramatically during its last quarter:

DEATH RATES (per 1,000)	MALE	FEMALE
1846–1850	24.1	22.6
1871–1875	23.3	20.7
1896–1900	18.8	16.6

R. B. Oram, "The Great Strike of 1889: The Fight for the 'Docker's Tanner,'" *History Today* (August 1964). See also the early chapters of Keith Hutchison, *The Decline and Fall of British Capitalism* (New York, 1950).

Improved public health measures were largely responsible. Pure water and reasonably effective drains were now widely available. Smallpox vaccination had become general and the isolation of victims of infectious diseases a commonplace. Infant mortality remained high; but there were no serious cholera or smallpox epidemics after 1871, and the number of deaths from typhus, typhoid fever, scarlet fever, and tuberculosis were all on the decline.

The result of a falling death rate would have been a rapid rise in the population had it not been for two compensating factors. One was emigration; during the later decades of the nineteenth century, a continuing stream of migrants sought their fortune in the United States, Canada, Australia, New Zealand, and to a lesser extent, in South Africa and South America. Over a million and a half left the British Isles during the 1870s, two and a half million during the 1880s, and another two million during the 1890s. In part, this outflow was balanced by immigration. Irishmen continued to flock to England; and throughout the century, Britain served as a refuge for small groups of Continental exiles, as it had for Flemings in the sixteenth century and for French Huguenots in the seventeenth. Between 1870 and 1914 some 120,000 Jewish refugees from Eastern Europe found a new home in Britain, especially in London's East End, where they played an economic and, in due course, a cultural role comparable to their counterparts in the lower East Side of New York City.

The other compensating factor was a falling birthrate, partly because men and women were marrying later and having fewer children. Whereas the average married woman of the 1860s had had six children, her granddaughter four decades later had only three. Although the decline in the birthrate was evident in all classes, it affected most rapidly the business and professional elements, who, by the turn of the century, often had no more than two children per family. One reason for this decline was the growing availability of contraceptive knowledge. Perhaps more significant was the desire to make use of it. The very availability of new consumer comforts and conveniences provided an incentive for having a smaller family. A greater number of benefits could be bestowed on children if there were not so many of them. Nor did thrift any longer seem as great a virtue as it had to the mid-Victorians. In the world of corporate rather than individual enterprise, it was becoming more difficult to gain status and success by business frugality. "Comparable satisfactions had to be sought in other ways, and it was becoming easier to find them through conspicuous consumption than through the conspicuous creation of an independent fortune and position to be bequeathed to a numerous progeny." [2]

---

[2] William Ashworth, *An Economic History of England, 1870–1939* (London, 1960).

The decline in the size of middle-class families had other implications. Houses and rooms no longer needed to be so large, and there was no longer so great a demand for domestic servants. These had traditionally been drawn from the countryside, the daughters of tenant farmers and farm laborers. As agriculture declined, so did the number of farm girls. As late as 1880, one out of every six English and Welsh workers was in domestic service. That ratio was henceforth to drop steadily. Since birthrate and death rate both declined, the overall population of the United Kingdom—except for Ireland—continued to increase almost as rapidly as earlier in the century. In 1871 there had been twenty-two and a half million Englishmen and Welshmen. Three decades later there were thirty-two and a half million, a larger proportion of whom were mature adults and a smaller proportion dependent children.

No step did more for the emancipation of the middle-class woman than the reduction in the size of her family. By the late nineteenth century a movement to insist upon equal rights for women in the law and in politics was also in full swing. Queen Victoria herself was no admirer of the emancipated female, and she was "anxious to enlist everyone who can speak or write to join in checking this mad, wicked folly of 'Women's Rights,' with all its attendant horrors." She could not, however, halt the Married Women's Property Act of 1882 or the opening of civil service positions to women; nor could she stop the drive for women's suffrage which John Stuart Mill had helped launch in 1867. Unmarried women had been made eligible in 1870 to vote for schoolboard officials. They had been given the right to vote for town councillors in 1882 and county councillors in 1888. The Local Government Act of 1894 not only made both single and married women eligible to vote for district and parish councillors but also made them eligible to stand for election. Only Parliament remained beyond their direct influence. Educational doors had also been opening, as both Oxford and Cambridge added women's colleges and lower level girls' schools multiplied. Instrumental in bringing a comparable emancipation in female clothing was the growing popularity of bicycling and of athletics in general. "So much of our success depends on quickness of movement and suppleness of body," explained Lady Milner, a staunch advocate of women cricketers, "that I may be pardoned for pointing out that if we are steel-bound and whale-bound throughout, the free use of our limbs which the game demands is rendered impossible."

The increasing popularity of sports for both sexes helped change the way Englishmen spent their Sundays. Whatever may be said about the religious spirit of late Victorian England, such measurable activities as churchgoing were clearly on the decline. A survey of 1902 showed only one out of five Londoners were in church on an average Sunday, a far smaller percentage than that revealed by the Religious Census of 1851. The type of family prayers described by Tocqueville in the 1830s was part of a fading way of life. The sale of religious books was declining and, conversely, that of novels and works of history rising.

The intellectual questioning of Biblical doctrine evoked by "higher criticism" and by Darwinism contributed to the decline. So did the ritualistic tendencies of the Anglican Church. The stressing of vestments, episcopacy, and the sacraments tended to alienate many laymen who interpreted this emphasis on ritual and form as a sign that the Church of England was out of tune with the times, both politically and socially. Englishmen might continue to be baptized, married, and buried under its auspices; in all other respects, however, its influence had begun to wane.

The nonconformist chapels remained strong, but they too were growing less quickly than the population. Many an able young man of lower-class origin who earlier in the century had been drawn to the nonconformist ministry was now drifting toward secular interests. He might become a trade-union leader or enter politics or, now that so many of the legal and educational barriers had been lifted, he might even enter a profession; and he or his children might, at least for social reasons, actually join the Church of England. The sharp mid-Victorian social and political distinction between "church" and "chapel" was thus beginning to blur; but particular measures involving pub licensing or the role of religion in education did, at least temporarily, resharpen the distinction; and in Wales, nonconformity remained closely allied with a revived spirit of Welsh nationality.

By the 1890s there was a widespread hedonistic reaction against the stricter ethical code of Victorianism. The disenchanted young man of the late nineteenth century was typified by the Prince of Wales, the future Edward VII, who became the leader of London's fashionable high society, a world which his mother neither approved nor understood. It meant horse racing, golf, tennis, and polo by day and restaurants and theatres by night. Edward VII is often credited with inventing "the weekend" as a peculiarly British institution.

For the urban classes on the lower strata of society, the end of the century marked the beginning of widespread participant and spectator sports. Although cricket remained largely a middle-class sport, football began to appeal to all elements of society. Each major city developed its professional team, and soon there were national teams to represent England, Scotland, Wales, Ireland, and the major colonies.

The discovery was made in the 1890s that the lower classes not only had a widespread interest in organized athletics but constituted a great untapped market of newspaper readers. The mid-Victorian papers, though not always as respectable in content as their format might indicate, had appealed primarily to the gentleman. The working-class reader might buy an occasional Sunday paper, and he had within his price range a great variety of penny serial novels and printed street ballads which dealt with those three universal and timeless best sellers: sex, crime, and violence. The man who united the respectable Victorian daily with the pulp literature of the street ballad to create the modern mass circulation newspaper was Alfred Harmsworth (1865–1922), a youthful ill-educated barrister's son who in 1896 founded the *Daily Mail* as a halfpenny morning paper. The *Daily Mail* combined a simplified presentation of old-style news with "human interest" stories and prize competitions in such a fashion as to attract an increasing number of readers and, not surprisingly, an increasing number of advertisers. Within three years, the *Daily Mail* had a circulation of half a million copies. Newspapers had become big business; and although Lord Salisbury dismissed the *Daily Mail* as "written by office-boys for office-boys," Harmsworth's shrewdness won him a fortune, a peerage (as Lord Northcliffe), and the flattery of emulation by his fellow press lords who by the early twentieth century dominated the British newspaper scene.

The Decline of Laissez-Faire

Perhaps the most significant late Victorian transformation was one of social and political attitudes, specifically a strong current of opposition to the prevailing "laissez-faire" preconceptions of most mid-Victorian economists. Laissez-fairism, as we have already noted in Chapter 3, was never so all-inclusive as popular stereotype would have it, yet it was dominant. Individual enterprise seemed to be the key to both production and general prosperity; and the occasions on which the state might intervene were carefully circumscribed. The creed of the classical Victorian economists—though still doctrinally defended by political philosophers like Herbert Spencer—was coming under increasing assault as having failed to create a society worthy of men liberated by science from the slavery of life on a subsistence level.

The men who decried Victorian-Liberal economics most loudly were avowed socialists. Utopian socialism had been professed by Robert Owen half a century earlier, and Christian

Socialism had been advocated by Charles Kingsley and others a generation earlier. But it then died out, and only in the 1880s did organized socialism reappear in the British Isles. Karl Marx, strangely enough, had little to do with the English socialist revival. London was his home in exile for three decades, but he always remained a foreigner there, and no English translation of *Das Kapital* was attempted until some years after his death in 1883. Yet most of the factual data for his interpretation of history and his moral condemnation of capitalism was gleaned from British publications during daily sojourns to the British Museum, the country's largest library. Some years ago a prospective biographer of Karl Marx went up to the oldest attendant in the Reading Room and asked him whether he remembered a bespectacled and bearded little man, who used to sit every day at seat G7. After a bit of thought, the attendant said: "Ah yes, sir, I remember: a Mr. Marx it was, wasn't it? He came in every day like clockwork for years, and then one day he didn't come in, and no one's ever heard of him since."

The story may be apocryphal, but it illustrates Marx's elusive place in the modern British socialist tradition. The first professed Marxist Socialist was an ex-Tory businessman and journalist, H. M. Hyndman (1842–1921), who was wont in the 1880s to peddle his weekly paper *Justice* for a penny a copy and to preach class revolution while dressed in top hat and frockcoat. He wrote a popularization of Marx's ideas entitled *A Textbook of Democracy: England for All* and founded a small group of devotees who came to be known as the Social Democratic Federation. Since Hyndman neglected in his book to mention Marx's name, Marx promptly disowned him and excommunicated the first Marxist Party in England.

As significant as Hyndman's difficulties with his spiritual godfather was his conversion to the socialist cause of William Morris (1834–96), a man of much greater talents than Hyndman himself. Morris had led an artistic reaction against the absence of design in mid-Victorian furniture and carpetry. He sought to empty the mid-Victorian living room of its litter of manufactured knickknacks. Morris' socialism was less concerned with material gain for the working population than with a somewhat utopian readjustment of society that would make all men happy and self-reliant in their work. He hoped to return to an idealized world of individual medieval craftsmanship which he believed the industrial revolution had destroyed. Morris cooperated with Hyndman for three years and then they split, if only because Morris was not fundamentally in accord with Marx's vision of "scientific socialism." "I do not know what Marx's theory of value is," Morris burst out on one occasion, "and I'm damned if I want to know."

More influential than either Hyndman or Morris was the Fabian Society, a small group of intellectuals including George Bernard Shaw, H. G. Wells, and Sidney and Beatrice Webb. Like most nineteenth-century socialists, the Fabians tended to dwell more on the evils of capitalism than on the details of the socialist utopia of the future. Beatrice Webb, herself the daughter of a well-to-do manufacturer, explained her own conversion this way:

> I used to ponder over the ethics of capitalist enterprise as represented by my father's acts and axioms. . . . He thought, felt, and acted in terms of personal relationships and not in terms of general principles; he had no clear vision of the public good. . . . Hence he tended to prefer the welfare of his family and personal friends to the interests of the companies over which he presided, the profits of these companies to the prosperity of his country, the dominance of his own race to the peace of the world. . . ." [3]

The Webbs agreed with Hyndman in their definition of socialism — "It is an organized attempt to substitute ordered cooperation for existence for the present anarchical competition for existence"—but they were far apart on tactics. Hyndman's small band of followers looked forward militantly to the day of proletarian revolution; and they were half fearful that such capitalist concessions as an eight-hour working day would delay the coming of class war. The Fabians, on the other hand, wanted to use existing government machinery to forward the cause of economic equality by legislating against poverty and by bringing all major industries under the control of a democratically elected government. They sought no revolution; rather they wished to permeate the existing parties and organizations and gradually to wear down the opposition, just as the Roman general Fabius Cunctator in the third century B.C. had worn down the onslaught of Hannibal and eventually defeated him. In the words of one hostile critic, the Fabians "expected, by cautious and indeed almost imperceptible degrees, eventually to achieve a beatific state of intolerable bureaucracy."

The most successful late nineteenth-century socialist was a Lancashire journalist named Robert Blatchford, whose *Merrie England* (1894) explained in simple good-humored language that society as then constituted was unjust. It sold over a million copies. Although not even Blatchford converted the mass

[3] Beatrice Webb, *My Apprenticeship* (London, 1926).

of workingmen to socialism, some of the socialist groups developed useful collections of economic statistics on income
distribution in society and on the operation of the Poor Law.
The Fabians, who were instrumental in founding the world-
renowned London School of Economics, in this respect followed
in the footsteps of Benthamites like Edwin Chadwick. Nor were
the Fabians afraid of using humor as a weapon. One of their
favorite tactics was to try to show that socialism, far from being
a radical foreign innovation, was already a successful English
institution. Wrote Sidney Webb in 1889:

> The practical man, oblivious or contemptuous of any
> theory of the general principles of social organization,
> has been forced, by the necessities of the time, into
> an ever-deepening collectivist channel. Socialism, of
> course, he still rejects or despises. The individualist
> town councillor will walk along the municipal pave-
> ment, lit by municipal light and cleansed by municipal
> brooms with municipal water, and seeing, by the munic-
> ipal clock in the municipal market, that he is too early
> to meet his children coming home from the municipal
> school, hard by the county lunatic asylum and the mu-
> nicipal hospital, will use the national telegraph system
> to tell them not to walk through the municipal park, but
> to come by the municipal tramway, to meet him in the
> municipal reading-room, by the municipal museum, art-
> gallery, and library, where he intends to consult some
> of the national publications in order to prepare his next
> speech in the municipal town hall in favour of the na-
> tionalization of canals and the increase of Government
> control over the railway system. "Socialism, sir," he
> will say "don't waste the time of a practical man by your
> fantastic absurdities. Self-help, Sir, individual self-
> help, that's what has made our city what it is."

Webb's parable was a shrewd one, for the late nineteenth century saw a notable expansion in the social duties undertaken
by urban municipalities. It was under the mayoralty (1873–
76) of Joseph Chamberlain, for example, that Birmingham took
over the private gas- and waterworks and demolished over forty
acres of slums in order to build model homes for workingmen.
In the 1880s Birmingham took the lead in providing municipal
electric lighting and in operating the street railways. Successive
acts of Parliament had ended most limitations upon the powers
of municipal councils, and thereafter they were permitted to
put out bond issues to pay for long-term capital improvements.

By 1900, the new London County Council had come to epitomize progressive municipal administration in matters of education, health, and housing. Although Chamberlain accepted "gas-and-water socialism" as a description for the kind of work he had pioneered in Birmingham, he preferred to compare his city to a large corporation. "The leading idea of the English system of municipal government," he explained, "may be that of a joint-stock or cooperative enterprise in which every citizen is a shareholder, and of which the dividends are receivable in the improved health and the increase in the comfort and happiness of the community."

More immediately influential than professed socialists or reluctant municipal officers swept along by the course of events in helping to change the prevailing attitude toward government intervention in the economy were a host of pamphleteers, politicians, socially-conscious clergymen, and secular social reformers. Highly significant was *Progress and Poverty* by Henry George, an American whose panacea for poverty was the elimination of all taxes except a single tax on land and whose book was a bestseller in England throughout the 1880s. Though not a socialist, George helped undermine the doctrine of laissez-faire by his insistence that poverty was a man-made evil which could be eradicated by social action. In a very real sense, poverty was rediscovered in late Victorian England. The upper middle-class manufacturers who had moved to the suburbs a generation before were sharply reminded that there remained at least three out of ten Englishmen who lived close to the subsistence level. Andrew Mearns' pamphlet, *The Bitter Cry of Outcast London*, led to a Royal Commission on the Housing of the Working Classes (1884) which included such luminaries as Sir Charles Dilke, the Prince of Wales, Lord Salisbury, and the theologically conservative but socially radical Roman Catholic prelate, Cardinal Manning. Another Royal Commission called attention to the plight of the "sweated workers," men and women who worked not in factories but at home. There they produced cheap clothing, shoes, and furniture under extraordinarily ill-paid, unhealthful, and unregulated conditions. In 1889, Charles Booth published the first of eighteen exhaustive volumes on the *Life and Labour of the People of London*. Booth's work and B. Seebohm Rowntree's comparable study of the City of York (1901) are pioneer examples of detailed sociological investigation.

The implication of all such studies was that economic suffering was man-made and could and must be cured by human action. Not all reformers, however, were agreed as to the particular means. Private charity organizations continued to flourish. In 1878 after years of evangelical mission work in the East

End of London, "General" William Booth, an Anglican clergyman, founded the Salvation Army to provide succor and, if possible, a new start for the down-and-outers at the bottom of the English social ladder. Six years later, anxious not only to relieve symptoms but remove causes, another Anglican clergyman, Canon Barnett, founded Toynbee Hall, the prototype of subsequent settlement houses throughout the world. Barnett's plan was to settle a "colony" of social workers, preferably university graduates, among the poor and thereby try to bridge the chasm of class indifference and ignorance and offer an opportunity for intellectual and material improvement.

In some ways it may seem surprising that what Beatrice Webb called "the humanitarian upsurge of the 'eighties'" should have taken place at a time when statistically the average workingman was clearly improving his standard of living. The explanation lies partly in the sense of uncertainty and insecurity which the "Great Depression" fostered among many Englishmen, but economic motivation was only half the story. The desire to save the bodies as well as the souls of those groups in society who had not shared in the general rise of living standards proved to be a powerful motive for many earnest people who had either forsaken orthodox religion and sought secular substitutes or felt that, as clergymen, their Christian faith required them to relieve suffering in the world around them. The notable improvement in the condition of the working classes did not in late Victorian England keep pace with humanitarian conceptions of what that position should be.

Social Reform and Politics

The workers who were members of trade unions were not at first particularly attracted by the social creed of either socialists or social reformers. The prosperous '60s had been climaxed by a burst of union organizing, and the total membership in the Trades Union Congress grew from 114,000 to 735,000 between 1868 and 1873. The next fifteen years were to prove less favorable to union growth, and TUC membership first declined sharply and then began to grow again at a much slower pace. For the most part, the TUC continued to represent the aristocracy of skilled labor, men who were essentially satisfied with the capitalistic organization of industry, who preferred negotiation to strikes in dealing with their employers, who voted Liberal in politics, and who had little inclination to have Parliament legislate on hours and wages.

The new unions of the later 1880s and 1890s were, however, of a different social and political complexion. They were usually made up of less skilled and less highly paid workers. Their leaders were far more class conscious, more favorable toward strikes, more distrustful of the goodwill of their employers, and therefore more intent on parliamentary action. One of the first of the new unions was the London Dock Workers. Traditionally, the London docker had been exposed to all the vagaries of laissez-faire economics; there was no continuity of employment, and a host of men competed daily for whatever work was available. In 1889 the dockworkers demanded a minimum wage of six pence an hour ($12\frac{1}{2}$ cents in terms of the American dollar of the day), at least four hours of work at a time, and extra pay for overtime. When their demands were refused, they struck, and for five weeks the Port of London was virtually closed to all traffic. The strike caused hardships for many Londoners, not least of all for the strikers themselves; but eventually a committee of citizens, including the aged Cardinal Manning, succeeded in bringing about a settlement. The dockers, beneficiaries of the financial aid and sympathy of many middle-class Londoners, won their six pence an hour and most of their other demands.

The success of the Dock Strike provided a stimulus for other new unions among office clerks, teachers, and shop assistants (store clerks), some of whom worked an incredible 86 hours a week. Such organizations and a revived miners' union caused the TUC membership to rise from 750,000 in 1887 to over 1,500,000 by 1892. It also inspired the idea that workers should have representatives of their own in Parliament rather than vote for Liberals or Conservatives. The first such representative was Keir Hardie, a Scottish miner who was elected in 1892 and who astonished the House of Commons by entering the chamber wearing a miner's cap and a tweed jacket rather than the traditional top hat and frock coat. In 1893, under Hardie's influence, an organization known as the Independent Labour Party was set up. It was the first "popular" socialist party founded in England, and it derived its strength from trade unions and nonconformist chapels. Yet for the moment its own popularity was open to question in that it could boast but a single Member of Parliament. In the general election of 1895, all of its 28 candidates were defeated, including Hardie himself. Imperialist excitement largely explains the election returns of 1895, but during the Boer War plans were laid to create a real labor party that could win votes. Three elements – socialist intellectuals (especially the Fabians), the trade unions, and Hardie's Independent Labour Party – met to organize a Labour Representation Committee for the purpose of seeking the nomination and election of labor candidates to Parliament. That Committee was to become the nucleus of the twentieth-century British Labour Party.

Although no significant separate Labour Party emerged in Parliament until 1906, the two major parties were deeply affected by the gradual shift of sentiment in favor of a greater degree of government regulation of the economic scene. The Liberals were caught in a dilemma; if they were to survive they would have to listen to the voice of the masses; but the traditional Liberal political philosophy exalted not social welfare but individual freedom from archaic legal and economic shackles. A veteran of many of those earlier conflicts, John Bright, expressed the opinion in 1883 that no political issues remained upon which great conflicts were likely to arise.

Yet at this very time, the opinion was obviously gaining weight that the economy of an industrialized country produced problems for which the answers of traditional liberalism seemed insufficient. The highly touted "freedom of contract" which all adult laborers enjoyed might well be illusory when factories employed thousands of men. Either such men would organize — and both large unions and employer associations might require government regulation—or else they might demand the setting of minimum standards by the government. Nor could "natural" monopolies such as telegraph and telephone companies, railways, and electric power companies be treated by the state as if they were small shopkeepers. Finally, the Liberals faced the paradox that the electorate that emerged from the extension of the franchise in 1867 and 1884 might wish to use its vote for purposes opposed to traditional liberalism.

Some pragmatic Liberals began to shift their outlook. John Morley, a member of Gladstone's last Cabinet, illustrates such a change of attitude with his comments on Britain's housing problem in 1883: "I am beginning to doubt whether it is possible to grapple with this enormous mass of evil in our society by merely private, voluntary, and philanthropic effort. I believe we shall have to bring to bear the collective force of the whole community, shortly called the State, in order to remedy things against which our social conscience is at last beginning to revolt." It was in this spirit that the Liberals sponsored the Irish Land Acts of 1870 and 1881 and that they hesitantly began the regulation of the labor of adult men (rather than merely women and children) in the Employers' Liability Act of 1880, which permitted an employee to sue his employer for compensation for industrial accidents, even if a fellow employee was technically at fault. By 1891, the Liberals were even tentatively advocating a mandatory eight-hour workday. It was a Liberal Chancellor of the Exchequer, Sir William Harcourt, who in the Budget of 1894, introduced in regard to "death duties" (inheritance taxes) the principle of a graduated tax, the key to all future efforts to redistribute wealth. Liberals found comfort in the teachings of a new generation of economists like Henry Sidgwick, who gave marked emphasis to John Stuart Mill's distinction between the production of wealth, which society ought to leave alone, and the distribution of wealth, which society might well regulate. Sidgwick noted that not all individuals could look after themselves, that some types of state intervention (such as compulsory education) actually encouraged individual self-help rather than hindered it, and that in particular cases social needs must take precedence over private profit.

The Conservatives had fewer doctrinal difficulties in going against the tenets of laissez-faire than did the Liberals, but they did face the practical problem of being increasingly the party of big landowners and big businessmen whose privileges would have to be restricted and whose property would have to be taxed if the goals of the social reformers were to be achieved. Disraeli's paternalistic "Tory democracy" was never completely forgotten in the decades that followed his death, and the irrepressible Joseph Chamberlain added a new dose of the same tonic to political conservatism.

Although the Irish issue and Gladstone's longevity had pushed him into an alignment with the Conservatives, his absorption with imperial problems never overshadowed totally his interest in municipal and national social reform and his willingness to break with old-style assumptions. The question of the hour, Chamberlain had declared in 1885, was "What ransom will property pay for the security which it enjoys?" Noting in 1891 that one out of every four Englishmen over sixty was on poor relief, Chamberlain was the first important British statesman to advocate a system of government-sponsored old age pensions. As Cabinet minister in a largely Conservative Cabinet, Chamberlain helped pass the Workmen's Compensation Act of 1897, which made it compulsory for employers to pay the costs of industrial accidents and thus greatly strengthened the Employers' Liability Act of 1880.

For a time in the 1890s public preoccupation with social reform gave way to preoccupation with imperialism, but the ideological shift which was to cause Britain to establish the fundamentals of a welfare state in the early years of the twentieth century had already taken place. In the words of one historian, "The Poor had become Labour and Labour had become the People, a power which could not be ignored." Declared Sir William Harcourt, the Liberal, in 1889: "We are all Socialists now." The analysis was succinct but misleading. Harcourt's thought was more moderately expressed by the Conservative Prime Minister, Lord Salisbury, when he concluded that in many areas "the policy of laissez-faire can no longer be pursued without disaster to the State."

Chapter 12

THE ROCKY ROAD TO THE Welfare State

THE YEARS before 1914 are nostalgically remembered to-day by a diminishing band of men and women as an era of peace, dignity, and stability, an age when European influence and European values were dominant throughout the world and, most prominently, an epoch which knew nothing of world wars or cold wars. The age did have some of these qualities, and we are not wholly wrong if we visualize it in terms of an Edwardian upper class dancing the "Ascot Gavotte" in "My Fair Lady" fashion. Yet contemporary Englishmen were as likely to see themselves living in the dawn of a new age as in the Indian summer of an old. In the field of social reform, the transformation of attitudes which had taken place in the late Victorian years was to lead in the early years of the new century to a body of laws and institutions which by 1914 had laid the foundations of the welfare state. Like most momentous developments, the foundations of the welfare state, and the accompanying social and intellectual unrest, were as much the product of the accident of personalities and events as of premeditated calculation.[1]

---

[1] The 1900–14 domestic scene is dealt with in greatest detail in the final two volumes of Elie Halevy's *History of the English People in the Nineteenth Century: Imperialism and the Rise of Labour (1895–1905)*, and *The Rule of Democracy (1905–1914)*, Paperback edition (London, 1961). Briefer accounts are supplied by Ensor and by Colin Cross, *The Liberals in Power* (London, 1963), and in the early chapters of three surveys of twentieth century Britain: Alfred Havighurst's

Edwardian Prosperity

A significant backdrop for social and political change was provided by the paradoxical period of "Edwardian Prosperity." Just as historical accident had identified the later part of Victoria's reign with the curious "Great Depression," so it was to identify the reign of her son Edward VII (1901–10) with a period of economic boom. The association is not altogether specious. Whereas Queen Victoria had conveyed the image of the rather formidable and moralistic mother (and grandmother) of her people, Edward conveyed rather the impression of the genial uncle who enjoyed life and who liked to see his people enjoying life also.

Most of the economic statistics of the first fifteen years of the twentieth century substantiate the widespread impression of prosperity. In contrast to the last decades of Victoria's reign, prices were rising rather than declining and so was the margin of business profit. Agriculture was still in the doldrums; but the decline had been halted, and cattle raisers who fed their herds on imported grains were doing well. The value of exports (discounting inflation) grew by one third; as late as 1913 Britain still produced 27 percent of the world's exports of manufactured articles. American and German competition was still increasing, and Britain's relative economic position continued to decline; but if Britain was no longer the world's workshop, she was at least "its warehouseman, its banker, and its commission agent." Britain remained by far the world's greatest shipbuilder and maintained the largest merchant marine. Although an Italian, Marconi, invented radio, it was the British who first put it to practical use as a method of keeping in touch with ships at sea. Contributing notably to the atmosphere of prosperity was a revival in large-scale English foreign investment. The net balance of foreign investment had been £764 million in 1872; it was £2,431 million in 1902 and £3,568 million by 1912.

The period of Edwardian prosperity, though real enough for many British merchants and corporations, rested at least in part on unstable foundations. The upsurge of financial investment abroad, where a better monetary return could be expected, tended to discourage investment in industry at home. This in turn contributed to a noticeable rise in the rate of obsolescence in many British industries in comparison with Amer-

---

Twentieth Century Britain (Evanston, Illinois, 1962); D. C. Somervell, *British Politics Since 1900,* New and Revised Ed. (London, 1953), and Charles Furth, *Life Since 1900* (London, 1956). In *They Saw It Happen, 1899–1940* (Oxford, 1960), Asa Briggs supplies an instructive collection of primary source excerpts.

ican and German ones. United States cotton mills had adopted the latest ring-spinning machinery; but the Lancashire cotton firms continued to rely on early nineteenth-century mules. Coal-cutting machines were becoming prominent in the United States, whereas the English mineowner was continuing to rely almost solely on hand labor. Yet coal mining was more important than ever in the British economy, because by the twentieth century the export of coal had become one of the most significant ways in which Britain paid for her imports. There was still plenty of coal underground, but mine shafts had to be sunk deeper and deeper and coal seams often slanted at sharp angles that made it difficult to use machinery, even if machinery had been available. The result was that productivity per coal miner, which had been steadily rising during the nineteenth century, was now on the decline. In 1881 output per man per year had been 403 tons; in 1901 it was 340 tons; in 1911, 309 tons. Mine workers' wages were frozen, and company profits were declining. It is not surprising then that the mining industry gave rise to more legislation between 1906 and 1914 than any other industry or that two decades later it inspired the only general strike in British history and that in 1946 it became the first major British industry to be nationalized.

The most paradoxical aspect of Edwardian prosperity was that unlike the middle and later years of Victoria's reign, wages only barely kept pace with rising prices and that real wages for a majority of English workingmen did not rise at all. The average worker may have labored shorter hours and may have enjoyed a few more social services, but his family's income stood still at a time when other groups in society seemed obviously to be prospering.

The failure of real wages to rise proved a potent stimulus to overseas emigration, and between 1900 and 1914 more than four and a half million people left the British Isles, an all-time high. In contrast to their nineteenth-century predecessors, a majority of them (56 percent) settled within the British Empire; this fact was a source of deep satisfaction to imperial federationists like Joseph Chamberlain.

The causes of the failure on the part of real wages at home to continue to increase are complex. An attitude of complacency on the part of managements which failed to replace obsolete machinery halted the rise in productivity. An acceptance by many laboring men of the doctrine of the classical economists that there was only so much work to go around (and that if he did less there would be more for his fellows) tended similarly to discourage a rise in productivity. Also relevant was the fact that the "terms of trade" had once again turned against Britain. It now required relatively more British exports to pay for a given quantity of imports. Whatever the precise cause, the failure of wages to keep up with profits produced for the middle classes the aura of prosperity while at the same time fostering on the part of laboring men not only emigration but considerable social unrest and an increasing demand for social reform legislation.

While it was no longer exclusively landed in its economic interests, there was still a class of gentlemen at the top of the British social ladder, and for them life in Edwardian England could be very comfortable indeed. Despite the complaint of one lady about "domestic servants now so difficult to get, and so exacting when found," many country estates still boasted large staffs whose function it was to provide "ordered luxury and plenty of punctual meals and silent service" for the master and his wife, their children, and a great host of guests. In London there were full-time nannies to care for the children, and during the London "season" there was a glittering round of formal teas, luncheons, dinners, and formal dances. Horse-drawn hansom cabs clattered along London streets; and although the first gasoline-driven omnibuses entered London transit service in 1905, the individual automobile remained a noisy luxury. The rich man's car, as it sped along unpaved streets, frightened the casual passerby and covered him with dust on a dry day and water on a rainy one; it seemed a visible symbol of arrogant wealth. At the very time that many "gentlemen" were becoming more conscious of social problems, they often unwittingly aggravated class feeling in this manner.

"Ladies were ladies in those days," recalls Darwin's grand-daughter in her revealing account of a late Victorian and Edwardian girlhood.[2] Ladies did not do things themselves. They told other people what to do and how to do it. The author's Aunt Etty never made a pot of tea in her life. She never traveled in a cab or in a train without her maid. She never sewed on a button or mailed a letter, and she never put on a shawl or answered a doorbell except on those rare occasions when no maid was immediately at hand.

If life was luxurious for the upper classes, it remained reasonably comfortable (if somewhat stereotyped) in middle-class suburbia, where families lived in semidetached houses with tiny, manicured fenced-in gardens, and children played with scooters, tricycles, and hoops on the sidewalks of the quiet residential streets. Here too there was considerable entertaining—amateur dramatics, music, and tennis. Yet the middle class was by no means rich. Forty-four of the forty-five million people who lived in the British Isles in 1911 still had an income

---

[2] Gwen Raverat, *Period Piece* (London, 1960).

of less than $15 a week (in terms of 1911 dollars). Many of the lower middle-class clerks and teachers, anxious to preserve their social status, found themselves affected by the tendency of "real wages" to stay the same; and they were increasingly fearful of talk of new taxes to pay for battleships and social legislation.

At the bottom of the pyramid were the working classes, whose life continued to be mean and bleak. Their world was the endless, ignoble acres of narrow two- and three-story row houses with their multitude of chimney pots which made up metropolitan London and the industrial cities of the Midlands. Englishmen were slow to take to apartments and much preferred a house, however small or dingy. While only a minority of working-class families were in any sense on the edge of starvation, life remained extremely simple; and prolonged illness, unemployment, or old age could push most families below the poverty line. The average work-week was still 54 hours, and Sunday remained the only full day off. Paid vacations were still unknown, and few working-class families ever had occasion to venture far beyond the neighborhoods in which they lived or worked.

The Cultural Revival

If the brilliance and glitter of Edwardian society were largely limited to the privileged few, this did not make it any less real. It was connected, moreover, with a remarkable revival in English music and English drama. British painters were largely content to follow the lead of the French along the road to Impressionism and Cubism, but English composers for the first time since Purcell in the seventeenth century played a distinct role in European music. Sir Arthur Sullivan (1842–1900) had aspired to serious composition, but he remains best remembered for the delightfully satirical operettas he wrote in collaboration with W. S. Gilbert (1836–1911). Sir Edward Elgar (1857–1934), on the other hand, represented by such works as the violin concerto, the cantata "The Dream of Gerontius," and the *Enigma Variations* for orchestra, became a distinguished individual member of the late romantic movement. Frederick Delius (1862–1934), who was born in Bradford and spent much of his life near Paris, composed a number of impressionistic tone poems in a highly personal style. Ralph Vaughan Williams (1872–1958), who was to become one of the great symphonic composers of the twentieth century, began during the Edwardian years to incorporate into his music long-neglected English folk tunes.[3]

These same years saw three great English playwrights, James Barrie (1860–1927), John Galsworthy (1867–1933), and George Bernard Shaw (1856–1950) at the height of their powers. While Barrie tended toward whimsy and Somerset Maugham (1872–   ), who in 1908 had four plays running at once in London, was a master at the comedy of manners, Galsworthy and Shaw were characteristically concerned with the social problems of the age. Galsworthy's *Strife* (1909) was an attack upon prevailing relations between capital and labor, and his *Justice* (1910) criticized prison conditions. Shaw was both willing and eager, in a completely un-Victorian fashion, to thrust his dramatic stiletto at every available accepted institution, be it private property (as in *Major Barbara*) or class relations (as in *Pygmalion*), or militarism (as in *Arms and the Man*). He was ever the enemy of pretence and hypocrisy, and he succeeded in both entertaining and puzzling his upper- and upper-middle-class audiences. "One really doesn't quite know what to think," was the reaction of a typical Edwardian playgoer.

The revival in drama was matched by a revival in novel writing. Joseph Conrad (1857–1924), Pole by birth and English-man by adoption, added a touch of subtle psychological analysis to tales pitting man against nature in distant lands. Arnold Bennett (1867–1931) was more typical in his concern with life in provincial industrial towns which is reflected in novels like *Old Wives' Tale* and *Clayhanger*. Galsworthy began his masterly multivolume study of British upper-class life, *The Forsyte Saga*, with *The Man of Property* (1906). Most representative of the widespread early twentieth-century attitude that while serious social problems existed, they could be solved by appropriate legislative remedies and the education of the common man was H. G. Wells (1866–1946). He wrote a prodigious number of fantasies and realistic novels—such as *Mankind in the Making* (1903) and *A Modern Utopia* (1905), nearly all of which sought to advance the goal of social regeneration. Less hopeful of social progress but no less articulate were Hilaire Belloc (1870–1953) and G. K. Chesterton (1874–1936). The former a Roman Catholic by birth, the latter one by conversion, both sought their utopias in the Middle Ages rather than in the twentieth century. Although they participated in the literary flowering of the Edwardian years, Belloc and Chesterton were less representative of the prevailing social attitudes. More typical of the latter was Leonard T. Hobhouse, journalist and Professor

---

[3] A. L. Bacharach, *British Music of Our Time*, new ed. (Hammondsworth, Middlesex, 1951).

of Sociology at the University of London, who in his *Democracy and Reaction* (1904) sought to disentangle nineteenth-century liberalism from doctrinaire laissez-faire attitudes or Social Darwinist doctrine. He saw the liberal and socialist ideals as complementary; both opposed the growing power of wealth, which he diagnosed as the greatest menace to the working of popular government.

The Conservative Decline (1900–1905)

The government in power when the new century began was that of Lord Salisbury, and he, though in no sense a conservative diehard, was still very much part of a tradition harking back to William Cecil, Salisbury's sixteenth-century forebear, a tradition combining the life of a landed aristocrat with a career of public service. A peer as Prime Minister had come to seem anachronistic to many Englishmen, and Salisbury proved to be the last. His final ministry was dominated by Joseph Chamberlain; but the latter was by this time far more involved with schemes of imperial federation than new programs of social reform. Salisbury's coalition of Conservatives and Liberal Unionists—the two did not finally and officially coalesce until 1912—had received a strong vote of confidence in the "khaki election" of 1900, held in the wake of the Boer War victories. The popular vote margin—2,400,000 to 2,100,000—was not nearly so impressive as the margin in Parliamentary seats, but the opposition remained weak. The Liberal Party was still sorely divided between "Liberal Imperialists" and "pro-Boers." When Salisbury retired from the Prime Ministership because of ill health in 1902, the most obviously qualified successor was Joseph Chamberlain; but he was not really trusted by his political colleagues and, in the event, he made no real fight for the position. The Prime Ministership was thereupon inherited by the longtime Conservative leader of the House of Commons, Salisbury's nephew Arthur James Balfour. Balfour was a genial fifty-five-year-old bachelor, a brilliant and charming conversationalist who possessed shrewd political insight and whose writings gave him some claim to be considered a professional philosopher. Yet philosophical detachment was not the most useful talent for a twentieth-century political leader; and Balfour, as things turned out, presided over three successive years in which his party lost political strength, a process climaxed by the overwhelming Liberal triumph and Conservative defeat of January 1906.

That Liberal triumph was far less the result of the development of a positive Liberal program than of a capitalization upon the political errors committed, often for the worthiest of motives, by Balfour's ministry. The first of these was the Education Act of 1902. Its main objective, that of raising educational standards in Britain, was beyond cavil. The means used for that purpose proved highly controversial. The local school boards established by the Forster Education Act of 1870 were abolished as too small for the purpose; and the national primary education system was put into the hands of the elected county and borough councils. These councils were also authorized to enter the field of secondary education, hitherto almost solely in the domain of private academies, and to set up their own secondary schools. The number of students in such institutions consequently increased from 94,000 in 1905 to 200,000 in 1914.

The controversial aspect of the act was that it authorized the new educational authorities to give grants to voluntary church-affiliated schools (mostly Anglican) so as to raise the salaries of their teachers and limit the size of their classes to the level of the state schools. Since at the time the act was passed, more children went to "voluntary" schools (3,000,000) than to "board" schools (2,600,000), this meant that in many districts a child of nonconformist parents was required to attend a school in which he was taught Anglican doctrine and had to attend Anglican services.

The nonconformists had objected to the principle of tax funds for church schools in 1870; now they were doubly outraged. Under the direction of a Baptist minister, Dr. John Clifford, they organized and protested. "What is at stake is not education merely," declared Clifford, "but chiefly our retention of that divinest gift to man; the right to the free, unfettered and full use of his inmost soul. If we are men, we shall not submit to be robbed of that." A Passive Resisters' League refused to pay taxes which would go to church schools. The League became so influential, especially in Wales, that Balfour's ministry felt compelled to pass special enforcement legislation. The Education Bill, its beneficial provisions overlooked, reconverted many a straying Liberal Unionist to the political faith of his fathers.

The Licensing Act of 1904 had a similar result. The question of whether a pubkeeper's license, granted by local authorities, was a permanent right or one that could be revoked without compensation had long been an open legal question; but the House of Lords ruled in 1891 that pub licenses were limited to a year at a time. Temperance advocates, stronger than ever, welcomed the decision as opening the way to an immediate reduction in the number of establishments selling alcoholic beverages and their entire prohibition in the near future. The

act of 1904 took the right of licensing out of the hands of the immediate local authorities and placed it in the hands of the
Justices of the Peace meeting in quarter sessions. It provided,
moreover, for a fund levied on the brewing trade itself to com-
pensate owners whose licenses were taken away. The act was
clearly defensible and worked over the long run to reduce the
number of pubs without injuring individual pub-owners; but
temperance advocates denounced the measure as "a brewers'
bill." Men who were convinced that the elimination of drink-
ing might make all other measures of social reform unnecessary
saw the bill as "endowing the devilish trade." The Licensing
Bill thus won the Liberals additional staunch recruits.

In the meantime the Conservative Party had been split on
an issue far more explosive than alcohol. Joseph Chamberlain,
the man who in 1886 had divided the Liberal party by refusing
to follow Gladstone on Irish Home Rule, in 1903 resigned from
the Cabinet and divided the Conservative party by publicly
advocating tariff reform. After half a century of free trade, he
wanted Britain to return to protection. His reasoning was simple
enough. Let Britain set up a tariff wall taxing all imports including food. Then let the government knock holes in the wall
to admit food and manufactures from the colonies at a lower
rate of duty. The result would be a customs union covering a
quarter of the globe and four hundred million people. Just as
the German *Zollverein* of the 1830s had led to the German Empire of the 1870s, so, Chamberlain argued, the British customs
union would in due course lead to a politically united empire.
In the meantime, the extra revenue the government would acquire from the tariffs could be used for social reforms such as
old age pensions.

Chamberlain soon won over many members of his party;
but a significant number, including the Duke of Devonshire,
the man who as Marquess of Hartington had joined Chamberlain's secession from the Liberals, did not go along. Balfour
vainly sought to steer a middle course. The country as a whole
seemed unready to turn its back on free trade, an action which
Sir Henry Campbell-Bannerman, the Liberal Party leader, compared to "disputing the law of gravitation." "I don't think they
will vote for Protection," explained Chamberlain's own brother
Arthur, "because I can't think they will be so silly as to ask the
government to tax the food they eat, the clothes they wear and
the commodities they use, on the promise of the politicians that
their wages will rise."

There indeed lay the crux of the matter. No matter how
eloquently Chamberlain sang the praises of tariff protection
and imperial federation, he found it difficult to deny that the
most immediate result of tariff reform would be more expen-

sive food. Thus Chamberlain's Tariff Reform League was soon countered by a Free Food League; and during the election campaign, Herbert Asquith, the former Liberal Home Secretary, stalked Chamberlain from town to town rebutting his arguments and contrasting, by means of placards and actual loaves of bread, the "Big Loaf" of Free Trade with the "Little Loaf" of Protection. Chamberlain did not really expect to convert the country immediately. What he hoped was that the Liberals would briefly take over, would demonstrate their inability to govern, and that a Conservative Party by then pledged to Protection would thereupon replace them. Balfour, though he did not take sides on the question of tariff reform, had similar expectations of Liberal incompetence. He therefore resigned in December 1905 without first calling for a general election. Perhaps, he thought, the Liberals might find it impossible even to construct a Cabinet.

The Liberal Revival (1905–1908)

Conservative hopes were soon confounded. Sir Henry Campbell-Bannerman was named Prime Minister by King Edward VII, and he soon put together one of the ablest Cabinets in British history. Campbell-Bannerman had impressed most of his colleagues as a rather lackluster figure, but behind the scenes he had done much to heal the split in Liberal ranks created by the Boer War. He was a millionaire who had inherited his fortune from his father, a Glasgow warehouseman; he had been a member of Gladstone's later ministries and had served as M.P. for the same Scottish borough since 1868. Campbell-Bannerman was similarly constant in his personal habits. Every summer for thirty-four years he accompanied his invalid wife to the Bohemian health resort of Marienbad. Each year was like the last year in Marienbad because the couple always occupied the same rooms in the same hotel. Yet in politics, he welcomed innovation; by temperament and conviction he "was possibly the truest radical ever to become Prime Minister of Great Britain." His appointment as Prime Minister transformed his manner from one of ineffectuality into one of decision and authority, and he had no fear that the more flamboyant or more articulate members of his Cabinet would overshadow him.

These included Herbert Asquith as Chancellor of the Exchequer, Sir Edward Grey as Foreign Secretary, and R. B. Haldane as Secretary for War. The Lord Privy Seal and Liberal leader in the Lords, the Marquess of Ripon, had the distinction of having served in the same Cabinet as Palmerston and of being the son of a man who had been an M.P. with Fox. Herbert

Gladstone, the able son of a distinguished father, was appointed Home Secretary, and David Lloyd George, a dynamic Welshman, was named President of the Board of Trade. Another young M.P., Winston Churchill, who had switched from his father's Conservative party on the issue of Protection, joined the Ministry as Under Secretary for Colonies; he was to join the Cabinet proper two and a half years later. Perhaps the most remarkable of Campbell-Bannerman's appointments was that of John Burns as President of the Local Government Board. Burns, a onetime member of Hyndman's Social Democratic Federation, had been a leader of the London dock strike of 1889 and was the first manual laborer ever to enter a British Cabinet. Paradoxically enough, he proved far less radical a political innovator and far more the captive of the permanent officials of his department than his aristocratic colleagues.

As soon as the Cabinet had been firmly installed, Campbell-Bannerman asked the king to dissolve Parliament and call for new elections. The brief campaign concentrated on the issues already outlined – the Education Act, the Licensing Act, and the tariff issue. The subject of imperialism emerged in the form of "Chinese slavery": had the Conservative Government been right to sanction the importation into South Africa of 46,000 Chinese coolies to work under conditions of semislavery in South Africa's gold and diamond mines? To the Liberals this smacked too much of the concept that labor was a commodity.

While the import of election billboards featuring sinister Chinese may not have been clear to every voter, most other issues were; and the election results were equally straightforward. The Liberals had won by a landslide: Liberals, 401; Irish Nationalists, 83; Labour Party, 29; Conservatives, 132; Liberal Unionists, 25. The popular vote margin was, as usual, not quite so decisive (3.3 million votes for the first three parties and 2.5 million for the remaining two); but it too was unmistakable. The Liberals had captured every seat in Wales, four fifths of all the Scottish seats, and, for the first time since 1880, a bare majority of English seats as well. The Parliament of 1906 included at least 300 new M.P.s. It was, in some ways, the first truly middle-class parliament in English history, made up to a large extent of lawyers, journalists, and teachers, all of whom worked for a living and many of whom were extremely sympathetic to the idea that Members of Parliament should be paid. The Liberal contingent included only a minority (one in three) who had attended a public school. Never since the Parliaments of Oliver Cromwell had so many religious nonconformists sat in the House of Commons.

One election result which caused considerable public comment was the arrival on the parliamentary scene of a separate

Labour Party of 29 members. True, they dutifully hired the traditional top hats for the occasion, but their appearance as professed working-class representatives was a novelty. Labor's success at the polls was not only a reflection of the hard work done by the Labour Representation Committee but also the result of the Taff-Vale decision by the House of Lords in 1901 which decreed that an employer could sue a labor union for damages caused by an individual member of that union. The decision once again threw the legal status of trade unions into doubt, and many a worker decided, for the first time, that since the prevailing Conservative government seemed unwilling to reverse the judicial verdict by legislation, a separate Labour Party was needed.

A less advertised explanation for the presence of labor M.P.s in 1906 was a secret compact in 1903 between Herbert Gladstone, then chief Liberal whip, and Ramsay MacDonald, the secretary of the Labour Representation Committee. They agreed that in a certain number of constituencies, Labourites and Liberals would not compete with each other and thereby risk a Conservative victory. The compact aided both parties in 1906 and provided the Labourites with at least 16 of the 29 seats they won that year. The Labourites could not afford, of course, to publicize an arrangement which seemed to make them no more than a Liberal appendage.

The new Liberal Ministry soon set to work. It had no prepared social program; but its supporters included many impatient, reform-minded idealists, and it was conscious of the presence of the new band of Labourites, ready to criticize as too tame every projected reform. In imperial policy, the Ministry was Gladstonian in outlook. At the fifth Colonial Conference of Prime Ministers (1907), it happily accepted the substitution of the term "dominion" for "colony" when referring to self-governing parts of the Empire. In South Africa, Sir Henry Campbell-Bannerman — who had shown strong sympathy for the "pro-Boers" of his party a few years before — brought to an end the importation of Chinese coolies and insisted on the rapid establishment of autonomy in both the Transvaal and the Orange River Colony. Conservatives protested, but ex-Boer generals such as Louis Botha and Jan Christiaan Smuts cooperated willingly. A constitutional convention in 1908 among representatives of the four South African colonies led in 1909 to the establishment of the Union of South Africa to take its place with its sister dominions as an autonomous member of the British imperial family.

The successful reconciliation of Briton and Boer after so many years of conflict was long regarded as a triumph of British liberalism; but in the retrospect of half a century, the triumph seems hollow. The spirit of Paul Kruger ultimately proved stronger than that of Campbell-Bannerman. Neither Briton nor Boer concerned himself at the time with the legal status of the native black population. In the Treaty of Vereeniging, which had ended the Boer War, the British government had indeed specifically pledged itself not to enfranchise the Bantus. A Labour Party motion to give the vote to black South Africans on terms of equality with the British and Boer population was consequently little heeded and easily defeated.

In India, the new Liberal Ministry also turned away from the paternalism represented by the Viceroyalty of Lord Curzon (1900–05) and returned to a policy of cautiously developing the machinery for self-government. "We have had imposed upon us by the unlucky prowess of our ancestors," wrote John Morley, the Secretary of State for India," the task of ruling a vast number of millions of alien dependents," and it was his hope to win the support of the more moderate leaders of educated and nationalistically inclined Indian middle classes. These had been convinced by British defeats in the Boer War and Russian defeats in the Russo-Japanese War that neither Britons nor white men generally were imbued with the innate superiority which they had so often claimed. The reforms put into effect by the Liberals in 1909 did much to reconcile the Indian National Congress leaders for the moment. Henceforth, there was to be at least one Indian in the Viceroy's Cabinet and two in the Secretary of State's Advisory Council in London. The provincial and central legislative councils were enlarged to include a greater number of elected members.

Extremists like B. G. Tilak, who sought immediate independence and were willing to use terroristic methods to obtain it, lost support for the time being; and when King George V visited India in 1911 formally to assume the Emperorship and receive the homage of Indian princes, he was hailed by hundreds of thousands of Indians. A step taken by the king-emperor which was popular with the Indians, though resented by many English civil servants, was to move the capital of British rule from sophisticated Calcutta to historic Delhi. There a British architect, Sir Edwin Lutyens, planned the handsome public buildings, the wide avenues, and circular colonnades of New Delhi which were first to serve the British Raj and later the rulers of the new Republic of India.

Back at home, the Conservatives quickly rallied in defeat. Joseph Chamberlain, whose native Birmingham had remained loyal to him despite the Liberal landslide elsewhere, was ready to replace Balfour as leader on a platform of "tariff reform"; but on July 11, 1906, three days after the City of Birmingham celebrated Chamberlain's seventieth birthday with extraordinary enthusiasm, that difficult political warrior was struck down by a paralytic stroke, and though he lingered on until 1914, his political career came to an abrupt end. Arthur James Balfour thus remained the leader of the Opposition, and a year later he decided to embrace the doctrine of tariff protection as his own.

By then he had also learned to use the House of Lords as a means of blocking Liberal bills which the Conservatives could not stop in the House of Commons. The traditional upper chamber—in which the Liberals were a small minority and which had not rejected a single measure during the previous ten years of Conservative rule—was now used as an adjunct of the Conservative Party. In 1906, the Lords vetoed an Education Bill to relieve nonconformists of their objections to the 1902 Bill. All further attempts to amend the religious provisions of that bill proved equally unavailing. Another bill, to end plural voting by individuals who owned property in several constituencies and had the right to vote in each, was similarly thrown out by the Lords. In 1907 two bills to extend the rights of Scottish tenant farmers were turned down. The same fate befell a 1908 Licensing Act by which the Liberals hoped within a few years to close 32,000 pubs, one third of the country's establishments serving alcoholic beverages.

Campbell-Bannerman was outraged. It was all very well for the House of Lords to argue that on issues which had not been subject to public debate the peers should serve as a chamber which gave public opinion time to make itself felt. But the country had just expressed its opinion on measures like the Education Act of 1902 by electing an overwhelming majority of Liberals. He moved a resolution that the power of the House of Lords be so restricted by law "as to secure that within the limits of a single Parliament the final decision of the Commons should prevail." The House of Commons approved the resolution by a vote of 432–147, but for the moment he refrained from carrying the fight to the House of Lords. To appeal to the country in a new general election so soon again seemed undesirable, and even risky, and for two years the issue of the House of Lords hung fire.

The House of Lords in any event did not veto a number of measures likely to be of special appeal to workingmen, a group of voters many Conservatives sought to win, or rewin, to their side. In 1908 an eight-hour day for miners was established by law. For the first time since the repeal of the Elizabethan Apprenticeship Statutes, the hours worked by adult males were brought under governmental supervision. At the Board of Trade, David Lloyd George established a reputation for constructive statesmanship by sponsoring the first Census of Production in Britain (a comprehensive statistical survey of British industry) and by codifying merchant shipping legislation and reforming patent law. Lloyd George went on successfully to mediate a railway and shipyard strike and to supersede the chaos of private dock companies along the Thames with a single Port of London authority, virtually a measure of nationalization. In the meantime, Herbert Asquith at the Exchequer had introduced a precedent-breaking Old Age Pension scheme into the 1908 Budget. All British citizens over seventy years of age with a weekly income of ten shillings ($2.50) or less were to be entitled to a weekly pension of five shillings ($1.25) from the government. The sums were small, even by 1908 standards, but the scheme which immediately benefited five million citizens was at least a start; and for the first time the obligation of society to take care of its elderly citizens was accepted by the state as a matter of right rather than of charity.

Asquith, Churchill, and Lloyd George

By the time the Old Age Pension scheme had become law in 1908, Campbell-Bannerman was dead. His logical successor as Prime Minister, both in the eyes of King Edward VII and his Liberal party followers was Herbert Henry Asquith (1852–1928), a Yorkshireman of nonconformist origins who had worked as an obscure London lawyer, commuting each night to a small house in Hampstead, where he kept chickens in his back garden. He was elected to Parliament in 1886, became a Cabinet Minister six years later, and, three years after the death of his first wife, married Margot Tennant, a brilliant society girl. His pro-Government stand at the time of the Boer War had alienated many Liberals; but those wounds had healed by 1908, and Asquith had won a deserved reputation as a parliamentary debater and as Chancellor of the Exchequer. He never became a popular hero, perhaps because he lacked a certain imaginative flair which Britain's greatest Prime Ministers have all possessed. He did, however, have the ability to manage men; and he was so able an orator and could support a case with such lawyerlike precision and conviction that his predecessor nicknamed him "The Sledgehammer." At one public meeting Asquith spoke eloquently for an hour in support of the Government's Licensing Bill. He reinforced his case with reams of facts and strings of statistics. When an admiring woman spectator came up to him afterwards and asked whether she might have his notes as a souvenir, he handed her a scrap of paper on which were scrawled three words: "Too many pubs."

Asquith's Prime Ministership began in April 1908, and was

to be the longest continuous Prime Ministership since Lord Liverpool's a century before; but this was by no means obvious at the time. A recession had raised unemployment figures to close to ten percent. The government was losing by-elections right and left, and the tariff reformers were winning new converts. Conservative strategists felt increasingly confident that a new general election would return their party to power with a comfortable majority. Under the circumstances Asquith was ready to listen to two members of his Cabinet who were searching for ways of reviving the government's sagging fortunes.

One of these men was David Lloyd George, who now became Chancellor of the Exchequer; the other was Winston Churchill, who replaced Lloyd George as President of the Board of Trade. As a grandson of the eighth Duke of Marlborough, Churchill had had no youthful contact with lower-class life and was regarded by his erstwhile Conservative colleagues as a turncoat. But Churchill shared with Lloyd George a restless urge to seek out and apply new ideas, and in 1909 he discovered and pushed two far-reaching concepts. One of these was suggested to him by a young journalist and amateur sociologist named William Beveridge (1879–1963), who in 1909 published a book entitled *Unemployment*. Beveridge met Churchill at one of the many dinners Beatrice and Sidney Webb gave for intellectuals and politicians and convinced him that the Government should sponsor a network of Labour Exchanges, offices where the unemployed might register for jobs and employers might make known their needs. Churchill pushed a measure calling for such a network through Parliament in 1909 and appointed Beveridge the first Director of Labour Exchanges. The new offices could not as such create employment; but they could spare unemployed men the daily drudgery of walking the streets in search of work. Employers were similarly benefited. The Labour Exchanges were a still novel example of government offices whose purpose it was not to tax people or sell them things — like the post office — but to serve their welfare. They were also the necessary prelude to an even bolder proposal, the establishment of a scheme of unemployment insurance.

Churchill's other proposal dealt with the regulation of the "sweated" trades. A Royal Commission two decades earlier had deplored the fate of this new generation of domestic workers but nothing had been done. In 1908, however, a "Sweated Trades Exhibition," sponsored by the Liberal *Daily News* called attention anew to the fact that the fine clothes worn by a middle- or upper-class woman might well have been stitched by starving wretches slaving sixteen hours a day in East End cellars for less than a penny an hour. Churchill's Trade Boards Act of 1909 established government commissions for the tailoring, paper box, lace, and chain trade to set minimum wages and maximum hours.

In the meantime the new Chancellor of the Exchequer had not been idle at his post. Lloyd George, the orphaned son of a Welsh village schoolmaster, had been raised by a shoemaker uncle and was a genuine "man of the people" in a sense that Churchill could not be. He rose in politics as the champion of Welsh nonconformity, though in fact he had little religious faith, and as the symbol of militant teetotalism, though in private he enjoyed his glass of champagne. Lloyd George possessed the voice and the magnetic personality which could sweep an audience into an emotional frenzy. He outraged his Conservative opponents from the start by his public radicalism; yet in private negotiation, he could be an adept mediator and a mollifying persuader. It was Lloyd George's radicalism, however, which was most apparent in the renowned "People's Budget" of 1909.

Lloyd George had a number of purposes in constructing his budget. One was to raise £16 million extra in order to build additional warships and to pay for old age pensions and other social services. "This is a War Budget," he emphasized. "It is for raising money to wage an implacable war against poverty and squalidness." Secondly, he saw the Budget as a means of translating into action a longstanding Liberal campaign promise to deal with selfish Conservative landlords. Thirdly, he saw the Budget as a way of capturing the attention of the electorate by a dramatic measure of reform.

The Budget introduced a number of new taxes. A "supertax" to be paid by the very wealthy established the concept of progressive taxation for income as it had earlier been established for inheritance. Moreover, death duties were raised as high as 25 percent for those leaving estates of over a million pounds. A new tax on gasoline and automobiles was introduced for road-paving purposes. Most controversial of all was a tax on land, a 20 percent levy on the unearned increment of land value (to be paid whenever real estate changed hands) and a small duty on the capital value of undeveloped lands and minerals. It was these last taxes which raised the greatest outcry, if only because they would have entailed a precise valuation of all the landholdings in the country.[4] The Conservatives in the House of Commons resisted the budget every step of the way; but after seventy sittings and 554 divisions, the Budget was passed in November 1909 by a vote of 379–149. Three and a half weeks

---

[4] The most controversial tax, that on the unearned increment of land, proved to cost more to administer than it contributed in revenue. It was later repealed.

later the House of Lords overwhelmingly rejected the Budget, 350–75.

The Revolt of the Peers

It has sometimes been argued that Lloyd George introduced the Budget of 1909 with the purpose of goading the Lords into vetoing the measure. This seems unlikely, if only because Asquith, who supported his Chancellor of the Exchequer all the way, did not think the House of Lords would do anything so obviously unconstitutional. To deprive the government of revenue was tantamount to voting it out of office. Never since the Glorious Revolution had the House of Lords laid claim to such a power, and not since Gladstone had introduced the consolidated annual budget of 1861 had the upper House tampered with any revenue measure. By 1909, however, the peers had become so fearful of the threat to their purses and Conservatives generally had become so frightened by the thought of socialism, that they did not heed the consequences. Dozens of peers who had never bothered to attend the House suddenly appeared to cast their vote.

Once the prospect of a House of Lords veto loomed, Lloyd George was happy enough to goad the peers on. "The peers may decree a revolution," he declared, "but the people will direct it. If they begin, issues will be raised that they little dream of.... It will be asked why 500 ordinary men, chosen accidentally from among the unemployed, should override the judgment—the deliberate judgment—of millions of people." Immediately after the unprecedented veto, Prime Minister Asquith moved and carried in the House of Commons a resolution declaring the peers' action "a breach of the Constitution and a usurpation of the rights of the Commons." Shortly thereafter he asked the king to dissolve Parliament. A new general election was to resolve the conflict of "The Peers against the People."

The key issue was the Budget, but the future role of the House of Lords was involved as well, and Lloyd George continued to speak scornfully of the qualifications for the upper House. "No testimonials are required. There are no credentials. They do not even need a medical certificate. They need not be sound, either in body or in mind. They only require a certificate of birth, just to prove that they are the first of the litter. You would not choose a spaniel on these principles." The Conservatives, in turn, charged the Liberals with a "conspiracy" to substitute single-chamber government for Britain's traditional system and renewed their championship of Chamberlain's policy of "tariff reform."

The results were disappointing to both major parties:

Liberals	275
Conservatives	273
Irish Nationalists	82
Labour Party	40

In one sense the Liberal position had been upheld. The parties that wished to limit the power of the House of Lords, the Liberals and the Irish and the Labourites, had a large majority. Yet it was clear that Asquith could not act alone; he had to depend on the support of the smaller parties. The only way to assure Irish cooperation for the Budget was to promise a new push for Irish Home Rule. The only way he could win labor support was to propose further social legislation. The Conservatives had staged a remarkable revival, but they too felt frustrated. Only a year before, they had expected to win the forthcoming general election; even after the election of January 1910 they could not foresee that Asquith might manage to keep a Liberal Cabinet in office for more than half a decade more.

The Government's immediate project was to enact the controversial Lloyd George Budget. With Irish help, it easily passed the Commons, and a considerably chastened House of Lords accepted it without a division after a single day's debate. Willingness to accept a "People's Budget" was not sufficient, however, to stave off constitutional nemesis, for the House of Commons quickly passed a Parliament Bill to limit the powers of the House of Lords permanently. Henceforth the upper House might delay money bills (including budgets) for at most one month. Other bills were to be limited to a delay of two years and to become law without the approval of the Lords provided that three successive sessions of the Commons had passed the same measure. Finally the bill required a general election at least every five years, rather than every seven years.

The question of the hour became whether the House of Lords would acquiesce in its demotion to second-class status or whether it would fight. Many peers suddenly became interested in alternate schemes of reform which would have retained the power of the House of Lords but changed its structure: that the right to vote be restricted to certain peers only; that a given number of life peers be added to the hereditary peers, etc. None of these proposals came to fruition.

Yet a number of Liberal and Conservative leaders were disposed to seek a compromise solution to the constitutional dilemma, and their opportunity came in the summer of 1910.

King Edward VII had died unexpectedly in April; the new king, George V, called upon the leaders of the two major parties to seek a mutually acceptable compromise proposal for the sake of the national interest. A consequent series of secret conferences came close to resolving the crisis. Provisional agreement was reached on a procedure for settling disputes between the two houses which would have involved joint sittings for most disputed bills and popular referenda for constitutional changes.

The conferences were going so well, in fact, that Lloyd George, switching from the role of radical agitator to persuasive manipulator of power, proposed a Liberal-Conservative coalition ministry in which Asquith would move to the House of Lords and continue as Prime Minister while Balfour would lead the House of Commons. In return for Conservative support for their social reforms, the Liberals would accept a Conservative proposal for compulsory military service (in emulation of Continental armies) and promise to consider tariff reform. Ultimately, both the attempt to evolve a compromise plan for dealing with the House of Lords and Lloyd George's surprising coalition proposal proved abortive. Balfour was too fearful that his party would lose its identity and the Liberals too worried that such a coalition would destroy any chance of Home Rule for Ireland.

The Conference having broken down, and the House of Lords having defeated the Parliament Bill, Asquith advised the king to dissolve Parliament and call another election, the second within the year. The specific issue presented to the electorate was whether the House of Lords was to be permanently curbed or not. If the Liberal Ministry were to be returned to power, the king promised to create – if necessary – a sufficient number of peers to ensure the passage of the Parliament Bill by the House of Lords. This was an eventuality King George V wished desperately to avoid, but he considered himself to have no constitutional alternative. For the moment, however, the king's promise was kept secret.

The second election proved in many respects a replica of the first. For the Liberals the crucial problem was the necessity of curbing the authority of the House of Lords; for the Conservatives, it was the danger of Home Rule for Ireland, which seemed sure to follow. The Labour Party had its own interests – specifically the Osborne Judgment of 1909 in which the House of Lords (in its role of supreme court) had held illegal the contribution of trade union funds to political candidates and to Members of Parliament. As a result, the party had almost no funds and some of its M.P.s who had no income of their own, were in particularly dire straits. There is considerable evidence that while such issues very much concerned the politicians at Westminster, the average voter was becoming apathetic. Although a number of seats changed hands, the overall results of the election of December 1910 were almost identical to those of the previous January:

Liberals	272
Conservatives	272
Irish Nationalists	84
Labour Party	42

According to the traditional rules of politics, the Conservatives should now have conceded the battle. But they refused to recognize the reality of their defeat. They did not know that the king had already given Asquith a pledge to create enough peers to end their control of the House of Lords. Many of them felt the Liberals were somehow "cheating" by relying for their majority upon two such splinter groups as the Labour Party and Irish Nationalists. Certain Conservatives, convinced that their leaders—A. J. Balfour in the Commons and Lord Lansdowne in the Lords—were not providing sufficiently vigorous party leadership, hoped that continued resistance to the Parliament Bill would necessitate yet a third general election.

"The House of Lords," Lloyd George had observed in 1908, "is not the watchdog of the Constitution; it is Mr. Balfour's poodle." [5] Now the "poodle" began to bite its erstwhile master, as a group of Conservatives appeared who ignored Balfour's advice and preferred if necessary "to die in the last ditch." "The Ditchers," under the eighty-eight-year-old Lord Halsbury, stood firm against the "Hedgers," who preferred the retention by the House of Lords of a suspensive veto to being swamped by four hundred new peers.

The "Ditchers" did not really believe that Asquith would dare to recommend the mass creation of peers; but the Prime Minister was serious and had secretly prepared a list which included some of Britain's most eminent men—Bertrand Russell, then most noted as mathematician; Thomas Hardy, the novelist; Gilbert Murray, the philosopher; G. P. Gooch and J. A. Spender, the historians; and J. M. Barrie, the playwright. Plans were even being prepared by the Government's First Commissioner of Works to enlarge the Lords' chamber so as to seat the new peers. The crisis reached its climax when the "Ditchers" emasculated the Parliament Bill with amendments. Asquith privately informed the Conservative leaders that he would ask

---

[5] Roy Jenkins' *Mr. Balfour's Poodle* (London, 1954) is a comprehensive and readable account of the whole constitutional crisis of 1909–11.

the king to fulfill his promise unless the amendments were dropped; but when he rose in the House of Commons to move the rejection of those amendments, outraged Conservative M.P.s greeted his motion with a chorus of shouts, catcalls, and denunciations. For the first time in British history, a House of Commons refused to let a Prime Minister speak, and after half an hour of tumult the Speaker suspended the sitting. Balfour had earlier counseled the Conservative peers simply to abstain and let the Liberal peers pass the controversial bill; but as the "Ditchers" remained adamant, he now felt forced to ask some Conservatives to vote for the measure they despised. The final vote took place during a heat wave on August 10, 1911. Outside, the temperature stood at 97—it was the hottest day in the records of the London weather bureau—and the temperature inside was even hotter. The outcome was uncertain until the last moment, but in the end the Bill was passed, 131–114. Every Liberal peer had been mustered, and eventually the Liberals were joined by twenty-nine Liberal Unionist peers, the two archbishops, and eleven of thirteen bishops. The "Ditchers" had been defeated and no mass creation of peers was required.

The Twentieth-Century Constitution

The Parliament Act of 1911 had an important effect both upon the nation's constitution and upon all of its political parties. It belongs with the Reform Acts of 1832, 1867, and 1884 as a key measure which helped make Britain a political democracy. The statute made a matter of law what had long been a matter of practice, the preeminence of the House of Commons; yet despite the fears of many Conservatives, it did not lead to the total abolition of the traditional two-chamber structure of the government. The House of Lords retained its powers to amend, its suspensive veto, and its position as a reservoir of Cabinet members.

The constitutional crisis had also shown once again that if the monarch were to remain above politics, he would have to abide by the decisions of the Cabinet which possessed the confidence of a parliamentary majority. The monarch retained in practice three rights—"the right to be consulted, the right to encourage, the right to warn." Half a century before, Walter Bagehot had so defined the limits of monarchical authority, but George V was the first English king to have read Bagehot or to think of himself as a constitutional and limited monarch who reigned but did not rule.[6] The change has been aptly described:

---

[6] Harold Nicolson, *King George V* (London, 1951).

> In the eighteenth century the prime minister got his importance from the fact that he was the only person in the realm who had the right of constant access to the monarch; today the monarch gets his importance from the fact that he is the only person in the realm who has the right of constant access to the prime minister.

The one other right which a British monarch retains is that of nominating a new Prime Minister when the dominant party in Parliament is suddenly deprived of its leader by death or resignation.

With the passage of the Parliament Act and the decision made during the same year to pay all members of Parliament £400 annually, all but one of the Chartist demands of the 1830s and 1840s had been substantially accomplished. Even the last, annual elections, had been tried in 1910; but neither M.P.s nor the electorate saw great value in repeating that experiment. The House of Commons of 1911 was made up much less of individually independent members than of members pledged to support their party. As a result it was no longer so much the House of Commons which controlled the Cabinet as it was the Cabinet which now controlled the Commons. Admittedly, ministers still had to justify their policies to members of their own party, but the possibility of Parliament voting "no confidence" in a ministry had now almost disappeared. The odium of party disloyalty was too great an electoral handicap. Thus by 1911 the real check upon a ministry was less the House of Commons than the electorate, which could and did exercise its power firmly but intermittently.

The Prime Minister of 1911 remained in theory no more than first among equals; the concept of collective Cabinet responsibility remained. Yet insofar as the Prime Minister had a dominant voice in the choosing and placing of his colleagues, he obviously approached the powers of an American President; and insofar as he was not only chief executive but by definition leader of the majority in the legislature, his authority was often more effective than that of an American President. Some Prime Ministers saw their role primarily as chairman of the board and spoke little. Others saw themselves as leaders of the nation in all but ceremonial matters which could safely be left to a figurehead monarch.

The Parliament Act of 1911 had its more immediate political repercussions as well. In the Conservative Party the irate "Ditchers" launched a "B.M.G." campaign: "Balfour Must Go." As always the somewhat detached philosopher, Balfour refused to combat the movement, and in November 1911 he resigned as party leader. As matters turned out, his political career was far from over. His successor was Andrew Bonar Law (1858–1923), a Member of Parliament for eleven years who had been born in Canada, raised in Scotland, and had never held ministerial office. Under Law, a morose and solitary man, the mood of violence which had crept into the Conservative Party was to grow even stronger.

As for the Liberals, they had to pay off their political debts. The Lords had been chastised and chastened only with the full cooperation of the 42 Labour and 84 Irish Nationalist M.P.s, and each group now demanded its reward, the first in the form of social legislation, the second in the form of Home Rule. With Lloyd George still Chancellor of the Exchequer and Winston Churchill now Home Secretary, the ministry introduced a bill calling for two precedent-breaking social reforms, national health insurance and unemployment insurance. Both proposals were in part the consequence of the Poor Law Commission Report of 1909, which was published after four years of hearings. Both the Majority and Minority Reports recommended extensive changes in the operations of the 1834 Poor Law. The Minority Report, written by the Webbs, indeed proposed the scrapping of the Poor Law concept altogether in favor of separate government-sponsored social services dealing with illness, unemployment, and old age. The old workhouse, whose conditions were by definition to be worse than those which the lowest paid wage earner could afford, was to give way to "the national minimum" below which no citizen was to be allowed to fall. Neither set of recommendations was, for the time being, put into effect; but the Minority Report gave additional sanction to the establishment of state services.

In setting up a national health service, Lloyd George was also much impressed by the successful operation of a similar scheme in Germany. Since a host of voluntary societies already provided members of the working class with sickness and death benefits, Lloyd George decided to incorporate these societies into a national scheme which would apply to all workers who earned less than £160 ($800) a year. Each employee would contribute 4d. a week, each employer 3d., and the national government 2d. In return the employee would obtain free medical care from the doctor on whose panel he was enrolled and weekly sick pay when he was out of work because of illness. The act passed Parliament with relatively little difficulty, though there was great opposition for a time from the employers of domestic servants and from the British Medical Association. The doctors were soon won over by the fact that the Government was prepared to pay them more per panel patient than voluntary societies had ever done. The act applied almost immediately to fourteen million people, one third of the population, and in due course became the basis for the far more comprehensive National Health Service established in 1948.

The other part of the National Insurance Act of 1911 provided the first national program of unemployment insurance. In contrast to old age pensions and health insurance, Britain was in this matter blazing a new trail rather than following the example of Germany, and the project was seen at the time as "a risky adventure into the unknown." For the moment it was limited to some 2,250,000 workers in the construction, engineering, shipbuilding, and vehicle building industries. The unemployment insurance fund was created by equal contributions from employer, employee, and the state. In return, an insured worker who lost his job could expect a weekly payment of 7s. for up to fifteen weeks a year. Although the contributory principle at the time bitterly split the small Labour Party — Ramsay MacDonald favored it and Philip Snowden wished all expenses to come from the National Exchequer — the principle of dividing costs among employer, employee, and state was to become the basis of all future advances to the welfare state.

The National Insurance Act of 1911 proved to be the last major social reform enacted by the Liberal Government, but there were a number of minor measures. The Osborne Judgment of 1909 was partially repealed by a Trades Unions Act of 1913 which provided that trade unions might collect money for political purposes if they placed it in a separate fund and if they gave each member the option of "contracting out." Shop Assistants (i.e. retail clerks), a class of workers who lacked union organization and were often greatly exploited, were given a compulsory half day off in addition to Sunday; thus arose the British custom of an "early closing day" (not necessarily on Saturday) for all stores. An act of 1912 provided a compulsory minimum wage for miners. Another Liberal measure, one more in line with nineteenth-century tradition, was the Welsh Disestablishment Bill of 1912. The purpose of the bill was to deprive the Church of England of its special privileges and some of its property in Wales, where its adherents numbered at most only one quarter of the population. The measure passed the Commons but was until 1920 halted in the Lords.

Suffragettes and Syndicalists

By 1912 the dynamism of reform was exhausted. The Liberal Party had taken a series of giant strides along the road to the welfare state, but much of the party remained middle class in leadership and Victorian in inclination and viewed the whole social reform program with deep misgivings. Moreover, the time and energy of the Liberal Cabinet was increasingly involved in the attempt to preserve law and order in the face of a growing number of civil disobedience campaigns. The catcalls and clamor that had greeted Asquith in the House of Commons during the debate on the Parliament Bill seemed to herald an era of militancy and even violence in which at times all precepts of Victorian respectability and moderation were thrown to the winds. Beneath a surface gaity, the "Revolt of the Peers" was followed by comparable revolts by suffragettes, syndicalist union leaders, and Irish Ulstermen until these domestic tempests were suddenly submerged within that far greater and more frightful storm of violence called World War.[7]

In some ways the most sensational, if not the most serious, problem confronting the Liberal Government was how to deal with the suffragettes and their demand for political equality between the sexes. The National Union of Women's Suffrage Societies dated back to the 1860s and had won in the late nineteenth century a number of successes on the level of local government. The Women's Social and Political Union, founded in 1903 by Mrs. Emmeline Pankhurst (1857–1928), the widow of a Manchester doctor and a onetime member of Keir Hardie's Independent Labor Party, proved to be a far more militant organization. By 1908 a clear distinction had grown up between the respectable "suffragists" and the bellicose "suffragettes" led by Mrs. Pankhurst and her daughters Sylvia and Christabel.

In 1905 they began a regular program of interrupting Liberal speakers with the cry "Votes for Women." All Liberals were heckled, those who openly supported women's suffrage, such as Sir Edward Grey and Lloyd George, and those who seemed opposed, such as Asquith. The heckling was limited to Liberals on the grounds that so long as the Liberals constituted the Government they alone could provide women's suffrage. The difficulty faced by the Liberals was that so long as the vote was still granted on the basis of the ownership or rental of property, then to give the vote to women would mean enfranchising only a minority (women property-owners) who would in all likelihood proceed to vote Conservative. The alternative was a bill to enfranchise all adults equally, but for this there was little popular pressure. A number of suffrage bills passed the House of Commons between 1907 and 1913, but none was enacted into law.

---

[7] George Dangerfield provides a penetrating, if perhaps unduly gloomy, account of the era in *The Strange Death of Liberal England* (London, 1935). Also relevant is Roger Fulford's *Votes for Women* (London, 1961).

After 1910 the tactics of the suffragettes grew more violent. They broke the windows in No. 10 Downing Street and embarked on an orgy of window smashing in London's shopping districts. "The argument of broken glass is the most valuable argument in modern politics," explained Mrs. Pankhurst. They chained themselves to railings in Parliament Square. They dropped acid into mail boxes. They slashed pictures in public art galleries. From her Paris hideout Christabel Pankhurst began in 1912 a campaign of arson. Empty houses in different parts of the country were burned; so were several churches, a school, and a railway station. When arrested and put into jail, many suffragettes would go on hunger strikes; and the government, anxious not to have them die in jail, employed for a time the questionable method of forced feeding.

Although such aggressive tactics initially inspirited the women's suffrage cause and helped the passage in 1907 of an act making women eligible to serve as town and county councillors, eventually they hindered the cause. To the most militant suffragettes, like the young lady who threw herself before the horses on Derby Day 1911 as a voluntary martyr, the vote was a badge of equality rather than the means to any particular end. Riotous agitation came in fact not only to dominate the cause but to contradict it, for possession of the vote presupposes the rule of free persuasion. Yet the suffragette leaders proclaimed by word and deed that the way to get results was through violent action. "The militants will rejoice when victory comes," wrote Christabel Pankhurst, "and yet, mixed with joy, will be regret that the most glorious chapter in women's history is closed and the militant fight over—over, when so many have not yet known the exaltation, the rapture of battle. . . ."

If the combative suffragettes were a nuisance to the government, the mass labor strikes of 1911 and 1912 threatened the entire economy of the country. Here too a mood of violence and frustration was evident, frustration with the failure of wages to keep up with rising prices, irritation with the peaceful and seemingly ineffectual methods of the Labour Party. For the time being, a number of trade union leaders came to prefer direct action to parliamentary pressure. Some of them, men like Tom Mann of the engineers and A. J. Cook of the miners, became convinced syndicalists. They saw the trade union not as a pressure group but as a potential unit of government. They saw the class struggle as a war which should be fought with a series of militant strikes all leading up to a general strike which would bring the capitalist parliamentary system to an end and somehow bring into being a syndicalist utopia. Orthodox socialists distrusted the syndicalists, and most of the trade union members did not fully understand the ultimate aims of their leaders. They did prove, however, increasingly sympathetic to the appeal to violence. Whether the motive for strikes was wages or forced unionization of the unorganized workers or sympathy with the grievances of other laborers mattered little. Often, indeed, strikes began in defiance of the national union leadership.

In 1910 a strike of Lancashire cotton workers, which began over a question involving the duties of one man, idled 120,000 workers. A strike by a handful of miners in South Wales who were dissatisfied with the rate of pay on a particular seam of coal resulted in a "sympathy" walkout by 30,000 miners. A seamen's strike in Liverpool during the summer of 1911 led to rioting. The army was called in; strikers stoned the troops and burned trains; two men were killed and two hundred wounded. During the same summer Britain experienced its first general railway strike. Late in the year, a weavers' strike idled 126,000 workers for a month, and in March 1912 a general miners' strike involved 850,000 men. This particular dispute was finally settled by an act of Parliament setting up district conferences to decide on minimum wages along lines the government had proposed before the strike began. Later in 1912 a dock strike began on the technical issue of whether one particular foreman had the right to work as a regular union hand. The strike evoked little public sympathy and collapsed after six weeks. The year 1913 saw the organization of a "Triple Alliance" of miners, railway men, and transport workers, each of which continued to have its list of grievances and the leaders of which looked ahead to a general strike late in 1914.

While some of these strikes were successful in winning specific gains, others were not. Still others demonstrated the unwieldiness of a strike involving hundreds of thousands of men in settling fairly technical contract details. The union leaders often lacked both the freedom and the flexibility to bargain effectively. The strikes did, however, reinforce a sense of working-class consciousness and, since the rate of unemployment was low, they went hand in hand with a steady growth of trade union membership. Between 1910 and 1914 membership in unions affiliated with the Trades Union Congress (and almost all were) increased from 2,300,000 to 4,000,000.

Ireland Again

Of all the pre-World War I revolts, it was the Irish question which by 1914 represented the greatest threat to parliamentary government and which brought Britain closer to genuine civil war than it had been at any time since the seventeenth century.

The issue had slumbered since Gladstone's Second Home Rule Bill had been defeated by the House of Lords in 1893. The Irish Nationalist party had remained strong in Parliament and, under the leadership of John Redmond (1856–1918), it waited patiently for the day when the Liberals would be powerful enough to overawe the House of Lords. In 1911 that day seemed at hand; and during the parliamentary session following the passage of the act curbing the upper house, Asquith introduced and the House of Commons approved a Home Rule Bill. The Lords refused to pass it, but they could only delay it for two years. It was clear to everyone that in 1914 Home Rule would automatically become law.

By 1914, however, the question was no longer simply one of Home Rule but of what to do about Ulster, the counties of northeastern Ireland in which non-Catholics were dominant. A fanatical lawyer named Edward Carson (1854–1935) organized an Ulster Unionist Council which proclaimed a provisional government in case Home Rule became law. On his knees in Belfast's City Hall he signed an Ulster Covenant – in emulation of the Scots Covenant of 1637 – binding himself to use "all means which may be found necessary to defeat the present conspiracy to set up a Home Rule Parliament in Ireland." Almost half a million Ulstermen signed the document. Unauthorized military drilling began. It took the Liberal Government some time to realize that if Home Rule for Ireland became a reality, it might have to be defended by armed force. The Conservative Party, moreover, was encouraging rather than discouraging talk of violence and military resistance in Ulster. "There are things stronger than Parliamentary majorities," declared the party's leader, Bonar Law. "I can imagine no length of resistance to which Ulster can go in which I should not be prepared to support them."

By the spring of 1914 the Liberal Government began to toy with a plan permitting the Ulster counties to "contract out" of Home Rule for a period of six years; but for Carson this concession was not enough. Then the Government decided on a show of force, only to be met with the most serious of all the examples of insubordination, violence, and disrespect for authority and order – "mutiny" within the army itself. A group of officers in Ireland resigned their commissions rather than be faced with the possibility of having to fight the Ulster Loyalists. It was becoming desperately clear that Home Rule which for so many years had been a parliamentary problem was now, on the threshold of its enactment, passing beyond the ability of Parliament to enforce.

Irish Nationalists in the South now began to emulate the Ulster volunteers in the North. Both sides smuggled in arms from abroad, and although Home Rule became law in May 1914 its precise implementation remained in doubt during the spring and summer of that year. Violence continued to flare in Ireland as a conference of party leaders sought a compromise solution. Carson demanded the permanent exclusion of Ulster from an autonomous Ireland. Redmond, his authority among Irish Nationalists already weakened by his attempts to cooperate loyally with the Liberal Government, could not consent to any permanent partition. As still another conference session broke up in deadlock and the members rose to go, the Foreign Secretary announced that he had just received bad news – the text of an ultimatum which the Austrian Government had sent to Serbia the day before. The specter of a general European war suddenly darkened the conference chamber.

Thus the rocky road toward the welfare state and toward the fulfillment of the uncompleted tasks of nineteenth-century liberalism came into sudden conjunction with the road to war. The "revolts" of the peers, the women, the workers, and the Irish (the last involving an extraordinary degree of scorn for parliamentary procedure by the Conservative Party) were all to be put in the shade by the conflagration of the next four years. They reflected nonetheless a widespread resentment of authority and a deliberate flouting of accepted mores and canons of respectability by large numbers of British citizens. Yet in the midst of these disturbances, in an unsystematic trial and error manner, the Liberal Government had instituted a series of far-reaching social reforms. Their potential scope was not always appreciated at the time, and even their immediate benefits tended to be downgraded. But in the retrospect of half a century these constructive steps loom larger than do either the surface glitter and stability of upper-class Edwardian society or the often irrational revolts against authority which seem at first glance to dominate the pre-World War I domestic scene.

Chapter 13

The Road to War

In the retrospect of more than half a century, 1914 remains preeminent as a demarcation point, as the year which saw the beginning of the First World War, the war that was to destroy the "old order" in Europe, the war that was to topple four empires and bring in its wake untold misery and destruction as well as death to nine million men and injury to twenty-two million others. Its long-range consequences were to include the rise of totalitarian dictatorships in Europe, the awakening of militant nationalism in Asia and Africa, a second world war, and a cold war. To call the war of 1914–18 the First World War is technically misleading. The wars of the eighteenth century—the War of the Spanish Succession, the War of the Austrian Succession, the Seven Years' War, and the War of the American Revolution—had all been fought on at least three continents as well as the high seas. It was the lapse of a century since the last world war—the Napoleonic—and the achievement in the meantime of an unprecedented potential for military destruction which caused Europeans of 1914 to look upon their world war as unique.[1]

---

[1] The causes of World War I are discussed in thousands of books. Luigi Albertini provides the most detailed account based on the fullest use of government archives in *The Origins of the War of 1914* (Eng. trans., 3 vols., London, 1952–57). This topic is taken up with various degrees of insight in the books by Ensor, Strang, Taylor, and Seton-Watson referred to earlier. E. L. Woodward's *Great Britain and the German Navy* (London, 1935) is relevant. So are the memoirs of Sir

The causes of World War I have been analyzed and disputed by at least two generations of historians; and while this chapter justifiably concentrates upon Britain's role, the wider problem of causation cannot be avoided. There is much about the immediate causes of the war, like the assassination of Archduke Franz Ferdinand, which partakes of the fortuitous. Yet the decisions made by the chancellories of the great powers during the last days of July and the first days of August 1914 can be explained only in the light of assumptions and preconceptions which went back in some cases half a decade, in others half a century. Britain's ultimate entry involved elements — such as concern with the Low Countries and with the European balance of power — which went back half a millenium.

The Web of Diplomacy

As recently as the 1890s, Britain had seemed relatively aloof from the power blocs into which continental Europe was organizing itself. The extent of such "isolation" can easily be exaggerated, however. Britain's interest in the Near East, shown in 1878 at the Congress of Berlin, her involvement with the great powers on the Egyptian Debt Commission, and the secret Mediterranean Agreements with Austria and Italy in the 1880s all demonstrated Britain's involvement with the Continent. Every diplomat prefers to be a free agent, but at times the pressure of national security seems to dictate a more or less binding alliance with another power. It was fear of French military revenge (a fear made plausible by the forcible takeover of Alsace-Lorraine in 1871) which prompted Bismarck's Triple Alliance with Austria (1879) and Italy (1882). It was a French desire to escape diplomatic isolation and a suspicion, shared by Russia, of British ambitions overseas which prompted the Franco-Russian Alliance of 1894. The desire to escape binding commitments in unforeseen circumstances caused British statesmen to eschew such alliances until a number of events of the mid and late 1890s led in due course to a reappraisal.

What G. M. Young called "that passionate jealousy of England which for a generation was the most widely diffused emotion in Europe" was brought home to Englishmen by a variety of incidents: the Venezuela Boundary Dispute of 1895, which

Edward Grey (Lord Grey of Fallodon), *Twenty-Five Years*, and G. M. Trevelyan's *Lord Grey of Fallodon* (London, 1937). Barbara Tuchman provides a highly illuminating and readable account of the immediate antecedents of the war in *The Guns of August* (New York, 1962) (Paperbound).

aroused widespread anti-British sentiment in the United States; the telegram sent by Emperor William II to President Kruger at the time of the Jameson Raid; the Fashoda incident which brought France and England to the brink of war; and finally, the Boer War. Each demonstrated anew the perils of diplomatic isolation.

In 1901, Joseph Chamberlain grasped the bull by the horns and publicly proposed an alliance with Germany (and, if possible, with the United States as well) as the most logical step for Britain to take in view of her longstanding rivalry with France and Russia. His suggestion was but the latest of a number of approaches in such a direction. Bismarck had hoped to attach Britain to his Triple Alliance in the 1880s but had been unable to overcome Britain's fears that any such alliance would commit her to support Austrian ambitions in the Balkans. In 1901 it was the German government which hesitated to agree to any arrangements which did not involve Britain's complete adherence to their Triple Alliance. It did not wish to provoke unnecessary antagonism toward Germany on the part of Russia, Britain's perennial rival in the Near East and along the Indian frontier. Later historians were to criticize German successors to Bismarck for successively antagonizing first Russia, the world's greatest land empire, and then Britain, the world's greatest sea empire. Yet German diplomats remained confident in 1901 that Britain's conflicts with Russia and France were too deep-seated to make possible any diplomatic outcome other than an ultimate British adherence to Germany's Triple Alliance on German terms.

That the attitude of the British public had undergone a fundamental change was shown by the relatively cool reception which Chamberlain's proposal of an Anglo-German entente received in British newspapers. There had been too many examples of German hostility in Africa and in the Near East, where German diplomats and a German military mission had supplanted their British counterparts at Constantinople. German opinion might well have proved equally hostile, for nowhere on the Continent did envy of Britain stir more breasts than in Germany. The Emperor was representative of many of his countrymen in his frequently expressed feeling that German industrial and military power had thus far failed to elicit the worldwide respect and recognition which they merited. Germany had been expanding its markets throughout the world with little difficulty, but Britain retained the largest colonial empire and possessed the mightiest navy, London remained the financial capital of the world, and an occasion such as Victoria's Diamond Jubilee conveyed an impression of romantic glory which William's Berlin could not match. It was this sense of psychological rather than any specifically material frustration which caused German publicist Friedrich Naumann to declare in 1900: "If there is anything certain in the history of the world, it is the future outbreak of a world war, i.e. a war fought by those who seek to deliver themselves from England."

A consciousness of diplomatic isolation and an awareness that an alliance with Germany was impractical led Britain in the course of the first years of the twentieth century to resolve various overseas anxieties which from time to time had threatened war with France and Russia. Yet the first break with diplomatic isolation came not in the form of an understanding with a European nation but in the form of an alliance with a country which a generation before would not have been regarded as a "power" at all, much less a great one, Japan. The last years of the nineteenth century had brought a disintegration of the "open door" trading policy which Britain had fostered in China. As a result of the Opium War of 1839–42 and the Treaty of Tientsin of 1859, major Chinese ports had been opened to the commerce not only of Britain but also of the major Continental nations and the United States. Yet for a long time British trade was preponderant, and partly as a consequence, Japan, Russia, Germany, and France during the 1890s all began to seek more permanent concessions (involving railroad building and mining) and to look forward to the eventual division of all China into foreign "spheres of influence." The British, though deploring the tendency, joined in it by securing what was in effect a "sphere of influence" over the Yangtse Valley.

The alliance with Britain in 1902 was welcomed by the Japanese in that Britain, unlike Russia, France, and Germany, had not sought to deprive Japan of the spoils of its military victory over China in 1895. Britain had, moreover, been the first European power to give up its claims of "extraterritoriality" (special judicial treatment for its citizens) in Japan. The treaty provided for mutual aid if either nation were attacked in the Far East by two other powers. In thus engaging in advance to take military action under circumstances not precisely foreseen at the time the treaty was signed, Britain was clearly embarking along a new diplomatic path. The immediate result was to enable the British government to feel more secure about its interests in the Far East and thus to withdraw most of its naval forces from the area. For Japan the treaty was an assurance that if rivalry between Russia and Japan over Manchuria led to war, Russia's ally France would be deterred from entering on the Czar's side.

The Russo-Japanese War of 1904–1905 fulfilled this expectation. It also had two other results which were ultimately less helpful to British interests. By defeating the world's greatest land power, the Japanese demonstrated to nonwhite peoples throughout Asia that European overlordship rested more on temporary technological advantage than on innate racial superiority. No other single event may have done more to awaken the hopes of Asian nationalists under Western domination. Secondly, by frustrating her ambitions in the Far East, the war rekindled Russian ambitions in the Balkans, thereby making more likely a conflict with Austria which might well involve all Europe.

At the very time that the British government was successfully mending diplomatic fences in the Orient, it embarked upon a similar endeavor with the United States. The Venezuela Boundary Dispute of 1895 having been settled, essentially to British satisfaction, by arbitration, the government sought to forestall all future quarrels which might injure Anglo-American relations. Unlike other European powers, Britain remained friendly to the United States during the Spanish-American War; and in the Hay-Pauncefote Treaty of 1901, the Salisbury government gave up all claims to a share in an American-built Panama Canal. The following year, when the Venezuelan dictator, Cipriano Castro, defaulted on debt payments, British ships joined German ships in a naval blockade of Caracas; but unlike the German ships, they withdrew in deference to the American fear that such action violated the Monroe Doctrine. A year later the British representative on an international commission to resolve a long-slumbering dispute concerning the boundary between Alaska and British Columbia bent over backwards to side with the American as opposed to the Canadian position.

The ultimate justification for such a pro-American policy was the belief that the fundamental interests of the two countries were broadly the same and that their relations should not therefore be marred by minor irritants. No formal alliance resulted, but at least one United States Senator spoke of an *entente cordiale* between the two countries as early as 1898. Early in the new century the British naval squadron was withdrawn from the Caribbean Sea, leaving it essentially an American lake, and by the time World War I broke out in 1914, the two countries could look back upon a generation of friendly relations.

The Triple Entente

In the search for friends in a diplomatically uncertain world, it was apparent that eventually Great Britain would have to choose between Germany and France. Though to many Englishmen France remained the historic national enemy and to many Frenchmen Britain remained "perfidious Albion," diplomats in both countries were prepared to reexamine old assumptions. For a man such as French Foreign Minister Delcassé, fear of Germany in Europe took precedence over fear of Britain in Africa; and in 1900 he commenced a deliberate policy of reconciliation. In his English counterpart, Lord Lansdowne, he found a receptive spirit who arranged in 1903 for a state visit to France by King Edward VII. This was a task the monarch found most congenial for, unlike his mother, he had always been a Francophile. The royal visitor's initial reception in Paris was cold. "The French don't like us," remarked a worried aide. "Why should they?" replied the king, bowing and smiling unperturbedly from his carriage. He made numerous public appearances and everywhere made graceful and tactful speeches in French about his friendship and admiration for his hosts. By the end of his visit a notable change of attitude had come about, and Parisian crowds were shouting "Vive notre roi!" [2]

King Edward's visit paved the way for the Anglo-French Entente of 1904. In return for acknowledging Britain's paramount role in Egypt, France received a similar British recognition of her position in Morocco, a state which like China and the Ottoman Empire seemed to be on the eve of disintegration. After long negotiation, other disputes, ranging the world from Madagascar to Siam and from the islands of the South Pacific to the Newfoundland fisheries, were resolved in similarly amicable fashion. Although Delcassé's ultimate hope was that the entente would align Britain with France diplomatically, this was not Lansdowne's expectation. He viewed the treaty as a settling of old differences—comparable to the Heligoland Treaty with Germany (1890) and the Hay-Pauncefote Treaty (1901) with the United States—and not as a step toward an Anglo French alliance. That the entente could lead, however, in the direction of alliance was made clear the following year, when Emperor William II of Germany challenged the French right to establish a protectorate over Morocco by making a flamboyant visit to the port of Tangier. He succeeded in forcing the resignation of Delcassé as Foreign Minister and compelled the French to let the future of Morocco be determined by an international conference at Algeciras, Spain. The Germans hoped that their diplomatic initiative would once again drive a wedge between Britain and France, but in this expectation they were disappointed; for Britain gave France strong diplomatic support, and the new entente was materially strengthened.

---

[2] Sir Edward Magnus, *King Edward VII* (London, 1964).

By the time the Algeciras Conference met in 1906, Balfour's Conservative Government had fallen and Lansdowne's post as Foreign Secretary had been taken over by the Liberal Sir Edward Grey (1862–1933), who was to hold it for the next ten fateful years. Grey too looked upon the entente with France more as the settlement of past differences than as the prelude to a firm alliance, and he repeatedly explained to the French that no British government could undertake a binding committment to France. Parliament would not accept such an agreement. Impressed by the Morocco crisis of 1905–06, Grey did, however, come to look upon Germany as the greatest potential European troublemaker; and he foresaw the possibility that Britain might in the indefinite future find it necessary to ally herself with France in a war against Germany. If such a war should ever come about, Grey believed that Britain should have the option either to aid France or to stand aside. Should the decision be to help France, such aid would only be meaningful if French and British generals had held secret conversations to discuss methods of possible military cooperation. Such confidential discussions began in 1906. They were intended as no more than the means to one of several possible ends, but they created in many English minds the impression that Britain was in effect allied with France, and they undoubtedly encouraged the French to believe that in a showdown with Germany, Britain would side with her channel neighbor.

Once Britain was diplomatically associated with France, it was only a matter of time before she found it expedient to settle her international differences with France's continental ally, Russia. The rivalry between Britain and Russia in the Near East, on the Indian frontier, and in the Far East had been even more unremitting than the comparable conflicts with France; but prolonged negotiations led to the Anglo-Russian Convention of 1907. The convention eased Britain's fears for the safety of the Indian frontier by recognizing her right to determine the foreign policy of Afghanistan and resolved another conflict by dividing Persia into a large Russian sphere of influence in the north, a smaller British sphere of influence in the south, and a neutral zone in between. Though some diplomats henceforth spoke of a Triple Entente of Britain, France, and Russia to counterbalance the Triple Alliance of Germany, Austria-Hungary, and Italy, Grey himself disliked the phrase. The convention with Russia seemed to him to be at most a settlement of past differences, not a promise of future cooperation. And indeed, the sense of common culture and shared political aspirations which some Englishmen felt for France could much less readily be extended to an aristocratic Russia which had crushed the Revolution of 1905 and remained the prime example of European despotism. When King Edward VII went off on a state visit to St. Petersburg in 1908, several Labour Members of Parliament protested against the idea of His Majesty "hobnobbing with bloodstained creatures." Though the king was his gracious self and dutifully danced the "Merry Widow Waltz" with the czarina, the pre-1914 tie between Britain and Russia never became more than a polite formality.

Anglo-German Rivalry

While Sir Edward Grey at the Foreign Office was very much involved with the various diplomatic crises that beset early twentieth-century Europe, the average Englishman tended ordinarily to be more concerned with domestic affairs. The one issue of foreign policy which did, however, awaken his interest and which more than any other convinced him that Germany had become Europe's chief troublemaker was the Anglo-German naval rivalry. In the late nineteenth century, Admiral Tirpitz had convinced the Kaiser's government that only if Germany built a large navy could it make its diplomatic weight felt. If Admiral Tirpitz expected the British government to permit its navy to be overtaken in size and fire power, he reckoned without Sir John Fisher (1841–1920), the First Sea Lord from 1904 to 1910 and from 1914 to 1915.

In the face of the German naval menace, Fisher argued that the English navy should be reorganized and rebuilt. Rather than having British squadrons spread throughout the world, he believed that most of the fleet should be concentrated in the North Sea to meet any threat from Germany. A new naval base was established at Scapa Flow in the Orkney Islands north of Scotland. From there the navy could intercept a German fleet steaming out into the North Sea or attempting to pass through the English Channel. Fisher ruthlessly scrapped hundreds of outmoded naval vessels and secretly planned the *Dreadnought*, the prototype of the twentieth-century battleship which dominated the seas until 1945. A number of successively improved iron battleships had been built during the late nineteenth century, and British expenditures on the navy had edged upward from the late 1880s on; but the *Dreadnought* surpassed all its predecessors. Its ten twelve-inch guns possessed more than twice the firing power of earlier ironclads, and the ship had the added advantage of being able to run on oil as well as coal.

It was obvious that if the Germans wished to prolong the naval race, they too would have to build dreadnoughts. This decision, in turn, would force them to widen the Kiel Canal, the

German water artery between the Baltic and the North Sea. In the meantime the new Liberal Government temporarily halted the Fisher program of building four dreadnoughts a year and initiated attempts to reach an agreement with Germany placing a ceiling on the size of both navies. But Emperor William II made it clear that he "did not wish good relations at the expense of the fleet." A sudden realization in the winter of 1908 that Admiral Tirpitz's shipbuilding plans would enable Germany to overtake Britain in the number of dreadnoughts within two years caused alarm, first in a divided Liberal Cabinet and then in the British press. Public pressure eventually forced the Government to begin laying the keels of eight great battleships rather than the four initially planned. "We want eight and we won't wait," went the contemporary music-hall refrain.

This is how the naval race progressed over the next few years:

NUMBER OF DREADNOUGHTS IN OPERATION

YEAR	BRITAIN	GERMANY
1910	5	2
1911	8	4
1912	12	7
1913	15	10
1914	18	13

By 1914 France and the United States each possessed eight comparable battleships and Japan five.

The navy necessarily retained a different meaning for Britain than for Germany. Britain by 1914 was so dependent upon imported food that should she lose control of the seas it would mean starvation. Moreover, a German navy large enough to control the Channel would enable the German army to capture London. Yet no degree of British naval superiority could ever enable a British army to capture Berlin, for in 1911 the German army (including trained reserves) comprised 4,800,000 men. The comparable British force was confined to 380,000 men. Though the Anglo-German naval rivalry was clearly a factor which exacerbated relations between the two countries, it is difficult to see how the men responsible for British national security could have responded to the German challenge except by seeking a program of naval limitation and, that failing, by persevering in their own naval-building program.

Although certain Englishmen were tempted from time to time to emulate the large conscript armies which had been characteristic of continental nations for half a century, the principle of voluntary recruitment was retained during the decades before World War I. The relatively small British army was reorganized during these years, however, by the Secretary for War, Richard Burdon Haldane,[3] so as to make it potentially a more efficient fighting force. For the first time a general staff was set up along Prussian lines and a Military Intelligence Branch associated with it. An expeditionary force of six infantry divisions (with associated artillery and cavalry contingents capable of rapid mobilization) was set up, and the older militia was replaced by a fourteen division Territorial Army to take over home defense in wartime. Officer's Training Corps programs were established in most "public schools," designed to produce tens of thousands of commissioned officers for modern war. In 1911 the Royal Flying Corps was founded to assist the army in reconnaissance work, and that same year a little-noted measure, the Official Secrets Act, reversed traditional judicial procedures by making it necessary for anyone accused of attempting to transmit secret military information to a foreign state to prove his innocence. Mass conscription had not been adopted, but Britain was adapting its military forces with reasonable efficiency for the possible demands of twentieth-century warfare.

Although domestic problems remained uppermost in the mind of the average Englishman, every so often an international crisis would flare into the headlines. The Bosnian Crisis of 1908 was one example; on that occasion Austria weakened Russian prestige in the Balkans by proclaiming the full annexation of Bosnia-Herzegovina, the Turkish territory it had been "occupying" since 1878. Another crisis captured the headlines in 1911 when the German gunboat, *The Panther*, appeared off the coast of Morocco at Agadir in an effort to reassert and dramatize German influence in North Africa. Lloyd George gave public expression to the concern of his countrymen: "Britain should at all hazards maintain her place and prestige among the Great Powers, and if a situation were to be forced upon us in which peace could only be preserved by the sacrifice of the great and beneficent position that Britain had won by centuries of heroism and achievement – then I say emphatically that peace at such a price would be a humiliation intolerable for a great country like ours to endure." These ringing phrases sounded more like Palmerston at his most bellicose than like an ex-"pro-Boer" Liberal who belonged to the pacifist wing of his party. But times had changed and so had Lloyd George. Each international crisis seemed to elicit greater tension and excitement.

Sometimes World War I is seen as the inevitable result of two increasingly rigid alliance systems meeting in inevitable

---

[3] He was created Viscount Haldane in 1911.

head-on collision. Yet neither the Triple Alliance nor the Triple Entente was ever as rigid or stable as it seemed at the height of a temporary and often deliberately manufactured "crisis." No state could ever be totally assured of the support of its supposed allies. No nation ever wished to break all ties with states in the other camp. Nor in one very real sense, could they; for the monarchs of pre-1914 were almost all related. Not for nothing has Queen Victoria been called the "Grandmother of Europe."

Emperor William II of Germany, who in his earlier days had written dutiful "Dear Grandmama" letters to Victoria, continued during the early years of the twentieth century to write similarly personal letters to his cousin, Czar Nicholas II of Russia. He would write in English, addressing the czar as "Dearest Nicky" and signing the letters "Your affectionate friend Willy." Envy of his Uncle Edward VII, who regarded William as the *enfant terrible* of Europe, did not prevent him from wearing his scarlet British Field Marshal's uniform and proudly taking his place of honor in the imposing monarchical funeral cortege that followed his uncle's coffin through the streets of London in May 1910. Torn like so many of his countrymen between feelings of envy and admiration for Britain, William for once was satisfied that his assigned role at the funeral befitted his station, and he wrote to Berlin from Windsor Castle: "I am proud to call this place my home and to be a member of this royal family."

Stronger even than links of monarchy were ties of trade and finance. International commerce was growing everywhere; and although German competition caused grave alarm for some English businessmen, it never caused as much general concern as German naval competition. When in the summer of 1914 Britain agreed not to hamper the building of a projected Berlin-to-Bagdad Railway, she acknowledged the fact that Germany had peacefully supplanted Britain as the most influential foreign economic influence in Turkey. Furthermore Britain was Germany's best customer, while Russia was Germany's single most important supplier of food and raw materials. During the years 1912–14, as Germany apparently came to accept the impossibility of surpassing British naval power, Anglo-German diplomatic relations improved. Both countries cooperated in limiting the scope of the Balkan Wars of 1912–13, and by June 1914 one leading German diplomat spoke of the "pleasant cordiality of Anglo-German relations." World War I was far less the inevitable outcome of economic rivalries or of inflexible alliances than the result of mediocre statesmanship and the subordination of true national interest to ephemeral notions of national prestige.

EUROPE IN 1914

TRIPLE ALLIANCE
Germany–Italy–Austria-Hungary

TRIPLE ENTENTE
England–France–Russia

The Lights Go Out

The assassination of the Austrian Crown Prince in Sarajevo on June 28, 1914, alerted the chancellories of Europe to the probability of another international crisis; but the absence of an immediate diplomatic reaction by Austria gave the political atmosphere a deceptive calm. Two weeks after the assassination, Lloyd George could assure an audience that the international sky had never looked bluer. Behind the scenes, however, the Austrians were planning to make use of the assassination to crush their pesky southern neighbor, Serbia, once and for all; for the assassin had been a young Bosnian who hoped to make Austrian-controlled Bosnia part of a greater Serbia. Having obtained the promise of full support from their German ally, the Austrians on July 23 issued a 48-hour ultimatum to Serbia demanding the suppression in Serbia of all anti-Austrian publications and the punishment of all teachers who spoke out against Habsburg domination, and the acceptance of Austrian officials to enforce Serbian compliance to these demands. The Serbian reply was unexpectedly conciliatory. The Serbs accepted all Austrian demands except the entry of Austrian officials on Serbian soil and even on this point agreed to refer the matter to the international court at the Hague. Austria, however, pronounced the Serbian reply to be unsatisfactory, and on July 28 she declared war; a day later her guns began shelling Belgrade.

Russian reaction to Austro-Hungarian aggression in the Balkans was immediate and decisive — first she declared a partial and then a general mobilization of her forces. In the meantime Sir Edward Grey desperately sought to reconvene the London Conference which had satisfactorily resolved the Balkan Wars of the year before. Germany, insisting that the conflict concerned only Austria and Serbia, turned down the invitation. In the face of what appeared to be Germany's refusal to prevent a wider war, Sir Edward asked both France and Germany to respect Belgian neutrality. France agreed, Germany was noncommittal. By July 30, the German civilian government did indeed belatedly caution Austria to go slow; but its advice was secretly superseded by Count von Moltke, the chief of the German general staff, who urged Austria to mobilize against Russia and promised unconditional German aid. By the summer of 1914 the German general staff had clearly convinced itself that a general European war was inevitable in the near future and that the relative military position of Germany and Austria-Hungary was as favorable then as it was ever likely to be. The German general staff was in no sense responsible for the assassination of the Austrian archduke nor was it directly involved in the preparation of the Austrian ultimatum; but once the occasion for war arose, it welcomed the opportunity. Neither the weak-willed Emperor nor his civilian Chancellor found himself able to make a stand for good sense.

Military time tables dictated the scenario that then unfolded. The German war plan against France and Russia required an immediate push to Paris which was expected to fall within six weeks. Once France had been knocked out of the war, the full might of the German army could be turned against the larger but more slowly assembled Russian forces. After ultimatums demanding an immediate halt to Russian mobilization and an immediate promise of French neutrality were not answered to German satisfaction, Germany declared war on Russia and began its attack in the west.

The British Cabinet, its peace efforts unavailing, was painfully divided on the subject of whether to aid France in case of German attack. A majority of the Liberal Government was averse to intervention. London bankers, fearful that war would "break down the whole system of credit with London as its center," pleaded with the Government to remain neutral. At the same time the French ambassador frantically begged for aid, and uninformed members of the Cabinet suddenly became aware of the extent of the Government's secret military conversations with France. Not only had the generals been preparing a plan for sending a British Expeditionary Force to France, but the admirals had in effect allotted the Mediterranean Sea to the French Fleet and the English Channel to the British. If a German fleet were now to steam down the English Channel to shell unprotected French ports, could Britain justify a position of standing aside?

Though the First Lord of the Admiralty, Winston Churchill, placed the navy on a precautionary war footing, Asquith's Cabinet was still undecided on August 3, when Grey addressed an expectant House of Commons. Speaking slowly but with evident emotion, Grey asked the House to approach the crisis from the point of view of "British interests, British honor, and British obligations." He related the history of the military conversations with France but made clear that no secret engagement restricted Britain's choice of action. Yet he urged that Britain must take a stand "against the unmeasured aggrandizement of any power whatsoever."

> I ask the House [Grey went on] from the point of view of British interests to consider what may be at stake. If France is beaten to her knees ... if Belgium fell under the same dominating influence and then Holland and then Denmark ... if, in a crisis like this, we run away

from these obligations of honor and interest as regards
the Belgian Treaty ... I do not believe for a moment
that, at the end of this war, even if we stood aside, we
should be able to undo what had happened, in the course
of the war, to prevent the whole of the West of Europe
opposite us from falling under the domination of a single
power ... and we should, I believe, sacrifice our respect
and good name and reputation before the world and
should not escape the most serious and grave economic
consequences.

Grey clearly won the support of the House of Commons, and
after he sat down first Bonar Law, on behalf of the Conservatives, and then, in a signal act of courage, John Redmond, on
behalf of the Irish Nationalists, announced their support.
Only Ramsay MacDonald, the head of the Labour Party, dis-
sented; but even he soon proved to be part of a minority within
his own small party.

By the time Grey spoke, the German Government had
asked for the right to cross Belgium; but Belgium's King Albert,
on the grounds of his country's permanent neutralization by
international agreement, refused his consent and requested
British diplomatic support. On the morning of August 4 news
came that a German invasion of Belgium had nonetheless begun. The British government thereupon mobilized its army
and sent an ultimatum asking the Germans to withdraw from
Belgium by 12 P.M. No reply was received, and at midnight of
August 4, 1914, Britain found herself at war with Germany.

The German invasion of Belgium, a country whose neutrality Britain had guaranteed in 1839, resolved the Cabinet's
dilemma. Although two members of the Cabinet resigned,
Germany's violation of international agreement enabled the
British Government to enter the war with a substantially unified
populace staunchly behind it. It might have been difficult to
persuade the British public on grounds of self-interest alone,
but the issue of Belgium now added the all-important moral
factor to the decision.

Since it was clear both in London and Berlin that Britain's
entry into the war was directly tied to Germany's invasion of
neutral Belgium, the question necessarily arises: why did the
Kaiser's Government make what appears in retrospect a monumental blunder? The answer is that the German war plan
for the west, the Schlieffen plan, left no alternative. Only by
passing through Belgium could the German army hope to capture Paris in six weeks. Moreover, although German generals
were fully aware that British participation would necessarily

follow, the significance of the British military contribution was discounted in advance. The English army was, after all, in Emperor William II's words, "contemptibly small."

Though anticipated by the German generals, the British declaration of war infuriated the German populace. The immediate origins of the war of 1914 had nothing to do with a direct Anglo-German rivalry, for no outstanding issue between the two countries was remotely worth a war; but once Britain declared war, England became immediately the most hated of all Germany's enemies. The English action was felt to be an act of treason to the "Nordic race," and the deity was called upon to punish the perfidy—"Gott Strafe England!" The Kaiser demonstrated his own incompetence anew by making the least profound of possible comments about the origins of the war. "To think," he lamented, "that George and Nicky should have played me false! If my grandmother had been alive she would never have allowed it."

Whatever the immediate chain of events and the last minute soul searchings, Britain's decision to enter the war followed logically from the historic British preoccupations with the independence of Belgium—a significant factor as early as the onset of the Hundred Years War with France in 1337—and with the fear of a Europe dominated by a single power, whether it be the Spain of Philip II, the France of Napoleon I, or the Germany of William II or his successors. Whatever may be said for some members of the London populace who, like their counterparts in Berlin, Vienna, Paris, and St. Petersburg, cheered the onset of war as exciting sport, Britain's governmental leaders were aware of the gravity of their decision. An English publicist, Norman Angell, had vividly portrayed the horrors of war between industrialized nations in *The Great Illusion* (1910); and though other generals were more hopeful, Lord Kitchener, Britain's new Secretary for War, predicted a conflict that would last at least three years. As the sky darkened on the night of August 4 and the time limit of Britain's ultimatum to Germany to halt her invasion of Belgium drew inexorably to an end, Sir Edward Grey stood by a Whitehall window. Sadly he turned to an aide standing at his side and spoke the words that were to become the epitaph of nineteenth-century Europe and the Victorian and Edwardian eras: "The lamps are going out all over Europe. We shall not see them lit again in our lifetime."

Chapter 14

Britain and 𝕸𝖔𝖗𝖑𝖉 𝕸𝖆𝖗 𝕴

The Fighting Fronts (1914–1915)

Once war had been declared by Britain on August 4, the contingency plans worked out with the French general staff were, with minor revisions, put into effect. Three divisions, and after brief hesitation a fourth – 100,000 men in all – of a British Expeditionary Force under Field Marshal Sir John French were safely transported under naval cover across the Channel. By August 22 the British forces were taking their assigned place on the left of the French front. They had little opportunity to establish themselves, for rapidly advancing German troops had already captured or bypassed all major Belgian fortifications. No sooner had the British forces crossed into Belgium than they began, together with their French allies, a general strategic retreat.

The main thrust of the German attack was still toward Paris in accordance with the Schlieffen plan, which came within an eyelash of succeeding. But on the outskirts of Paris at the Battle of the Marne the Allied forces (predominantly French) under General Joffre held firm. During the second week of September the German onslaught was halted and in some places pushed back. Frustrated in their attempt to reach Paris, the German army turned west toward the Channel and captured the Belgian ports of Zeebrugge and Ostend. But after heavy fighting at what came to be known as the first battle of Ypres in October and November of 1914, the British managed to halt the German advance. Half the British regular army was destroyed, but a tiny corner of western Belgium was saved, and so were the vital French ports of Dunkirk, Calais, and Bologne. By the spring of 1915 the war in the west was bogged down amidst miles of trenches, barbed wire, and machine-gun positions that stretched from Switzerland to the North Sea.[1]

With the exception of a few generals such as Lord Kitchener, neither the Allied nor the German leaders had expected such an impasse. Most generals and civilians were guided in their thinking by the wars of the mid-nineteenth century, which had almost invariably been quick and often decided by a single battle. The American Civil War, with its virtual four-year stalemate on the eastern front between Richmond and Washington, offered military food for thought of a different order, but European strategists had paid the American ordeal little heed.

What had happened was that a twentieth-century defense had stymied a nineteenth-century offense, and what most men had expected to be a swift surgical operation was turning into a slow bleeding to death. On both sides, the generals refused to acknowledge military reality. Instead they excused the stalemate on the ground that they lacked the men and the guns to carry out the strategic doctrines on which they had been trained. They planned and hoped for a successful frontal breakthrough; but though they spent tens of thousands of lives and hundreds of thousands of artillery shells, they repeatedly failed. Battle was no longer the decisive factor. "Europe was locked in gigantic siege operations, in which victory would come by the attrition of manpower, industrial resources, food supplies, and morale, rather than by generalship." [2]

Though baffled on land, Britain immediately put to use her overall naval superiority to drive Germany's merchant marine from the high seas and to enforce a strict blockade to prevent Germany and her allies from importing foodstuffs or munitions from abroad. In the meantime, isolated German war-

---

[1] Winston Churchill's *The World Crisis* is a detailed four-volume history of the First World War (London, 1931). Cyril Falls' *The Great War: 1914-1918*, Paperbound ed. (New York, 1961) provides a concise single-volume military history. Sidney Pollard's *The Development of the British Economy, 1914-1950* (London, 1962) includes an instructive discussion of the economic implications of World War I. Wartime politics is taken up in R. H. Gretton, *A Modern History of the English People, 1880-1950* (London, 1930) and in biographies such as the one of Lloyd George by Thomas Jones (New York, 1951) and of Asquith by Roy Jenkins (London, 1964). Lord Beaverbrook's *Politicians and the War* (London, 1928) and *Men and Power* (London, 1956) provide a "behind the scenes" account.

[2] William B. Willcox, *Star of Empire* (New York, 1950).

THE Western Front: 1914-1918

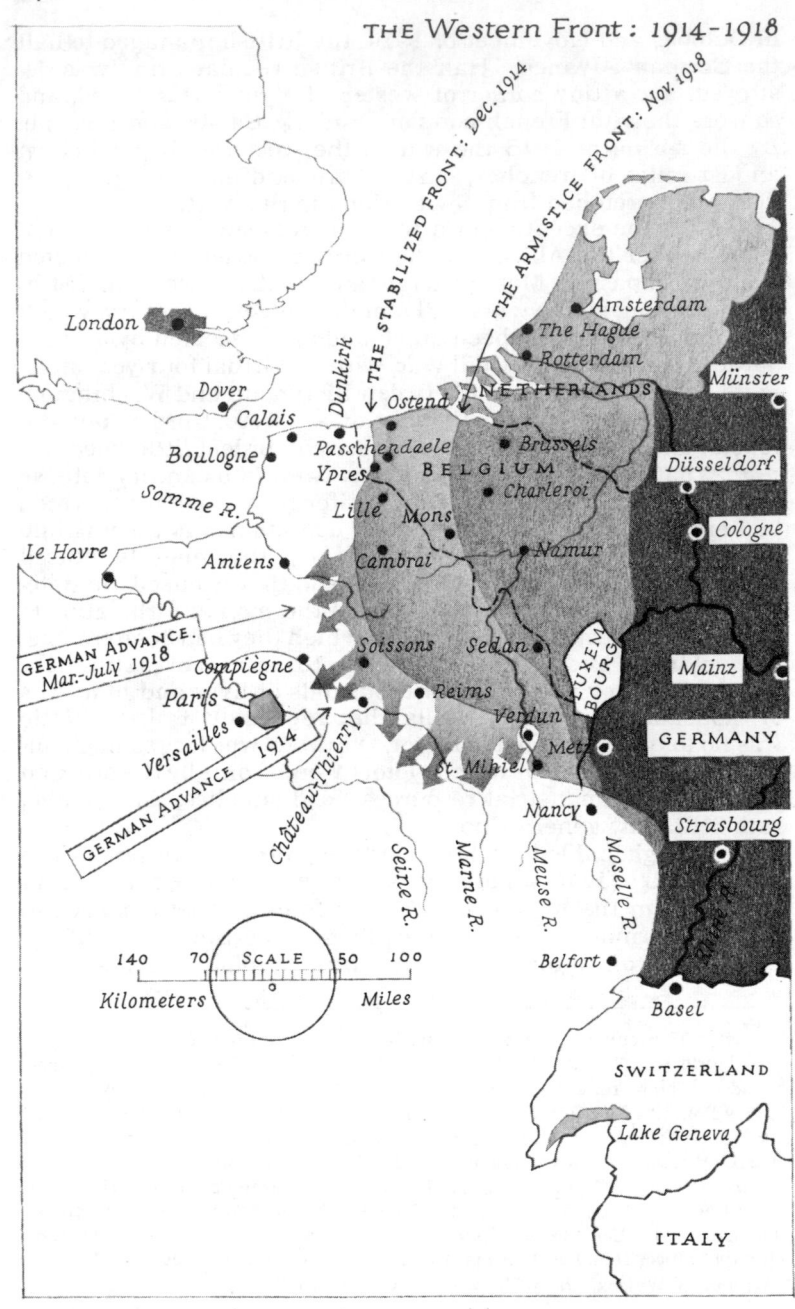

THE STABILIZED FRONT: Dec. 1914

THE ARMISTICE FRONT: Nov. 1918

London

Dover

Calais

Boulogne

Dunkirk

Ostend

NETHERLANDS

Amsterdam

The Hague

Rotterdam

Münster

Düsseldorf

Cologne

Passchendaele

Ypres

Brussels

BELGIUM

Charleroi

Lille

Mons

Somme R.

Le Havre

Amiens

Cambrai

Namur

GERMAN ADVANCE.
Mar.-July 1918

Compiègne

Paris

Versailles

GERMAN ADVANCE 1914

Soissons

Reims

Château-Thierry

Sedan

Verdun

St. Mihiel

LUXEMBOURG

Metz

Nancy

Mainz

GERMANY

Strasbourg

Seine R.

Marne R.

Meuse R.

Moselle R.

140   70   SCALE   50   100

Kilometers   Miles

Belfort

Basel

SWITZERLAND

Lake Geneva

ITALY

ships were hunted down or forced to seek refuge in neutral ports, where their crews were interned, until the greater part of the German navy was blockaded in its home waters. The inability of the German Government to send assistance to its overseas colonies meant that these fell into Allied hands during the next few years, the one exception being German East Africa, where a small German force succeeded in holding out as long as the Fatherland.

Early in 1915 the Allies made their major attempt to out-flank the entire Western Front by attacking what seemed to be the weakest link among the Central Powers, Turkey. For decades the preservation of the Ottoman Empire had been a major object of British foreign policy. By the turn of the twentieth century, this aim no longer loomed so large, and the Anglo-Russian Entente of 1907 necessarily made the defense of the Dardanelles against Russia a less pressing concern. This same entente had convinced the dominant forces in the Turkish Government by 1914 that their salvation now lay with Germany. The Allied naval and land attack upon the Dardanelles thus had the paradoxical purpose of opening that waterway to Russia. The Russians were eager for closer military cooperation and easier communications with the Western Powers and strongly favored the plan. Its chief defender in London was Winston Churchill, the First Lord of the Admiralty, who had become aware sooner than most of his colleagues of the stalemate that lay ahead in France.

The operation was badly mismanaged. The British and French fleets, seeking to force their way through the Straits, withdrew because of losses at the very point that the Turkish defenders were ready to give in. The Allies then decided to stage a land invasion instead; but by the time British, Australian, and New Zealand troops landed in April 1915, the Gallipoli peninsula had been well fortified and the Allied forces found it impossible to storm the almost impregnable hilltop positions which overlooked their small beachhead. Heavy fighting in Poland prevented the Russian armies from lending support; and after clinging to their beachhead for several months, the Allies were forced, in December 1915, to evacuate Gallipoli. Fifty-five thousand men were lost in a campaign which from the start had been strongly opposed by the French Government and by the more conservative military leaders in Britain. Winston Churchill became the scapegoat for the debacle and lost his position as First Lord of the Admiralty.[3]

---

[3] Alan Morehead, *Gallipoli* (London, 1956).

The Home Front (1914–1915)

Within Britain itself, once war had begun, all the animosities which had troubled the immediate prewar domestic scene were subordinated to what Winston Churchill was to call "a higher principle of hatred." Trade unions called off pending strikes. Political parties agreed upon an electoral truce. John Redmond, the Irish Nationalist leader, and Sir Edward Carson, the Ulster leader who had dallied with rebellion in the interest of preserving the Anglo-Irish union, both turned their energies to recruiting army volunteers. Suffragette leaders newly released from jail devoted themselves to winding bandages, organizing war relief, and asking young men why they were not at the front. All over the country recruiting posters depicting the stern and imposing features of Lord Kitchener, the Minister for War, bore the same message: "Your Country Needs You." "Oh, we don't want to lose you but we think you ought to go," went the words of one music-hall ballad. For the time being, Britain insisted upon preserving its volunteer army tradition, and between 1914 and 1916 more than two million young men enlisted in the army, a number demonstrating a remarkable and widespread sense of youthful idealism. Wrote Rupert Brooke in 1914:

Now, God be thanked Who has matched us with His hour
And caught our youth, and wakened us from sleeping.

The immense changes which world war was to bring to the economy and the political life of the nation were not at first appreciated. Some businessmen, once the initial shock of war had worn off, thought in terms of "business as usual" and found solace in the thought that much German overseas trade would now fall into British hands. It soon turned out, however, that British industry had not the capacity to gear itself to full war production and at the same time continue its traditional role of exporter. Nor was the requisite shipping available. The result was that German and British markets in Canada and Latin America were largely taken over by businessmen from the United States. Japanese businessmen filled a similar role in the Far East.

One major industry which felt the effects of war at once was the railways. In accordance with a standby measure dating back to 1871, they were immediately taken over by the Government on a rental basis and for the first time operated as a single system. As overseas freight rates doubled and tripled in the early months of 1915 because of submarine damage, the Government also took over refrigerator ships. Eventually all ocean-going vessels were placed under government control. Labor unions had, in the meantime, become increasingly disturbed by the way in which the manpower shortage had caused the managements of the war industries to "dilute" union standards by recruiting laborers from other industries and lower-paid women workers. In reaction to the threat of labor unrest, the Government utilized its powers under the comprehensive Defence of the Realm Act to obtain a trade union conference agreement in which unions pledged to abandon the use of the strike in wartime, to accept government arbitration in all disputes, and to relax traditional union rules. In return the Government promised that such concessions would not be used to depress wages, that the financial benefit of such union concessions would accrue to the state rather than to the employers, that the suspended rules would be restored when peace came, and that postwar preference in rehiring would be given to prewar employees.

The difficulties encountered by Local Armaments Committees, made up of employers, workers, and government representatives in giving force to this agreement led to a more direct measure of government control: a Ministry of Munitions. It provided for the limitation of profits in war industries and also restricted the right of workers to move from one such industry to another. Such imposition of government control on labor and management alike did not curb all labor discontent—a major strike in the Welsh coalfields broke out in July 1915—but it did mark a notable and largely successful step in the mobilization of domestic resources for military purposes.

Just as the initial surge of patriotism had begun to fade on the industrial scene by the spring of 1915, so did the comparable truce in domestic politics. The Conservatives under Bonar Law became frustrated by their inability to influence policy-making directly. The war, moreover, was clearly not leading to any speedy victory. The first major reconstruction of the Government, in May 1915, was precipitated by the resignation of the aging First Sea Lord, Admiral Fisher. Fisher had been restored to his former post in 1914 because his successor, Prince Louis of Battenberg, bore too German-sounding a name. Fisher and his civilian superior, Winston Churchill, found themselves continually at odds. Churchill favored the Gallipoli invasion while Fisher preferred an even more dramatic venture which would have been even less likely to succeed: a landing of Russian troops under British naval protection on the Baltic Coast near Berlin.

The apparent failure at Gallipoli prompted Fisher's resignation, and Bonar Law, the Conservative leader, took advantage of the situation to demand a change in the Cabinet. It now became a three-party coalition. Asquith remained as Prime Minister but Bonar Law became his deputy. Lloyd George assumed the significant new post of Minister of Munitions, and Arthur Henderson joined the Government as President of the Board of Education, the first member of the Labour Party to gain Cabinet office. John Redmond declined Asquith's comparable invitation to the Irish Nationalists. In the meantime, Winston Churchill was demoted to a minor office and soon left London for a year in the trenches in France. Lord Haldane was similarly forced out of the Cabinet; the creator of the British Expeditionary Force in France had become the victim of widespread newspaper criticism because in his youth he had received his higher education at a German university.

The Rise of Lloyd George

The grueling months of war stretched into years, and by the summer of 1916 victory seemed as distant as ever. On the Western Front the long drawn-out Battle of the Somme which began on July 1 of that year cost the British 400,000 casualties; and although it aided the stalwart French defense of Verdun to the southeast, it failed to bring about a decisive change in the battle lines. Both in the United States and in Europe there was occasional talk of a compromise peace; but Germany would accept only a peace which recognized its military advances in the east and west. The Allied leaders, in turn, found it impossible to justify to their peoples a peace which preserved and strengthened the very Prussian militarism for whose destruction they were asking such enormous human sacrifice.

A prolonged war which brings no victory invariably injures the reputation of the government which conducts it, and in the fall of 1916 two of Britain's "press lords," Lord Northcliffe and Sir Max Aitken (the future Lord Beaverbrook) launched a newspaper campaign to replace Asquith as Prime Minister. He seemed too undramatic and too ineffectual to be an appropriate war leader. Much more fitting seemed David Lloyd George, the fiery Welsh orator whose popular reputation had been made by the "People's Budget" of 1909 and reinforced by his success as Minister of Munitions in overcoming a notorious shell shortage. That there should be a shortage of artillery ammunition was not surprising, considering that in three weeks of the Battle of the Somme the British army fired more ammunition than it had during the entire three years of the Boer War. In the summer of 1916, when Lord Kitchener was drowned while on his way to Russia in a warship which struck a German mine, Lloyd

George became Secretary for War as well. In the autumn he proposed that a special four-man War Cabinet be created to run the war with himself in charge. Asquith rejected the proposal as an unconstitutional abdication of his own responsibilities. Lloyd George thereupon submitted his resignation, and the Conservative members of the Cabinet did likewise. Asquith consequently sent in his own resignation also. King George V requested the Conservative leader, Bonar Law, to form a government; when the latter declined, Lloyd George was left as the logical choice. He was offered the Prime Ministership and accepted the task.

The erstwhile radical and pacifist, the scourge of dukes and terror of millionaires, thus became head of a Coalition Cabinet in which Conservatives predominated. Both Herbert Asquith and Sir Edward Grey found themselves out of office, but Asquith, though deeply hurt by his dismissal, loyally asked his followers to support the new Prime Minister. As matters turned out, however, the wounds which the events of December 1916 opened in the Liberal Party were never completely to heal. The manner and the consequences of Lloyd George's elevation to the Prime Ministership probably did more than any prewar event or historical force to start one of Britain's major political parties on the road to disintegration.

In 1916, admittedly, most Englishmen were more concerned with country than with party; and if Lloyd George should indeed prove to be the man who could win the war, all else might be forgiven him. That he was imbued with driving energy, with boundless self-confidence, and with unshakable resolution became evident almost at once. He organized a small War Cabinet along lines he had previously proposed, and for the time being the House of Commons fell very much into eclipse. "The Wizard of Wales" seemed to personify, indeed, the "total war" which the conflict with Germany and her allies had become.

By the time Lloyd George became Prime Minister, much of the legislation converting England into a warfare state was already in the statute book. Railways and munitions plants were under government control and the free market of peacetime capitalism had been drastically curbed. If Lloyd George never imposed the degree of compulsion upon British labor which the law empowered him to decree, it was because he preferred to exert his own vast powers of persuasion. "When the house is on fire," he had insisted in 1916, "questions of procedure and precedence, of etiquette and time and division of labour must disappear." Such questions never did disappear altogether, and the last years of the conflict were filled with sporadic stoppages and often "unofficial" strikes; but for the average workingman, the full employment and overtime work resulting from the war brought a rise in living standards relative to other groups in the population. The organized labor movement as a whole gained similarly, as union membership doubled in four years (1914–18) from a little over four million to a little over eight million. A host of minor grievances, however, including war fatigue and the conviction that labor was more severely restricted than management, left a legacy of ill will which erupted the moment the war was over.

Swollen wartime wage packets went hand in hand with shortages of consumer goods and with the increased taxes necessitated by the abrupt rise in government spending. The British wartime budget of 1917–18 (£2,700,000,000) was more than thirteen times as large as the peacetime budget of 1913–14. The standard rate of the income tax rose from 1s.2d. in the pound in 1914 (approximately 6 percent) to 3s. in 1915–16, 5s. in 1917–18, and 6s. (30 percent) in 1918–21. Even that sum proved insufficient to pay for the war on a pay-as-you-go basis. Over the 1914–20 period, the government did succeed in paying for some 44 percent of expenditures by current taxes, but the remainder had to come from borrowing. The cost of servicing a new national debt of seven billion pounds proved a heavy burden for postwar Chancellors of the Exchequer, though it is difficult to see how such a burden could have been avoided. Relative to Britain's wealth and population, it was, moreover, no heavier than that which Britain's Napoleonic War government had left to its successors.

One area of regulation in which the Government may well have lagged behind popular demand was in control of prices. The first three years of the war saw prices rise more than 25 percent per year, but it was only in 1917 that attempts were made to impose government price controls. By then wheat, meat, tea, and sugar were all in short supply, and long queues stretched in front of every food store. Attempts to encourage grain production at home only partially made up for the losses imposed by German submarine warfare; and in early 1918 the Government, in the person of Lord Rhondda, the Minister of Food, established rationing for meat, sugar, butter, and margarine. The system, which had each consumer register with a particular retail store, proved generally equitable and caused the queues to disappear.

The complete mobilization of the economy which constituted total war at home was only a reflection of the manner in which new means of warfare were obliterating the traditional distinction between soldier and civilian. From early 1915 on, fleets of as many as sixty Zeppelins (lighter-than-air dirigibles) dropped bombs on London and other English cities. In 1917 airplanes supplemented Zeppelins, and one German bomber raid resulted in the death of 120 school children in London's East End. The Zeppelin raids were initially regarded by most Englishmen more as a risky type of entertainment than as an act of war, but the bomber raids came to seem less an act of war than the random murder of women and children.

War on Sea and Land (1915–1917)

The same breaking down of traditional demarcation lines involved in the bombing of civilians was implied by the German decision in the spring of 1915 to embark upon unrestricted submarine warfare. The German government defended the step as justifiable retaliation for the increasingly successful British naval blockade. Of the German fleet, only the submarines were still at sea; only submarines could break Britain's economic links with the outside world. International law provided that a warship encountering an unarmed merchant vessel should fire a warning shot across its bow, board the ship, and search for contraband. If contraband was found, the vessel might be taken as prize or sunk, so long as provision was made for the crew. If no contraband was found, the merchantman was to be permitted to go on its way. Unrestricted submarine warfare meant that there was to be no warning shot, no search, and no provision for the crew or passengers — only a torpedo blast and a watery grave in the North Atlantic.

The German government argued, cogently enough, that a submarine could not act as if it were a battleship. Its effectiveness depended not on armament but upon speed and surprise. The Allied reaction, and, for that matter, the reaction of most Americans, was that the military nature of the submarine did not excuse its violation of international law. The German sinking in May 1915 of the *Lusitania*, the largest passenger liner still at sea, with the loss of more than a thousand civilian lives, thus prompted a much greater sense of outrage than did the death of tens of thousands of soldiers in the trenches of Northern France. The warnings of the American government were indeed so strong that the German government quietly ordered its submarine commanders to cease attacking passenger vessels for the time being.

In May of 1916 while unrestricted submarine warfare was in abeyance, there occurred the greatest naval battle of the war, the Battle of Jutland. The main German fleet had remained in its home base, awaiting the gradual attrition of British naval strength. Seeking to speed the process, a small German squadron sailed into the North Sea to lure the British battle cruiser fleet into the path of the main German dreadnought fleet. Quite accidentally, it turned out that heavy British battleships as well as the less heavily armed battle cruisers were in the same area, and the snare originally set for the English turned out to be a trap for the entire German High Seas Fleet. The stage seemed set for the greatest sea battle of all time, with more than 250 vessels of all sizes taking part. During the night, however, the German fleet succeeded in evading the British ships and managed to return to its home base. The battle thus ended on a strangely inconclusive note, and the British commander, Admiral Jellicoe, was afterwards much criticized for his inability to take advantage of the opportunity to destroy German naval strength. The British lost fourteen ships, the Germans eleven. On the other hand, the German fleet never successfully ventured into the North Sea again, and British naval superiority remained unchallenged on the high seas if not always in the waters beneath.

The last proviso is important, for in the beginning of 1917 German unrestricted submarine warfare was renewed. For a time one merchant ship in every four which left the British isles was sunk, and the loss of shipping in April 1917 — 870,000 tons — was so severe that the prospect of starvation became a genuine one. The same month (largely as a response to unrestricted submarine warfare) the United States entered the war on the Allied side, and American naval cooperation, combined with the development of new weapons such as the depth charge and the revival of old methods such as the convoy system, gradually brought the submarine menace under control. Nonetheless, the British merchant fleet was hard hit. Seven million tons of British shipping were lost during World War I, 38 percent of the prewar merchant fleet, the world's largest.

In the meantime, the war had still to be won. Lloyd George's Government was committed to the idea of a knockout blow and never seriously considered the possibility of a negotiated peace. The only drawback to such a militant position was that no one had a plausible plan to win the war. The secret had not been found in the Dardanelles, nor had it been discovered in an equally ill-fated attempt to launch a Balkan invasion from Salonika in Greece. Nor did new allies necessarily provide the key. Italy, an erstwhile member of the Triple Alliance, had entered the war on the British-French side in May 1915, but the Austro-Italian front soon became as stalemated as the older Western Front. The entry of Romania on the Allied side in August 1916 led only to the conquest of that Balkan country by the Central Powers. By the spring of 1917, Russia was engulfed by revolution; and although the Liberal Russian Government which emerged from the "February Revolution"

Shipping in wartime. The Cunard liner "Mauretania," camouflaged in dazzling diamonds in order to avoid the fate of her sister-ship "Lusitania."

Recruiting poster portraying Lord Kitchener.

insisted on abiding by all the military and diplomatic pledges given by its Czarist predecessors, domestic disorder made Russia an ever less reliable ally; and after the "October Revolution" of the Bolsheviks, it ceased to be a combatant at all.

From the point of view of France and Britain, the loss of Russia was counterbalanced by the entrance of the United States; but for the moment this brought little help in terms of manpower. The bulk of the British forces remained immobilized on the Western Front; and for Field Marshal Sir John Haig, who had replaced French in December 1915, it was the Western Front which retained paramount importance. The "Pyrrhic victory" of Verdun in 1916 had decimated the French forces, and by 1917 more than half of the Western Front was manned by British troops. For the first time since the Middle Ages Britain had become a great land power. It was under Haig's leadership that the British summer offensive of 1917 was conducted. The results were just as disappointing and grisly as the Somme campaign of 1916—a few muddy acres around Passchendaele in Belgium and 400,000 British casualties. As Lloyd George saw it, England could afford no more such triumphs. Possibly if the tank, a British invention, had been used with greater perceptiveness in 1916 and 1917, it might have revealed an escape from the impasse of trench warfare, but it was to be German rather than British generals who twenty years later were first to exploit its potential power.

Much of the idealism which the war had first evoked had begun to erode by 1917 and 1918, and a mounting hatred of the death and destruction which had been wrought found expression in the literature of the period. For a man like H. G. Wells, initial idealism gave way to the eventual conclusion that the war itself, "that whirlwind of disaster," had become the enemy. Bertrand Russell lost his lectureship at Cambridge because of his pacifist views and was jailed "for statements likely to prejudice recruiting and discipline of His Majesty's forces." Lytton Strachey and Aldous Huxley were conscientious objectors. Others, though serving in the armed forces, expressed their opposition in print. John Buchan, often remembered as a pro-imperialist writer, expressed his disillusionment in his autobiography: "I acquired a bitter detestation of war, less for its horrors than for its boredom and futility.... To speak of glory seemed a horrid impiety."

It seems fair to conclude, however, that for the average Englishman the hope remained that the human and material costs of the war would be at least partly compensated for by the prospect of a better life to come. The war brought new prosperity and respectability for agricultural laborers at the same time that high taxes and a shortage of domestics were making traditional country house life difficult or impossible to maintain for the upper classes. Class lines were being blurred in business and politics as well as in the army. Wartime shortages and the growing popularity of ready-to-wear clothes encouraged Englishmen of all ranks of life to dress increasingly alike.

The Lloyd George Ministry heeded the widespread feeling that the war should mark the beginning of a new world as well as the destruction of an old. In 1917 it appointed a Minister of Reconstruction to centralize postwar planning of industrial conditions, housing, public health, and transportation facilities. In 1918 it asked Parliament to place on the statute books two major pieces of legislation which, in their way, constituted a climax to the prewar Liberal program. One was the Representation of the People Act of February 1918, which for practical purposes eliminated all property qualifications for male voters over the age of twenty-one. The multitude of restrictions which the Reform Act of 1884 had left were abolished and the Chartist ideal of the 1840s was at last achieved. Women over thirty were similarly enfranchised, and though the age differential remained because of the fear that English politics might be taken over by a new race of Amazons, men and women for the first time in British history became politically equal. Thus the aim which the prewar suffragettes had been unable to achieve by agitation was granted to women en masse as a reward for their patriotic wartime efforts as factory workers, nurses, auxiliary soldiers and sailors, police, omnibus and railway girls, and as workers – often for the first time – in a host of other traditionally masculine preserves. The other major legislative measure was the Education Act of August 1918. Though it was never fully implemented during the interwar years, the Act called for the establishment of state nursery schools for the very young, the extension of the legal age of schooling to 15, and the increase of teachers' salaries and pensions.

The End of the War

Much of this postwar planning took place at a time when the war was far from over. As 1918 began, Britain and France had lost their most important ally, Russia, and gained an equally important associate, the United States. The question of the moment was whether Germany would be able to rush to the Western Front the vast armies hitherto tied up in the East more quickly than the United States could speed its newly trained recruits across the North Atlantic. Before either eventuality had occurred on a large scale, President Woodrow Wilson of the United States had issued his "Fourteen Points." The American preoccupation with spelling out the purposes of the war impelled the British Government to issue its own statement of war aims. Britain's original aims of 1914, as expressed by Asquith, had been the recovery of Belgium, the security of France, the rights of small nations, and the destruction of Prussian military domination. However, for many Britons victory *per se* remained always the overriding, if inconclusive, purpose of the war; and only in October 1917 did the British government commit itself to so specific a goal as the French recovery of Alsace-Lorraine.

The question of Allied war aims was considerably muddied in the eyes of most Americans and of many left-wing Englishmen when the revolutionary Soviet government released early in 1918 the texts of secret treaties which the Czarist government had signed in the course of the war. The treaties assumed that upon an Allied victory both the Ottoman and Habsburg empires would in all likelihood break up and that it was desirable to plan for the disposition of the territories involved. The treaties, despite the interpretations subsequently placed upon them, were not the cause but the consequence of World War I; and some of their provisions were less signs of Allied greed than of mutual Allied distrust. The promise that Russia might at long last occupy Constantinople was agreed to by Britain in order to reassure the Czarist government that the Gallipoli invasion, if successful, would not entail the permanent British takeover of Turkey. The promise of part of the Austrian Tyrol to Italy was intended as an incentive to gain Italian support for the Allied side. The ultimate breakup of both the Habsburg and Ottoman empires had less to do with secret treaties, however, than with the longstanding nationalistic ambitions of Czechs, Poles, Serbs, Romanians, and Arabs and with the fact that both these empires chose the losing side in the war.

The Fourteen Points demonstrated the curious ambiguity which marked the United States' entry into the war. Wilson had long urged a "peace without victory"; and the Fourteen Points of January 1918 implied that, even though the United States was now militarily associated with the anti-German side, Americans still saw themselves above the battle, fighting not for reasons of self-interest but in order "to make the world safe for democracy." Some historians have long urged that American entry into the war *was* a matter of self-interest—Wilson had himself said: "England is fighting our fight!"—but American war aims were not ordinarily expressed in this fashion. Englishmen in general and Lloyd George in particular could sympathize with many of the Fourteen Points, such as the doctrine of national self-determination as a basis for changing the boundary lines of Europe and the establishment of a League of Nations, a proposal which had been advocated for a number of years by influential Englishmen. But the British Government was far less certain than Wilson seemed that the war had been the result of secret diplomacy, and it could not accept Wilson's insistence upon "absolute freedom of navigation upon the seas, alike in peace and war." To accept this provision, Lloyd George pointed out, would mean that Britain would deprive herself of the right to enforce a naval blockade, one of her major war weapons against Germany. Equally unacceptable to much Western European opinion was the implication that Belgium and France deserved no compensation or reparations for the immense material and human damage done by the German invaders.

The German government answered the Fourteen Points with an all-out drive for total victory. In the East, Germany imposed the Treaty of Bucharest upon Romania and the Treaty of Brest-Litovsk upon Russia. Their purpose was to convert the Balkans and much of prewar European Russia into German satellite states. Then in March of 1918, with her Eastern Front secure, Germany launched her last great offensive of the war. A rapid advance was made in the Somme area, where the depleted British forces retreated in the face of superior German numbers; and German guns with a seventy-mile range began to shell Paris. The threat of a breakthrough between the British and French forces impelled the Western Allies at last to entrust the strategic direction of the war in the west to one man, General Ferdinand Foch. A more drastic conscription act in Britain made every man between 18 and 55 liable to military service, and 355,000 British reserves which had been kept at home because of Lloyd George's fears of General Haig's intentions were now sent to the Continent. In April, American troops first took active part in the fighting and during the next three months over 600,000 additional American troops crossed the Atlantic.

In May and June the Germans succeeded in making small advances, but by July the tide had turned. The Allied side had now achieved technological superiority, and in August General Haig's forces, successfully using tanks, began a general offensive in the Somme region. The German forces slowly retreated along the whole Western Front and by early September the German army chiefs informed their Government that peace had to be made at once. The Kaiser's Government, which had scorned the Fourteen Points in January now accepted them in October "as a basis for peace negotiations." The British Cabinet issued a reminder that "the pronouncements of President Wilson were a statement of attitude made before the Brest-

Litovsk Treaty [and] the enforcement of the peace of Bucharest on Roumania. . . . They cannot, therefore, be understood as a full recitation of the conditions of peace."

In the meantime, the Austrians had suffered a major defeat on the Italian Front, and an Allied advance from Salonika in Greece had pushed Bulgaria out of the war. A long drawn-out British campaign against the Ottoman Empire in the Near East, in the course of which British Colonel T. E. Lawrence had roused the Arab tribes against their Turkish suzerains, was climaxed in October 1918 by the capture of Damascus. On October 31 Turkey left the war. In Germany itself, four years of unremitting war effort had likewise taken their toll. The reconstruction of the Government in October 1918 only fanned the fires of domestic discontent. In early November a naval mutiny began to spread inland; Emperor William II was forced to abdicate; and early on November 11 it was announced that representatives of the German Government had agreed to terms which amounted to a virtual "unconditional surrender."

Six million Britons had served in the armed forces. Of these 750,000 had lost their lives (88 percent were killed in action), and 1,700,000 had been wounded. For the moment, all that the living could think of was that the ordeal was over at last. As the bells announced the Armistice, London's streets became "a sea of laughing, joking people" dancing and singing in the streets and on buses. The horrors of the past and the fears for the future evaporated for the moment in "a triumphant pandemonium."

Chapter 15

THE CONSEQUENCES OF THE 𝔓𝔢𝔞𝔠𝔢

THE ENERGIES of the inhabitants of a country engaged in all-out war may be repeatedly buoyed up by the prospects of victory; but when the moment of victory arrives, it is discovered that the triumph is hollow and that the problems of peace are more frustrating than the problems of war. The exultant Englishmen of Armistice Day, 1918, were soon to discover issues that transformed "victory" for some into a tawdry, second-rate achievement. The war was over but the nation now faced the difficulties of restoring international stability and of facing the perennial Irish Question, the frustrations of domestic reconstruction, the perils of economic boom and bust, and the uncertainties entailed by a political party structure undergoing a fundamental transformation.[1]

The Election of 1918

One of the first acts of peace was to call a new election, and on November 21, 1918, the voters went to the polls to replace a

[1] The best account of the interwar era is Charles Loch Mowat, *Britain Between the Wars, 1918–1940* (London, 1955). Robert Graves' and Alan Hodge's *The Long Week-End: A Social History of Great Britain, 1918–1939,* Paperbound Edition (New York, 1963; first published 1940) is lighthearted but revealing. More specialized aspects of the early postwar age are taken up in Lord Beaverbrook's *The Decline and Fall of Lloyd George* (London, 1963), Robert Blake's *The Unknown Prime Minister* (London, 1954), a biography of Bonar Law, and Richard Lyman's *The First Labour Government* (London, 1958).

House of Commons that had been sitting for eight years. Lloyd George, now "the prime minister who won the war," dramatically sought a popular mandate for his coalition ministry and authority for himself to negotiate the peace abroad and begin the work of economic reconstruction at home. The wartime coalition government had included Liberals, Conservatives, and even Labourites, but not all these groups joined forces for the election. The Conservatives under Bonar Law continued to give loyal support to Lloyd George, but the prewar Liberals did not. The rift between Asquith and Lloyd George opened in 1916 had not been bridged and in 1918 it was deepened when Asquith asked for a Select Committee of Inquiry into a military incident on the Western Front and Lloyd George angrily denounced the request as "a conspiracy to overthrow the Government." In the resultant parliamentary division the Liberal Party split down the middle.

During the general election in November, only those Liberals who had supported Lloyd George in that division were granted certificates of political loyalty—popularly known as "coupons." The 106 Liberals who had not, the Asquithian Liberals, ran a separate slate of candidates. So did the Labour Party, which for the first time designated candidates in a majority of constituencies and which had reorganized itself and its platform so as to lessen the influence of the giant trade unions and increase the influence of individual workers and intellectuals, especially the Fabian Society. Henceforth the Labour Party program openly called for the "common ownership of the means of production." The war had confirmed the expectation of most Labourites that such industries as coal, railways, and power could be operated efficiently by the state, and the party advocated the expansion of such nationalization in the interest of workers' welfare. The party also supported the old Fabian demand of "a national minimum" of social services and the distribution of surplus wealth—by means of a sharply progressive income tax and a capital levy—for the common good.

In contrast to Labour, Lloyd George and his coalition teammates spoke more vaguely of their long-range social goals and more specifically of their immediate foreign policy aims: to try Emperor William II, to punish those guilty of atrocities, and to make Germany pay for the cost of the war "to the uttermost farthing." As the campaign progressed, the Prime Minister's utterances, carefully attuned to the popular mood, became ever more extravagant; "Heaven only knows," he later confided, "what I would have had to promise them if the campaign had lasted a week longer." The Asquithian Liberals denounced the "ish election" as a deliberate attempt to crush all independent political opinion, and Asquith prided himself upon remaining a Liberal "without prefix or suffix."

It may well be that the electorate was not so aroused by the election as the more flamboyant newspaper headlines of the time seemed to indicate. Only 57.6 percent of the eligible voters, who included six million newly enfranchised women, participated, and the result was an overwhelming triumph for the Lloyd George coalition. It elected 484 members, 338 of whom were Conservatives; and the Conservatives elected an additional 48 members as well. The Labour Party, whose popular vote had increased almost six times since 1910, elected 59 M.P.s, the largest opposition group. Yet its principal figures, MacDonald, Philip Snowden, and Arthur Henderson, were all defeated. While the Lloyd George Liberals had become the prisoners of the Conservative majority in the coalition, the Asquithian Liberals managed to elect only 26 members, not including the former Prime Minister himself. A similar upheaval overtook the longtime Liberal allies, Redmond's Irish Nationalists. All but seven of them were defeated by the revolutionary Sinn Feiners, who refused to take their seats at Westminster. The new House of Commons, whose majority overflowed three quarters of the chamber, was thus a very different body from its predecessor. It included a host of new members – such as an unusually large number of (usually Conservative) company directors – but it lacked the cohesion which the traditional nineteenth-century party system had provided. A final *finis* had clearly been written to the prewar era, but the political shape of the new age seemed far from certain.

Lloyd George at Paris

The one prewar Liberal who had escaped unscathed from war and general election was David Lloyd George. He set forth to Paris to make the peace with the apparent support of a large majority of his countrymen. The Paris Peace Conference of 1919 inevitably evoked recollections of a similar gathering at Vienna a little more than a century before. Once again a coalition in which Britain had played a leading role, on sea and land, had emerged victorious and had succeeded in preventing a single power from dominating the European continent. Once again there were representatives from many lands; but it was the leaders of but a few, the Big Five in the earlier instance and the Big Three in the latter, who made the major decisions.

The differences between the two peace settlements were as notable as the similarities. In 1815 Czarist Russia had been one of the victorious allies; in 1919 Communist Russia had withdrawn in defeat from a war it considered to be nothing more than a power struggle among capitalist states headed straight for eventual revolution and destruction. In 1815 the defeated power, France, had helped negotiate the peace. In 1919 the defeated power, Germany, was forced to accept the consensus reached by the victors. In 1815 the Big Five had all been European; in 1919 the Big Three included an all-important non-European power, the United States of America.

The Big Three among the victorious powers did not find it easy to reach a common accord at Paris, if only because they had drawn conflicting lessons from the years of war. The French, who had suffered most, whose soil had been the scene of the most severe fighting, and who had witnessed a generation of young men killed or crippled, drew but one lesson: Germany must never again be allowed to possess the power to invade France. At best, Germany should be cut up; at the very least, she should be deprived of her right to a standing army. A binding anti-German alliance uniting France, Britain, and the United States seemed to be the best guarantee of French security. In contrast, the United States, whose ratio of casualties to population had been only 1/50 as great as France's, had not fought consciously for material gain. Her cities had not been destroyed, nor had her people faced the prospect of starvation by submarine blockade. Consequently, she was willing to assist in the building of a new and better Europe, but not to the extent of signing an entangling alliance. Ultimately, indeed, even the slight limitation upon national sovereignty which membership in the new League of Nations would have entailed proved a stumbling block to the United States Senate.

Britain, whose cost in casualties had been half as great as France's but twenty-five times that of the United States, took a diplomatic stand somewhere between the other two. Britain had some foreign ambitions, and certain former Ottoman and German colonies were eventually added to the British Empire as League of Nations mandates. In regard to Europe itself, however, the British attitude proved more closely akin to the American than to the French. Some of England's chief objectives—the defeat of Germany, the restoration of Belgian independence, the surrender of the German fleet, the abdication of William II—had all been achieved by the time the diplomats met at Paris. Britain, though she had not fought the war to break up the Austrian Empire, could sympathize with the Poles, Czechs, Serbs, and Romanians who had thrown off generations of German, Russian, and Magyar rule. Though Lloyd George did not have such high hopes for the League of Nations as Wilson, he was quite willing to associate Britain with the new organization. Lord Robert Cecil, the younger son of Prime Minister Salisbury, who became the British representative to the League, was a convinced Wilsonian idealist. Lloyd George was no more eager than Wilson to sign a binding military alliance with France. He was less fearful of the new German Republic than was France, and he soon came to realize that Germany could not both be destroyed as a viable state and be expected to pay huge reparations or buy British goods. Once Germany had accepted the peace terms, Lloyd George promised in March 1919, Britain would do "everything possible to enable the German people to get on their legs again. We cannot both cripple her and expect her to pay."

The resultant treaty was necessarily a compromise, not sufficiently idealistic to please Wilson and taking insufficient heed of the needs of French security to please Clemenceau. Even Lloyd George, once he returned to London, was criticized. "I think I did as well as might be expected," he replied, "seated as I was between Jesus Christ and Napoleon Bonaparte." The main territorial and disarmament provisions of the Treaty of Versailles with Germany (and the comparable treaties with Austria and Hungary) were not so severe as a generation of critics inside and outside Germany was to contend. The provisions for reparations proved indeed both politically unenforceable and economically impractical—the coal which Germany had to export to Italy as a reparations payment, for example, deprived Britain of a former export market—and only a small percentage of the thirty-three billion dollar reparations bill was ever to be paid.

One factor of instability promoted by the Paris Peace Settlement was the new and untried governments set up in Eastern Europe. Old habits of obedience had been ended and traditional channels of trade were blocked by new tariff walls. Yet the new boundaries reflected much more adequately than those of 1914 the national preferences of the East European peoples. A second and much greater factor of instability was the fact that while the great powers of 1815 had all participated in and been substantially agreed upon the settlement of Vienna, three of the big powers of 1919 were clearly not satisfied with the Paris Peace Settlement. The Italians, one of the victors, regarded themselves deprived of legitimate gains in the Adriatic. The Russians clearly wished to bring within the boundaries of international communism all the lands the Czars had controlled and more besides. Finally, the Germans were soon to argue that international equity required the restoration of their fleet, their colonies, and at least some of their lands in Eastern Europe, where a Polish "corridor" now separated East Prussia from the rest of Germany.

For the moment neither Germany nor Russia had the power to change the settlement, and a long era of at least relative peace seemed a reasonable hope in the summer of 1919. A balance of power of sorts had returned to the continent of Europe, and British statesmen could once again afford to turn their attention to other matters. One of these was the British Empire, upon which World War I had had a paradoxical effect. On the one hand that empire had grown, so that a map of the world painted in 1919 could show more areas than ever "painted red" in the traditional imperial sense. The new acquisitions admittedly were neither colonies nor protectorates but League of Nations mandates, a status midway between colony and international trusteeship, in that a specific mandatory power had practical control but owed ultimate responsibility to the new international organization. In the Near East three of the Arab states which had hitherto been parts of the Ottoman Empire came under British auspices as class "A" mandates or protectorates soon to gain independence: Palestine, Trans-Jordan, and Mesopotamia (henceforth Iraq). In Africa, parts of former German Togoland and Kamerun (Cameroons) and all of German East Africa (Tanganyika) became class "B" mandates, in which the mandatory power was granted "full powers of administration and legislation."

For the older British dominions and for India, the war had provided both an opportunity to demonstrate their loyalty to the mother country and an incentive to develop a new sense of separatism. The government in London might still have claimed in 1914 the technical right to involve all the dominions in war, but it could clearly not have compelled their military aid. Yet tiny New Zealand sent 112,000 troops to fight overseas, almost as large a percentage of her total population as was recruited for the armed forces in the British Isles themselves; and even larger contingents (representing a somewhat smaller percentage of the total population) were sent by Australia, Canada, and South Africa. Almost the entire professional Indian army (80,000 Europeans and 230,000 Indians) was sent to Europe or the Near East. The motives ranged from traditional loyalty by emigrant sons and daughters and outrage at German militarism to a desire (in India at least) to be rewarded with a greater degree of self-government.

War weariness at times sapped the spirit of imperial unity overseas just as it encouraged political discord at home. Some South African Boers wished to take advantage of the conflict to regain their republican status; but other Boer leaders, like Botha and Smuts, working in cooperation with South Africans of English origin, kept South Africa in the war. Both New Zealand and Canada adopted military conscription, in emulation

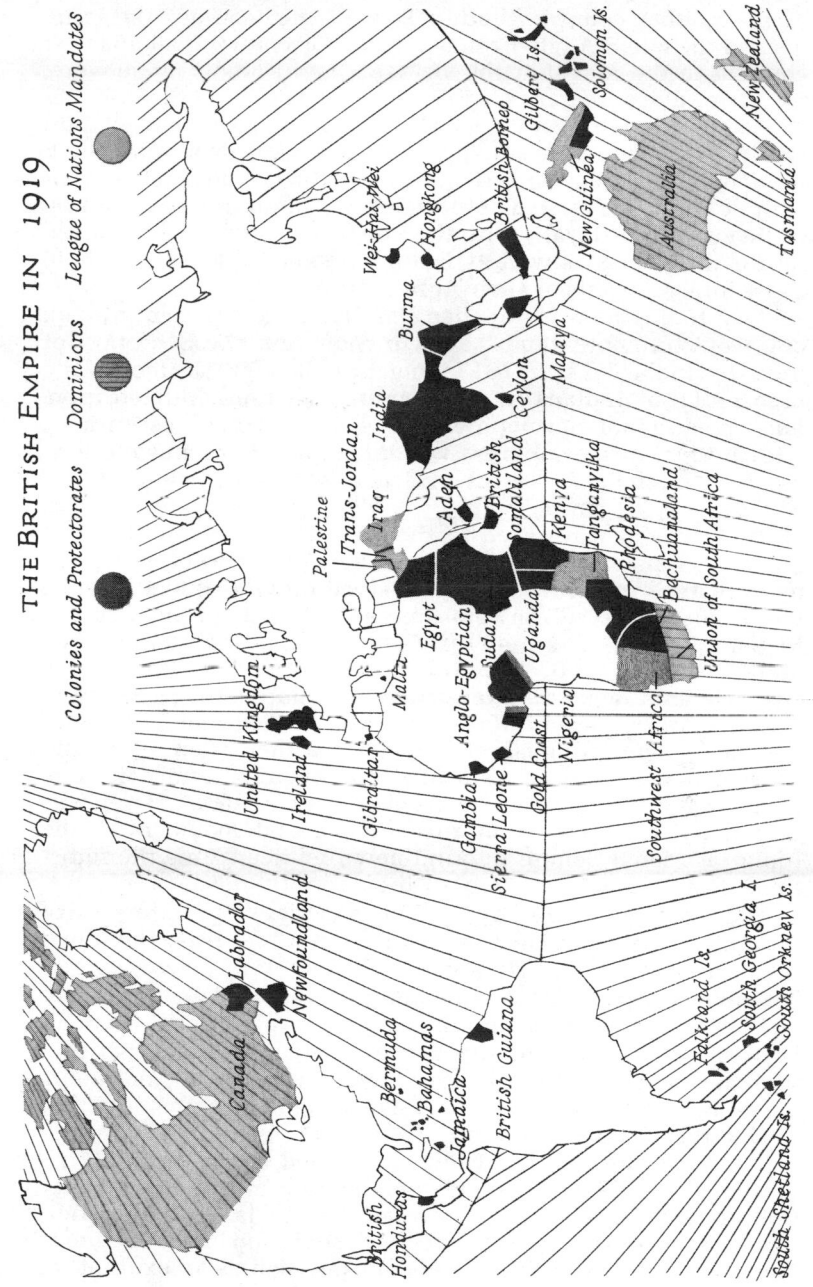

THE BRITISH EMPIRE IN 1919

Colonies and Protectorates   Dominions   League of Nations Mandates

United Kingdom
Ireland
Gibraltar
Malta
Palestine
Trans-Jordan
Iraq
Aden
British Somaliland
India
Burma
Ceylon
Malaya
British Borneo
Wei-Hai-Wei
Hongkong
Gilbert Is.
Solomon Is.
New Guinea
Australia
New Zealand
Tasmania
Kenya
Tanganyika
Rhodesia
Bachuanaland
Union of South Africa
Egypt
Anglo-Egyptian Sudan
Uganda
Nigeria
Gold Coast
Sierra Leone
Gambia
Southwest Africa
Canada
Labrador
Newfoundland
Bermuda
Bahamas
Jamaica
British Guiana
British Honduras
Falkland Is.
South Georgia I.
South Orkney Is.
South Shetland Is.

of the mother country, though in the latter country the issue opened the latent Anglo-French rivalry. French Canadians took comfort in the fact that the British Empire and France were, for once, allies, but they still opposed conscription if only because the French Third Republic was anticlerical rather than loyally Catholic. Australia, whose Labour Party was much influenced by emigrant Irishmen, narrowly voted down conscription in two national referendums. In all other ways Australia cooperated loyally with the imperial war effort, and indeed all the dominions as well as India found cause to take pride in the military exploits of their fighting men.

In India, the war impelled the British government to spell out its future intentions. Edwin Montagu, the Secretary of State for India, did so in 1917 when he called for "the increasing association of Indians in every branch of the administration, and the gradual development of self-governing institutions, with a view to the progressive realization of responsible government in India as an integral part of the British Empire." The same spirit characterized the Montagu-Chelmsford Report of 1918 which in turn led to the Government of India Act of 1919. "Transferred" powers were henceforth to be exercised by ministries responsible to the elected provincial legislatures, while only "reserved" powers remained directly in the hands of British officials. The inauguration of this new system of "dyarchy" was marred by "the Amritsar Massacre" in that Punjab city. General Reginald Dyer ordered his native troops to fire at a rioting mob. Nearly 400 people were killed and 1200 were wounded. Some Englishmen applauded the action as having averted a second Indian mutiny, but Asquith termed it "one of the worst outrages in the whole of our history." Dyer was ultimately dismissed from the service, and members of the Indian National Congress found new fuel to enflame the sometimes fitful nationalistic zeal of their countrymen.

For a time in 1917 and 1918 an Imperial War Conference of Dominion Prime Ministers and representatives from India met regularly in London. They generally met with Lloyd George's five-man War Cabinet as an enlarged Imperial War Cabinet. Such wartime planning promised to revive Joseph Chamberlain's hope of a federal supergovernment for the British Empire, but the entry of the United States into the war and the increasing interest in the prospective League of Nations tended to sidetrack such speculation.

The dominions and India demanded, and eventually received, the right to separate membership at the Paris Peace Conference; and Canada, Australia, New Zealand, South Africa, and India were granted separate representation in the League of Nations. Many Americans saw this decision as an example of

British duplicity in that it increased British representation, and the multiple membership in the League was often cited by opponents of the League as a reason for steering clear of the venture. In fact, the initiative for separate representation had come from Canada; it was less a tribute to Lloyd George's Machiavellian cunning than a reflection of political embarrassment. Dominion status henceforth was to connote a high degree of foreign policy autonomy as well as domestic independence. In this sense the First World War effected a giant stride toward the gradual transformation of the British Empire into what some men in 1918 were beginning to call the British Commonwealth of Nations.

A Solution for Ireland

As so often before in British history, the most troublesome of imperial problems provoked by war was the one next door in Ireland. While Redmond and his fellow Irish Nationalists had sought to rally their countrymen to the British cause as the only way of winning home rule without splitting their island, the revolutionary members of Sinn Fein ("Ourselves Alone" in Gaelic) preferred to take advantage of the war by accepting German aid as some of their predecessors had once sought Spanish or French help. By the spring of 1916 little German support had been forthcoming and a majority of Sinn Fein leaders were in jail. A minority, however, succeeded in April 1916 in launching "the Easter Rebellion" in Dublin. A republic was declared, but within a week the insurgents had been defeated. The mass of Irishmen might have remained acquiescent had not the British government decided to execute fifteen of the ringleaders. Another leader, Eamon de Valera (1882–   ) escaped by reason of American citizenship, and he henceforth led the movement for complete independence. In 1916 began the six-year "Time of Troubles" in Irish history which was to inspire so much of twentieth-century Irish literature; by 1918 much of southern Ireland had become in effect an occupied country.

The General Election of 1918 sealed the doom of Redmond's constitutionalist policy. The Sinn Feiners elected were pledged to sit in a parliament in Dublin but never in Westminster, and in January 1919 those not in jail or in hiding renewed their declaration of independence and attempted to set up their own parliament in Dublin. The result was savage civil war between the British "black and tans" (soldiers whose uniforms combined the khaki of the British army with the black caps and belts of the Royal Irish Constabulary) and the Irish Revolutionary Army.   No traditional rules of war restrained the consequent tactics of ambush, plunder, burning, and seizure of hostages.

In the middle of this civil war, the Parliament at Westminster replaced the Home Rule Act of 1914 — which had never been put into effect — with the Home Rule Act of 1920.   This provided for two Irish parliaments, one for the twenty counties of the south, the other for the six Ulster counties of the north, with authority over all activities except defense, currency, and tariffs.   These were to remain in the hands of the Westminster Parliament, in which the Irish were to retain limited representation.   The Northern Irish accepted the plan; thus the section of the island which had so long fought the concept of Home Rule now paradoxically received it.   The Sinn Feiners, on the other hand, rejected the plan as a political mockery and a criminal effort to partition the island.   The Sinn Fein Dail (Parliament) claimed to be the Government of all Ireland, and the civil war continued.

Sir Henry Wilson, the Chief of the Imperial General Staff, urged that the Government must either "Go all out or get out." Lloyd George, though in part responsible for the civil war, ultimately preferred the latter alternative.   The protracted fighting not only alienated public opinion in the United States and in the Empire but also caused a similar sense of revulsion in England itself.   A number of newspapers, the Archbishop of Canterbury, and King George V all spoke in favor of a peaceful settlement.

Protracted negotiations in 1921 by Lloyd George and Sinn Fein representatives led to a treaty giving the new Irish Free State dominion status in the Empire.   Men like Arthur Griffith and Michael Collins preferred the substance of complete independence to the letter, if only because a total military triumph was beyond their power.   Reluctantly they also acquiesced in the right of the Northern Irish Parliament to exempt itself from the new Irish Free State, a right it immediately exercised.   For DeValera and the more radical Sinn Feiners, the treaty seemed a betrayal, and the year that followed the withdrawal of British troops saw an outbreak of civil war among Irishmen even more fierce and damaging than the fighting of the previous years. Only after Collins had been killed in ambush and Griffith had died of heart failure did DeValera call off armed resistance. Ultimately even he came to realize that the Treaty of 1921 had given at least to the twenty counties of southern Ireland independence in fact, and that the tenuous bonds which still tied the Irish Free State to Britain — such as the required oath of loyalty to King George V — could be cut step by step in a constitutional fashion.   In some respects, the centuries-long "Irish Question" had been resolved in 1922 by a combination of violence and compromise.   Partition remained a stumbling block; but as feelings gradually mellowed, some Irishmen began to realize that, politically independent or not, they remained tied to Britain by economic interest, by language — for the attempt to supplant English completely with Gaelic did not succeed — and by a common heritage of legal and political institutions.

The Twenties: Economy and Society

Although the inhabitants of England and Scotland could not help but be concerned with Irish affairs during the immediate postwar period, they were even more engrossed with events on their own island. Although the Government had promised returning veterans "to make Britain a fit country for heroes to live in" and had set up a separate Ministry of Reconstruction to provide schemes for government-aided housing and town planning, it looked forward with some foreboding to the sudden demobilization of millions of war veterans at a time when the specter of socialist revolution seemed to haunt the Continent. The reconstruction proposals had assumed the existence of a stable economy and the continuation of some form of wartime rationing and price controls. Instead, there was an immediate demand for a general relaxation of controls, and Britain was caught up for a year and a half in an unprecedented economic boom.

Returning veterans might not find "civvy street" paved with gold, but for the moment they had no difficulty locating jobs, as many large companies worked overtime filling orders for civilian goods and pouring capital into plant expansion. The result was a widespread inflation which carried wholesale prices to 225 percent of their prewar level. Labor unions, which had gained 50 percent in size since 1914, found their energies diverted from long-range goals of nationalization to the more immediate problem of keeping the pay packets of their members in line with rising prices. Strikes were endemic — an average of 49 million working days a year were lost to strikes in 1919–21, a figure more than twice that of even the most turbulent prewar year and ten times as high as any year of the 1930s, 1940s, or 1950s. In the midst of such militancy, a spirit of class consciousness became more evident than ever in British history.

During the immediate postwar boom it was found uneconomic to build the working-class houses for which the Housing and Town Planning Act of 1919 had called; and once the bubble burst, the Government found budget retrenchment the only answer to declining revenues. Initially the slump of 1921 was seen as but a temporary phenomenon. Only when it be-

UNEMPLOYMENT IN BRITAIN BETWEEN THE WARS *

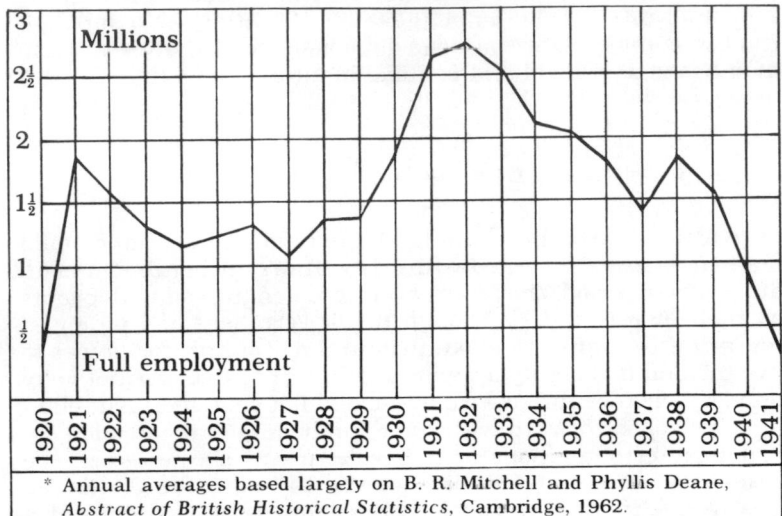

* Annual averages based largely on B. R. Mitchell and Phyllis Deane, *Abstract of British Historical Statistics*, Cambridge, 1962.

came clear that Britain could not pull herself out of the economic doldrums and did not seem to be benefiting from the world boom of 1925–29 did pessimism about the future of the economy become prevalent.

During the thirty years from 1883 to 1913, only one man in twenty had been unemployed; during the postwar years of 1921–38, unemployment was the fate of one man in seven. Such economic waste was the by-product of persistent difficulties in three of Britain's most important nineteenth-century industries – coal mining, cotton manufacturing, and shipbuilding. The problem was only in part alleviated by vigorous industrial and technological development in certain newer industries and by a general rise in the standard of living.

The economic slump of 1921 did not at first dim all postwar reconstruction hopes. Although the reorganized railways were returned to private ownership and the coal mines, despite the pleas of the miners and a majority of a government-appointed "Sankey Commission," remained unnationalized, the Housing and Town Planning Act of 1919 became only the first of numerous such interwar statutes. The Industrial Courts Act of 1919 permanently increased the power of the Ministry of Labour to mediate in labor disputes. The slump of 1921, although it dampened labor militancy and brought about a downturn in trade union membership, was not followed by a decline in real wages. Prices often fell more quickly than wages, and the

$46\frac{1}{2}$–48 hour working week became standard in British factories.

Perhaps the most significant of the immediate postwar social service measures proved to be the Unemployment Insurance Act of 1921, which extended the scope of the initial act of 1911. As the number of unemployed remained at a million or more from 1921 on, this statute became for many Englishmen the most meaningful of all government welfare measures. Unemployment benefits made up an ever increasing portion of the national budget. The £500,000 of benefits paid in 1913–14 swelled to £53,000,000 in 1921–22. The dole was to be the butt of many a wry joke during the 1920s and 1930s, but it remained a government recognition that neither private charity nor the poorhouse could be the sole refuge for those out of work. They had a "right" to such help, and those afflicted came to accept it as such.

The war, which helped cause the postwar boom-and-bust cycle and which accentuated Britain's decline from its unrivaled pre-1914 international trading position, also accentuated many long slumbering social changes. Four years of war blurred outward distinctions of class and of sex. The mass consumption of readymade clothing softened social differences in dress, and first the cinema and later the radio provided a common intellectual denominator for all elements of society. The lower-class deference which Walter Bagehot had discerned in the 1860s was far less evident in the 1920s, and the phrase "I know my station" was increasingly reserved for revivals of Gilbert and Sullivan operettas. The Edwardian upper class, though not overthrown by the war, had seen a pitifully large number of its sons killed in battle, and the large landowner with strong ties to the business world now had to rub shoulders in popular esteem with movie stars and heroes of "the now all-important world of sport." The columnist and the gossip writer had found a niche in the newspaper world, and "society" was increasingly becoming "people worthy of a columnist's respectful attention."

The foothold which many middle-class women had gained in the business and professional world was to some extent retained. The law which provided votes for women was matched by others which admitted women to the courtroom both as lawyers and as jurors; but the advocates of "equal pay for equal work" found big businessmen and trade union leaders less sympathetic than politicians. Even in politics, the hopes of the prewar suffragettes remained, in one respect, disappointed. Women M.P.s, like the Virginia-born Lady Astor, who was elected to the House of Commons in 1919, continued to be the exception rather than the rule. The female ideal of those who "thought modern" in the 1920s became the "flapper": the easygoing, sporty young woman with a boyish figure who wore short hair and short skirts and who dispensed with chaperones.

Divorces were made easier to obtain, but the only legally accepted causes remained adultery and desertion; and despite the fears of an older generation of moralists, the number granted in any given year during the 1920s remained below 5000. Psychoanalysis became fashionable. Dr. Marie Stopes gave new prominence and respectability to the practice of contraception for married people, and by 1930 the Anglican Church had given the practice its somewhat hesitant blessing. Old barriers were collapsing in the upper-class nursery as well. Children were no longer barred from eating or conversing or playing games with their parents until they had reached late adolescence. With the falling birthrate, children were in some cases enjoying a scarcity value they had hitherto lacked.

For the English, the 1920s were less the "Roaring" than the "Careless" Twenties. While older standards did not disappear altogether, there was both in literature and in life a change of attitude which the war had at least promoted. It was the attitude of somewhat cynical and superficially gay disillusionment embodied in the phrase "Life's too short" and in the adjective "bittersweet," which became the title of one of Noel Coward's popular musical comedies. The war had demonstrated that neither life nor property was sacred, and the postwar period provided an incentive to seek "psychological compensation" for social tensions in idle amusements. Yet the very fact that so many Britons were able to do this reflected a reasonably high standard of living. Comfort as well as social satire could be derived from the fact that when the newspaper headlines screamed ENGLAND IN PERIL or CAN WE AVOID DISASTER? the reference was not to a new military or diplomatic catastrophe but to the results of a cricket match.

The Fall of Lloyd George

The economic slump which began in 1921 could not help but weaken the political position of the powerful coalition ministry which had governed Britain under Lloyd George's leadership since the general election of 1918. Not that the Prime Minister became personally unpopular. He was still "the pilot who weathered the storm," and published reports stating that individuals whom he had recommended for the knighthood and the peerage had paid large sums into his party war chest (£150,000 per barony) hurt his reputation little. Admittedly, he had been less successful than he wished in restoring Europe to perfect harmony. Problems of German reparations and inter-allied war debts hampered the restoration of the prewar system of international trade. Anglo-French distrust added to the lack of international stability, since Britain and France were the two great powers in the League of Nations. Britain went so far in 1922 as to offer France the diplomatic guarantee against Germany which she had been demanding since 1919; but when the offer was not accompanied by a military convention that accorded with French wishes, the arrangement fell through. A war between Greece and Kemal Ataturk's new Turkish Republic was still going on in the Near East, and Lloyd George was widely, though perhaps unjustly, criticized for his handling of the "Chanak affair." He had warned the Turks not to attack the area of the Dardanelles then occupied by British troops pending a final peace settlement. He then discovered that the French and most of the dominion prime ministers were unwilling to pledge support if the stand led to war. Though Lloyd George's intransigence restored British international prestige in the Near East and led to the resolution of the Near Eastern war in the Treaty of Lausanne (1923), his countrymen tended to view his policy as dangerous brinkmanship.

Although most of the leaders of the Conservative Party continued to favor the Coalition arrangement, an increasing number of Conservative backbenchers did not. They feared the permanent eclipse of an independent Conservative Party, even though many prewar Liberal-Conservative differences had disappeared and even though the rise of a professedly socialist Labour Party seemed to dictate fusion with the Liberals. Moreover, Lloyd George's greatest diplomatic achievement, the Irish Treaty of December 1921, seemed to many old-guard Tories to be a sellout of their "unionist" principles. Finally, for Conservatives like Lord Beaverbrook, the editor of the influential *Daily Express,* Lloyd George's unwillingness to meet economic problems with a full-fledged program of tariff protection and imperial preference provided an adequate reason for wanting him out of office.

Ultimately, it was the decision by Bonar Law to support the backbench revolt which led the Conservative Party in 1922 to leave the Coalition. The resignation of his chief Cabinet ministers forced Lloyd George to resign as well, and the king asked Bonar Law to head the new, purely Conservative, ministry. King George V fully expected to see the fifty-nine-year-old Lloyd George Prime Minister again — and so doubtless did Lloyd George himself — but matters worked out otherwise. Bonar Law's first decision was to ask the king to dissolve Parliament and call for new general elections on a platform that bore a close kinship to President Harding's "normalcy" in the United States: "tranquillity and freedom from adventures and commitments both at home and abroad."

Both Liberals and Conservatives stressed the danger of the Labour Party coming to power. That party in turn defended its policy as one of bringing about "a more equitable distribution of the nation's wealth by constitutional means. This is neither Bolshevism nor Communism, but common sense and justice." The results of the election (5½ million votes for the Conservatives, 4.2 million votes for Labour, 4.1 million votes for the Liberals) indicated that Britain's prewar pattern of two major parties and two minor parties had been replaced by a virtual three-party system. The Conservative popular vote plurality was, however, sufficient to give the Conservatives a decisive overall Parliamentary majority: 347 Conservatives, 142 Labourites, and 117 Liberals (divided between 60 Asquith Liberals and 57 Lloyd George Liberals).

Bonar Law's ministry proved to be a short one because the cancer of the throat which was to end his life in 1923 began to grow progressively worse during his term of office. Law did achieve one major foreign policy settlement, which proved for the second time in two years how much Britain had come to make good relations with the United States a cornerstone of her foreign policy. Although Britain had emerged from World War I with the royal navy still the foremost in the world, naval officials soon came to realize that both finances and Anglo-American relations made the goal of naval parity preferable to a new naval race. Thus at the Washington Conference of 1921–22, Britain, by accepting a 5–5–3–1.75–1.75 ratio of battleships with the United States, Japan, France, and Italy respectively, quietly agreed to end over two hundred years of naval supremacy. The same conference also replaced the Anglo-Japanese Alliance of 1902 with a more vaguely worded agreement involving the United States and France, as well as Japan and Britain, which guaranteed the status quo in the Far East. Japan had profited from its role as ally in World War I by usurping much of the influence formerly exerted by Germany and Russia in China, and the Washington Conference Treaties facilitated the furthering of Japanese espansionist ambitions. But this result was not obvious to the other major powers at the time.

A yet more notable example of British recognition of the political and financial importance World War I had bestowed upon the United States was the signing of a war debt agreement in January 1923. One of the economic heritages of the war was that Britain had become both a debtor and creditor nation. Her European allies owed her $10.5 billion, the Germans owed her $7.2 billion in reparations, but the United Kingdom itself owed $4.25 billion to the United States. Though Lloyd George had initially advocated heavy reparations payments, his Government soon came to realize that the immense burden of inter-European debt was proving an enormous obstacle to the restoration and growth of international trade.   In the 1922 "Balfour Note," Britain sought to cut the Gordian knot by offering to remit all Allied payments and German reparations payments to her if the United States remitted all British debts as part of an international financial settlement.   If the United States refused, Britain would ask of her allies only so much money as she had to pay to the United States.

Neither the French nor the Americans were sympathetic. The French felt that the United States should cancel all Allied debts as her contribution to a common cause to which France had committed more than her share of human lives; German reparations, on the other hand, were seen as a legitimate compensation for damage done and suffering incurred.   The American government viewed France and Britain as debtors, not as allies in a common cause.   "They hired the money, didn't they?" was President Coolidge's somewhat narrow reaction.   The settlement reached in Washington by Stanley Baldwin, the Chancellor of the Exchequer, provided for Britain to repay her debts to the United States over a 62-year period at $3\frac{1}{2}$ percent interest. Americans regarded the terms as a generous concession, and for the moment the settlement aided Anglo-American relations and safeguarded the British reputation for financial integrity.   By 1931 Britain had paid nearly $2 billion, a difficult task in view of the steep American tariff barriers.   Initially, the settlement also raised Baldwin's prestige, but it was to be much criticized later on when the United States concluded similar agreements with other European debtors on terms much less onerous than those imposed on Britain.

Bonar Law's retirement from the Prime Ministership in May 1923 forced King George V to name a successor, since the Conservative Party had no obvious candidate.   Lord Curzon (1859–1925), the Foreign Secretary (1920–24) and former Viceroy of India expected the call, but the nomination ultimately went to Stanley Baldwin largely because, in Curzon's biting words, Baldwin possessed "the supreme and indispensible qualification of not being a peer."   By 1923 it seemed no longer practical to most Englishmen to have a Prime Minister rule from the House of Lords, especially when the largest opposition party, the Labour Party, was virtually unrepresented there.   Baldwin (1867–1947), an M.P. since 1908, had reached Cabinet rank only in 1921 and was unprepossessing in appearance and undistinguished in intellect.   He established, however, a reputation as a man of moral integrity, common sense, and good will; and his precepts of "Faith, Hope, Love, and Work" as the remedy for the ailments which beset Britain and the world were sufficiently characteristic of the attitudes of a majority of his countrymen to cause one recent author to dub the 1920s and 1930s "The Baldwin Age" and another "The Age of Illusion." [2]

Stanley Baldwin's decision in the fall of 1923 to seek to unite his party and to meet the continuing problem of mass unemployment on a platform of full-fledged tariff protection did not prove similarly in tune with the views of his countrymen. The unexpected election of December 1923 did attract wavering Conservative leaders back to their party's standard, but at the same time it revived a potent prewar political controversy. The same issue which had reunited the Liberals of 1905 sufficed to cause the Asquith and Lloyd George Liberals to wage a strong antiprotection campaign under a common banner in 1923. Labourites also opposed protective tariffs; for them the remedy for unemployment lay not in tariffs but in socialism. The election results showed how a relatively small switch in popular votes in a few constituencies could completely alter the Parliamentary picture. There were now 258 Conservative M.P.s (formerly 346), 191 Labourites (formerly 142), and 158 Liberals (formerly 117).

The First Labour Government

Although Baldwin faced the new Parliament as Prime Minister, he resigned after a vote of "no confidence" by the combined Liberal-Labour opposition, and the king called upon Ramsay MacDonald, the leader of the Labour Party, to form a new government. That a "revolutionary socialist" should be named Prime Minister seemed startling to many Englishmen, and few Labour leaders had really expected that their distant vision of a Labour Government would become reality so soon. Asquith was begged by many to "save the country from the horrors of Socialism and Confiscation"; but a Conservative-Liberal coalition after an election fought on the issue of protection would have been as illogical as a Labourite-Liberal coalition. There was also a widespread realization that a Labour Government dependent on Liberal support would give the supposedly revolutionary party a taste of power while preventing it from enacting truly revolutionary measures.

The Labour Party of 1924 was, in any event, an amalgam of both moderate and radical trade union leaders, socialist intel-

---

[2] John Raymond (ed.), *The Baldwin Age* (London, 1960), and Ronald Blythe, *The Age of Illusion* (London, 1963).

lectuals, and recent converts from Liberalism who were attracted more by the party's humanitarianism and internationalism than by its socialism. While leaders like F. W. Jowett pungently criticized the "terrible tribute to Rent, Interest, and Profit" paid by the workers to "enrich mainly the class which has already more to spend than it can usefully spend," men like Sidney Webb struck a different note. "For we must always remember," he observed in 1923, "that the founder of British socialism was not Karl Marx but Robert Owen, and that Robert Owen preached not class war but the ancient doctrine of human brotherhood."

Ramsay MacDonald (1866–1937), the new Prime Minister, was the illegitimate son of a poor Scotswoman. A longtime party worker, he had received a great reputation for radicalism because of his opposition to World War I, but he proved in practice to be a political moderate as well as "the handsomest of all Prime Ministers"; and his new Cabinet of twenty included not only trade union members (five) but also ex-Liberals like Lord Haldane. A minor furor was raised in the party's ranks by the question of whether the Cabinet should wear formal dress to meet the king. Some did and others did not; the Cabinet eventually bought three uniforms of formal court attire to be worn in turn by whichever Cabinet members required them on specified occasions. "I could not help marvelling," noted J. H. Clynes, the new Lord Privy Seal, as he waited to be received by King George V, "at the strange turn of Fortune's wheel, which had brought MacDonald, the starveling clerk, Thomas, the engine-driver, Henderson, the foundry laborer and Clynes, the millhand, to this pinnacle. . . . "

The Labour Government of 1924 disappointed the expectations of its more enthusiastic supporters, but it did succeed in taking over the governmental reins, and it was able to record several minor accomplishments on the domestic scene. It raised unemployment insurance benefits, eased the conditions under which the elderly received their pensions, and enacted a new housing act which provided added government subsidies for the building of working-class houses under controlled rents. It repealed certain wartime tariffs and widened the educational opportunities of working-class children by increasing the number of "free places" in secondary schools and providing university scholarships.

MacDonald was his own Foreign Secretary and did his best to advance the task of European reconciliation. The American Dawes Plan to extend and regularize German reparations payment — largely written by Josiah Stamp, the British expert on the Dawes Committee — led, as a result of MacDonald's skillful diplomacy, to the withdrawal of French forces from the German

Ruhr into which they had moved the year before to force German compliance. The result was an Anglo-French reconciliation and the laying of the groundwork for the full readmission of Germany to the European diplomatic family. MacDonald gave full British support to the League of Nations and was the first British Prime Minister to attend its sessions in person.

The Labour Government's most controversial foreign policy innovation involved British relations with Russia. Although most Labour Party adherents had long since become disillusioned with their initial expectation that the Bolshevik Revolution would lead to a democratic socialist state in Russia, they repeatedly argued that the new Russian government ought to be recognized and dealt with like any other legitimate power. They saw no contradiction between their championship of Russian rights on the international scene and their quick decision to bar the new small British Communist Party from membership in the Labour Party. "A Communist," wrote J. R. Clynes in 1924, "is no more a Left Wing Member of the Labour Party than an atheist is a Left Wing member of the Christian Church." In 1921 the Lloyd George Government had given Soviet Russia *de facto* recognition and negotiated a trade agreement, but anti-British propaganda in the Russian press and various minor incidents kept relations strained.

As soon as the Labour Government took office in 1924 it extended *de jure* recognition to Soviet Russia and after lengthy negotiations in the spring and summer of 1924 it announced the signing of two treaties with the Soviet Union: first, a commercial agreement and second, a treaty promising that, in return for Russian consideration of the claims of British holders of Czarist bonds and former owners of property nationalized by Russia without compensation, the Government would recommend to Parliament a British guarantee of a sizable loan to the U.S.S.R. The treaty, which required Parliamentary ratification, was opposed by Conservatives and Liberals alike and might well have brought down the Government. What actually did do so, however, was the Campbell case, the decision by the Government to drop their prosecution of a Communist editor who had violated a statute of 1797 against incitement to mutiny by urging soldiers never to fire on fellow workers. Asquith's motion for a Select Committee of Inquiry was interpreted by MacDonald as an issue of confidence, and when the Labour Government was defeated he resigned from office. The result was the third general election in three years.

The Conservatives seized the opportunity to brand the Labourites as Bolsheviks, and they were given added ammunition when late in the election campaign the Zinoviev Telegram was published in the newspapers. Purportedly written by the Secretary of the Communist International, it strongly urged a Labour victory in Britain as necessary for the approval of the Russian Treaty which, in turn, would further "the revolutionizing of the international and British proletariat no less than a successful rising in any of the working districts of England. . . ." The Zinoviev letter has long been considered a prime factor in the Labour Party defeat in the general election. An analysis of the election returns of November 1924, however, indicates that a sharp decline in the Liberal Party vote—the voice of studious moderation in the midst of the "Red Scare"—was more significant. In comparison with the election of the year before, the Conservative popular vote increased by two million, but the Labour vote also increased by 1.2 million. The Liberal vote, however, declined by 1.2 million. The Labourites, who had benefited from the Conservative-Liberal split in many a three-cornered fight the previous year could do so no longer, and for the next five years the Government was in the hands of a massive Conservative Parliamentary majority: 415 Conservatives, 152 Labourites, and but 42 Liberals. The Liberal Party, the victim of war and personalities as well as of changing social conditions, had ceased to be a major party, and Stanley Baldwin was back as the head of what he promised would be a "sane, commonsense Government, not carried away by revolutionary theories or hare-brained schemes. . . ."

Chapter 16

THE FALSE DAWN AND THE GREAT
𝔇𝔢𝔭𝔯𝔢𝔰𝔰𝔦𝔬𝔫

STANLEY BALDWIN'S second ministry (1924–29) provided many Britons of the day with the impression that the domestic political and economic reverberations set off by World War I had died down. "The spirit of Locarno" added a glow of reconciliation to the international horizon. Only in retrospect did it become clear that the dawn was a false one and that the economic dislocations created by war had only been patched and not mended. The resulting international great depression, by bringing Adolf Hitler and his national socialist movement to power in Germany, was to lead directly to another World War.[1]

Baldwin's Cabinet included a number of notable personalities: two sons of Joseph Chamberlain, Austen as Foreign Minister, his half brother Neville as Minister of Health, and Winston Churchill as Chancellor of the Exchequer. Churchill's return to the party he had left in 1904 symbolized the erosion that had been taking place within the Liberal Party and the drift away from the Liberal camp toward either the Conservative right or the Labourite left. One of Churchill's first steps as Chancellor of the Exchequer was to prove highly controversial; he made the British pound once again freely exchangeable for

---

[1] The books by Mowat, Raymond, and Graves & Hodge referred to earlier are all relevant for this chapter. Detailed economic statistics are taken from Sidney Pollard's *The Development of the British Economy, 1914–1950* (London, 1962).

gold at the prewar ratio of $4.86. The return to the gold standard had for some years been the dream of such English financiers as Montagu Norman, the influential Governor of the Bank of England. It seemed at once the symbol of the revival of prewar economic and moral values and the step which would restore Britain's trade, prosperity, and prestige. In effect, the return to the gold standard at the old rate tended to overvalue Britain's exports by 10 percent, thus magnifying the problems faced by the country's exporters. At the same time the need to maintain a sufficient gold reserve kept interest rates at a high level, a factor discouraging industrial investment. It was a little like "putting on the brake while going up hill." Although 1925–29 saw the unemployment rate decline in comparison with the 1921–25 period, Britain did not experience an economic boom comparable with the Coolidge prosperity in the United States.

The General Strike and After

The restoration of the gold standard may have provided the illusion that normalcy had been achieved, but the troubles of the coal industry led, in May 1926, to a very abnormal event — the only general strike in British history. The coal industry had already undergone one damaging strike in 1921, when the mines had been returned to private ownership after being operated by the Government during the war. At that time wages had been cut, but the miners had been allowed to keep the seven-hour day they had gained in 1919. For a time, special conditions such as the decline in German coal production which resulted from the French occupation of the Ruhr in 1923 increased British coal exports. By 1925, however, the industry was again in the doldrums. British mines were lagging disastrously in technological innovation, many pits had closed, and 300,000 miners were out of work. The owners could see no way out but to reduce costs by again lowering wages or else restoring the eight-hour day. The Secretary of the Miners' Federation, A. J. Cook, responded with the battle cry: "Not a penny off the pay, not a minute on the day." A strike was only averted in 1925 when the Government appointed a Royal Commission under Herbert Samuel (1870–1963) to seek a solution while providing the coal owners with a subsidy to keep wages at their old rate.

The Samuel Commission reported the following March with various suggestions for increasing mine efficiency which would enable the industry to pay better wages but with no solution for the immediate problem. Both sides remained obdurate.

"It would be possible to say, without exaggeration," wrote Lord Birkenhead, "that the miners' leaders were the stupidest men in England if we had not had frequent occasions to meet the owners." No agreement could be reached, and on May 1, the day the temporary government subsidy ceased, the miners struck. They had been sufficiently shrewd to gain a pledge of support from the Trades Union Congress, and on May 4 a general strike began as well.

A sudden stillness descended upon the land. No trains moved, nor did trams or buses. No newspapers were printed. The docks were still, so were the steel mills. All construction work stopped and no men reported for work at the electric power plants or gasworks. Yet the general strike of 1926 proved to be among labor disputes what the Revolution of 1688 had been among political revolutions – bloodless and peculiarly English. The mass of trade union members were indeed faithful to the strike call, as much out of loyalty to their movement as out of a sense of passionate conviction concerning the coal miners' case. The rest of the public in turn remained loyal to the Government without feeling fanatical resentment against the mass of the strikers. Indeed, for many the days of the strike provided an unexpected and refreshing break with routine. Some London office workers were put up in hotels while others took pride in walking ten miles to work. University students on holiday attempted to load ships, and middle-aged businessmen realized childhood ambitions by serving as locomotive engineers. Though there were clashes between police and strikers in Glasgow and a few other cities, there was no loss of life. In some parts of the country strikers played football matches with policemen. Winston Churchill edited a Government newspaper, the *British Gazette*, while the Trades Union Council put out the *British Worker*. The only source of news for most people was the radio, though wireless sets were owned by less than one family in four.

Strangely enough, the one group in the country which was most uncomfortable about the strike was the Trades Union Congress. Its leaders had come face to face with a dilemma which – when a comparable strike was threatened in 1919 – Lloyd George had clearly outlined:

> . . . you will defeat us. But if you do so have you weighed the consequences? The strike will be in defiance of the government of the country and by its very success will precipitate a constitutional crisis of the first importance. For, if a force arises in the state which is stronger than the state itself, then it must be ready to take on the functions of the state, or withdraw and accept the authority

of the state. Gentlemen—have you considered, and if you have, are you ready?

A. J. Cook, a self-confessed "humble disciple of Lenin," might blithely declare "I don't care a hang for any government, or army, or navy," but most Trades Union Congress leaders were loyal parliamentarians and had no wish to stage a revolution. They insisted, indeed, that the strike was only a sympathy strike and not a general strike at all. Thus, as soon as Herbert Samuel put forward the compromise proposal that coal industry negotiations be resumed and that there be no changes in miners' wages until the money-saving provisions of his report had been adopted by the mineowners, the TUC leaders called off the strike.

It had lasted nine days, and individual strikes went on for several days more; but Baldwin specifically urged employers not to take advantage of the return to work to secure wage reductions, and most railwaymen and others were soon back at work under their old conditions. Neither the Trades Union Congress leaders nor the Prime Minister, however, could prevail upon the miners. They were adamant and for six months refused any proposal which involved the slightest reduction in pay. Eventually the resentful miners straggled back to the mines essentially on the owners' terms, which included a return to the eight-hour day. £60,000,000 in wages had been lost.

The following year, with Baldwin's acquiescence, though not with his encouragement, a Trade Disputes Act was passed which outlawed "general" and "sympathy" strikes and which decreed that union members could only be required to contribute to the Labour Party if they specifically indicated their wish to do so. Though the act was regarded as punitive by the Labour Party, which pledged itself to repeal the measure as soon as it could (and did so in 1946), the legislation had little immediate practical effect.

Although a number of intellectuals were attracted to the cause of the political left by the general strike, most Britons were satisfied by Baldwin's goal of "One Nation" divided neither by class nor ideology. "I am opposed to Socialism," the Prime Minister declared, "but I have always endeavoured to make the Conservative party face left in its anti-Socialism." As Minister of Health, Neville Chamberlain introduced several measures of social reform which adhered closely to the philosophy his father had espoused as a left-wing Liberal in the 1880s. The Widows', Orphans', and Old Age Contributory Pensions Bill provided pensions at 65 (rather than 70) and a form of social security to all those—about half the population—covered by the National Health Insurance Act of 1911. Chamberlain's Local Government Act of 1929 abolished the century-old Poor Law unions and transferred their powers and others to the county and county borough councils. The traditional source of income for these bodies, taxes on real estate, was sharply reduced and largely replaced by "block grants" from the National Treasury. The Electricity Act of 1926 gave a new public authority control over the national distribution of electricity generated in private or municipal plants, thereby creating a "national grid" which did much to enable Britain during the 1930s to catch up with the world's leading industrial nations in the utilization of electricity.

The Central Electricity Board, a public board appointed by the Minister of Transport, was to serve as a model for post-World War II measures of nationalization; but other legislative measures of the second Baldwin ministry harked back to an earlier age. The Reform Act of 1928, which gave the vote to women on the same basis as men was in some ways the climax of a process that had begun in 1832. The debate over the Prayer Book Bill of 1927 evoked an even earlier age, that of the Tudors, since its backers sought to gain parliamentary approval for a revised Book of Common Prayer. Slumbering evangelical passions were revived; the proposal was denounced as papistical, and the measure was defeated. Though religious questions could still stir up occasional furors, the trend in the direction of widespread religious indifference continued during the inter-war era.

The Spirit of Locarno

The spirit of relative domestic tranquillity which marked the later 1920s was echoed in international affairs. There Mac-Donald had done much during his brief Prime Ministership to ease old tensions. He went so far as to support the Geneva Protocol, which would have bound Britain automatically to go to war against any country which the League of Nations declared to be an aggressor. This was a form of "blank check" which most Englishmen still found difficult to sign; and Austen Chamberlain, the new Conservative Foreign Secretary (1924–29), therefore scuttled British support for the Protocol. He was, however, willing to apply the principle of the Protocol to one particular area, Germany's western frontier; in 1925 at Locarno, Switzerland, Germany, France, Belgium, Poland, and Czechoslovakia solemnly pledged not to go to war with each other and to arbitrate all disputes. Great Britain and Italy specifically guaranteed Germany's western frontier; France, which had alliances with Poland and Czechoslovakia, did the same for the eastern borders. Consequently, Allied troops were withdrawn from the German Rhineland and Germany was admitted to the League of Nations. Though the Locarno Treaty involved an element of wishful thinking—it deliberately ignored Germany's evasion of the disarmament clauses of the Treaty of Versailles—the "spirit of Locarno" was not wholly bogus. Germany faithfully paid its reparations payments under the Dawes Plan, and Foreign Ministers Stresemann of Germany, Briand of France, and Chamberlain of England conferred regularly and amicably at Geneva. Although specific disarmament proposals often foundered, Britain joined France, the United States, and twelve other powers in signing the euphoric (and unenforceable) Kellogg-Briand Pact of 1928 which "outlawed war as an instrument of national policy."

A comparable tranquillity affected the British Empire during the later 1920s. The Imperial Conference of 1926, recognizing the changes brought by World War I, defined the dominions as henceforth "autonomous Communities within the British Empire, equal in status ... united by a common allegiance to the Crown, and freely associated as members of the British Commonwealth of Nations." The definition was given parliamentary sanction in the Statute of Westminster of 1931. Whatever troubles might still plague the world, that of world war seemed far in the distance by the end of the 1920s. As John Buchan concluded in 1929, "civilization has been saved, and, on the whole, the nations are once more a stable society."

The Second Labour Government

Secure in the knowledge that the Conservative Party had at least helped to save civilization, Baldwin called an election in 1929. The Conservatives offered the electorate the comforting slogan "Safety First," while the Labour Party pledged "to end the capitalist dictatorship in which democracy finds everywhere its most insidious and most relentless foe." It was an apparently reviving Liberal Party which under Lloyd George's direction offered the most precise proposals for coming to grips with such problems as the continued high level of unemployment. The Liberals suggested that industries of public concern be placed under public boards, that employer-worker councils be expanded, and that the Bank of England's credit powers, public works, and deliberate deficit financing be employed by the government in order to assure full prosperity.

The election results were inevitably disappointing to the

Liberals. They had regained some ground since 1924, but they won only 59 parliamentary seats. Stanley Baldwin's Conservatives retained 261, and Ramsay MacDonald's Labourites gained 287 and became for the first time the largest parliamentary party. MacDonald became Prime Minister for a second time, relying upon Liberal support (or acquiescence) to stay in power.

The Second Labour Government was beset by the same misfortunes which were to cloud the reputation of the Hoover Administration in the United States. Within a matter of months after its accession to office in May 1929, the Government witnessed the stock market crash in the United States and the collapse of the whole artificial international financial structure of the 1920s. American loans to Germany ceased; so in due course did German reparations payments to France and Britain; and at length to complete the circle, so did French and British repayments of World War loans to the United States. All the economic statistics skidded steadily downhill; and if Britain's relative descent by 1932 was less precipitous than that of the United States, it was only because she had not really participated in the preceding economic boom.

	BRITISH WHOLESALE PRICES	PERCENT UNEMPLOYED	INDEX OF INDUSTRIAL ACTIVITY[2]
1929	100.0	10.4	118.7
1930	87.5	16.1	107.4
1931	76.8	21.3	86.8
1932	74.9	22.1	81.1
1933	75.0	19.9	89.3

The total value of Britain's exports dropped by half between 1929 and 1932; and so did the production of iron and steel. Over three million tons of shipping were laid up and shipbuilding came to a virtual standstill. J. H. Thomas, who had been appointed Lord Privy Seal in order to be "minister of employment" found his problem multiplying as unemployment figures soared: one million in June of 1929, 1,500,000 in January of 1930, 2,500,000 in December of 1930. By mid-summer of 1932 almost one Englishman in four (and one Welshman in three) was out of work, and almost seven million people of a total population of 45 million subsisted solely on the dole.

The depression shattered the nineteenth-century assumption that markets would continue to expand along with man's productive capacities. The defenders of laissez-faire capitalism were everywhere placed on the defensive; yet the attempts of a

---

[2] Pollard, p. 225.

professedly socialist Labour Government to deal with the depression proved as unavailing as those of the Republican Hoover Administration in the United States. A new Housing Act, a compulsory 7½-hour (rather than eight-hour) day in the mines, and an increased Treasury grant to the overburdened Unemployment Insurance Fund proved mild palliatives at best. The failure of the MacDonald Government to do more is explained partly by the fact that it was a minority government, partly by the fact that many Labour leaders, though socialists, shared most of the orthodox financial tenets of the time. Philip Snowden, the Chancellor of the Exchequer, was as convinced as Herbert Hoover that the Government's duty was, if at all possible, to balance its budget and to adhere to the gold standard as a bastion of financial integrity.

In the face of mounting economic crisis, ministerial unity began to dissolve. The youthful Sir Oswald Mosley (1896–   ) resigned from the Cabinet on the grounds that the Government was insufficiently dynamic to meet the problem of unemployment. Mosley, who had originally entered Parliament as a Conservative, resigned from the Labour Party to form his own "New Party" and eventually became the leader of the British Fascist Union. The Liberals were also split, and Conservative ranks were temporarily brought into disarray by the attempt of two "press lords," Lord Beaverbrook and Rothermere, to found their own United Empire Party on a platform of imperial protectionism.

The event which ultimately toppled the Labour Government was the financial crisis precipitated in the summer of 1931 by an international run on the gold reserves of the Bank of England. England had seemed the financial Rock of Gibraltar until 1931. Since most of its private banks were organized into five nationwide amalgamations which could look for emergency support from the Bank of England, the country had undergone no rash of bank failures as in the United States. Because of its own loans to continental banks, the Bank of England was, however, seriously affected by the failure of Austria's largest banking firm, the Credit Anstalt, and by a rash of bank failures in Germany.

The fact that the 1931 Budget could not be completely balanced weakened foreign confidence in British financial stability; so did the prediction in July by a government-appointed committee headed by Sir George May that much bigger deficits were in the offing. The Government was advised to make stringent economies (notably in unemployment insurance funds) in order to balance the budget and restore foreign confidence in British financial stability. The Labour Cabinet struggled for three weeks to find ways of cutting expenses. Substantial economies were agreed upon, but the ministry ultimately split upon the necessity of slashing benefits to the unemployed. Mac-Donald and Snowden insisted that some such reduction was necessary, but nine members of the Cabinet refused to agree. That a Labour Government should be responsible for deliberately injuring the interests of jobless laborers was an irony too poignant to be borne.

The National Government

MacDonald submitted his resignation but was asked by the sovereign, King George V, to head a new National Government instead. It would be a temporary government of personalities, four Labourites, four Conservatives, and two Liberals, which would meet the financial crisis as a coalition, just as the coalition government of 1915 had faced the military crisis of World War I. Thereafter it would resign and normal party politics would be resumed.

MacDonald agreed, and his decision was almost immediately denounced by the Executive Committee of the Labour Party as a betrayal; two months later he and his colleagues in the National Government were expelled from the party. Mac-Donald went down among his longtime compatriots as a traitor to his cause. The fictionalized account of his career – the novel and film "Fame Is the Spur" – presents him as the boy from the bottom of the social ladder corrupted by the desire to win the plaudits of Britain's high society. MacDonald, however, saw himself as placing country above party; and it has been cogently argued that, keeping in mind the predominant economic convictions of the time, a National Government was the best possible solution.[3] Although MacDonald initially expected the coalition arrangement to provide only a brief political interlude after which he would rejoin the Labour Party, the National Government survived under Conservative domination until the end of the decade.

Within a month, the new National Government, having won a vote of confidence in the old Parliament, introduced a new Budget and promptly went off the gold standard. The Budget increased taxes and cut all government salaries (including those of teachers) and all unemployment benefits by 10 percent. A "means test" sought to reduce the dole for any of the long-term unemployed who had alternate means of support. The Budget was no surprise, but the decision to go off the gold

---

[3] R. Bassett, *Nineteen Thirty-One: Political Crisis* (London, 1958).

standard was, to say the least, paradoxical. It was the result of a new run on the pound by foreign investors frightened by exaggerated reports of a naval mutiny in the Scottish port of Invergordon. With an "orthodox" government in power, the Bank of England assented to a step which only a month before it had regarded as revolutionary. Although it shocked foreign financial opinion, the decision no longer to exchange British currency for gold on demand made surprisingly little difference. The value of the pound fell on the international exchange, but domestic prices were little affected and British exporters derived a limited benefit. The British example was followed by the United States two years later.

Widespread Conservative pressure caused the National Government to call for a new election in October 1931, and to seek a vote of confidence from the electorate as a single coalition somewhat as the Lloyd George Government had done in 1918. It did not try to formulate a single program, and MacDonald simply asked a "doctor's mandate" to diagnose and prescribe for the depression. The result was an overwhelming victory for the National slate: 556 (472 of whom were Conservatives) as against 56 for the Labour opposition. The popular vote margin, $14\frac{1}{2}$ million to 6 million, was not quite so overwhelming, but decisive enough. The Parliamentary Labour Party, now headed by George Lansbury (1859–1940), the only undefeated anti-MacDonald Cabinet member, was angry and frustrated. The election all but destroyed what was left of the Liberal Party, which found itself divided into three tiny splinter groups: Sir John Simon's National Liberals who were already all but indistinguishable from the Conservatives, the Samuel Liberals, who were partners in the coalition government, and Lloyd George's family Liberal Party of four members (Lloyd George, his son, his daughter, and his son's brother-in-law). The National Government may have reflected British popular opinion well enough, but the lack of an effective alternate government or opposition party was to prove an element of weakness as well as strength.

Early in 1932 the National Government in its Import Duties Act proposed, as one method of curing the Depression, that the United Kingdom return to the system of protective tariffs which had been abandoned during the 1840s. The first digressions from the policy of free trade had come with the "McKenna Duties" during the First World War; and those duties, largely retained during the 1920s, had given some protection to the automobile industry. Yet as late as 1930, 83 percent of all British imports had been completely duty free, and the decision to return to a policy of protection represented a major change of principle. Most of the Conservatives in the National Government had long favored such a step, and Neville Chamberlain— as the new Chancellor of the Exchequer—took pride in the opportunity of introducing the bill his father had championed so long. Only the Labourite Philip Snowden and the Liberal Party representatives in the Cabinet objected, and they were permitted for the time being to dissent publicly, a temporary break in the century-and-a-half-old tradition of Cabinet unanimity.

The act imposed tariffs ranging from 10 to $33\frac{1}{3}$ percent on both industrial and agricultural imports, except for meat and wool. The bill enabled an Imperial Economic Conference at Ottawa in August 1932 to approach the elder Chamberlain's ideal of an imperial customs union. By then, however, many of the economic prerequisites for Chamberlain's neomercantilistic views had vanished; no one could seriously envisage Great Britain as the industrialized heart of an empire in which the dominions served merely as sources of raw material. All the dominions had their own infant industries to protect, as did India, whose production of cotton cloth had almost eliminated a once giant market for English textiles. Moreover, both Britain and the dominions had long established trading relationships with other parts of the world. Yet the act and the Conference did, to some degree, encourage a greater amount of trade within the Commonwealth. The return to protection was as much a political as an economic decision, for it gave the impression that the government was *doing something* in the face of economic crisis and joblessness.

It has been a common tendency among historians to contrast the National Government's policies in Britain unfavorably with Roosevelt's New Deal in the United States. The National Government, it is said, sought to wait out the depression—or to put it more bluntly, "Millions were starving but the Tories did nothing"—while in the United States Roosevelt was seeking to combat the depression with dynamic if sometimes contradictory measures. It is true that in Britain, unlike the United States, the same men were in power under a new guise. It is also true that Britain's National Government never embarked upon a full-fledged public-works program based on deficit spending. But even in the United States the desirability of deliberate deficit spending as a means of countering depression came to be accepted by most politicians only in the 1940s and by most big businessmen only in the 1960s. Churchill's statement of 1929 that "very little additional employment and no permanent additional employment can, in fact, and as a general rule, be created by State borrowing and State expenditure" was still accepted by most economists in the 1930s.

This thesis was strongly challenged by the Liberal economist John Maynard Keynes (1883–1946) in his *General Theory of Employment, Interest, and Money* (1936), the fullest elaboration of views first expounded in the 1920s. Keynes disagreed that economists had no more control over the ups and downs of the economy than meteorologists had over the alternations of rain and sunshine. Economic specialists could not only chart national growth and decline, but they could also advise the government how to stabilize the economy. Governments, he argued, should encourage deficit spending and low interest rates in time of depression, budget surpluses and high interest rates in times of inflationary boom. At first Keynes received an indifferent reception in Britain, if only because Conservatives were alienated by his emphasis upon the role of government in business and Labourites by his defense of capitalism and the role of the individual.

Although the National Government did not overtly subscribe to Keynes' views, its policies—tariff protection and a removal of the gold standard—did imply considerable management of the economy. So did the farm subsidy and marketing acts, tightened stock market regulations, and new housing acts. Of the four and a half million houses built in Britain between the wars, 1,400,000 were built by public authorities and another half million were constructed with the aid of government subsidies. One reason why the National Government does not seem more closely comparable to the New Deal is that so many New Deal measures—such as social security and unemployment insurance—had in fact been adopted by Britain before World War I. The proportion of the national income spent by British public authorities, local and national, rose steadily from 5.5 percent in 1913 to 13.0 percent in 1938. The table on page 288 makes clear the expansion of social services by the 1930s.

The Depression and British Society

The impact of economic conditions upon human beings can never be measured by statistics alone. It is not true that the unemployed starved during the Great Depression or that "the Tories did nothing," but it remains true that the problem of unemployment was ultimately resolved in Britain—as in the United States—only by a war. Moreover, prolonged and unrelenting unemployment put a lasting mark upon those British workingmen who experienced it. It left a sense of frustration and futility; it caused a loss of skills, of self-respect, and sometimes the onset of a physical deterioration. A situation in which the bread-winner was perpetually out of work warped traditional

SOCIAL SERVICES (in £ million)

PAYMENTS MADE BY THE GOVERNMENT	1913–1914	1933–1934
Poor Relief	16½	47
Health Insurance	14½	32
Old Age Pensions	10	58½
Widows', etc. Pensions	–	22½
War Pensions	–	44
Unemployment Insurance	½	88½
TOTALS	41½	292½

CONTRIBUTIONS LEVIED ON INDIVIDUALS[4]		
Health Insurance	17	26
Pensions	–	23
Unemployment Insurance	2	39½
TOTALS	19	88½

family relationships. To keep one's sense of respectability while living on the dole meant a degree of penny pinching which left room for none of the occasional luxuries which add spice to life.

Faced with the specter of joblessness and a falling standard of living, the British workingman was surprisingly moderate. There were occasional hunger marches on London from as far as Scotland and Wales, but only a small minority of the unemployed gave their political allegiance to either communism or fascism. Among university students and in certain intellectual circles it became fashionable to be a Communist sympathizer, to be, as it were, outside the ordinary political game, free to criticize and to speculate on new ideas. The U.S.S.R. again became the Mecca of the Left in the 1930s, and its record of political repression was ignored in favor of the economic efficiency promised by Stalin's five-year plans. The United States, in contrast, had been scorned by the British Left ever since the Sacco-Vanzetti Case of the 1920s; and even Roosevelt's New Deal was often dismissed as a "Fascist economy." From 1936 on, the Left Book Club — borrowing an American idea — faithfully supplied its 50,000 members with propaganda. In innumerable novels the hero, after a painful struggle of conscience between his materialistic and idealistic selves, joined

---

[4] The remainder of the expenditures were derived from regular taxation. The social services constituted almost 3/7 of the annual national budget in 1933–1934. 1/7 was devoted to defense expenditures and another 3/7 to interest payments on the national debt.

the Communist Party on the last page. ("Robert turned from the window. The sound of the unemployed Welsh miners' singing came faintly from below. 'All right, I'm coming with you,' he said simply.") [5] The Communist Party never attracted more than a few thousand card-carrying members; it elected only a single Member of Parliament during the decade; and it never succeeded in winning the Labour Party to the cause of a United Front against fascism; but its ideological influence was certainly significant.

An alternate cure for the ills of society was offered by Sir Oswald Mosley's British Union of Fascists. In emulation of Mussolini and Hitler they paraded in blackshirt uniforms, held theatrical floodlighted meetings, and in unison saluted their leader: "Hail Mosley!" The Fascists saw themselves as representatives of "Youth" and "Vigour" and spoke constantly of "Action" and "Getting Things Done." Mosley mercilessly taunted his former Labour allies who had resigned their governmental power in the face of the collapse of capitalism they had so long predicted: "What would you think," asked Mosley, "of a Salvation Army which took to its heels on the Day of Judgment?" Although the Union of Fascists had 20,000 members by 1934, their paramilitary organization, their overt anti-Semitism, and their bullying and violent tactics alienated most British opinion. "Mosley won't come to any good," predicted Stanley Baldwin in 1934, "and we need not bother about him." The Government did bother about him to the extent of passing a Public Order Act in 1936 which outlawed the wearing of political uniforms, but otherwise Baldwin's prediction was borne out by events.

There were numerous other fringe groups active in the 1930s, each with its own particular panacea for the nation's ills. The Distributionists saw industrialization as the enemy and echoed the early nineteenth-century Ludditos in their advocacy of peasant proprietorship and the wearing of handwoven clothes. The Social Credit Party saw the bankers as the enemy, wore green shirts, and sought to raise consumer purchasing power by distributing what they called "the national dividend." While such movements all betray a widespread disillusionment with politics as usual in the 1930s, they all proved in the long run to be lost causes.

A desire to be socially conscious and an affinity for the Left was found among a generation of new poets and novelists such as W. H. Auden, Stephen Spender, and Christopher Isherwood. George Orwell explored the theme of poverty in the large

---

[5] Michael Wharton, "A Few Lost Causes" in John Raymond (ed), *The Baldwin Age*.

city in such novels as *Keep the Aspidistra Flying* (1936). Yet other traditions persisted as well during the interwar era: the Freudian self-analysis of D. H. Lawrence (1885–1930); the experimenting in verbal techniques of James Joyce (1882–1941); and the explorations of a private world carried on by Virginia Woolf (1882–1941). And such Edwardian literary giants as Shaw, Wells, and Galsworthy remained active well into the 1930s or beyond.

Regarded as "Neither art nor smart" by the intellectuals but far more influential than the serious novel among the working classes, the cinema came gradually to replace the music hall as the chief source of popular entertainment. Far more acceptable to intellectuals was the BBC, the British Broadcasting Corporation begun in 1922 and established in its present form in 1927. The BBC was a monopoly established under the auspices of the state but not subject to its day-to-day control. It received its income not from advertisers but from license fees paid to the Post Office. There were three million licenseholders by 1929, nine million by 1938. In the words of Sir John Reith, who directed the Corporation from its founding until 1939, its governors "were not interested in the material welfare of the Corporation; their interest was in the intellectual and ethical welfare of the listeners." From the beginning, the pattern of programming was established as a combination of classical music, discussion and variety programs, weather forecasts, a children's hour, Sunday services, and programs for schools. Its faithful reporting of the statements of government and strike leaders alike during the General Strike of 1926 gave it a reputation for impartiality in reporting the news which was to make it the symbol of factual integrity for millions of Europeans in occupied lands during World War II. In the late 1930s the BBC began the first regular television broadcasts in the world.

The BBC is often credited with doing much to broaden the music taste of the British public. Certainly side by side with the world of popular song continued the English revival of classical music which had begun at the turn of the century. Ralph Vaughan Williams, William Walton, and Arnold Bax composed actively, and Sir Thomas Beecham (1879–1961) utilized his family medicine-pill fortune to found symphony orchestras. A division comparable to that between popular and serious music existed in the world of journalism. Britain could boast a handful of serious and well-edited newspapers and reviews; others, such as the weekly *News of the World* served primarily as a form of entertainment and as advertising billboards.

Whether the National Government was responsible or not, by 1935 a substantial recovery from the Great Depression was under way. The Budget of 1934 had restored the cuts in unemployment benefits and most of the salary reductions imposed in 1931. Unemployment in the depressed areas of Scotland, Wales, and Northwest England had been somewhat alleviated, and the rest of the country was beginning to enjoy a mild boom. Housing construction, much aided by government financing, helped employ millions of men and aided other industries as well. The automobile and steel industries were flourishing and by 1939 three million motor vehicles packed Britain's roads. Another relatively new concern, the electrical industry, helped to take up the slack of the older, dying businesses such as coal, textile, and shipbuilding. The 730,000 electrical consumers of 1920 had grown to over nine million by 1939, and many a British housewife had become accustomed to the same amenities — vacuum cleaners, refrigerators, and washing machines — as her American counterpart. As in most advanced industrial countries the number of people employed in service trades ranging from amusements and barbering to dry cleaning and automobile maintenance was growing more quickly than those employed in manufacturing. The fact that productivity per worker rose 50 percent between 1913 and 1939 is, of course, one explanation why the long stagnating index of industrial production could begin to rise sharply in the mid-thirties without restoring full employment.

INDEX OF INDUSTRIAL PRODUCTION IN U.K.
(1924 = 100) [6]

1913	94.2
1920	102.3
1924	100.0
1929	117.3
1931	99.0
1935	130.8
1937	153.1

Even if Britain's export trade was not reviving quite so rapidly as its industrial production, the average Englishman was benefiting from the fact that international "terms of trade" were once again shifting in Britain's favor. During the interwar era the cost of Britain's imports — mostly food and raw materials — was falling more rapidly than the cost of her exports. Thus it required in 1938 a volume of exports only 70 percent as

[6] Pollard, p. 96.

high as that of 1914 to "buy" the same volume of imports. The shift in terms of trade and the overall rise in productivity help explain why for all but the chronically unemployed, the 1920s and 1930s provided a notable rise in the standard of living.

The capitalism which had survived the Depression was at best a reasonable facsimile of its early nineteenth-century prototype, even if its critics gave it the same name. For one thing, some industries, most transport services, and many utilities were in the hands of public authorities. For another, manufacturing industries—85 percent of which were organized as corporations—were again shifting location. In the eighteenth and early nineteenth centuries, manufacturers had sought the coal mines and swift flowing rivers of England's north and northwest. The new and growing industries of the interwar era, however, were no longer tied to ports or coalfields; and they tended to move once again to the southeast. London, whose growth Tudor commentators had found "monstrous" in the sixteenth century grew more "monstrous" still in the 1930s. On the other hand, another sort of migration was slowing down — that of Englishmen going overseas. If only because Canada, Australia, and the United States were similarly depression-ridden, emigration was only a third as high in the mid-thirties as it had been in 1913.

Other tendencies were at work. The small individually-owned manufacturing concern had almost completely given way to the giant corporation, but the corporation in turn had also changed. The ownership of the shares was increasingly far removed from the actual exercise of control, which was left in the hands of essentially self-perpetuating Boards of Directors, who might own no property in the concern and were merely hired administrators. Another tendency was the increasing domination within particular industries by combines and cartels such as the ICI (Imperial Chemical Industries) in chemicals and the Lever Combine in soap. While as late as 1919 a government Committee on Trusts had deplored this movement toward monopoly, the government attitude altered during the Depression. In a fashion similar to Roosevelt's short-lived NRA, the Macmillan Committee of 1931 encouraged "desirable amalgamations and reconstructions designed to eliminate waste and cheapen costs." Large concerns could provide economic stability as well as mass packaging and national advertising. They could, and increasingly did, encourage the process of industrial research and discovery. The line between applied and theoretical science is often an ill-defined one, and it is probably not accidental that one of the founders of nuclear physics, Lord Rutherford (1871–1937), was an Englishman.

Moreover, British technologists were instrumental in the development of television and radar and in the forefront of airplane engineering.

Although the general movement in industry during the 1930s continued toward an oligarchical corporate structure, this tendency never went all the way. Large sectors of the economy remained unorganized; the individual entrepreneur still played a significant role on the retail level, and oligopolies often competed very genuinely with each other. In its modified form, the capitalist system in Britain proved far more flexible and adaptable than would have been expected by its depression critics.

Left to their own devices, it is difficult to say how successful or unsuccessful Britain's business leaders or its National Government would have been in guiding Great Britain into the 1940s. Unfortunately, economic affairs and domestic politics were not allowed to remain isolated from events abroad. By 1936 Britain faced a threat even greater than depression; she was confronted with the specter of German Hitlerism, Japanese expansion, and the coming of yet another world war.

Chapter 17

The 𝕾𝖙𝖔𝖗𝖒 Gathers Anew

In 1918 MANY Britons had shared with President Woodrow Wilson the hope that World War I would indeed prove to be "the war to end war." In 1928 Britain had joined the major nations of the world, including the United States and Germany, in pledging forever to "outlaw war as an instrument of national policy." And yet in 1939 Britain found itself at war again, a war which was to involve every continent, almost every country of the world, and which was never to be concluded by a peace treaty comparable to that of Paris or Vienna. Some of its momentous worldwide consequences have become clear only in the 1960s.[1]

---

[1] The most widely accepted version of the events leading up to World War II may be found in Winston S. Churchill's *The Gathering Storm* (London, 1948; available in paperbound edition), Vol. I of his *History of the Second World War*. Mowat provides some highly illuminating chapters. The appeasement policy is analyzed and criticized in Martin Gilbert and Richard Gott, *The Appeasers* (Cambridge, Mass., 1963). It is viewed with greater sympathy in the biographies of Neville Chamberlain by Keith Feiling (London, 1946) and Iain McLeod (London, 1960). Also relevant is J. W. Wheeler-Bennett, *Munich: Prologue to Tragedy* (London, 1948). The place of the monarchy in twentieth-century Britain is clarified in Harold Nicolson, *King George V* (London, 1951), J. W. Wheeler-Bennett, *King George VI: His Life and Reign* (London, 1958), and Lewis Broad, *The Abdication: Twenty-Five Years After* (London, 1961). The Labour Party during the interwar years is discussed in G. D. H. Cole, *History of the Labour Party Since 1914* (London, 1948) and in Vol. I of Alan Bullock's *Ernest Bevin* (London, 1960).

The Rise of Totalitarianism

For Britain, as for much of Western and Central Europe, the later 1920s seemed to bring an easing of international tensions and an apparent alleviation of some of the grievances (such as reparations) which the Treaty of Versailles had left in the minds and pocketbooks of the German people. Although the League of Nations did not live fully up to the hopes of its founders, it was a going concern; and although the dream of worldwide disarmament proved chimerical, Europe was at least spared an arms race comparable to that of the pre-World War I decade.

This false dawn was swiftly obscured by two related developments of the new decade: worldwide economic depression and widespread repudiation of liberal democracy. The first, the Great Depression, with its hundreds of bank failures, its thousands of bankruptcies, its millions of unemployed, its millions more with reduced living standards, helped swing the balance toward the second. Throughout the Western world, the response to the depression lay in economic nationalism, in building tariff barriers, and in the curtailment of political liberties.

The depression years accentuated the widespread repudiation of liberal democracy which had seemed to be the goal, if not the achievement, of most Europeans as recently as 1918. In Germany the extremist parties, the Communists and the National Socialists (Nazis), became increasingly popular, and a majority of middle-class Germans either supported or acquiesced in the take-over of political power by the Nazis and their leader, Adolf Hitler, in 1933. In him they found the self-appointed messiah who would save them from communism and who paradoxically promised higher salaries and lower rents, higher prices for retailers and cheaper food for workers, increased social services and lower taxes. Perhaps most important of all, his demagogic speeches and sense of mission enabled them to participate vicariously in a national cause which went beyond individual self-interest. Once admitted to power, the National Socialists rapidly eliminated by edict and street terrorism all overt internal political opposition.

Nationalism had once seemed an essentially liberal doctrine, and as recently as 1918 Woodrow Wilson had considered a Europe divided along lines of nationality as fully compatible with a world made safe for democracy. But the nationalism which flourished during the 1930s in Germany and Italy and Japan was in every sense antipathetic to the nineteenth-century democratic liberalism, with its emphasis upon the legal rights of individuals. It was, for that matter, equally opposed to theoretical Marxist communism, which stressed internationalism rather than nationalism. The result was a new type of fanaticism — racial, imperialistic, militaristic — a secular religion which provided dictators with a mass following.

The Great Depression and the rise of fanatical nationalism changed the entire background of European-diplomacy; but the makers of British foreign policy were slow to appreciate this fact. They came to realize only gradually that Germany's new rulers did not share their own assumptions about the use of reason in politics, about the desirability of compromise, and about liberal democracy as the best form of government. The British were deflected from strong initiatives in foreign policy by domestic economic problems, by difficulties in concerting policy with erstwhile allies, and by widespread pacifism. "From 1918 to 1939," wrote R. H. Tawney, "the loathing of war was unquestionably the most powerful, the most general and the most constant of political emotions."

The policy which resulted from these presuppositions is known as appeasement. Since 1939 that word has had a derogatory, an almost treasonous, connotation. This was not so in the 1930s. An appeaser then was merely a man who wanted peace. In any event, it may be a misleading use of hindsight to convey the impression that British foreign policy makers during the 1930s saw themselves as carrying out a single always consistent policy. Rather, like most diplomats at most times, they were faced with specific issues on specific occasions. Possibly they were too sensitive to the feelings of their electorate; it may be true to say that they generally took the easy way out; but final judgment can only be passed if the problems they faced are reviewed and analyzed.

In the Far East, Japan had as a result of World War I become the inheritor of European claims to spheres of influence in China. In 1931 she invaded Manchuria and transformed it into a puppet state. The League of Nations, on the basis of a report issued by an international commission headed by the English Earl of Lytton, condemned the Japanese action but found it impossible to enforce its views. Neither Britain nor any other major League power nor the United States was prepared to wage war for the sake of Manchuria. Nor was the imposition of economic sanctions palatable at a time when they might aggravate the economic distress brought on by the depression. The only concrete result of the adoption of the Lytton Report by the League of Nations was Japan's decision to leave the League and to continue gradually to expand its economic and political influence over a divided China.

The policy of orderly retreat followed by Britain in the Far

East was, in a sense, applied to India as well. There the leadership of the Indian National Congress fell into the hands of Mohandas K. Gandhi (1869–1948), a physically small and far from handsome man, who inspired millions of his countrymen with the dream of national independence. Gandhi's minimum demand was dominion status. When the Simon Commission was sent to review Indian governmental arrangements eight years after the passage of the Government of India Act of 1919, Gandhi protested the failure to include native Indians on the Commission with a campaign of civil disobedience, a boycott of English cloth imports, and a defiance of the government salt monopoly.

Although Gandhi and other Indian leaders were arrested from time to time, they were also permitted to play a political role; Gandhi himself participated in 1931 in the second of three Round Table Conferences which sought to draft a new Indian Constitution. Life in London did not change Gandhi's habitual asceticism, and he wore his traditional loincloth for a Buckingham Palace reception by King George V. The two men chatted politely enough, but the monarch felt compelled to warn: "Remember, Mr. Gandhi, I won't have any attacks on my Empire!" Gandhi replied politely: "I must not be drawn into a political argument in Your Majesty's Palace after receiving Your Majesty's hospitality."

The Round Table Conference could not reconcile all differences if only because many Conservatives (like Winston Churchill) were hostile to further concessions to Indian nationalism and because the Indian representatives themselves were divided between Hindu and Moslem, Brahmin and "untouchable." The statute which finally resulted, the Government of India Act of 1935, did not give India dominion status; but except for reserve emergency powers retained by British governors, the eleven provinces of British (as opposed to princely) India became virtually self-governing. Matters of defense and foreign policy remained, however, firmly in the hands of the British-controlled national government. Although the Indian National Congress initially chose to boycott the new constitution, it subsequently relaxed its stand, and millions of Indians participated in what was becoming at least partly their government. Hitler once privately recommended to the British a different mode of dealing with Indian nationalism: "Shoot Gandhi, and if that does not suffice to reduce them to submission, shoot a dozen leading members of Congress; and if that does not suffice shoot two hundred and so on until order is established. You will see how quickly they will collapse as soon as you make it clear that you mean business." No twentieth-century British government could reconcile such conduct with its principles; that is why it proved so susceptible to tactics of civil disobedience. The Government of India Act of 1935 thus remains a tribute to MacDonald's and Baldwin's diplomacy, a form of appeasement which has received less subsequent condemnation than British policy toward Germany.

Between 1933 and 1935, Hitler's Germany, in addition to crushing internal opposition, began to turn away from "the spirit of Locarno." In 1933, the year of his death, Lord Grey, the pre-World War I Foreign Secretary, declared hopefully: "The great security for peace at the present moment is that Germany is not armed and not in a position to go to war." Such security was soon to fade. Germany withdrew from the Disarmament Conference of 1933, resigned from the League of Nations that same year, and in 1935 announced that she would no longer abide by the disarmament provisions of the Treaty of Versailles. The building of an air force was in fact already under way, but now military conscription was reintroduced and the size of the army increased from 100,000 to more than 500,000 men.

The British and other Western governments protested, as did the Council of the League of Nations; but no meaningful steps were taken to halt German rearmament. Some Englishmen found it all too easy to go along with Hitler's reasoning that since his neighbors had not disarmed, he might rearm. By signing a Naval Agreement with Germany in June 1935, permitting Germany to build battleships and submarines but limiting a German navy to 35 percent of British tonnage, Britain gave implicit recognition to Hitler's right to violate the peace treaty. Britons took comfort in the thought that the agreement saved them from a naval race comparable to that preceding World War I. Since Hitler was, in any case, giving preference to land and air rearmament and since the limits allowed by the treaty would keep his shipyards busy for many years, the treaty was scarcely a meaningful barrier to his ambitions. It did, however, erode still further the ideal of "collective security" against aggression.

When the next challenge to international peace came, Britain reacted more forcefully. Mussolini's invasion of Ethiopia in the summer of 1935 was not a direct threat to Britain, but it impressed British opinion as a clear-cut moral issue. It seemed to be a flagrant violation of the sovereignty of a neighbor state, and Sir Samuel Hoare (1880–1959), the British Foreign Secretary, strongly urged collective League action against Italy. Such action was forthcoming in the form of financial sanctions, an embargo upon all goods imported from Italy, and a partial embargo upon goods exported to Italy. Sentiment hostile to international bullying was widespread in Britain, and for once the League of Nations seemed to be operating as intended.

The Election of 1935

It was while the Ethiopian crisis was still in the front pages that the General Election of 1935 took place. The Labour Party had strong hopes of regaining some of its pre-1931 stature. A new generation of leaders, Clement Attlee (1883–), Herbert Morrison (1888–1965), Stafford Cripps (1889–1952), and Ernest Bevin (1881–1951) among them, were moving to the fore. In the local elections of 1934, the Labour Party under Morrison's leadership had gained control of the London County Council. Comparable victories had given it a majority in more boroughs and county councils than ever before. Although the party was agreed upon the goal of peace and socialism, it still had its ideological left wing and right wing. Intellectuals like Cripps showed some affinity for semirevolutionary speculation, but trade union leaders like Bevin supported "common sense" and parliamentary democracy under all circumstances. For four years the parliamentary party had been led by George Lansbury, who, as a Christian pacifist, did not quite belong to either wing. At the party's 1935 conference, supporters of sanctions against Italy swamped advocates of the peace at any price policy put forward by Lansbury, and the latter resigned soon thereafter to be replaced by Clement Attlee, the party intellectual most acceptable to trade unionists.

It was the apparent popularity of its foreign policy stance and the obvious degree of economic recovery which caused the National Government to seek a new electoral mandate in November 1935. MacDonald had resigned as Prime Minister the previous June and had been replaced by his deputy in the National Government, Stanley Baldwin. The National Government's program stressed additional steps to speed economic recovery, support for the League of Nations, and a program of rearmament to keep air parity with Germany and replace obsolescent ships. The Labourites and the Liberals found at least some of their ideological clothes stolen and, as the campaign proceeded, increasingly attacked Baldwin and Neville Chamberlain, his Chancellor of the Exchequer, who had prepared the Defense White Paper for the year, as warmongers. Baldwin in turn sought to mollify the electorate by assuring it that he had no large-scale armaments in mind.

The election resulted in another overwhelming victory for the National Government. 428 of its supporters (387 of them Conservatives) faced an opposition made up of 157 Labourites, 17 Liberals, and a handful of independents. The popular vote margin was not nearly so decisive: there were $11\frac{1}{2}$ million Government supporters ($10\frac{1}{2}$ of them Conservatives) compared with 8.3 million Labour supporters and 1.4 million who voted Liberal.

The question relating to Ethiopia which neither Government nor opposition had truly asked during the general election was: what if economic sanctions proved insufficient? Would Britain, as the chief League military power, be willing to fight a war against Italy to prevent the absorption of Ethiopia? Sir Samuel Hoare thought not. "Keep us out of war," Baldwin had told him; "we are not ready for it." Since the French were even less eager to alienate Mussolini and drive him into the arms of Hitler, Hoare agreed upon a plan suggested by Pierre Laval, the French Prime Minister, according to which Mussolini was to give up his plans of conquest in favor of the cession of half of Ethiopia. When details of the Hoare-Laval plan leaked to the press, British public opinion was appalled by this apparent betrayal of preelection pledges. Baldwin's government felt compelled to repudiate Hoare, who resigned and was replaced as Foreign Secretary by Anthony Eden (1897–   ).

A victory had been won for principle but not for Ethiopia. While the League debated the imposition of further sanctions in the spring of 1936, Italy completed her military conquest. The sanctions imposed had not proved effective, if only because they did not include oil and could not be enforced upon either Germany or the United States. In July 1936, the British government and the League decided to end economic sanctions against Italy. Neville Chamberlain described them as "the very midsummer of madness." Although the sanctions had not helped Ethiopia, they had alienated Mussolini sufficiently to push him into an alliance with Germany, and in 1937 he and Hitler formed the Rome-Berlin Axis which was later joined by Tokyo as well.

Whether the government was arming fast enough was debated by contemporaries (and was to be debated by subsequent historians), but while the Labour Party systematically voted against defense expenditures the Government *did* keep its pledge to rearm. The defense budget rose from £127 million in 1935 to £343 in 1938 and £630 in 1939. Aircraft production quadrupled during the same period. Yet even in 1938, German war expenditures were twice as high as those of Britain and France combined.

The Abdication

In the year 1936 new storm signals from Germany were drowned out for many British citizens and for millions of others around the world by affairs monarchical. In January 1936, only half a year after King George V and his wife, Queen Mary, had marked their Silver Jubilee amidst great popular adulation, the old king, the embodiment of Victorian virtues, was dead. A state funeral followed, as did a new king, Edward VIII, who, as Prince of Wales, had often toured empire and commonwealth and who had been built up by newspaper publicity as a glamourous personality, handsome, athletic, versatile.

The new king *was* unconventional: he flew to his accession council by airplane; he liked to spend his leisure time gardening in a grubby shirt or eating dinners with small groups of friends in London flats; he rarely attended church; he had a freely avowed interest in the welfare of the miners in depressed areas of Wales; he preferred to live in Fort Belvedere, a military lookout post built by George II, rather than in Buckingham Palace. Most curiously of all, the king at forty was still single, the most eligible bachelor in all Europe. All European and American newspaper readers soon learned a fact from which British newspaper proprietors tactfully shielded their readers until late in November 1936: that the king was very much in love with Wallis Warfield Simpson, a commoner, an American, and a divorcee who in October 1936 had applied for a second divorce (from Mr. Simpson) in order that she might marry King Edward VIII. Stanley Baldwin was deeply perturbed as was the rest of the royal family and the Church of England. The king was its head. The Archbishop of Canterbury was to preside over the king's coronation the following year, but the Church did not recognize the propriety of divorce.

Once the case broke in the British press, the story rapidly reached a climax. The king hoped for a morganatic marriage in which Mrs. Simpson would not officially become queen. The king had his supporters: Lord Beaverbrook, Winston Churchill, and others who maintained "The King's Happiness Comes First" or asked that "God Save the King from Mr. Baldwin." It was Baldwin who was Prime Minister, however, and he refused to introduce a bill making a morganatic marriage possible. The dominions whom Edward served as monarch would not accept such a proposal, argued Baldwin, and neither would public opinion in Britain. "I believe I know what the people would tolerate and what they would not," he had confided to the king earlier, and he may well have been right.

If the monarch failed to accept the Prime Minister's advice, a constitutional tradition would be broken and the king would have to find another government capable of securing the support of a majority of the House of Commons. A general election would have to be fought on the issue of the king's private life. Edward did not wish to provoke a constitutional crisis of such dimensions, and on December 10 he abdicated the throne so that he could marry Mrs. Simpson. He was succeeded by his brother, the Duke of York, as George VI. The new king had long lived in the shade of his elder brother and was unduly modest about his own abilities. A model family man with a strong sense of duty, he served as ideal constitutional monarch during the fifteen years that followed.

Steps Toward War

Although the abdication crisis was clearly the biggest news story of the year if not of the decade, it was not perhaps the most significant. More fateful was Hitler's unilateral remilitarization of the German Rhineland. This was a clear violation of both the Treaty of Versailles and the Treaty of Locarno, and Hitler had promised to uphold the latter only a year before. Had the French immediately intervened, Britain might have been compelled to provide support. But the French hesitated, and the British did not find the cause worth risking military conflict. "After all," observed one English diplomat of the Germans, "they are only going into their own backgarden." The fortification of Germany's western frontier, however, had other noteworthy military consequences. It confirmed Hitler's prescience among German army leaders who had felt sure that the German bluff would be called, and it made possible subsequent German expansion eastward.

The year 1936 also brought the beginnings of the Spanish Civil War, a conflict between large sections of the Spanish army, supported by the Church, who fought under General Franco against the legitimate government of the Spanish Republic. To prevent the war from spreading, Britain joined twenty-six other nations in agreeing not to take sides. Traditional practice would not have dictated a policy treating legitimate government and rebel force alike and forbidding the former to purchase arms abroad; but in Anthony Eden's words, the hope was to preserve "peace at almost any price." Both Mussolini and Hitler soon broke their word. Mussolini sent five army divisions to fight on Franco's side, and Hitler sent technicians and materiel to be tested under actual war conditions. The Republican government, which as the war progressed fell increasingly under communist influence, received some aid from Russia and volunteers but no materiel from Britain and other countries of the Western world. For the Spanish Civil War kindled ideological passions in Britain in the manner that the Greek war of independence had inflamed the imagination of Byron. No other event of the decade became so burning a cause. In the process, some left-wing intellectuals endowed the Spanish Republic with virtues neither it nor any human society could have possessed. In some ways the Spanish Civil War proved to be a preview of World War II; but the outcome, Franco's victory in 1939, was less useful to the cause of the Axis powers in World War II than friend or foe would have anticipated in the 1930s.

The Road to Munich

In May, 1937, shortly after King George VI's coronation, Stanley Baldwin resigned from the Prime Ministership because of ill health. The logical choice as his successor was Neville Chamberlain, who thus obtained the prize which had eluded his father and half brother. Chamberlain had a deserved reputation as a highly competent department head, and on most issues of domestic and foreign policy he and Baldwin had seen eye to eye. But whereas Baldwin had been a sociable man who shunned foreign affairs, Chamberlain was a man with few close friends who approached the European scene with courage and astonishing self-confidence. His immediate experience had all been in domestic matters, but he soon in effect became his own Foreign Secretary—especially after Eden's resignation from that post in February 1938—and the foremost exponent of personal diplomacy in pre-World War II Europe.

Chamberlain faced his first major crisis when Germany annexed Austria in March 1938. The so-called "Anschluss" violated both the Treaty of Versailles and Hitler's pledges of only two years before. Britain and France did little except to agree to continue the talks between the general staffs of their armies, which had been resumed in 1936. In the course of the summer that followed, it became clear that the next trouble spot was to be Czechoslovakia, the nation in Eastern Europe with the greatest affinity for Western democracy. Czechoslovakia contained within its borders—established at Paris in 1919—more than three million German-speaking inhabitants (erstwhile subjects of the defunct Austro-Hungarian Empire) who were encouraged by Hitler agents to demand complete autonomy within their state and the ultimate right of "reunion" with Hitler's Germany.

Since German violence inside Czechoslovakia was likely

to serve as an excuse for an invasion by German troops, since France was treaty-bound to support Czech frontiers, and since Britain was equally bound to support France in case of war with Germany, Prime Minister Neville Chamberlain made it his special interest to seek a peaceful solution. Under Franco-British pressure, the Czechs offered the Sudeten Germans almost complete local autonomy; but for Hitler — who had ordered his generals to prepare for war by autumn—this was not enough. In mid-September Chamberlain flew to Berchtesgaden, Hitler's Bavarian mountain retreat, to hear from Hitler's own lips the demand that areas of Czechoslovakia in which Germans constituted more than fifty percent of the population be immediately incorporated into Germany.

Chamberlain, who peculiarly enough formed the impression on this occasion that Hitler "was a man who could be relied upon when he had given his word," returned to confer with the French and the Czech representatives. Only if the Czechs would accede to Hitler's dismemberment plans, the British and French representatives insisted, would the Western allies continue their support. The Czechs reluctantly acquiesced, and Chamberlain flew to Godesburg to meet Hitler a second time to announce Czech acceptance. Chamberlain discovered that Hitler had upped his price and demanded the Sudeten territories as of October 1 and not by means of the gradual transfer plan the Western allies had worked out. This was too much, even for Chamberlain, and he returned home. The Czech and French armies mobilized, as did the British fleet, and the Prime Minister was in the midst of explaining to the House of Commons that the British people might soon find themselves at war when a message was handed to him asking him to join a four-power conference at Munich to discuss the situation anew. The only result of that conference between Hitler, Mussolini, Chamberlain, and Daladier (the French Premier) was to postpone the German takeover of parts of the Sudetenland for ten days. Chamberlain and Hitler then went on to sign a joint declaration that there was to be no more war.

Chamberlain returned to London a conquering hero. Not since Disraeli had returned in triumph from the Congress of Berlin bearing "peace with honour" was an English statesman so universally acclaimed. For at the very brink of war, with German bombers only hours away, he had returned with "peace in our time." Winston Churchill, who as an independent Conservative backbencher had for several years criticized the Government's appeasement policy and the lagging pace of its rearmament efforts, was in a small but vocal minority when he described the Munich settlement as "a total and unmitigated defeat." As Churchill put it: "The German Dictator, instead

of snatching his victuals from the table, has been content to
have them served to him course by course. £1 was demanded
at the pistol's point. When it was given, £2 was demanded
at the pistol's point. Finally, the Dictator consented to take
£1 17s. 6d."

The End of Appeasement

Chamberlain's temporary popularity soon faded, for, as
things worked out, the Munich agreement precipitated the
breakup of the Czechoslovak state, and in March of 1939, German troops marched into Prague. The promises made by Hitler
at Munich had been broken within six months as had so many
earlier commitments. In March 1939 even Neville Chamberlain came to realize that his hopes had been misplaced, and
Britain began to speed up her preparations for war. In May,
conscription was reintroduced – for the first time in British
history in time of peace. Poland and Romania, one or the other
of which now seemed next on Hitler's list, were given guaran-
tees of support by Britain.

Attempts were made to reach an alliance with Communist
Russia and thereby reconstruct the pre-World War I Triple
Entente. The attempt failed, largely because Poland refused
to concede to Russian troops the potential right to cross Polish
territory to fight the Germans. In the light of post-World War
II events Polish misgivings are understandable. Agreement
with Russia failed ultimately not only because of mutual distrust but because Hitler offered better terms. The Hitler-Stalin
Non-Aggression Pact which surprised the world on August 24,
1939, gave Communist Russia a free hand (for the moment) in
all the lands of Eastern Europe (Finland, the Baltic States,
western Poland, and Bessarabia) which had been part of the
Russian Empire in 1914. Britain held firm to its guarantee of
Poland, however, and confirmed it with a treaty of mutual assistance on August 25. A last minute German demand for a
multitude of Polish territorial concessions had not even been
officially communicated to the Polish government when German
troops entered Polish territory and German airplanes began to
rain bombs on Polish cities on September 1, 1939. Two days
later Britain and France declared war on Germany. World War
II had begun.

The policy of appeasement had failed, but the policy must
not only be condemned but also understood. For a long time it
had the approval of a great majority of the British people, if
only because it had strong roots in British idealism. Many

Britons had come to think in the 1920s that Germany had been badly treated at Versailles; Hitler exploited this feeling of guilt in the 1930s. Many Britons had come to think that World War I had been caused by an excessive absorption with ideas of national prestige. Was it not better to attempt in a business-like fashion to bend over backwards to resolve every plausible national grievance which might lead to war? And German grievances – in the Rhineland, in Austria, in the Sudetenland – were, after all, cleverly based on an old liberal doctrine, national self-determination. Hitler found it easy to speak in Wilsonian terms.

Neither Baldwin nor Chamberlain was a pacifist, and although their rearmament program permitted Germany to gain air superiority and did not proceed at the pace which Churchill demanded, it was in tune with a public opinion which on the subject of weapons costs was probably even more cautious than the government leaders. Rearmament proceeded at a far more rapid pace than the official Opposition might have permitted had it been in power. The manner in which Czechs and anti-Nazi Germans were in effect handed over to Hitler was indeed callous; but a country which had suffered two and a half million military casualties less than a generation before might readily see a new war as an even greater evil. Perhaps Chamberlain was disingenuous when he spoke of the Czechoslovakian dispute in September 1938 as "a quarrel in a far away country between people of whom we know nothing"; but his feelings may well have been shared by a majority of his countrymen, and they were clearly shared by the Prime Ministers of the Commonwealth who almost invariably urged caution.

Of course the appeasers were under an illusion. Until 1939 they looked upon Nazi Germany as merely another state in the international balance of power, dictatorial at home but diplomatically sensible abroad. How successfully Hitler managed to sustain that illusion in German diplomatic documents has recently been demonstrated by one historian.[2] How reasonable he could seem in personal conversation was revealed by numerous private English visitors who could take satisfaction in his constant expressions of a desire for peace, his giving the English language first priority among foreign languages in German schools, and his apparent modesty. When one English visitor explained that Stanley Baldwin was a shy and modest

---

[2] A. J. P. Taylor, *The Origins of the Second World War* (London, 1961). But see H. R. Trevor-Roper's review in the June 1961 issue of *Encounter*, P. A. Reynold's "Hitler's War," *History* (Oct. 1961), and T. W. Mason, "Some Origins of the Second World War," *Past & Present* (Dec. 1964).

statesman who had never entirely got over his astonishment at finding himself Prime Minister, Hitler smiled and interjected, "And I also." (As one Englishman put it at the time, "It is all one to me whether the Nazis come and take us over or not, I've got my pension: they can't touch that.")

As a result some of the appeasers began to confuse means with ends. Nazi racial policies, concentration camps, and violent speeches were explained away as products of the exuberance of a revolutionary movement which would disappear as soon as Hitler acquired the maturity which accompanies power. For men such as Geoffrey Dawson, editor of the influential *Times* of London, the harassment of independent churchmen within Germany and the use of German planes to bomb defenseless Spanish towns during the civil war were less signs of a rising totalitarian force upsetting the prevailing balance of power than obstacles to the desired Anglo-German rapproachement. It was to become clear in retrospect that the apparent ragings in Hitler's book, *Mein Kampf,* were a more accurate indication of his ultimate ambitions than his tea talks with visiting Englishmen. Although Hitler might prove flexible in tactics, he never forgot his ultimate goal of dominating all of Eastern Europe even at the expected risk of a war with the West.

Thus the appeasers placed too much faith in treaties, underestimated the rapidity of German rearmament, and felt too secure about their own ultimate ability to defend themselves. They took too much comfort in the thought that whatever else he was, Hitler was at least an anti-Communist – until that illusion, too, was shattered by the Stalin-Hitler Pact. (That pact, in similar fashion, shattered the illusion of left-wing Labourites who had hoped to cooperate with the Communists in an anti-fascist "popular front.")

Yet whatever their mistakes or illusions, the appeasers must be credited with a genuine desire to preserve the peace. It was indeed the very failure of the appeasement policy which convinced the world that Hitler wanted war and that there was no alternative to military resistance. When war began in September 1939, there existed in Britain no desire for martial glory – as had stirred in some hearts in 1914 – but only a strong sense that justice lay entirely on the British side and an absolute conviction that Hitler's Germany could be stopped only by force of arms.

Chapter 18

THE AGE OF **Churchill**

FOR BRITAIN, World War II had many resemblances to World War I. Both were fought against the same enemy, Germany and her allies, who occupied the center of the Continent and relied upon vast initial superiority on land and upon submarine power at sea. In both wars Britain, France, Russia, and the United States fought on the anti-German side. In both wars Britain and her allies entered the conflict less well prepared than Germany and depended upon the command of the seas and the gradual utilization of resources outside Europe to build up a power sufficient to defeat the enemy.

Yet the two world wars had vast differences as well. Japanese military ambitions in Asia and the South Pacific and extensive fighting in North Africa caused the Second World War to live up to its name more truly than the first. New techniques — especially the coordinated utilization of the airplane and the tank—caused the second conflict to be far more a war of movement than the first. Britain came closer to defeat in 1940–41 than at any time in 1914–18 but ultimately won an even more complete victory in 1945 than in 1918—even if, like all twentieth-century military victories, it was a triumph tinged with tragedy.

Of all of Germany's enemies, only Britain and her dependencies plus four of her dominions were involved in the Second World War from its first week to its last. Canada, Australia, and New Zealand loyally declared war on Germany in September 1939 as did South Africa (by a narrow parliamentary margin).

India, to the displeasure of the National Congress, was also declared to be at war. The Irish Free State (Eire) remained strictly neutral, thereby depriving the Royal Navy of the use of Southern Irish ports.

As the war began, Neville Chamberlain was still Prime Minister, but he immediately recalled Winston Churchill to the post of First Lord of the Admiralty, the same position Churchill had held in 1914. "Winston is back" – the message was flashed from ship to ship. Since this one man, as statesman, as strategist, as diplomat, and as orator, was to lead his people through defeat to triumph and since he was afterwards, as historian, to chronicle that epic ordeal, it seems only fitting to write of Britain's involvement in World War II as the Age of Churchill.[1]

The "Phoney War"

It began in a peculiar fashion. Britain and France went to war on behalf of Poland, but they were in no position to save her from destruction. Within three weeks, Hitler's *Blitzkrieg* (lightning war) had overwhelmed the Polish army, whereupon Soviet Russia moved her troops westward to share in the partition of that unhappy land in characteristic eighteenth-century fashion. In the meantime, the British held air-raid drills, supplied civilians with gas masks, and evacuated some two million people (most of them children) from cities such as London which seemed the likely targets of German bombers. The Emergency Powers (Defence) Act of September 1939 gave the Government the powers it needed to control the civilian economy in the interests of war.

After the initial excitement produced by the declaration of war, there was a letdown. Germany, except for isolated submarine attacks, seemed to be in no mood to attack the West, and a certain leisureliness overtook the war effort. The number of men in uniform increased from half a million in the summer

---

[1] Churchill's six-volume *History of the Second World War* (London, 1948–1954) is available in paperback form. The best available biography of Churchill is Lewis Broad's two-volume study. British strategy is also discussed in detail in the two volumes by Arthur Bryant, based on the diaries of Lord Alanbrooke, head of the imperial general staff. The "Battle of Britain" is taken up in Drew Middleton's *The Sky Suspended* (New York, 1962), Hitler's invasion plans in Ronald Wheatley's *Operation Sea-Lion* (London, 1958), and the fighting in the West in Chester Wilmot's, *The Struggle for Europe* (London, 1948). Herbert Feis' *Roosevelt, Churchill, Stalin* (Princeton, 1957) details "Big Three" diplomacy. The impact of war upon domestic life is dealt with in W. K. Hancock and M. M. Gowing, *British War Economy* (London, 1949).

of 1939 to almost two million in the spring of 1940; but as of April 1940 there were still a million men unemployed. Munitions factories were not yet producing at full capacity. No special attempt was made to stockpile fats, sugar, timber, oil, or iron ore, even though the requisite shipping was available.

Britain sent a promised number of divisions to France, and the British and French general staffs coordinated strategy. But that strategy was the purely defensive one of awaiting a German assault behind the Maginot Line, a vast complex of tank traps, fixed artillery sites, subterranean railways, and living quarters, which paralleled the Franco-German border but failed to protect the Franco-Belgian border. Somehow the war was to be won by starving Germany into submission by economic blockade alone. Chamberlain privately questioned whether Germany had any intention of attacking the West at all; and a number of Englishmen, including Lloyd George, suggested that serious consideration be given to all German peace proposals. This the Government refused to do. Yet as the months dragged on, it did seem increasingly appropriate to call the war, as Americans were beginning to do, the "Phoney War."

War was indeed going on at sea; but on land and in the air there was a virtual standstill, and in England some of the evacuees began drifting back to their former homes. Fighting *was* going on in Northern Europe, where Russia took advantage of the Stalin-Hitler Pact to absorb the three Baltic states of Lithuania, Latvia, and Estonia and to launch an attack on Finland. There was strong Anglo-French sympathy for the Finnish cause; and a projected Allied expeditionary force to Finland was thwarted only by the refusal of Norway and Denmark to permit its transit and by the fact that the Finns made peace with (and ceded territory to) Russia in March, 1940.

The "Phoney War" ended suddenly on April 9, 1940. At dawn German naval units assaulted Copenhagen, Denmark, and all the major ports of Norway. Hitler's purpose was to prevent any Allied intervention in Scandinavia and to secure Germany's use of the iron ore supplies of neutral Sweden. The German invasion showed extraordinary coordination of sea, land, and air forces. Denmark surrendered within five hours, but the Norwegians held out for several weeks. For a time a British expeditionary force held on to outposts in central and northern Norway and at the same time managed to do much damage to the German surface navy. Half of her destroyers, three of her eight cruisers, and a battleship were destroyed. But German air superiority eventually forced a British withdrawal.

Churchill Becomes Prime Minister

It was the debacle in Norway which led to one of the most dramatic debates in the history of the House of Commons. Although an electoral truce had been declared in September 1939, Chamberlain had not been able to form a true Coalition Government. Neither the Labour Party nor the tiny remnant of the Liberal Party was represented in his Cabinet. The Labour Party therefore had no hesitation early in May about introducing a motion of censure of the Chamberlain Ministry. Liberals and independent Conservatives joined in. "The Government," declared Archibald Sinclair, the Liberal leader, "is giving us a one-shift war while the Germans are working a three-shift war."

The most scathing attack came from Leo Amery, a Conservative M.P. who had at one time been Chamberlain's Cabinet colleague. What was needed, declared Amery, was a government willing to match the enemy in fighting spirit, in daring, in resolution, and in the thirst for victory. He climaxed his speech by quoting the words which Oliver Cromwell had addressed three centuries before to the remnant of the Long Parliament: "You have sat too long here for any good you have been doing. Depart, I say, and let us have done with you. In the name of God, go." Chamberlain's Government had been accustomed to a majority of 200 votes or more; but in the vote of confidence of May 7, more than forty Conservatives voted with the Opposition and an even greater number abstained. The Government won the vote, 281–200, but the Labour Party continued to refuse participation in a coalition government under Chamberlain's leadership; and a public opinion poll showed that only 22 percent of the British public approved of Chamberlain as Prime Minister. On May 10, the same day that Hitler attacked Holland, Belgium, and France, Chamberlain resigned; King George VI, after first considering the naming of Lord Halifax, the Foreign Secretary, asked Winston Churchill to form a new government.

Churchill was 65 and until his return to the Admiralty the year before had not held Cabinet office for a decade; yet he was the man for the hour. In a sense his whole life, beginning with his service as soldier-correspondent in Cuba, India, and Africa in the 1890s, had been a preparation for the part he was now to play. He had always been a controversial figure; "I have," he said, "derived continued benefit from criticism at all periods of my life, and I do not remember any time when I was ever short of it." His brilliance and energy had long been recognized but also distrusted. He had devoted the 1930s to warning his countrymen against the menace of Nazi Germany; as early as 1932 he had prophesied that Hitler's demands would "shake to their foundations every country in the world." He had also spent his years out of office chronicling the deeds of his distant ancestor, John Churchill, the first Duke of Marlborough, who had served as leader of a European coalition battling the threat to the peace of an earlier age, Louis XIV. The new Prime Minister was a democrat by conviction but an aristocrat by birth and by training, and his self-confidence was never daunted by the fact that he happened to be in the minority at any given moment. In his sense of Britain's imperial mission, in his assurance that the struggle before him was one of *good* versus *evil* and that he was on the side of *good*, he personified the tradition of Cromwell, of Chatham, and of Pitt.

When he received the call from his sovereign to become Britain's wartime leader, Churchill was filled with a sense of quiet exhilaration. "I was conscious," he wrote later in his memoirs,

> of a profound sense of relief. At last I had the authority to give directions over the whole scene. I felt as if I were walking with destiny, and that all my past life had been but a preparation for this hour and for this trial. Ten years in the political wilderness had freed me from ordinary party antagonisms. My warnings over the last six years had been so numerous, so detailed, and were now so terribly vindicated, that no one could gainsay me. I could not be reproached either for making the war or with want of preparation for it. I thought I knew a good deal about it all, and I was sure I should not fail.[2]

Three days later he made his first appearance in the House of Commons as Prime Minister to outline his nation's problems and to define its aims. "I have nothing to offer but blood, toil, tears, and sweat." Long months of struggle and suffering lay ahead. "You ask, what is our policy: It is to wage war, by sea, land, and air, with all our might . . . against a monstrous tyranny, never surpassed in the dark, lamentable catalogue of human crime. . . . You ask, what is our aim? I can answer in one word: Victory, victory at all costs, victory in spite of all terror, victory, however long and hard the road may be. . . ."

"He mobilized the English language and sent it into battle," the late President Kennedy was to say of Churchill; and during the years that followed, radio enabled Churchill to become the inspiration not only of his own countrymen but of millions of Europeans and Americans as well.

---

[2] *The Gathering Storm,* p. 532.

For the moment, indeed, the English language was the most effective weapon Churchill had at hand. On the battlefield all his immediate hopes went awry. German armored battalions, supported by bombers and preceded by parachute units, conquered Holland in five days and Belgium in three weeks. By early June the German army was well inside France. This time there was no last stand at the Marne, for the Maginot Line had been outflanked and the Allied line broken. Italy's entry into the war on the German side prevented the use against Germany of French regiments stationed on the Italian border. On June 14, German troops entered Paris. Two days later, the last Premier of the Third French Republic was forced to resign, and his successor, the aged Marshal Pétain, signed an armistice with Germany according to which the German army, at French expense, was to occupy more than half of France, including the entire Atlantic coast, and to take over the French navy.

Churchill had appealed to the Belgians to continue to resist. He had appealed to Italy to stay out of the war. He had appealed to the French—in the French language—to become citizens of a joint Anglo-French union, to turn over the French fleet to Britain, and to keep up the battle in France's North African possessions. None of these appeals were heeded. The only comfort Englishmen could find in the events of May and June 1940 lay in "the miracle of Dunkirk." At that small French port, more than 300,000 British (and some French and Belgian) troops, surrounded on all sides by advancing German columns, were rescued by a motley flotilla of regular naval vessels, private yachts, trawlers, and motorboats. The success of this impromptu but superbly organized operation buoyed British spirits, even though it meant that 2,300 guns, 7,000 tons of ammunition, and 82,000 motor vehicles had been left to the enemy. Churchill freely admitted that Dunkirk was "a colossal military disaster. Wars are not won by evacuations."

The Battle of Britain

Hitler now bestrode the Continent from the North Cape to the Pyrenees, and in his shadow Mussolini sought to make the Mediterranean an Italian lake. Britain stood alone. London had become the home of numerous exiled kings and queens and of men like Charles DeGaulle (undersecretary of war in the last government of the Third French Republic), who attempted to rally the "free French." Britain had no ally left on the continent of Europe; she was subject to air attack from any point on the continent; and as in 1066 she was subject to the threat of invasion at once from Norway and from France.

314

"Very Well, Alone."   Cartoon by David Low
for the London *Evening Standard* (June 18, 1940).

Hitler, and many neutral observers, expected Britain to seek terms within a matter of weeks.   But Churchill stood defiant.   "We shall not flag or fail.   We shall go on to the end.   We shall fight in France, we shall fight on the seas and oceans, we shall fight with growing confidence and growing strength in the air, we shall defend our island whatever the cost may be, we shall fight on the beaches, we shall fight on the landing grounds, we shall fight in the fields and in the streets, we shall fight in the hills; we shall never surrender."   (See Low cartoon.) The British, who had been rather unimaginative in anticipating the coming of war, showed themselves equally unimaginative in failing to acknowledge that they had been beaten.

In the summer of 1940 Churchill took a number of desperate measures.   He had British troops occupy Iceland in order to anticipate any German venture in that direction and to safeguard North Atlantic sea-lanes.   At his command, the British navy destroyed or damaged the French fleets anchored in Oran (in French Algeria) and Dakar (in French West Africa) in order to prevent them from falling into German hands.   He sent men, guns, and tanks to Egypt (nominally independent since 1922 to hold the Suez Canal against an expected invasion from Italian Libya.   (See map.)

In the meantime, Hitler, wearying of Britain's obstinacy,

had given his general staff new secret orders. "Since England, in spite of her military hopeless position, shows no signs of coming to terms," he declared in mid-July, "I have decided to prepare a landing operation against England, and if necessary to carry it out. . . . The preparations for the entire operation must be completed by mid-August." Plans for what the Germans called "Operation Sea-Lion" were duly prepared, though Hitler's staff was handicapped by lack of time and by a relative lack of experience in the mounting of amphibious operations. The German high command realized that a successful invasion of England required air superiority over the Channel, and the demands of Operation Sea-Lion led necessarily to the Battle of Britain, the attempt to gain such air superiority and trammel Britain into submission by airpower.

Day after day, night after night—as many as 1,800 on a single attack—German bombers and fighter escorts streamed across the Channel to bomb and strafe British ports, airfields, and factories. Late in August, as a sign of impudence, British night bombers began to raid Berlin. Hitler was so enraged by this audacity that he ordered his bombers to pay less attention to vital military targets and concentrate all efforts upon the city of London itself; and on September 7–8, German bombs succeeded in setting much of central London aflame. The underground (subway) stations that served as nightly air raid shelters for the London populace did not save hundreds of people from being killed and thousands more from being wounded. (In the course of the war some 60,000 British civilians were to die as a result of air raids.) In the meantime, the alert had gone out along England's channel coast that thousands of landing barges had been sighted in the ports of northern France. Invasion seemed imminent. All directional signs were removed from hundreds of roads in southern England in order to confuse the enemy. Members of the Home Guard took their places along the beaches to await the invader, often armed with weapons little more complicated than the wooden pikes with which Harold's men had faced William the Conqueror in 1066.

The invasion never came. Hitler repeatedly postponed the date for a number of reasons, the most important of which may well have been the heroic resistance of the British air fighter command. Outnumbered four to one, the intrepid Hurricane and Spitfire pilots destroyed two German planes for every one of their own. "Never in the field of human conflict," declared Churchill, "was so much owed by so many to so few." German air superiority over the Channel was not achieved, and an increasing number of German invasion transports and barges were sunk in port. Neither industrial production nor civilian morale had been damaged by air raids to the degree that German planners had anticipated. Londoners digging in the rubble after a severe air raid often found King George VI at hand to commiserate or else a defiant Churchill puffing a cigar, his fingers formed in a "V for Victory" sign.

In mid-October, Hitler decided to postpone Operation Sea-Lion until the spring of 1941. He had been given his first great military rebuff, and his psychotic personality could not cope well with such reversals. Like the Battle of the Marne of September 1914 and the triumph over the Spanish Armada in 1588, the Battle of Britain of 1940 was a defensive victory. It halted the enemy in his tracks. It did not defeat him. But as did the victory over the Armada, so the Battle of Britain became a legend as well as a fact. It helped stiffen English resolution during the agonizing years of war that lay ahead, and it helped lead to Germany's ultimate defeat.

The War Economy

To write the history of a war only in terms of either barbarities and outrages or of courageous deeds and glowing words is necessarily a distortion of reality. Twentieth-century war is also a business which involves transforming a nation into one vast war-making machine. Such total mobilization overtook Britain during the winter of 1940–41 and the months that followed. Ordinary politics was adjourned for the duration of the war, as Labourites and Liberals became part of a genuine Coalition Cabinet. Churchill's inner war cabinet of five, in which Churchill served not only as Prime Minister but also as Minister of Defence, included two Labourites — Clement Attlee, the leader of the Labour Party, as Deputy Prime Minister, and Ernest Bevin, for many years the General Secretary of the Transport Workers Union and the outstanding trade unionist of the day, as Minister of Labour and National Service. Another Labourite, Herbert Morrison, became successively Minister of Supply, Home Secretary, and Minister of Home Security. Lord Beaverbrook, the politically independent "press lord," took on the all-important job of Minister of Aircraft Production. Under his auspices, British factories, which had produced 2,800 planes in 1938, built 20,000 in 1941 and 26,000 in 1943.

John Maynard Keynes became Economic Adviser to the Treasury. With his help and that of other economists, a national system of material allocation, rationing, and price control was set up which put the entire economy under government direction — if not, except for the railroads and the ports, under immediate government management. The right to conscript workers for munitions factories as well as for the armed forces was granted to the government by Parliament; some nine million men and women, one British citizen in five, were mobilized for the armed service, the auxiliary forces, or for munitions work. The right to conscript for nonmilitary activities was exercised sparingly; but the British economy was mobilized to an extent not matched by Germany, Italy, or Russia; and Churchill, though always subject to ultimate parliamentary control, became a dictator in all but name in his day-to-day conduct of the war.

Not only did the needs of war demand the continued expansion of the iron, steel, and aluminum industries, but they also dictated an expansion of agriculture. Not since the Napoleonic wars had the British farmer been given so great an incentive to increase acreage. In the course of the war, the number of acres in the British Isles devoted to grains and potatoes increased from twelve to eighteen million, thus saving vital shipping space. Thousands of city folk devoted weekends to spading and weeding their "allotments." Even the moat of the Tower of London became a vegetable patch. The number of tractors on British farms quadrupled, and farm laborers received the greatest boost in income and status in their often dismal history.

The Government was anxious not to alienate the labor movement, and except for one Welsh coal strike, World War II brought little of the industrial unrest which had marred the conflict of a generation before. Labor's belief in the justice of the war and the Labour Party's important role in the government were both conducive to this result. The Government did its best by means of rationing and price control to stabilize the cost of living; and by means of food subsidies, the official price index of daily necessities was kept steady from 1941 to 1945. Although real wages rose little if at all during the war, real earnings did rise in the sense that unemployment was now unknown and overtime pay became the rule. All major items of food, clothing, and furniture were rationed. All use of gasoline for civilian cars was banned, and restaurant meals were limited to 5s. ($1). Because of a shortage of newsprint, newspapers were reduced to four pages per issue. The only luxuries encouraged (though heavily taxed) were alcohol, tobacco, and the cinema. These presumably kept up civilian morale and absorbed excess spending power.

Wartime exigencies caused the national government to become involved in various health measures to an extent not known before. School meals became the general rule for rich and poor alike. Public nurseries helped working mothers, and cheap milk and vitamins were provided for children and expectant mothers. Factories were encouraged to provide doctors, nurses, and canteens. Deprived of their accustomed "sweets," English children could boast better teeth than ever before or since. These various measures, in spite of air raids, food short-ages, overcrowding, and strains on medical facilities, un-doubtedly brought an overall improvement in the health of British children. Infant mortality rates fell from 56 to 45 per thousand between 1937 and 1945. In Scotland, which had long lagged behind England in health standards, the improvement was even more noticeable.

In this wartime environment, class distinctions were sub-merged everywhere – air raid shelters, emergency hospitals, and evacuation centers were made available to all; the ration-ing system played no favorites; and the tax system tended more than ever before to equalize incomes. In this same atmosphere, the Coalition Government began, even sooner than during the First World War, to plan for the postwar world. Lord (formerly Sir William) Beveridge, the veteran Liberal social reformer, compiled the Beveridge Report (1942), which envisaged a com-prehensive public insurance system which would assure all Britons security from the cradle to the grave against all wants not of their own making. Although the report was prepared under government auspices and given much publicity, it was not given official approval by the Government. Such approval *was* granted to the main provisions of a second Beveridge Re-port on unemployment. Keynesian methods were to be used in the future to secure the permanent reduction of unemploy-ment to 3 percent or less of the British working force. The Education Act of 1944 set the school-leaving age at 15 (a goal achieved three years later) and secured the right of free sec-ondary education for all.

Before any postwar utopia could be achieved, the war had to be won, and not least among the problems faced by the Churchill Ministry was how to finance an economy in which fully half of the entire national output of goods and services was being devoted to the war effort. Initially the expectation of the Government had been that World War II would be fi-nanced in the same fashion as World War I had been – half by borrowing and half by increases in taxation. Upon Keynes' advice, the prime criterion of wartime financial policy became its success in counteracting the inflationary pressure being created by the disparity between rising wages and fewer con-sumer goods. The basic income tax rate was raised to 8s.6d. (42.5 percent) in the pound in 1940 and to 10s. (50 percent) in 1941. Many earlier tax exemptions were ended, and an excess profits tax of 100 percent was slapped on all corporate earnings in excess of prewar expectations. In 1943, at about the same time as in the United States, the "pay as you earn" withholding tax principle was introduced. Yet tax increases could not pay for the entire war effort, and the government channeled all savings either directly or indirectly (through banks) into the purchase of government bonds by prohibiting all ordinary capital investment.

The utilization of the taxes and savings of its own people was still not sufficient to finance the war. Even the borrowing of money from the dominions and other member countries of the Sterling Area (notably India and Egypt) was insufficient. The most vital outside source of war materiel was once again the United States; but when World War II began, the United States had made it far more difficult to purchase supplies than twenty-five years before. The neutrality legislation of the 1930s forbade private American corporations from lending money to European nations and private American ships from shipping goods to wartorn Europe. All purchases had to be made on a cash and carry basis. Only after the fall of France in June 1940 did the American government, increasingly conscious of the threat to its own military security posed by a European continent dominated by Hitler's Germany, gradually relax such restrictions. Three months later, the United States exchanged fifty of its overage destroyers for leases of military bases in British possessions in the Western Hemisphere.

In the meantime, large-scale British military purchases in the United States continued; but by the start of 1941 Britain's financial resources in the United States were exhausted. The country which during the Napoleonic wars had been able to shoulder the financial burdens of successive coalitions and which during World War I had still, in effect, been able to finance its own war effort, could no longer do so in World War II. The United States, under President Roosevelt's urging, responded in March 1941 with "An Act Further to Promote the Defense of the United States," popularly known as the Lend-Lease Act. The President promised "unqualified, immediate, all-out aid until total victory has been won." As Roosevelt phrased it in a homely analogy: if a neighbor's house was on fire, it was only right to lend him your garden hose.

The flow of lend-lease was slow at first; but before it ended, some $27 billion worth of goods had been sent eastward across the Atlantic. Although called "the most unsordid act" in diplomatic history and clearly essential to British military survival, the law did also impose onerous restrictions on British policy and ultimately involved some $6 billion of reverse lend-lease (from Britain to the United States), a sum which constituted as high a proportion of the British national income as lend-lease did of the American.

Despite the Lend-Lease Act, the United States in the spring of 1941 was still technically neutral and her war production facilities were still growing slowly. Britain remained the only major power actively resisting Axis expansion. The winter months had brought cheering news from Egypt, where a British force had chased an Italian army back into Italian Libya. Soon thereafter, British troops to the south liberated one of the earliest of the lands conquered by the Axis powers — Ethiopia was restored to King Haile Selassie.

The spring brought a reversal of fortune, however. German forces swept into the Balkans; and British efforts to make a last-ditch stand in mainland Greece or on the nearby island of Crete proved vain. Italian regiments in Libya were reinforced by German divisions under General Rommel, and the ill-equipped British forces were driven back into Egypt; only with difficulty could pro-British governments be kept in power in the Middle East. In the meantime, German bombing raids continued on a large scale. Plymouth, Liverpool, and Birmingham were all badly damaged; in London the chamber of the House of Commons was destroyed in May 1941, and for the next decade it had to utilize the House of Lords chamber for its meetings.

Forging the Grand Alliance

Late in the spring, German air raids began to let up, and on June 22, 1941, Hitler launched his invasion of Russia. Apparently underestimating the extent of Russian resistance, he hoped in a few bold strokes to win the wheat of the Ukraine, the oil of the Caucasus, and the greater part of Russia's industrial resources as well as the *Lebensraum* (living space) he had long claimed as the right of the German people. Once he dominated the Continent to the Ural Mountains, he hoped that even Britain would have to come to terms and that no full-scale invasion would be necessary. Perhaps indeed he expected to rearouse the latent strength of anticommunism in Britain. The gamble failed. The Russian army, though it ceded tens of thousands of square miles of territory, did not disintegrate. Churchill immediately pledged his aid to the U.S.S.R. Staunch anticommunist that he was, he saw Germany in 1941 as the far greater threat. It was German bombers, after all, which had been killing English civilians, just as it was the German government which was herding Jews and Slavs into concentration camps and which even then was embarking upon a policy of genocide and a type of barbarity which put to shame the much vaunted atrocities of the First World War.

"The Blitzed City"—London during World War II.
Etching by James Bone.

Thus Hitler's invasion of Russia forged the first link in the "Grand Alliance" which was ultimately to win World War II. As Churchill put it publicly: "Any man or State who fights on against Nazidom will have our aid." He also remarked privately: if Hitler invaded Hell it would be desirable to find something friendly to say about the Devil. British aid did go to Russia via the Arctic Sea and via Iran. In 1942 Churchill flew to Moscow to meet Stalin, and during the same year Britain concluded a twenty-year alliance with Russia.

Even before the United States and Britain had become actual military allies, Franklin D. Roosevelt and Winston Churchill became warm personal friends. Before the Second World War was over, Churchill was to hold nine meetings with the American President and to exchange 1,700 telegrams, telephone calls and letters. Their first meeting took place in August 1941 on a battleship off the Newfoundland coast. There the two statesmen composed "The Atlantic Charter," a document setting forth Anglo-American war aims. It rejected any territorial aggrandizement for either Britain or the United States and affirmed the right of all peoples to choose their own form of government.

On December 7, 1941, Japan forged the second link in the Grand Alliance. Her surprise attack on Pearl Harbor, followed as it was by an American declaration of war against Japan, a German and Italian declaration of war against the United States, and a British declaration of war against Japan, was the true turning point of the war for Britain.

No American will think it wrong of me [Churchill was to write] if I proclaim that to have the United States at our side was to me the greatest joy. I do not pretend to have measured accurately the martial might of Japan, but now at this very moment I knew the United States was in the war, up to the neck and in to the death. So we had won after all! After Dunkirk; after the fall of France; after the horrible episode of Oran [the destruction of the French navy]; after the threat of invasion when apart from the Army and Navy, we were an almost unarmed people; after the deadly struggle of the U-Boat War — the first Battle of the Atlantic, gained by a hand's breadth; after seventeen months of lonely fighting and nineteen months of my responsibility in dire stress, we had won the war. England would live; Britain would live; the Commonwealth of Nations and the Empire would live. ... Once again in our long island history we should emerge, however mauled or mutilated, safe and victorious. We should not be wiped out. Our history would not come to an end.[3]

Churchill immediately traveled to Washington in order, among other things, to address the American Congress. He did all in his power to buttress the links of Anglo-American understanding and often reminded his hearers that his mother had been American by birth and that he was himself "an English-Speaking Union." Britain and the United States drafted a pact in the name of twenty-six "United Nations"; and their respective war efforts became so intertwined that General George Marshall, the American Army Chief of Staff, could describe their cooperation as "the most complete unification of military effort ever achieved by two allied nations." Churchill also helped convince the American leaders that the defeat of Germany should be given first priority.

The immediate post-Pearl Harbor military prospects did not, admittedly, look bright. In the Far East, Japan rapidly overran not only the American Philippines and hundreds of other small Pacific islands but also the Dutch East Indies, British Malaya and Singapore, and much of British Burma. For the first time since the American Revolution, a substantial portion of the British Empire fell into enemy hands. In the meantime, America's own wartime requirements took precedence over Britain's needs. In the North Atlantic, continued German submarine successes produced the most serious shipping crisis of the war. German troops were again advancing in Egypt and in Russia, and men began to speculate about the fearful possibility of a linkup in India between German and Japanese forces.

The Road to Victory

Yet throughout the year, American productive capacities were being built up and the American armed forces kept growing. In the autumn of 1942 came the military turning of the tide. The Axis powers had attained their greatest territorial extent and almost simultaneously, in the Far East, in Russia, and in North Africa, the Allies began a counterattack. In November 1942 American marines landed on the island of Guadalcanal; it was to become the first of many islands to be recaptured from the Japanese. By then the mammoth battle of Stalingrad was under way. By the time it ended in February

---

[3] *The Grand Alliance,* pp. 606–607.

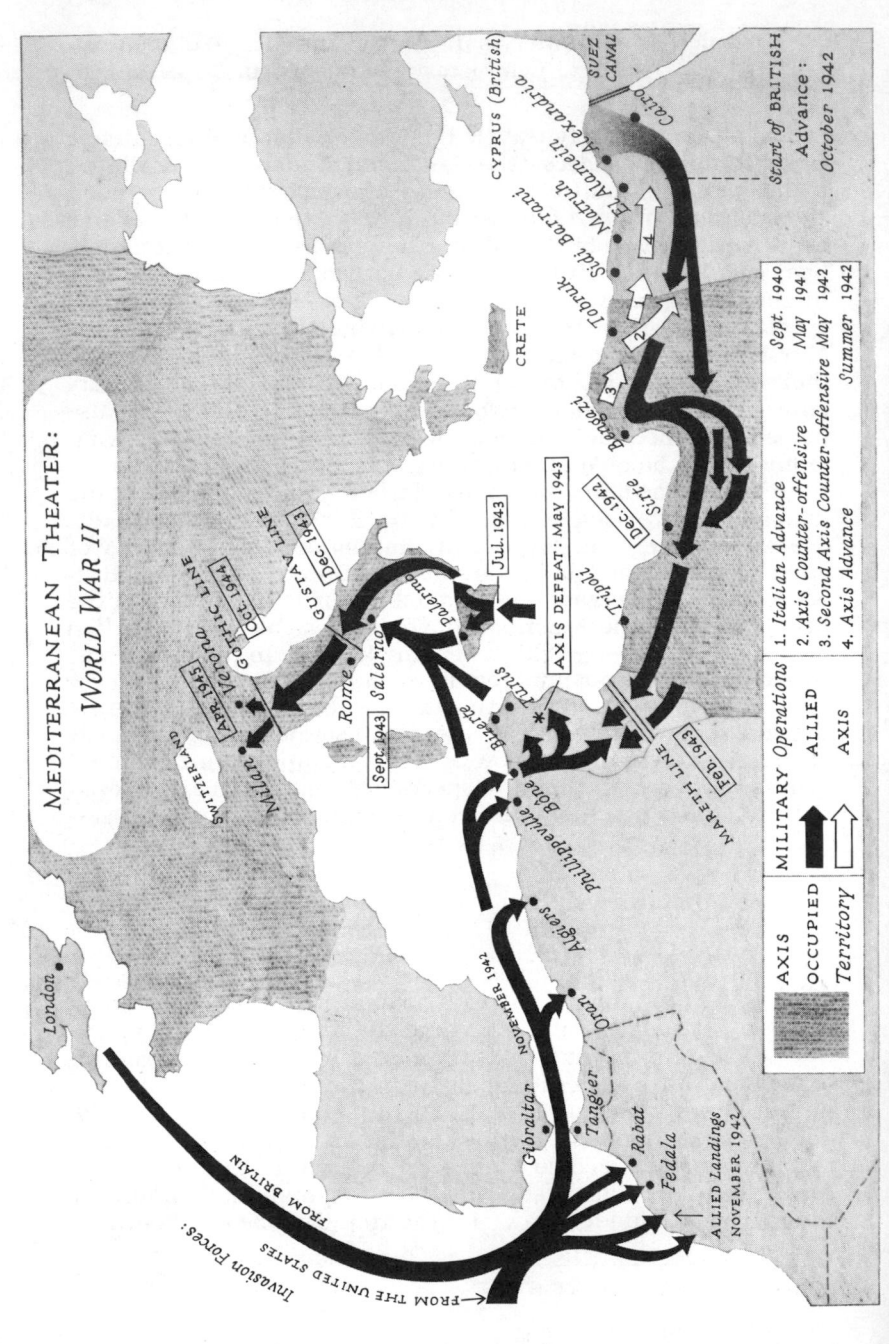

1943 the greater part of a German army had surrendered to the Russians and the remainder was retreating westwards. In October 1942 the British Eighth Army under General Bernard (later Lord) Montgomery (1887–) halted General Rommel's forces at El Alamein, seventy miles west of Alexandria, Egypt, and began a victorious drive westwards. In November 1942 Allied forces under General Eisenhower's command landed in Morocco and Algeria and began a drive which pushed all Axis forces in Africa into Tunisia and which, seven months later, in cooperation with Montgomery's Eighth Army, expelled them altogether from Africa. "Now this is not the end," proclaimed a jubilant Churchill on first hearing of the successful landings. "It is not even the beginning of the end. But it is, perhaps, the end of the beginning."

1943 brought a slow but steady Allied advance in the Mediterranean area and in Russia. Despite Russian urging, the western Allies did not yet feel themselves in a position to launch a full-fledged Second Front in France; but in July, American, British, and Canadian units invaded Sicily. Their invasion of Italy early in September was immediately followed by the overthrow of Mussolini and the signing of an armistice by a new Italian government. Churchill had long urged an attack against "the soft underbelly of the Axis," but Germany now treated its erstwhile ally as an occupied country; and powerful German resistance made the campaign up the Italian peninsula a costly one, reminiscent at times of the deadly trench warfare of World War I. Churchill hoped for an attack upon the Balkans as well, partly in order to prevent postwar domination of the entire area by Russia. In this case, he was overruled by the Americans, who, by virtue of the greater wealth and manpower at their command, had of necessity become the senior partner in the Anglo-American partnership.

Some of Churchill's strategic proposals were to receive critical scrutiny in postwar memoirs, but the value of his role in planning grand strategy and sometimes tactics as well is generally conceded as is his ever-present consciousness of the political probabilities of the postwar world. No permanent cleavage divided him from his generals, as had estranged Lloyd George from General Haig. Not that he hesitated to speak frankly to them at all times. For instance, when General Montgomery, the son of an Anglican vicar, boasted to Churchill: "I don't drink and I don't smoke and I am 100 per cent fit," the Prime Minister retorted: "I *do* drink and I *do* smoke and I am 200 per cent fit."

As 1944 began, almost all Allied planning was concentrated upon D–Day, the most massive and audacious amphibious invasion ever planned in military history. As Allied bombers became increasingly effective in disrupting the German industrial and transportation system, a million and a half American troops were landed in Britain in preparation for the grand assault on Normandy. It came on June 6, in the form of an armada of four thousand ships supported by 11,000 airplanes. Although there were setbacks after the initial landings, by the end of July the Allied forces had broken out of Normandy and had encircled the greater part of one German army. By late August, Paris was liberated and Hitler's forces were everywhere on the retreat eastwards.

Germany seemed on the point of collapse. But as German defensive lines began to resemble those of the First World War, they stiffened; and in the autumn the Allied drive in Belgium and eastern France was halted. During these weeks of apparent victory, Londoners and other Englishmen were exposed to a new threat, in some ways more unnerving than the nightly bomber raids of earlier years. These were the pilotless "buzz-bombs," rockets from France which descended suddenly from the stratosphere and did considerable damage. Once the launching pads in France of the short-range V-1 rockets had been captured, the long-range V-2 rockets fired from the German Ruhr continued to destroy and to disconcert for several months more.

In January 1945 a "Big Three" conference in the Crimea secured Russian agreement to a postwar international organization and Russian aid to the Far Eastern war, which was expected to continue for at least a year and a half after the war in Europe was over. Occupation zones for Germany were drawn up, and a government based on "free and unfettered elections" was promised for a reconstructed Poland, which was to cede its eastern lands to Russia and occupy former German territory instead.

A temporarily successful German counterattack in December—the Battle of the Bulge—had discouraged Allied strategists; and the sudden success of the Allies' late winter offensive came almost as a surprise. In March, the Allied forces crossed the Rhine, and on May 7, 1945, with Hitler and Mussolini both dead, the German high command conceded unconditional surrender. King George VI and his family—and Winston Churchill—waved to cheering crowds from the balcony of Buckingham Palace. The long-dimmed lights of Trafalgar Square and Piccadilly Circus gave way to floodlights as hundreds of thousands milled about in celebration of V-E Day.

For most of the British public, the war with Japan had always been of secondary importance; but the shift of men and materiel soon began; and by the time of V-J Day, less than three months later, over 650,000 British troops were engaged in the war against Japan. The British were especially active in Burma and Malaya and received the Japanese surrenders in French Indo-China and the Dutch East Indies. The perfection of the atomic bomb, in whose initial development British scientists had played a vital role, obviated the full-scale invasion of the main Japanese islands long thought necessary and brought the Far Eastern war to a relatively speedy conclusion.

The effects of World War II on Britain were manifold. 357,000 Britons had been killed (30,000 of them merchant seamen, 60,000 of them civilian air raid victims) and 600,000 more had been disabled. If the Second World War proved for Britain only one third as deadly as the first, it was because British troops had not had to undergo four years and more of continuous full-scale land fighting. The Sommes, Passchendaeles, and Verduns, of the First World War were called Leningrad, Moscow, and Stalingrad in the Second. Yet Britain's cities had been destroyed in a manner for which the earlier war provided no precedent. Her port facilities and her railways had deteriorated. She had a national indebtedness of twenty-five billion pounds and for the first time since the seventeenth century was, in terms of her total international accounts, a debtor country. She was still dependent upon the import of food and raw materials; yet most of the export industries with which she balanced accounts had been converted to military purposes, and the merchant marine which gained her "invisible earnings" was 30 percent smaller than it had been in 1938. The ghost of the Pax Britannica had been laid and naval supremacy conceded to the United States.

The problems of the peace—the long-range economic dislocations; the nationalist upsurge in Asia and Africa; and most notably, the "Cold War" that soon divided the members of the Grand Alliance—obscured so quickly the triumph of 1945 that its significance tends to be slighted. An Anglo-American alliance had been forged to end at last the schism that had divided the English-speaking peoples since 1775. A new and more comprehensive international organization had been created. In spite of overwhelming odds, Britain had emerged from World War II as one of the "Big Three," just as it had been one of the Big Three at Paris and one of the Big Five at Vienna. Finally, in the battle between a totalitarian, fanatical, nationalistic ideology and that of liberal democracy, it was liberal democracy which had emerged triumphant once again. Certainly British stubbornness in 1940 had something to do with that outcome. The Battle of Britain and the symbol of defiance it produced in the person of Winston Churchill, the greatest of all English war ministers, deserve the honored place they have attained in the collective memory of the British people and of free men everywhere. Britain's perseverance in the face of overwhelming odds has had its own effect upon the postwar world and has, despite setbacks, helped make the spirit of post-World War II Britain more hopeful and enterprising than the spirit of the 1920s and 1930s.

Chapter 19

The **Labour** Government

IT IS AN UNDERSTATEMENT to call 1945 an eventful year. It marked the end of the Second World War both against Germany and against Japan. It saw the organization of the postwar United Nations at San Francisco. It brought death for Mussolini and Hitler, and for Franklin D. Roosevelt, eulogized by Churchill as "the greatest American friend we have ever known." It marked the explosion of the first atomic bomb and thus ushered in what, in mingled pride and terror, we call "the nuclear age." In 1945 the foundations were laid for the "Cold War," the temperature of which was to rise and fall many a time during the years that followed. And for Britain 1945 signified a momentous general election, the first such election in a decade.

The General Election of 1945

Winston Churchill would have been happy to continue his Coalition Government until the war against Japan had been won, but the Labour and Liberal members of his Government preferred not to wait. Churchill therefore formed an all-Conservative "caretaker" Government in May, and elections were scheduled for July 5. In order to allow for servicemen's votes to be counted with the regular ballots, the actual tallying of the votes was held off until July 26. By that time Churchill was off at Potsdam to confer with Stalin and Harry S. Truman, the new President of the United States, in what proved to be the third and last of World War II's Big Three Conferences. Churchill returned to London to hear the returns: Labourites, 393 M.P.s; Conservatives, 189; Liberals, 12; various minor groups and independents, 46. The swing in the popular vote was not quite so dramatic, but significant enough. Labour advanced from 41 percent (in 1935) to almost 50 percent of the total popular vote. The Conservative vote declined from 55 percent to 40 percent.

As soon as the outcome of the election was clear, Churchill called at Buckingham Palace to tender his resignation as Prime Minister to the King. Hardly had he departed in his chauffeur-driven Rolls Royce than Clement Attlee drove up in his small family car to be named the new Prime Minister. Shortly thereafter Attlee set off for Potsdam to take his place as one of the Big Three.

The election results came as a dramatic surprise to most Britons and to most overseas newspaper readers as well. For Winston Churchill himself they were both a great surprise and a sore disappointment. As he was to write in his *History of the Second World War:* "... I acquired the chief power in the state, which henceforth I wielded in ever-growing measure for five years and three months of world war, at the end of which time, all our enemies having surrendered unconditionally or being about to do so, I was immediately dismissed by the British electorate from all further conduct of their affairs." The conclusion is at once succinct and misleading. For the campaign of 1945 was in no sense an anti-Churchill campaign. The Labourites were more than willing to acknowledge Churchill's great services as a war leader. One young Labour supporter, for example, shouted herself hoarse in Churchill's honor as he toured her city. "He's a marvel," she proclaimed, "and we owe him everything. But how old he looks! And how tired! What he wants is a good rest, and that is what we are going to give to him." [1]

The Labour Party was looking ahead to the postwar years, when the chief problems seemed likely to be domestic rather than foreign. And the Conservatives, contended the Labourites, had demonstrated during the 1930s their ineptitude in combatting unemployment as well as in preventing war. Labour

---

[1] D. C. Somervell, *British Politics Since 1900* (London, 1953). Ernest Watkins' *The Cautious Revolution* (New York, 1950) provides a comprehensive contemporary account of the postwar Labour Government. The essays in Michael Sissons and Philip French (eds.), *The Age of Austerity* (London, 1963) provide a more recent reappraisal. Also relevant are the books by Havighurst and Pollard referred to earlier and Maurice Bruce, *The Coming of the Welfare State* (London, 1961).

had a more specific electoral program and had retained during the war a much better organized party machinery. Churchill, moreover, found the abrupt change from world statesman to party spokesman a difficult one. When in one broadcast he predicted that in order to establish socialism the Labour leaders would have to rely "on some form of Gestapo," Hitler's dreaded secret police, the charge redounded against him. Attlee, Morrison, and Bevin had, after all, been his trusted Cabinet colleagues for half a decade, they had never revealed a Cabinet secret, and their patriotism was beyond cavil.

For the Labour Party, July 26, 1945, was its one great historic moment. For the first time in British history – and for the first time among the major democratic nations – a professed socialist party had won an overwhelming parliamentary majority. The election seemed to vindicate the pioneers who had organized the Labour Representation Committee in 1900 and to assuage the frustrations encountered by their successors of the 1930s who had rebuilt the party after MacDonald's "betrayal."

A few farsighted Conservatives were able to see a silver lining in the worst electoral disaster to befall them since 1906. The new government, they were aware, would not be able to concentrate only on "building socialism." It would have to deal with all the problems of postwar reconstruction, both physical and economic; and it might prove more successful in asking for necessary working-class sacrifice than a Conservative government. It would likewise have to deal with the monumental diplomatic repercussions wrought by war; and it might more readily achieve national unity against Russian expansion, if that were to prove a major postwar problem.

Though pledged to establish a "Socialist Commonwealth," the Attlee Ministry produced neither the shock nor the fear of complete social overturn which the first Labour Cabinet of Ramsay MacDonald had briefly occasioned. Yet Labour M.P.s did on one occasion jar the House of Commons by singing "The Red Flag" within the historic walls of Westminster Palace; and the background of the ministers gave some sanction to the party's claim to be "of the people." Eight of the thirty-seven ministers had at one time been coal miners; eleven had been active trade union leaders. While Hugh Dalton (1887–1962), the Chancellor of the Exchequer, and Sir Stafford Cripps, President of the Board of Trade, came from middle- or upper-middle-class backgrounds, Herbert Morrison, the leader of the House of Commons, had risen from a London slum, the son of a policeman and a housemaid. Ernest Bevin, who, as Foreign Secretary soon became the number two man in the government, had similarly risen from extreme poverty, as had Aneurin Bevan, the new Minister of Health. Bevan (1899–1960) was to play in the Labour Government of 1945 a role comparable to Lloyd George in the Liberal Government of 1906. Like Lloyd George, he was a Welshman and a spellbinding orator; none of the new ministers felt more conscious than he of having been the victim of social injustice, for his father had died early of a respiratory disease caught in the coal mines; and the gibes of no other Labour M.P. could so infuriate the Conservative opposition.

Attlee himself was of upper-middle-class background and had attended Oxford. He had been drawn to the Labour Party by his interest in social work and by the influence of the Webbs. No greater contrast to Churchill could have been imagined in physique or manner or oratorical power. "Mr. Attlee is a modest man," observed one of his aides to Churchill. Replied Churchill: "A modest man, but then he has so much to be modest about." To some extent, appearances were deceiving. Attlee's personality never imposed itself upon his countrymen as his predecessor's had done; but the man who had successfully led a difficult party for a decade was to guide an even more difficult Cabinet with a quiet demeanor but a firm hand.

Nationalization and Social Security

For a generation the Labour Party had pledged itself to nationalize the commanding heights of British industry. Its election victory in 1945 gave it the opportunity to pass the appropriate acts of Parliament. Nationalization meant that industries were to be operated by "public corporations" like the Tennessee Valley Authority in the United States and not directly by government departments. Former owners were to be compensated. Workers in nationalized industries had, as before, the right to bargain collectively and the right to strike. Henceforth, however, the motive of production was to be public service rather than private profit. The power of the capitalistic classes was to be curbed; and the ability of the government to counteract the ups and downs of the economy and to plan for the national welfare was to be enhanced.

The nationalization of the Bank of England in 1946 caused little visible change; the same man was kept as governor. Though originally a private institution, the Bank had long had unique public responsibilities. The confirmation of its public status, analogous to the Federal Reserve System in the United States, comforted those Labourites who had held a banker's plot responsible for the downfall of the Labour Government of 1929–31.

The first major segment of the economy to be nationalized was that of coal mining, for years the sickest of British industries. The easily accessible coal seams had long since been exhausted, and during much of the twentieth century the productivity of the mines had been declining. The industry, moreover, had the poorest record of labor relations, and the Miners' Union had long advocated nationalization. The act finally passed in 1946 provided that the more than 800 private coal companies, employing 765,000 workers, were to be replaced by a single National Coal Board appointed by the Minister of Fuel and Power and consisting of nine representatives of the various functions within the industry (such as finance, technology, labor, and marketing). The Board was to operate the mines subject to the general supervision of the Ministry.

Another act of 1946 placed the greater part of a much smaller but rapidly expanding industry, aviation, in the hands of three (and ultimately two) public corporations. BOAC (British Overseas Airways Corporation) had been created by the Chamberlain Government in 1939 but came into operation only in 1945. BEA (British European Airways) was set up in 1946. The overseas cable system was nationalized during the same year; the domestic telegraph system had been part of the Post Office since 1870. In 1947 and 1948 followed the nationalization of the electricity and gas industries. The establishment of the Central Electricity Board in 1926 had been a giant step in a direction completed by the act of 1947. The nationalized gas industry was left in the hands of twelve large autonomous regional boards. A much greater undertaking was the nationalization of inland transport. The consolidation of the four main-line railways left after the post-World War I amalgamations proved a fairly simple undertaking. Much more complicated was the nationalization of the hundreds of small trucking companies which had been feverishly competing with the railways since the 1920s. Inland transport also included docks and canals; and in terms of number of employees (888,000) and monetary value, the nationalization of inland transport was the largest of all such undertakings by the Labour Government.

Even after the program of nationalization was complete, some 80 percent of the British economy remained in private hands, and the most surprising result of nationalization for fervent advocates and die-hard opponents alike was how little difference it often made. Rational industrial planning might be made easier by nationalization, but the problem of financing the reequipment and modernization of wartorn railways and inefficient coal mines remained, as did the problem of labor relations. Many miners, it seems clear in retrospect, had envisaged nationalization as a form of "guild socialism," a concept popularized earlier in the century by G. D. H. Cole, in which they would somehow help run their own small coal company. But, although it provided them with indirect representation, the new National Coal Board proved often to be the old coal-owner writ large; it was "still the same bloomin' boss!" Even a staunch advocate of nationalization was forced to concede a decade later that the most notable failure of the government-controlled industries "has been their inability to evoke a new kind of response from the workers whom they employ." [2]

Although the life of the average Briton was not immediately affected by nationalization, it was very likely indeed to be affected by the National Insurance and the National Health Service Acts of 1946, twin pillars of the postwar welfare state. The first act consolidated steps taken by various British governments since the time of the Elizabethan Poor Laws to assume responsibility for the general welfare by providing security against unemployment, sickness and disability benefits, maternity and death benefits, and payments for retired persons, widows, and orphans. For the individual, all these were to be secured by the weekly purchase of a single insurance stamp. In practice, the insurance fund thus accumulated had to be supplemented by grants from the National Exchequer. The National Insurance scheme and associated schemes of family allowances and industrial injuries benefits, as supplemented by a National Assistance Board to help all those whose insurance benefits fell below a specified minimum, was compulsory and universal and embodied much of the first wartime Beveridge Report. Although the resulting social insurance program was far more comprehensive than the prewar program, it represented a smaller percentage of total government expenditure in 1950 (11.3 percent) than in 1938 (13.6 percent). Payments to the unemployed had dominated the interwar social insurance expenditures; but large-scale unemployment was absent from Britain's postwar economy.

Initially more controversial than the National Insurance system was the National Health Service which went into effect in 1948. It enabled all Britons regardless of class or status to enjoy free medical and hospital care. Within a year, 95 percent of the population had enrolled itself on the panel of the doctor of its choice. The doctor in turn was paid by the Health Service from Exchequer funds on the basis of the number of patients

---

[2] William A. Robson, *Nationalised Industries and Public Ownership* (London, 1960); R. Kelf-Cohen, *Nationalisation in Britain: The End of a Dogma* (London, 1959).

on his panel (a maximum of 3,500, an average of 2,200). Many British doctors had experienced the panel system under the working class health insurance act of 1911. The new act was much less cumbersome and much more comprehensive. It included the self-employed, the unemployed, and the dependent members of each family; and it provided for the care of teeth and eyes as well as ordinary medical care.

Although the British Medical Association had long favored a comprehensive national health service, it became fearful of the prospect during the 1940s. Long months of negotiation were required before Minister of Health Bevan could work out a formula to which a majority of doctors were willing to accede. In due course, 97 percent of British doctors joined the National Health Service. While it placed upper limits upon their income, it freed them from the problem of financially delinquent patients. "The absence of any financial barrier between doctor and patient," observed one physician, "must make the doctor-patient relationship easier and more satisfactory." [3]

Although the new National Health Service was handicapped initially by a severe shortage of hospitals, equipment, and staff, it soon became perhaps the single most popular measure of the Labour Government. Estimates of its cost, admittedly, soon exceeded expectations, for the sudden availability of free medical care revealed an unexpectedly high pent-up need and demand for dentures and eyeglasses. During the postwar years, thanks to the comprehensiveness of the National Health Service and to the great strides made in medical science, such formerly widespread diseases as tuberculosis, typhoid, diphtheria, and poliomyelitis were mastered. Although hospital construction remained slow and the problem of providing appropriate compensation to doctors and nurses at a time of inflation and rising expectations remained a troublesome one, the number of doctors increased rapidly (from 36,500 in 1948 to 49,000 in 1958). Infant mortality rates continued steadily to decline and life expectancy continued steadily to increase. By 1958, the average British man lived to age 69, the average British woman to 74.

Though the Labour Government made no attempt to nationalize land, it maintained the wartime emphasis given to British agriculture. It was far less successful with the building of houses. The war had resulted in a great housing shortage. The population had grown, but almost no new houses had been built during the war, and half a million houses had been destroyed by enemy action. Firm rent-control measures helped counter inflation but provided little incentive for new private

---

[3] Harry Eckstein, *The English National Health Service* (Cambridge, Mass., 1959).

building. As a result, the number of houses built annually during the later 1940s — mostly by local government authorities — was only half as large as the number built annually during the 1930s.

Austerity

All the Labour Government's plans of nationalization and socialist planning were increasingly handicapped and often overshadowed by the grave economic problems inherited from the Second World War. The underlying problem was easy to describe but difficult to resolve — a gap in the balance of payments. Britain's net annual income from overseas investments had decreased from £175 to £73 million since 1938, but the prices of necessary imports had increased fourfold. The immediate postwar years brought a worldwide shortage of the food and the raw materials which Britain needed to import; their price therefore had increased far more rapidly than the price of the manufactured goods which Britain was reconverting its industries to export. Thus the "terms of trade," which had been favorable to Britain in the 1930s and had helped to raise living standards for all but the unemployed, were now unfavorable. A government poster showed Britain in housewifely terms as a woman at a shop counter who had ordered more goods than she could afford to pay for. Only by raising exports by 75 percent above prewar levels could the international balance of payments be righted.

During the war, the payments problem had been greatly eased by American Lend-Lease aid. But in August 1945 the United States abruptly ended Lend-Lease, and Britain was faced with the immediate necessity of paying in dollars even for goods already in the country or on the way. Americans justified the sudden halt of Lend-Lease on the basis that the war was over and that they now had to think of their own domestic needs. But reconversion to peacetime industry was only beginning in Britain, and the dimensions of the economic problem were only just becoming clear. A British delegation headed by Lord (formerly Sir Maynard) Keynes went to Washington to seek a loan of 3.75 billion dollars. Months of difficult negotiation followed, because few Americans were yet conscious of the complexities of postwar European economic reconstruction. "Not one dollar for Britain," declared one American congressman, "as long as they have got the Crown Jewels in London." In July 1946 with the support of the Truman administration, the loan was successfully pushed through Congress, but only at the cost of fatally undermining Keynes' health and forcing the British delegation to accede to onerous restrictions. Only the rumbles of the Cold War—a Russian refusal to evacuate northern Iran and a plea by Joseph P. Kennedy, the former American ambassador to Britain, for aid to the United Kingdom as a bulwark against atheistic communism—turned the tide of Congressional opinion.

The American loan was at best a stopgap. Within nine months a billion dollars had been spent, but the imbalance in international payments was as great as ever. And Britons who had been looking forward to the easing of wartime restrictions were instead exposed to the full rigors of postwar austerity. In the summer of 1946, the Labour Government felt compelled to introduce bread rationing, a step which, Churchill testily reminded the country, his own government had been able to avoid even during the most difficult months of submarine warfare. During the winter of 1946–47, conditions reached their nadir. On a typical day in February, London's *Daily Telegraph* had the following headlines:

BREAD RATION MAY BE CUT
PEERS HEAR REVIEW OF 1947 FOOD OUTLOOK
LESS BACON AND HOME MEAT
BEER SUPPLIES TO BE HALVED IMMEDIATELY
SNOW FALLS IN LONDON

The last headline proved for the moment the most portentous, for the worst winter weather in a century prevented the movement of coal to the factories and electric plants and worsened what was in any event a dire fuel shortage. Railways were disrupted; gas and electricity supplies were sharply cut. The snows of winter were followed by the floods of spring, which killed sheep and cattle and inundated croplands.

In 1947 and 1948, food rations were reduced well below the wartime average to thirteen ounces of meat, eight ounces of sugar, one quart of milk, and one egg per week per person. Bread became one of a maximum of three dishes in a restaurant meal, and someone who ordered bread with the main dish discovered that he had forfeited his right to dessert. The food shortage posed a peculiar dilemma for advertisers who sought to resume prewar traditions but found the demand for their products far exceeding the available supply. Our milk chocolate is wonderful, exulted one manufacturer, but unfortunately we "are only allowed the milk to make an extremely small quantity, so if you are lucky enough to get some, do save it for the children...." For the most part, however, even children were forced to substitute carrots for prewar "sweets" and oranges, grapes, and bananas. The average housewife spent at least an hour a day waiting in a queue, clutching her various ration books and mentally juggling ration points as well as prices. Shortages were no longer explained on the basis of "don't you know there's a war on?" Now the favorite phrase was "all the best goes for export." The food shortage implied drabness rather than actual starvation, but in the summer of 1946 Prime Minister Attlee suggested that those British citizens who felt quixotically impelled to send food parcels to the Continent—where some people were worse off—might do more good simply by eating less.

Various spectacular government efforts to solve the food problem met with indifferent success. A giant peanut-raising scheme in East Africa (part of the sterling area) failed to get off the ground. Nor did the government succeed in making some readily available whalemeat a permanent part of the British diet. In 1947 the Government imported large quantities of canned "snoek," a tropical fish from South Africa, as a substitute for meat. Although the fish was given considerable publicity, with a ministerial snoek-tasting party and government-published recipes for "snoek piquante," snoek turned out to provide more food for cartoonists and music-hall comedians than for ordinary people. The trouble with snoek, as even one Labour minister conceded, was that it was "palatable, but rather dull." A few years later the large stocks of canned snoek which remained unsold were reduced in price, given new labels, and sold as "selected fish food for cats and kittens."

The food shortage was accompanied by a notable shortage of clothing. "We must *all* have new clothes," confided King George VI to Attlee in 1945; "my family is down to the lowest ebb." Clothes, like food, were rationed on a points system; and in 1947 when Princess Elizabeth, the heiress to the throne, was married to Lieutenant Philip Mountbatten, it was officially announced that for the occasion the Princess had been given 100 clothing coupons, bridesmaids 23 coupons each, and pages 10 coupons each. The clothing shortage caused the new women's fashions of 1947 to become an issue of state. Few people objected to women looking more feminine; and they were happy enough to see rounded shoulders and nipped-in waists replace the angular uniform look which women's clothing had taken on in wartime. But the fact that the "New Look" instigated by Paris designers involved a six- to eight-inch lengthening of skirts caused dismay at the Board of Trade. Material was already in short supply; now it would make fewer garments. Paris designers won out over government officials, however, and after an unavailing propaganda campaign, even the Board of Trade was forced to concede: "We cannot dictate to women the length of their skirts."

In 1947 the use of gasoline for civilian cars was entirely

prohibited (after a brief postwar respite) and newspapers were restricted once more to four-page issues. Tobacco taxes were raised by 43 percent, and for some months a 75 percent import duty was placed on American films in order to discourage the consumption of two products which used up so many of the again dwindling supply of dollars. The fuel shortage led to occasional factory shutdowns and to sporadic cuts in the electricity supply. As during the war, it was deemed unpatriotic to fill a bathtub with more than a few inches of water; and to turn on an electric heater in the summer was made a criminal offense. For a time all right of foreign travel for nonbusiness or nonmilitary purposes was suspended.

The member of the Labour Government who, first as President of the Board of Trade and from 1947 on as Minister of Economic Affairs and Chancellor of the Exchequer, came to epitomize the spirit of austerity was Sir Stafford Cripps. He was lean in appearance and ascetic in habit, and his earliest ambition had been to be a churchman rather than a politician. His confidence in his own rightness made him a difficult colleague but an inspiring leader. One can detect admiration as well as criticism in Churchill's comment: "There, but for the grace of God, goes God." Thought too intellectual by some, Cripps was yet the most successful of the Labour ministers in appealing to the better natures of his countrymen; for he sought to make them understand the restrictions of austerity as joint contributions to a national revival. Cripps, a left-wing party heretic during the 1930s, was willing and able to ask miners to work an extra half hour a day and could address the Trades Union Congress in terms which David Ricardo would have understood. "There is only a certain sized cake," he told the labor union leaders, "and if a lot of people want a larger slice they can only get it by taking it from others."

In 1948 and 1949, the economic situation gradually began to improve, not least because the United States had come to realize that only substantial American assistance could truly revive the floundering European economies. The European Recovery Program, or Marshall Plan, came into effect in 1948 and did much to encourage European economic cooperation and to break the vicious circle of shortages in one sector of the economy which impeded the recovery of another. Britain received $2,700,000 in American aid between 1948 and 1951.

Britain did have to undergo one last major "dollar crisis" in the summer of 1949 when an American recession depressed the flow of British exports. After a long delay for fear of incurring the stigma of fiscal irresponsibility, Sir Stafford Cripps persuaded the Labour Government in September 1949 to devalue the pound in terms of the dollar from $4.03 to $2.80. The devaluation had no immediate effect within Britain or in the sterling area countries which followed suit. It did, however, make British goods cheaper in dollar countries and imports from the United States dearer in the United Kingdom. Potentially it also discouraged foreign investment in Britain. The only alternative to devaluation would have been the raising of domestic interest rates in such a fashion as to produce widespread unemployment. To the Opposition, devaluation was proof that "Socialism has failed." But the government preferred to risk inflation rather than permit the revival of large scale unemployment. In the words of one Labour M.P., "We devalued money because we will not devalue men."

Not all Englishmen met the perils of adversity in the proverbial fashion by pulling in their belts, putting their shoulders to the wheel, making the best of a bad job, and keeping their upper lips stiff. The multitude of restrictions could not help but invite some violations. In 1946 groups of squatters settled in expensive but unoccupied houses in central London, while others made deserted army barracks their home. The squatters were evicted from the London homes, but the use of army barracks as emergency housing was eventually legalized. Black marketeers were active, and the "spiv" enjoyed a temporary notoriety. He was the sort of man who smuggled liquor from France by motorboat, hijacked a truckload of chocolates, ferried illegal immigrants, transacted unlawful currency exchanges, and often got away with his misdeeds. Twice as many criminal acts were recorded in 1948 as in 1937, and people spoke of a postwar "crime wave." In similar fashion, some businessmen began to employ "expense accounts" as a method of evading taxes. Yet the majority of the population abided by a rationing system which was deemed onerous but equitable and which did, by and large, live up to the Labour Government motto: "Fair shares for all."

Although the Attlee Government inspired a high degree of political idealism, it did not inspire a new literary mood. More people than ever were reading books—the Penguins had launched the "paperback revolution"—but the most notable literary luminaries of the time were prewar authors such as Evelyn Waugh, Graham Greene, and Elizabeth Bowen. They — and on a more popular level, authors such as Angela Thirkell — commemorated the passing of the old aristocracy or celebrated the resistance of old country families and other members of the upper middle classes to engulfment by the values of "mass society." Labour Party intellectuals had themselves long had an ambivalent attitude toward these same masses; on the one hand they wished to identify with them; on the other, they wished to uplift them, and it was more than coincidence that in 1946 the BBC introduced its "Third Programme," a broadcast service of abstruse music, high-level lectures, and discussion which in practice appealed to at most two percent of the total listening audience.

The postwar English theatre reacted against the naturalistic productions of the 1930s in favor of free verse plays like Christopher Fry's *The Lady's Not for Burning* (1949) and T. S. Eliot's *The Cocktail Party* (1949). Eliot, an American expatriate, had by this time become "perhaps the most influential highbrow on either side of the Atlantic, the focus of intelligent reaction against the new mass society." In the meantime, the English film industry underwent its own notable artistic, if not financial, renaissance and brought world renown to such actors as Laurence Olivier and Alec Guiness. And by the end of the decade, television, reintroduced by the BBC in 1946, seemed likely to replace the cinema as the mass entertainment of the future, just as the cinema had replaced the music hall.

Imperial Twilight: Asia and the Near East

One accomplishment of the post-World War II Labour Government likely to be permanently remembered is the peaceful granting of independence to India. World War II had imbued Indian National Congress leaders with a grim determination to bring their long and largely nonviolent drive for national independence to a triumphant conclusion. The decision of Churchill's wartime government to defer any decision on independence until after the war did little but add fuel to Indian discontent. The Labour victory in the British general election of 1945 was decisive in determining that the British Empire in India would end. The Labour Party had long pledged itself to procure self-government for India, and Attlee himself had been a convert to such a policy ever since a visit to India in 1927. Post-World War II Britain, despite the oft-voiced suspicions of Americans and Russians, among others, had neither the military power nor the economic strength nor the desire to hold India by force. The two-century-old empire in India may have been first won by force but it had been held less by military power than by prestige and by widespread Indian acceptance. Once British prestige (and that of the West generally) had been dissipated by two world wars, the granting of independence was ultimately the only solution in keeping with Britain's own political ideals and institutions.

The question from July 1945 on was not whether, but how? Was independent India to be maintained as the single political unit which British rule had fashioned or was it again to be divided, as so often in its history, along religious and linguistic lines? The National Congress Party under Gandhi and Nehru continued to agitate for complete unity, but Mohammed Ali Jinnah's Moslem League was stronger than ever and as fearful as before about the perils of Hindu domination. In 1946 Jinnah briefly acceded to a single India in which the separate states would be largely autonomous except for a central government which controlled defense and foreign affairs. When Nehru thereupon demanded a stronger central parliament, Jinnah reneged and began to press openly and with increasing adamance in favor of a separate Moslem state, Pakistan.

The impasse was broken early in 1947 by Attlee's declaration that India would have independence by 1948 at the latest and by his appointment of Admiral Lord Mountbatten (1900–) as Viceroy to bring matters to fruition. Mountbatten, a great-grandson of Queen Victoria, lived up to his reputation for speed and decision as well as personal charm by working out — together with V. P. Menon, his secretary — a partition plan and then convincing not only Nehru and Jinnah but also the Labour Government and the Conservative Opposition of its viability. The act of independence was passed by Parliament without division, and August 15, 1947, was celebrated as Independence Day by Indians and Pakistanis alike.

The one aspect of the transfer of power which afterwards evoked the greatest criticism was that insufficient provision had been made for the migration of Moslem minorities in India to Pakistan and of Hindu minorities in Pakistan to India. Although the leaders of both new states had promised protection to minorities, neither community felt safe, and amidst sporadic rioting, some ten and a half million people migrated from one state to another. Gandhi's pleas for tolerance helped limit the violence in the Bengal region; but at least 200,000 persons perished in communal rioting on the subcontinent. Clearly, neither Hindu nor Moslem leaders had anticipated such violence on the part of their followers. Yet had the British sought to delay their departure, they might simply have become the victims of a renewed sense of distrust and — as happened to the Dutch in Indonesia and the French in Indo-China — the villains in an Indian Civil War.

As it was, both India and Pakistan, and nearby Ceylon, agreed to remain within the Commonwealth of Nations. Nehru even suggested Mountbatten as India's first Governor-General. The status of a dominion was exchanged early in 1950 for that of a republic associated with the Commonwealth of Nations and recognizing the British monarch as head of the Commonwealth, a new status which stretched still further but did not sever completely the political ties which had bound Britain and India for so long.

As Nehru had foreseen, but many of his countrymen had not, independence was a beginning and not an end. It did not by itself resolve the problems of industrialization or of keeping the growth of food supply in line with a still burgeoning population. And inevitably, independence dissipated the strong bond of unity which the struggle against British rule had fashioned. Two decades later, however, India remains the world's most populous democracy and retains the parliamentary government and the civil service system inherited from Britain. In a linguistically divided land, English is still the closest approach to a national language among India's small educated minority.

Although Pakistan later substituted a more authoritarian presidential system for its parliamentary structure, it too has retained many British institutions, as has Burma, which received its independence in January 1948 but which declined to keep any association with the Commonwealth. Though prompted by domestic economic difficulties as well as by longstanding political principles, and though marred by violence between Hindus and Moslems, Britain's peaceful transfer of power in India remains an extraordinary example of enlightened statesmanship.[4]

This statesmanship was far less evident in the Near East, specifically in Palestine, where the British had been dominant since their occupation of Jerusalem in 1918 and their assumption of a League of Nations mandate in 1919. The Balfour Declaration of 1917 had pledged the establishment of a national home for the Jewish people in Palestine. At the same moment when the British government was seeking to win the support of Jews throughout the world by this move, it was also encouraging an Arab national revival against the Ottoman Empire; consequently successive British governments soon found themselves trapped upon the horns of a dilemma (largely of their own making). Although the 1920s brought much economic progress to Palestine, clashes between the growing number of Jewish immigrants and the resident Arabs became ever more frequent during the interwar years. A British plan of partition was rejected by the Arabs in 1936, and in a 1939 White Paper, the British Government announced its intention of creating a single independent state predominantly Arab in population. Jewish immigration was limited to 1,500 per month until 1944, when it was to be halted altogether. This policy appeared need-

---

[4] V. P. Menon, *The Transfer of Power in India* (London, 1952); Michael Edwardes, *The Last Years of British India* (London, 1963).

lessly heartless to those relatively few Jews who succeeded in escaping from Nazi persecution.

Tensions in Palestine itself eased somewhat during the Second World War; but with the end of hostilities, Zionist aspirations for an independent Jewish state revived. It seemed imperative to provide a homeland for those Jewish refugees who had survived the Nazi gas chambers, but the British Government remained reluctant to alienate Arab opinion by again permitting unrestricted Jewish immigration. The desire to maintain oil concessions in the Near East, fear for the safety of the Suez Canal, pro-Arab sentiment on the part of some British officials, and a genuine sense of being a neutral party above the battle all played a role in formulating British policy. By 1946 more than 100,000 English troops occupied Palestine. Ernest Bevin, Labour's Foreign Secretary, felt sure at first that he could resolve the dilemma; but both he and many of his countrymen were increasingly frustrated as Jewish terrorist groups attacked isolated groups of British military personnel and on one occasion blew up the largest hotel in Jerusalem. The deaths of British soldiers led to a number of anti-Semitic outbursts within Britain and a resentment on the part of Bevin against a widespread pro-Zionist attitude in the United States.

The British government's handling of the Palestine issue showed the same blindness to the reality of Jewish nationalism which had in earlier years been shown toward Irish nationalism. In 1947 the United Nations voted for a partition plan which would have provided the Jewish population with an independent though territorially almost indefensible state. The Arab states refused to acknowledge the decision, and Britain abstained, announcing that she would end her Palestine mandate in 1948. Bevin's expectation was that without British protection, the Jews would be driven into the sea and that only by withdrawing their army could the British prove how necessary their presence was. An Arab-Jewish War did break out in April 1948; but contrary to British anticipations, the beleaguered Jewish forces not only emerged victorious but upset the original boundaries established by the U.N. and forged a state with a viable and defensible frontier. An independent state of Israel was proclaimed, and Chaim Weizmann, the naturalized British citizen (and chemist) who had helped secure the Balfour Declaration, became the country's first president.

While Palestine proved in some ways to be the Labour Government's "Irish Question," actual Anglo-Irish relations were more harmonious. During the 1930s, the independent Irish Parliament had removed most of the links which still bound Ireland to Britain after the treaty of 1922. The Parliamentary oath of loyalty to the British monarch was abolished; so was the post of Governor-General and the right on the part of an Irish citizen to avail himself of the British Privy Council as a final court of legal appeal. After 1937 when a new republican constitution was adopted by the Irish Free State, the only remaining link was that British diplomats continued to represent Ireland in those countries to which Ireland sent no envoys of her own. Ireland broke this last tie in 1948, and Britain in the Ireland Act of 1949 acknowledged that the Irish Republic had ceased to be part of "His Majesty's Dominions" but guaranteed to the Northern Irish that their part of the island would remain part of the United Kingdom so long as their Parliament wished it. The Ireland Act also stated that though the Irish Republic was completely independent, its citizens were not to be regarded as foreigners in England. They retained, and still retain, free access as visitors or immigrants and, if resident in the United Kingdom, they have the right to vote in British elections. Moreover, the economies of Britain and the Irish Republic remain tightly intertwined.

The Cold War

The force of nationalism, which the British had first been compelled to acknowledge in Ireland during the nineteenth century and which had spread by the late 1940s to much of Asia and the Near East, was one of the great determining forces of the post-World War II world. The other was the "Cold War" between Russia and the Western allies. In one sense, the Cold War was implicit in the very manner in which World War II had come about. Although the fact was little recognized at the time, World War II had ceased, from 1940 on, to be a war which the Western democracies could win in any absolute sense. By then they were badly outmatched, and of the big powers on the democratic side, only Britain and potentially the United States remained. On the totalitarian side stood Germany, Italy, Japan, and Russia. If these four states could ever fully ally, the cause of Western democracy was lost. The only manner in which Britain and the U.S.A. could possibly defeat Germany and Japan was by means of Russian aid. Soviet Russia had disturbed much of Western opinion ever since the Communist Revolution of 1917 by its internal economy and its disregard for civil liberties. But in the years before World War II, Russia had not overtly attacked its neighbors. Germany had, and was necessarily deemed the more powerful and more obvious threat to world peace.

The problem, however, was this. If the Western democracies could win the war only by allying themselves with one of the nondemocratic powers, then quite obviously the ultimate victory would strengthen the nondemocratic power at the same time that it strengthened the democracies. In the long run, this was exactly what happened. Germany and Japan were defeated, but in the process Russia filled the vacuum of power created in Eastern Europe and (for a briefer time) in parts of Eastern Asia.

During the war there had been hopes in the West, especially in the United States, that the Grand Alliance of the war years might prevail in the postwar years. This hope was soon shattered, however; and in the very process of attempting to provide peace treaties for the nations involved in World War II, the Foreign Ministers of the Big Three found themselves increasingly at odds. Peace treaties were achieved for Italy, Finland, Hungary, Bulgaria, and Romania in 1947; but Russia refused to sign the 1951 settlement with Japan.

No peace treaty was achieved for occupied Germany at all. Instead the supposedly temporary zones of military occupation became fixed and eventually fortified boundaries – the American, British, and French zones of occupation being joined into the Federal Republic of (West) Germany in 1949. At the same time the Soviet Zone was transformed into a so-called People's Republic which was in practice a Soviet satellite. Although the Soviet Union had pledged itself to support "free elections" in Poland and the other countries of eastern Europe, it became clear between 1945 and 1948 that the Soviet definition of the phrase differed greatly from the British or American. Coalition governments were gradually subordinated to complete Communist Party domination, and with the active or passive assistance of the Red armies of occupation, Poland, Hungary, Romania, Bulgaria, and Yugoslavia all became Soviet satellites.

The one exception was Greece. Here Churchill, looking ahead more pragmatically than Roosevelt to the probabilities of the postwar world, had in 1944 struck an unofficial bargain with Stalin. If Russian influence was to predominate in Romania, Hungary, and Bulgaria – and Churchill did not see how this could be prevented at a time when the Red Army was occupying these areas – then British influence should predominate in Greece and influence in Yugoslavia should be divided on a 50–50 basis. Reports of such an arrangement were anathema to liberal opinion in both Britain and the United States; but as a result, British troops were sent to Greece in 1944 and became involved on the side of the anti-Communist government in a confused, cruel, and protracted Greek civil war.

The Labour Government inherited the problem in 1945, and though unsure how democratic the Greek government was and unhappy about the decision of the Greeks (in a plebiscite) to restore their king, it continued British support. The only alternative seemed to be a Communist takeover. Between 1944 and 1947, successive British governments spent £87 million on military and economic aid to Greece and forgave the Greeks another £46 million in war debts. As Bevin told a Labour Party Conference: "We cannot afford to lose our position in the Middle East; our navy, our shipping, a great deal of our motive power for our industry, in the shape of oil, are there. . . . The standard of life and the wages of the workmen of this country are dependent upon these things. . . ." The words might have been those of Palmerston; the only difficulty was that gunboat diplomacy was no longer sufficient to uphold British influence and that Britain's economic resources were sorely strained.

In 1946, the year in which Winston Churchill made famous the phrase "iron curtain" in a speech in Fulton, Missouri, some Americans began speaking of a "cold war" between Britain and Russia in the Balkans and in Iran in which the American role was that of bystander. For the moment at least, there was a pronounced American tendency toward bringing armies back home and limiting commitments abroad. For a time Bevin was almost as fearful of American isolationism as of Russian expansion. But in the spring of 1947 the British Government convinced the United States that the United Kingdom could no longer provide the economic and military support necessary to assure that Greece and its neighbor Turkey were kept out of the Russian sphere. The result was the Truman Doctrine, an American decision to take Britain's place in those two countries. Henceforth the United States was to be "the leader of the free world" in the "containment" of the Soviet expansion, and Britain was forced by economic necessity to become a junior partner in the Western Alliance.

Bevin was subject to severe criticism by left-wing members of his party, men who sought to explain away Stalin's actions in a manner analogous to the manner certain Conservatives had sought to explain away Hitler's actions a decade before. The Labour Government, however, cooperated loyally with the United States in the various measures that followed. The Marshall Plan of 1948 was not initially a Cold War measure, but the economic recovery it promoted in Western Europe clearly weakened the power of the large Communist parties in France and Italy. The Berlin air lift of 1948–1949 successfully repulsed a Russian attempt to drive the Western Powers out of their place in that isolated and divided city. The North Atlantic Treaty Organization of 1949, a military alliance among the United States, Canada, Britain, and the states of Western Europe was prompted largely by the Communist takeover in 1948 of Czechoslovakia, the most democratic of pre-World War II states in

Eastern Europe and the last to fall behind the iron curtain. Britain cooperated with the United States in combatting, under U.N. auspices, the invasion of South Korea launched by Communist North Korea in 1950. By this time, the Cold War was in full swing and the pattern of the postwar world had apparently been set.

The Elections of 1950 and 1951

In the meantime, the Labour Government had embarked upon the enactment of its last major piece of domestic legislation. In October 1948 it introduced its bill to nationalize the iron and steel industry. Labour had pledged itself to nationalize steel in its 1945 election program. Its leaders contended that the steel oligopoly ought to be the servant and not the master of the people and that only nationalization could provide security against the operation of otherwise uncontrollable economic forces. The Conservative opposition had criticized earlier nationalization measures in a halfhearted manner, since in the case of coal and electricity Labour had so obviously built upon Tory foundations. Now, however, they launched an all-out attack against this latest proposal, for steel was not an unprofitable public utility. It was a prosperous and efficient manufacturing industry in whose modernization and expansion large sums had recently been invested. Unlike the mines, its labor-relations record was good, and Conservative speakers could point to specific steel union leaders who were antagonistic or apathetic toward nationalization. With the Labour majority in the House of Commons still huge, the steel nationalization bill passed easily; but the Government did agree to a House of Lords request that its operation be held up pending another general election.

Fearing a House of Lords veto, the Labour Government had in 1947 introduced an act which limited the suspensive veto power of the upper house from two years to one. The bill became law in 1949. It followed the tradition of the Parliament Act of 1911, just as Labour's Representation of the People Act of 1948 followed the steps of the Reform Acts of 1832, 1867, 1884, 1918, and 1928. The act of 1948 eliminated the right of plural voting (for persons who had a home in one parliamentary district and a business in another) and the right, instituted under King James I, of separate parliamentary representation for the graduates of the universities of Oxford and Cambridge. There was also a complete redistribution of seats, and the number of M.P.s was reduced from 640 to 625, each representing approximately 56,000 persons.

The Conservatives had long been looking forward to the general election which was held in February 1950. After initial discouragement, the party had, under the chairmanship of Lord Woolton, refurbished its national and constituency organization and revitalized its research bureau. From the time of the fuel crisis of early 1947, the Conservative opposition had, with increasing effectiveness, protested against government restrictions and the necessity of having to "Starve with Strachey and Shiver with Shinwell," the Ministers of Food and Fuel, respectively. The Government was castigated for mismanaging the economy and Britain's position in the world and for placing, in the case of steel nationalization, power and ideology above the national welfare.

The Labour Government defended its record by observing that the perils of postwar reconversion had been successfully weathered and that production totals had reached a point almost 50 percent above those of 1938. The country had remained free from large-scale unemployment and large-scale industrial unrest; and the government's social insurance measures and national health service had guaranteed all British citizens against domestic perils not of their own making. The election results were far from satisfactory for either side: Labour, 315; Conservatives, 298; Liberals, 9. Almost all the independents elected in 1945, including two Communists, were defeated, and almost 84 percent of the electorate voted, an all-time record.

Although the election produced a virtual stalemate, party discipline was sufficient to enable the Labour Government to limp along for another sixteen months and to pass its controversial steel nationalization bill. A public corporation, the Iron and Steel Federation, took over the stock of the private companies, but for the moment their day-to-day management was little disturbed. The return of at least partial prosperity enabled the Government to end many of the restrictions of the austerity period. Bread rationing ended in 1948 and clothes rationing in 1949. In 1950 all limitations were removed from restaurant meals, and rationing ceased for milk, flour, eggs, and soap. London's water fountains and bright lights were turned on again. The Festival of Britain of 1951 commemorated the hundredth anniversary of the Great Exhibition of 1851 with exhibitions illustrating "British Contributions to World Civilization in the Arts of Peace." Though the exhibition was well attended and provided London permanently with the beautiful Royal Festival Hall, the spirit of overriding self-confidence of 1851 was absent.

The Labour Cabinet of 1950–51 was gravely weakened by the resignations of Sir Stafford Cripps and Ernest Bevin for reasons of health and by the resignations of Aneurin Bevan and

Harold Wilson (1916–   ), the youthful President of the Board of Trade, for reasons of policy. Bevan and Wilson objected to the charges for spectacles and dentures which Hugh Gaitskell (1906–1963), who had replaced Cripps as Chancellor of the Exchequer, had proposed in his 1951 Budget. The left-wing segment of the party, which Bevan represented, was also generally unhappy with the staunchly pro-American foreign policy of the Attlee Government and with rearmament expenditures prompted by the Korean War. Faced with a serious rift within his party which made it difficult to control Parliament with so slim a majority, Attlee decided in September 1951 to call for a new general election.

The campaign rehashed the issues of the year before. The Government saw the choice as one between "Forward with Labour" rather than "Backward with the Tories." Churchill, accused by Labour's left wing of being a "warmonger," was still seeking redress for the defeat of 1945 and spoke more moderately and more effectively than he had in 1945 or 1950. The Conservatives, he indicated, would accept the social services and almost all nationalization proposals already enacted except steel. The true choice, Churchill contended, was that Conservatives offered a ladder (on which everyone could rise), while Labour offered merely a queue (in which everyone took his turn). The results of the election were again very close: Conservatives, 321, Labour, 295, Liberals, 6. Labour still had a slim overall popular vote plurality, and only one voter in eighty had switched from Labour to the Conservatives since the previous general election; but this was sufficient to make Winston Churchill Prime Minister again at the age of seventy-seven.

The Labour Government had accomplished much in six years: it had nationalized most of the service facilities of the state; it had successfully presided over the dissolution of Britain's Asian Empire; and, although it had not transformed Britain into a "Socialist Commonwealth," it had made the welfare state a reality.

Chapter 20

A New Age of 𝔓𝔯𝔬𝔰𝔭𝔢𝔯𝔦𝔱𝔶: Paradoxes and Portents

THE NARROW Conservative victory in the general election of October 1951 was to lead to thirteen years of Conservative rule, the longest continuous period of predominance by one party since before 1832. Few political leaders of either major party would have considered such a prospect likely in 1951. The main themes of those years proved to be three: the gradual transformation of the economy and spirit of austerity into one of affluence; the continued evolution (or devolution) of the British Empire into a Commonwealth of independent nations; and the search by British diplomats for a meaningful role in an atomic age dominated, until the early 1960s at least, by the U.S.A. and the U.S.S.R. The period also brought the beginnings of a mood of self-questioning within Britain of what the fundamental goals of a materially sufficient twentieth-century industrialized society ought to be.[1]

---

[1] The events discussed in this chapter are not yet "history" in the customary sense of the word, but the following books may prove helpful. For political history, R. T. McKenzie, *British Political Parties*, 2nd ed. (London, 1963); for social history, Harry Hopkins, *The New Look: A Social History of Britain in the 1940's and 1950's* (London, 1964); for diplomatic history, John Lukacs, *A History of the Cold War* (Garden City, N.Y., 1962), the Earl of Avon (Sir Anthony Eden), *Full Circle* (London, 1960), Terence Robertson, *Crisis: The Inside Story of the Suez Conspiracy* (New York, 1965), and, more mundanely, C. M. Woodhouse, *British Foreign Policy Since the Second World War* (London, 1961). John Strachey's

The End of Austerity

The very slenderness of the Tory triumph of 1951 made it unlikely that a major policy turnabout was in store; and the early budgets of Richard A. Butler (1902–   ), Churchill's new Chancellor of the Exchequer, so resembled those of Hugh Gaitskell, the last Labour Chancellor, that the word "Butskellism" was coined. Yet after the immediate international payments crisis of 1951 had been resolved, there was a notable change in mood; in the course of the next few years, much of the framework of postwar austerity was dismantled. In 1952 income taxes were cut. Ration controls were removed from one food item after another until in the summer of 1954 the British housewife, after almost a decade and a half, was given the right to throw away her family's ration books and her husband was actually encouraged to build a new home. The first steps were also taken to dismantle the complex rent control system, whose origins went back to the First World War. The more fundamental transformations wrought by the postwar Labour Government were, however, largely kept intact. The only changes in the National Health Service were the addition of a charge of one shilling (14 cents) and later two shillings per drug prescription and in 1957 the partial return of the system to the insurance principle in lieu of the payment of all expenses by the National Exchequer. The construction of projected public health centers still tended to lag, however, as did the building of hospitals.

Except for the iron and steel industry and, partially, the trucking industry, the new Conservative Government did not attempt to reverse the Labour Government's program of nationalization. (An act of 1953 restored the steel industry to private hands under "an adequate measure of public supervision"; the actual process of denationalizing took a decade.) Nationalization was proving neither a cure-all nor a notable drawback for either the coal industry or the railways. Coal mine productivity even rose slightly during the 1950s, though the market was no longer growing. The railways, slowly converting from steam power to diesel or electric power, were hampered by a lack of capital, by renewed motor vehicle com-

---

The End of Empire (London, 1962) and Margery Perham's *The Colonial Reckoning* (London, 1963) throw light on the topics indicated. Drew Middleton's *These Are the British* (New York, 1957) and Anthony Sampson's *Anatomy of Britain* (London, 1962) are both illuminating analyses of Britain's social and political structure. The annual edition of *Britain: An Official Handbook* prepared by the Government's Central Office of Information provides many useful statistics. The 1963 edition was utilized in the preparation of this chapter.

petition, and by a public insistence that branch lines continue to operate even when, in strict economic terms, they no longer paid their way.

The oldest of Britain's "nationalized" concerns, the Post Office, retained its reputation for efficiency. The Post Office Savings Bank, which celebrated its centenary in 1961, utilized a central accounting system to enable any of its twenty-two million depositors to make deposits or withdrawals at any of the United Kingdom's 20,000 post offices and remained in this sense the largest banking institution in the world. The most productive of the nationalized industries was the Central Electricity Authority which, among other things, pioneered in the utilization of nuclear energy for nonmilitary purposes with its power plant at Calder Hall, Cumberland, in 1956.

Diplomatic Triumphs and Defeats

The second Churchill Ministry provided the opportunity not only for the relaxation of austerity measures but also for the evocation of a prewar note of pomp and circumstance in the solemn state funeral accorded to King George VI early in 1952 and in the triumphant coronation provided for his daughter Queen Elizabeth II in the summer of 1953. "I suppose that you and I have witnessed the coronation of the last British sovereign," wrote the historian Macaulay to a friend in 1837; but a century and a quarter later the monarchy, however altered as an institution, was as popular as ever in British life. Churchill, who had served in the armies and briefly in the Parliament of Queen Victoria, now had the opportunity of leading his fellow Prime Ministers of the Commonwealth, including Nehru of India, in the royal procession which marked the crowning of Victoria's great-great-granddaughter. The Westminster Abbey ritual followed a tradition dating back to the Anglo-Saxon kings.

Like Elizabeth I, Elizabeth II became monarch in her twenty-sixth year, and men began to talk of a new Elizabethan Age. Although one of the new Elizabethans, Sir Edmund Hillary, conquered Mount Everest in 1953 and another, Roger Bannister, became in 1954 the first man to run the mile in less than four minutes, the new age provided relatively fewer opportunities for individual daring. In the diplomatic arena, it seemed to promise little but prolonged and often futile negotiations on the Foreign Minister level. Churchill's hope of setting up another Big Three meeting in 1953 after the death of Stalin proved vain, partly because of the stroke suffered by Churchill in July of that year and partly because of the brief tenure of Stalin's immediate successor, Georgi Malenkov.

Yet Stalin's death did much to lessen the tensions of the Cold War. It helped bring the Korean War to an end in the summer of 1953. A year later, the efforts of Sir Anthony Eden, Churchill's Foreign Secretary, brought at least a temporary close to the prolonged war which French forces had been fighting in what once was French Indo-China. Part of the area, North Vietnam, was acknowledged as under Communist control, but the others, Laos, Cambodia, and South Vietnam, retained varying degrees of autonomy.

From time to time, Britain also acted the role of diplomatic broker closer to home. Churchill had himself been a prime mover in the post-World War II forces working for Western European Union; Britain had joined with France, Italy, Belgium, the Netherlands, and Luxembourg in an organization by that name in 1948. Britain did not, however, join the projected European Defense Community of 1952–54. Its purpose was to integrate the military forces of a rearming West Germany within a multinational European force. When the French Parliament rejected the E.D.C. project which its own government had helped formulate, American Secretary of State Dulles threatened "an agonizing reappraisal" of American commitments to Europe. Anthony Eden broke the resulting impasse by promising to keep British troops on the Continent indefinitely as a pledge of support, provided the French would accept West Germany as part of the North Atlantic Treaty Organization. West Germany was admitted into NATO in 1955.

In order to give force to its own foreign policy initiatives and in order to advertise to the world that Britain was still a great power, the Churchill Government tested Britain's own atomic bomb in 1952 – the Labour Government had earlier decided to undertake its production – and in 1955 Churchill announced that Britain would build a hydrogen bomb as well. Such a weapon was successfully tested in 1957.

In April 1955 Churchill retired from the Prime Ministership in his 81st year. Only Palmerston and Gladstone had held the office at a more advanced age. Eden, Churchill's second in command for a decade and a half, was the obvious successor. The Conservative Party could claim a number of economic and diplomatic successes; and Eden, suave and debonair in appearance but never a genuinely popular figure, easily led his party to its second straight general election victory in 1955. The Labour Party had developed no dramatic new program, and its slogans of "nationalization" and "full employment" had lost much of their charm and novelty. It was, moreover, internally divided by the left-wing Bevanite faction. The electorate proved relatively apathetic, and only 76.8 percent voted. Both parties lost votes, but the Conservatives lost fewer and therefore led their rivals 49.7 percent to 46.4 percent in the popular vote and 347 to 277 in parliamentary seats.

The new Prime Minister was immediately involved in the type of activity for which he had won the greatest renown, diplomacy. In May 1955 the Big Powers agreed to an Austrian peace treaty, and after seventeen years of occupation—first German and then Russian and Western—Austria once again became an independent (and neutral) state. The Austrian peace treaty led to a "Big Four" meeting at Geneva in July 1955, with President Eisenhower, Prime Minister Bulganin (accompanied by Khrushchev), Prime Minister Eden, and Premier Faure of France in attendance. "The spirit of Geneva," though it led to a state visit to Britain by Bulganin and Khrushchev, did not endure; nor did it bring closer the possibility of German reunification on terms which both the Soviet Union and the Western Powers would accept. Yet it did represent the implicit acknowledgment that—though the word might be suspect—coexistence was preferable to codestruction.

In the course of 1956, East-West relations, Britain's role in the Near East, and Anglo-American friendship all received rude shocks. Although Britain had helped inspire twentieth-century Arab nationalism, the Palestine dilemma of the 1940s had damaged British prestige in the area. Only long negotiations had enabled Britain to save the Anglo-Iranian Oil Company from the nationalizing plans of Premier Mossadegh of Iran in the early 1950s. An Egyptian revolution in 1952 replaced the complaisant King Farouk with the militant Colonel Nasser, who in 1954 obtained an agreement from Britain to withdraw the last of its military forces from Egypt in return for his promise not to nationalize the international Suez Canal Company.

By June 1956, when the last British troops withdrew from the Canal Zone, both Russian and American missions were already competing against each other in the Nile Valley. In July, however, after Secretary of State Dulles announced that the United States would not after all build a high dam at Aswan for Egypt, Nasser, in violation of the 1954 treaty, retaliated by nationalizing the Suez Canal. France and Britain decided not to acquiesce in this apparent *fait accompli;* but their attempts to arouse world opinion against the Egyptian dictator received only indifferent backing from the United States. Partly in concert with Israel, which was fearful of Russian arms shipments to Egypt, secret plans for a military operation were drawn up. On October 29, Israeli forces launched an attack across the Sinai desert. The next day Eden announced that France and Britain were intervening between Israel and Egypt and would temporarily occupy the Suez Canal.

The Suez intervention was to be criticized alternatively for its immorality and for its failure. Clearly Britain expected American acquiescence, if not support; instead, Secretary of State Dulles teamed up with the Russians in the United Nations to condemn the Anglo-French intervention and to save Colonel Nasser at the very same time that Russian tanks were crushing a Hungarian revolution in the streets of Budapest. When the British and French governments agreed to a cease fire on November 6, their forces had failed to occupy all of the Canal Zone, and the Egyptians themselves had blocked the waterway. A face-saving formula, worked out largely by Canadian Foreign Minister Lester Pearson, had U.N. forces replace the Anglo-French invaders.

In the Near East, the intervention had marred a widespread British reputation for fair dealing, while its failure had lowered British prestige. Back home, the affair sparked comparable criticism. Labour Party leaders denounced the intervention; Aneurin Bevan, for one, condemned the use of "epic weapons for squalid and trivial ends." Labour found it difficult to capitalize upon Eden's embarrassment, however, since many of its followers proved clearly sympathetic to the assertion of British power. Conversely, the intervention pleased the diehard imperialists in the Conservative ranks, but at least forty Conservative M.P.s threatened to desert the Government unless the troops were withdrawn. Prime Minister Eden, whose vacillation had been at least partly responsible for the fiasco, now became physically ill, resigned his office in January 1957, and retired from active politics by moving to the House of Lords as Earl of Avon.

For the first time since 1923, a monarch was given the duty to choose a Prime Minister without an obvious candidate being in sight. Richard A. Butler seemed the most likely selection, but, acting presumably upon the advice of Lord Salisbury (the Conservative leader in the House of Lords) and Sir Winston Churchill, Queen Elizabeth nominated Harold Macmillan (1894–   ). Macmillan, a book publisher by profession and first elected M.P. in 1924, had won renown as Churchill's Housing Minister and soon succeeded in restoring confidence both in his party and in his country.

In the early months of 1957, public opinion polls had revealed a sizable shift toward the Labour Party; but as the Suez crisis receded in the public memory and times remained prosperous, Macmillan's stock rose. An amiable Edwardian facade hid a shrewd and at times ruthless politician who increasingly impressed his party followers as a veritable "Supermac." His Labour Party counterpart in the 1959 general election was Hugh Gaitskell, the onetime economics instructor who had won out in a three-cornered party election over Morrison and Bevan upon Attlee's retirement from the party leadership in 1955. Gaitskell, though impressive in his intelligence and sincerity and though successful in rewinning the allegiance of Aneurin Bevan (who had once called him a "desiccated calculating machine"), was unsuccessful in completely uniting his party or in countering Macmillan's program of "peace" and "prosperity." In 1959, for the third time in a row, the Conservative Party won a general election; and for the fourth time in a row, it gained seats. It attracted 49.4 percent of the popular vote to Labour's 43.7 percent. In the House of Commons it now possessed a majority of 365 to 258.

The Mid-Century Commonwealth

While the Suez crisis had no long-range political effects within Britain, it clearly did have long-range effects in the British Empire. "I did not become the King's First Minister in order to preside over the liquidation of the British Empire," Winston Churchill had declared in 1942. And indeed, he lived up to his word. In neither of his two ministries did any British dependency gain independence; the devolution of the greater part of the Asian empire had taken place during the Labour Ministry. And during Churchill's Government of 1951–55, Britain withstood assaults on its remaining empire by successfully suppressing a Communist revolution in Malaya and the "Mau Mau" revolt in Kenya.

During the second half of the decade, the situation changed. In 1956 the onetime Anglo-Egyptian Sudan was set up as an independent republic, and a long drawn-out rebellion against French rule began in Algeria. Nasser's survival of the Suez invasion strengthened anew his own prestige; and once Africa north of the Sahara had gained its independence, could Africa south of the Sahara be far behind? The Macmillan Government, despite the reservations of some of its supporters, decided to embark upon a gradual program of independence within the Commonwealth for almost all of the African dependencies, rather than await the otherwise inevitable native rebellions.

In few of these areas had British influence ever been as pervasive or as longstanding as in India; but in all of the new African countries — whose boundaries were often the accidental by-products of nineteenth-century European diplomacy — British governmental and educational institutions had made some impact. Ghana (formerly the Gold Coast) began the process of independence in 1957. Nigeria, Britain's most populous West

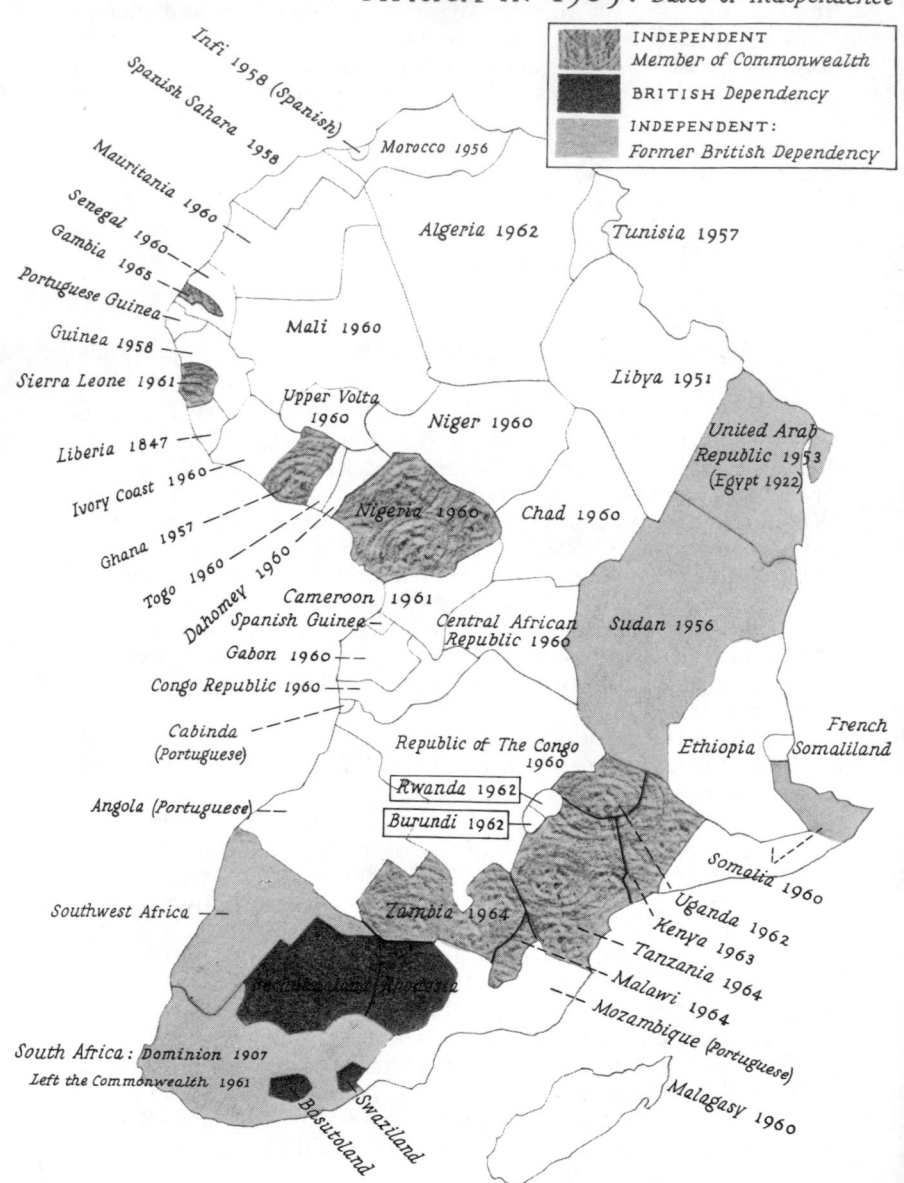

AFRICA IN 1965: *Dates of Independence*

INDEPENDENT
Member of Commonwealth

BRITISH *Dependency*

INDEPENDENT:
Former British Dependency

Infi 1958 (Spanish)

Spanish Sahara 1958

Mauritania 1960

Morocco 1956

Senegal 1960

Gambia 1965

Portuguese Guinea

Algeria 1962

Tunisia 1957

Guinea 1958

Mali 1960

Libya 1951

Sierra Leone 1961

Upper Volta 1960

Niger 1960

United Arab Republic 1953 (Egypt 1922)

Liberia 1847

Ivory Coast 1960

Ghana 1957

Nigeria 1960

Chad 1960

Togo 1960

Dahomey 1960

Cameroon 1961

Central African Republic 1960

Sudan 1956

Spanish Guinea

Gabon 1960

Congo Republic 1960

Cabinda (Portuguese)

Republic of The Congo 1960

Ethiopia

French Somaliland

Angola (Portuguese)

Rwanda 1962

Burundi 1962

Somalia 1960

Southwest Africa

Zambia 1964

Uganda 1962

Kenya 1963

Tanzania 1964

Rhodesia

Malawi 1964

Mozambique (Portuguese)

South Africa: *Dominion 1907*
Left the Commonwealth 1961

Swaziland

Basutoland

Malagasy 1960

African dependency, gained freedom in 1960, as did British Somaliland, which became part of the republic of Somalia. Tanganyika, one of Britain's League of Nations mandates, gained its independence in 1961; three years later it formed a union with the erstwhile British protectorate of Zanzibar to become Tanzania. Sierra Leone, which had been founded as a colony for freed Negro slaves in 1787, became independent in 1961. Uganda and Kenya followed in 1962 and 1963 respectively, and tiny Gambia in 1965. Back in London in 1965 the Colonial Office ceased to be a separate ministry in the government.

For a time British members of both political parties harbored the hope that in a divided world the Commonwealth could act as a bridge between nations of different races and stages of economic development. In a tour of the Union of South Africa in 1960, Prime Minister Macmillan sought to convince the government of that state that it too should heed "the winds of change" that were sweeping the continent; but South Africa, controlled since 1948 by the (Boer) Nationalist Party, adamantly adhered to its policy of "apartheid" (racial separation in theory, white supremacy in practice). In 1961 South Africa declared itself a republic and severed all ties with the Commonwealth. South Africa remains part of the sterling area and Britain maintains as dependencies in South Africa the enclaves of Basutoland and Swaziland and, as a protectorate, the neighboring state of Bechuanaland. Further to the north, the British Colonial Office encouraged the development of a multiracial Central African Federation of the Rhodesias and Nyasaland. The racial strain, however, proved too great, and in 1964 the Federation split — Northern Rhodesia becoming the independent state of Zambia, and Nyasaland the independent state of Malawi. Only Southern Rhodesia (now called Rhodesia) remained an autonomous British dependency under white settler control. [See map of African Commonwealth countries.]

A comparable process of imperial devolution was going on elsewhere. On the Mediterranean island of Cyprus, a prolonged struggle for reunion with Greece on the part of the leaders of its Greek-speaking majority was confused by the desire of the British to maintain the island as a naval base and by the fact that the Turkish minority on the island strongly opposed annexation by Greece. In 1960 Cyprus became an independent member of the Commonwealth; but the renewal of civil war between Greek and Turkish inhabitants in 1964 indicated that no final solution had been found. A contemplated Federation of the (British) West Indies broke down, but Jamaica and Trinidad-Tobago received independence as separate states in 1962. In the Far East the territory of Malaya received independence in

1957 and, by the addition of Singapore and British dependencies in Borneo, was transformed into the Federation of Malaysia in 1963.[2]

The average American may regard the Commonwealth of the mid-1960s as little more than a face-saving device to cushion the psychological impact on Britain of imperial renunciation. While the member states which have not declared themselves republics retain the office of governor-general and although the citizens of some (like Australia and New Zealand) retain the right of final legal appeal to the Judicial Committee of the Privy Council in London, most of the political bonds are so amorphous as to seem unreal. Certainly the Commonwealth states rarely form a single voting bloc in the United Nations. Yet the English language, British parliamentary institutions, and elements of the English law and civil service system remain common to most members of the Commonwealth. There are other links as well, athletic ties in the form of international cricket matches and educational ties stemming from the fact that many African universities began as branch colleges of the University of London.

There also remain strong commercial bonds in that all Commonwealth countries except Canada (but including Eire, South Africa, and Burma) are still part of the sterling area and settle their international payments in English pounds. In the late 1950s at least half of Britain's imports and exports went to and came from Commonwealth countries. In the postwar period the United Kingdom has become increasingly generous with loans and grants to foster the economic development of its onetime colonies. The annual expenditure on such loans and grants rose from £52 million in 1952–53 to £150 million in 1960–61. They involve teachers, technicians, and the British equivalent of the American Peace Corps. Military aid was involved as well in 1962 when India's frontiers were invaded by Chinese troops, and in 1964, when the newly independent governments of Tanganyika and Kenya asked assistance in putting down internal army officer revolts. In similar fashion, military help was offered the Federation of Malaysia in the face of Indonesian aggression in 1964.

Finally, Britain's immigration policy has helped maintain a sense of Commonwealth unity. Until the passage of the Commonwealth Immigrants Act of 1962, all Commonwealth citizens had free access to the United Kingdom itself. The act restricted, but did not end, such immigration. Regular conferences among

---

[2] In the summer of 1965 Singapore withdrew from Malaysia and was recognized as a separate independent member of the Commonwealth.

Commonwealth Prime Ministers continue to be held, following the tradition begun by Joseph Chamberlain in 1897. However inchoate in organization, the Commonwealth remains a meaningful element of the present and a noble ideal for the future as well as a shadowy relic of the past.

The Macmillan Era

For a majority of the inhabitants of Macmillan's Britain, the Commonwealth remained a subject of only sporadic interest. They were more immediately affected by the pleasures and paradoxes of a new age of prosperity. Although some of the old industries, like coal, shipbuilding, and cotton textiles, continued to languish, the oil refineries and the manufacturers of airplanes, electrical equipment, automobiles, and plastics flourished. The annual production of steel more than doubled between 1946 and 1964; and Britain maintains the largest nonferrous metals industry in Europe and the largest woollen textile industry in the world. As a result of higher productivity, the gross national product rose 32 percent between 1950 and 1961.

The lot of the average English family correspondingly improved. The 1950s witnessed a housing boom, and by 1961 one family in four lived in a post-World War II dwelling. The scars of war disappeared from central London and central Birmingham; a new cathedral replaced the one destroyed at Coventry; and if the new architecture sometimes jarred with the Edwardian, Victorian, and Georgian buildings amidst which it rose, it also marked the almost complete eradication of the urban slums which had for so long seemed the necessary consequence of big city life. While Britain, no more than the United States, could completely overcome the problems of suburban sprawl, the insistence on "green belts" around the major cities and the development of distinct "New Towns" under a parliamentary act of 1946 limited the disfigurement of the countryside.

The by-products of the affluent society also included increasing numbers of supermarkets and other self-service stores, the growing use of hire purchase (installment-plan buying), the general acceptance of an annual two-week vacation for most families, and, by 1962, the ownership of a television set by four families in five. It also meant eleven million automobiles by 1964, more cars per mile of road surface than could be found in any other country. It meant a gradual change of diet—a smaller consumption of potatoes and bread and a larger consumption of meat and eggs and fruit and the largest consumption of chocolates and candy per person to be found anywhere in the world. It meant larger sums placed in savings accounts and invested in stocks, and even greater sums of money given to football pools, horse race betting shops, and bingo parlors (the last two having been legalized by the Betting and Gaming Act of 1960).

Affluence also implied a greater interest in education, especially on the university level. Britain's educational growth did not parallel the post-World War II educational revolution in the United States, but by the mid-1960s, Oxford, Cambridge, London, and the Scottish universities had been joined by twenty "redbrick" universities in England's major cities, as well as by 158 teacher training colleges and over 600 technical colleges of various kinds. Although the universities remained self-governing, most of the expenses were underwritten by the National Exchequer and four out of every five students received government aid.

In the meantime the population was still slowly growing by some two million persons per decade. The great nineteenth-century emigration had ended by 1931; and although British citizens were still moving to Canada, Australia, New Zealand, and the United States, this emigration was more than balanced in the 1930s and 1940s by Continental refugees and in the 1950s by several hundred thousand West Indians and Pakistanis. Yet the agricultural improvements induced by World War II and postwar policy enabled Britain to produce one half of its own food in the 1960s, whereas three decades earlier it had produced only one third.

At least a partial explanation for the prosperity of the Macmillan era lay in the fact that the terms of trade which had been so oppressive in the 1940s once again favored Britain. The cost of imports fell, and the value of exports rose. British investments abroad grew more quickly than foreign investments in Britain, and by the mid-1960s, Britain was once again a net creditor country. (British investments in American companies, for example, rose from a little over one billion dollars in 1950 to almost two and a half billion dollars in 1961; no other country had so sizable an investment in the United States.)

Possibly the most significant by-product of the new age of prosperity was a gradual mellowing of the class consciousness which once divided England into "two nations" and which even in the 1930s seemed a permanent aspect of the British scene. Blue-collar wages were catching up with white-collar wages; and, more significantly, the relative number of factory workers was steadily declining, and the number of salaried office workers, professionals, and people active in the service trades significantly rising. If the mass of the British population had not yet become as outwardly "middle class" as that of the United States, then all the signs were pointing in that direction.

Critics of the 1950s

The new age of prosperity was accompanied by its critics, just as an earlier Victorian age of prosperity had its critics. There were those who objected that Britain's economic growth, though impressive in comparison with certain earlier periods, was not nearly so rapid as that of many other European countries. It compared unfavorably with the economic miracle of West Germany, for example. England's business managers seemed too bound by custom and too attached to the British tradition of exalting the amateur to attend (or to encourage the creation of) schools of business administration. The trade unions, in turn, seemed too conservative in outlook and still too much haunted by the possibility of unemployment to welcome labor-saving machinery and techniques.

Britain, it was observed with even greater cogency, had not yet managed to combine full employment and economic growth with price stability. Thus while personal income rose 106 percent between 1950 and 1961, retail prices went up 54 percent, and successive Chancellors of the Exchequer seemed destined time and again to chart a "Stop-Go" policy. Thus when bank rates were low, domestic investment was encouraged, but sooner or later imports would rise more quickly than exports and endanger Britain's international balance of payments. A new budget would then impose steeper taxes and higher bank rates which in turn would restrain imports and inflation but at the same time discourage domestic employment and the investments upon which ultimate economic growth depended. In Britain and the prospering countries of Western Europe, as in the poorer nations of Asia and Africa, there was "a revolution of rising expectations" which caused first one group and then another to push for wage increases. Necessarily there was pressure upon the government not to let its employees and old-age pensioners fall behind. As each element of the population successfully agitated for higher wages, the national income rose faster than national productivity, and inflation ensued. In the face of this inflationary spiral, there was pressure to devise a "national incomes policy" which would somehow make the divisions of the national pie at any given time less dependent upon the particular pressure which specific organized groups could exert. In 1962 the Government established the National Economic Development Council—known popularly as "Neddy"—to formulate such a plan. The possibility, however, of a workable national incomes policy in a society antagonistic to authoritarian regulation remained an open question.

Criticism of a different order was voiced by those who echoed the century-old warnings of Thomas Carlyle and Matthew Arnold. They argued that the entire ethos of British society was becoming purely materialistic and that in a society in which only wealth gave satisfaction, no man could ever feel secure in his status or content with his lot. What Britain seemed to require was a fundamental religious revival; but despite the temporary attraction of visiting American evangelists like Billy Graham, postwar Britain underwent no such religious revival or even growth of regular churchgoing as took place in the United States. The Church of England still baptized a majority of Englishmen and perhaps married and buried them, but no more than three million of its members were faithful adherents. The Church still owned vast property, and the activities of the Archbishop of Canterbury continued to receive much publicity — as when in 1960 he held the first meeting with a Roman Catholic Pope since Henry VIII's break with Rome—but the effect of the Church upon the day-to-day lives of its supposed members had long since been subordinated to a variety of secular influences. The nonconformist denominations—now generally known as the "Free Churches"—remained part of the religious scene but (even if the Presbyterian Church of Scotland is included) could count less than three million active members. The Roman Catholic Church was still growing slowly; but it too could claim the allegiance of less than one person in ten. The Jewish community grew to 450,000 and became as a result of immigration and of Nazi extermination the largest Jewish community in any European country outside Russia. Immigration from Pakistan and other countries made Islam the religion of some 200,000 citizens of the United Kingdom.

Critics of Britain's materialism could also point to the rising crime rate. Affluence seemed to encourage juvenile delinquents like the leather-jacketed "Mods" and "Rockers" of the early 1960s, and the number of indictable offenses rose from 500,000 per year in 1947 to 800,000 in 1961. Yet some comfort could be taken from the fact that Britain's total prison population was in 1962 only one third as large as that of the State of California; in a year in which the United States experienced 9,000 murders, Britain counted only 173. The murder rate in Britain had been twice as high a hundred years before and fifty times as high in the fifteenth century.[3]

As recently as 1955, one foreign commentator observed of Britain's writers: "Never has an intellectual class found its

---

[3] Christopher Hibbert, *History of Crime and Punishment* (London, 1963).

society and its culture more to its satisfaction." A year later John Osborne's play "Look Back in Anger" took London by storm, and what one literary critic was to call "the Angry Decade" was well under way. For a significant group of authors, the welfare state was somehow not enough. Playwrights such as Arnold Wesker and novelists like Alan Sillitoe began to rediscover the working class and to take pride in their own proletarian origins.[4] Many intellectuals in the period after Suez became suddenly aware that Britain was still, in fact if not in law, ruled by a privileged elite, now called "the Establishment," an amalgam of "Top People" in government, in industry, in the BBC, in the Church of England, and in the offices of the *Times* of London. Nine tenths of the recruits for Britain's Foreign Office posts still came from a few exclusive fee-paying "public schools"; so did 80 percent of all Conservative M.P.s elected in 1955. A majority of Prime Minister Eden's Cabinet came, indeed, from a single such school, Eton.

Education appeared to symbolize this continued inequality. The Education Act of 1944 had seemed at last to make a reality of the theory of universal free secondary education for British boys and girls. Yet every school child's life was apparently determined by the test he had to take in his twelfth year — the "eleven plus" examination — which destined three in four for the terminal "secondary modern" school while permitting one in four to go on to the academically far more respectable grammar school and possibly to a university. For some British critics the solution lay in the comprehensive American high school, which was then undergoing its own share of criticism (for different reasons) on the other side of the Atlantic.

The old aristocracy had not indeed disappeared, although the domestic servant class was all but gone and although many a peer was now making ends meet by charging tourists half a crown (35 cents) a head to tramp through his ancestral halls. "It was impossible to foresee in the spring of 1944," marveled Evelyn Waugh in 1960, "the present cult of the English country house.... The English aristocracy has maintained its identity to a degree that then seemed impossible." Yet any impression that there was no social mobility in Britain was misleading. More than half of Britain's thousand peerages had been created after 1906; and, measured in terms of the percentage of children of working-class parents who ended up in white-collar jobs (30 percent), there was as much social mobility in post-World War II Britain as in the United States.[5]

---

[4] James Gindin, *Postwar British Fiction* (Berkeley & Los Angeles, 1964).
[5] Seymour Martin Lipset, *Political Man: The Social Basis of Politics* (Garden City, N.Y., 1960).

The hero of Osborne's "Look Back in Anger" was apparently in despair because his generation had been deprived of the opportunity to participate in grand causes, such as the depression era hunger marches or the Spanish Civil War. In the late 1950s, such a cause was found in the Campaign for Nuclear Disarmament, a group headed for several years by an Anglican clergyman, Canon John Collins, and an octogenarian rationalist philosopher, Lord (Bertrand) Russell. Its aim was to "ban the bomb" on a worldwide basis, and, if that were impossible, to have Britain disarm herself unilaterally and to separate from the American bloc and take refuge in strict neutrality between East and West. The annual protest marches to London from Aldermaston, the British Atomic Energy Authority's chief research laboratory, grew year by year; and in 1960 the unilateral disarmament forces succeeded in having the Labour Party's annual conference adopt their position by a narrow majority. Gaitskell, the leader of the party in Parliament, regarded the policy as mistaken and dramatically vowed to "fight and fight and fight again and bring back sanity and honesty and dignity." A year later he succeeded in having the annual conference reverse its policy stand. The unilateral disarmament movement split in the early 1960s between "civil disobedience" extremists and more moderate forces and tended to decline in significance after the signing in 1963 of the international treaty banning nuclear testing in the atmosphere.

The nuclear disarmament movement had been fed by a sometimes overt and sometimes latent spirit of anti-Americanism which during the 1950s had been given added force by the strength of "McCarthyism" in the United States and by the apparent ideological inflexibility of Secretary of State Dulles. Englishmen also tended to deplore examples of American influence ranging from chewing gum and television serials to "rock and roll" music. In the category of popular culture, the British, of course, reciprocated not only with Dame Margot Fonteyn and the Royal Ballet and with British actors (Rex Harrison, Richard Burton, Peter O'Toole, and Peter Sellers all but monopolized the annual American Academy Award given in 1965 for the best actor) but also with the mop-headed Beatles and their musical kindred, whose American tours delighted thousands of screaming American teen-agers if not their parents.

On the diplomatic level, the British Foreign Office generally maintained close relations with the United States. Its diplomats did tend to view the United States as too much given to ideological rigidity—Britain, for example, had "recognized" Communist China as early as 1949—but it was their belief that they could more readily influence American policy as loyal allies than as a neutral third force.

Britain and Europe

A controversy of even greater moment than nuclear disarmament arose in the summer of 1961, when Prime Minister Macmillan announced that Britain was applying for membership in the European Economic Community, the "Common Market" consisting of France, West Germany, Italy, Belgium, the Netherlands, and Luxembourg. Since 1957 the Common Market had been embarking on a program of lowering economic barriers in such a fashion as to create a single economic (and potentially political) unit out of Western Europe. Britain had refused to join in 1957 but had instead set about creating a European Free Trade Association out of Britain, Sweden, Norway, Denmark, Austria, Switzerland, and Portugal – the "Outer Seven" as opposed to the "Inner Six."

The Common Market proved to be politically the more meaningful and economically the more stimulating organization, and by 1961 the Macmillan Government became convinced that it would be preferable for Britain to remain a strong power within this new European community than a weak power outside it. The decision to begin negotiations set off a political furor inside Britain. The Government was criticized for forsaking the Commonwealth, for ignoring the interests of Britain's farmers, and for being willing permanently to subordinate Britain's national sovereignty to the Economic Community's governing council without even first holding a general election. The Government's decision did indeed raise one of the oldest questions in British history: whether Britain's destiny, as in Roman times and in the days of Henry II or Henry V, resided on the European continent, or whether, in the tradition of the Elizabethan seafarers of the sixteenth century it lay, and continued to lie, beyond the seas.

Right-wing Conservatives (like Lord Beaverbrook) joined hands with staunch Labourites (such as Lord Attlee) in opposing Britain's entry into the Common Market; but it seemed likely in 1962 that the long drawn-out negotiations which Edward Heath (1916–   ) was carrying on in Brussels would culminate in Britain's entry. A bracing effect on Britain's economy was expected to follow, as were such logical by-products of unity with Europe as the adoption of a common time zone, the metric system, a decimal coinage system, and the building of a tunnel under the English Channel. Then in January 1963 President DeGaulle vetoed Britain's entry. DeGaulle's own ideal, it was clear, was not a supranational community at all – the Common Market Treaty had been signed before he became President in 1958 – but a strong Continental coalition dominated by France. He was suspicious of the non-European interests of "the Anglo-

Saxons" (the British and the Americans) and of the "special relationship" which British leaders had sometimes claimed with the United States.

DeGaulle's action was part of a wider international pattern which by the early 1960s was dissolving the bipolar power relationship of the Cold War. The immense potential destructive force of the nuclear bomb had paradoxically limited the actual power of both the United States and the Soviet Union. After the confrontation in 1962 between President Kennedy and Premier Khrushchev over the sending of Russian long-range rockets to Cuba had ended with a diplomatic Russian withdrawal, it seemed increasingly clear that a nuclear stalemate might continue for decades. In the process, both of the big postwar power blocs began to disintegrate. In the East, Communist China and the Soviet Union were increasingly at odds and the Soviet satellites of Eastern Europe showed signs of growing national independence. In the West, the North Atlantic Treaty Organization, now that it seemed less vital, was similarly undermined by an obvious French desire to limit direct American influence in Europe. The newly independent nations of Asia and Africa were often happily playing East against West in order to advance their individual interests. In the world of the 1960s, beset by the problems of an ever rising population and an ever growing gap between the wealth of the rich nations and the poverty of the poor, old-style diplomacy came to be of renewed importance. Now that two powers no longer predominated, a host of slightly lesser powers could exercise their influence, and Britain was clearly one of them.

By vetoing Britain's entry into the Common Market, DeGaulle had in his own fashion temporarily resolved a major political controversy within Britain — a controversy which seemed likely to reemerge some time in the future — but only at the cost of damaging the reputation of the Macmillan Government back home. Its position was further undermined in the summer of 1963 by the Profumo Affair, a scandal which involved a Minister of War, a Russian naval attaché, and a variety of "call girls." No actual breach of military security was disclosed but the widespread public shock at the revelation of a Cabinet Minister who in denying the affair had knowingly lied to his Cabinet colleagues in private and to Parliament in public demonstrated anew the high degree of confidence the British citizen had in the rectitude of his public officials. Profumo immediately resigned his office, and in September 1963 so did Prime Minister Macmillan, increasingly plagued as he was by physical and political ailments.

An End and a Beginning

His successor was a surprise: the slightly built and self-effacing Foreign Secretary, the 14th Earl of Home (pronounced Hume), who resigned his peerage to return to the House of Commons as Sir Alec Douglas-Home. A year earlier he could not have done this; but a battle fought by Anthony Wedgwood Benn (1925–   ), a Labour M.P., against being forced to enter the House of Lords (and resign his seat in the House of Commons) upon his father's death in 1960, had led to a new Peerage Act which relieved the members of the upper house of the political disadvantage of their titles. The House of Lords itself had been democratized a few years earlier, when in 1958 the first life peers, two of them women, were admitted to that venerable assembly.

Though the selection of Sir Alec Douglas-Home displeased such veteran party leaders as Iain McLeod, who refused to join his Cabinet, Sir Alec strove with considerable skill to mend party fences and to reduce the underdog status to which public opinion polls and by-election defeats had condemned his party. He put off the general election until the last legal month, October 1964, in the hope of staving off what appeared to be inevitable defeat.

The election was hotly debated. It involved not only Douglas-Home but also Harold Wilson, the man who had been voted Labour Party leader after Hugh Gaitskell's untimely death in January 1963, and Jo Grimond, the leader of a still small but revitalized Liberal Party. The results were very close: Labour, 317; Conservative, 304; Liberal, 9. The total popular vote showed no notable swing to Labour, but disenchanted Conservative voters had switched to the reviving Liberal Party in sufficient numbers to provide the Labour Party with a plurality of the popular vote and a slight overall Parliamentary edge. Despite the narrow margin of victory, the new Prime Minister, a self-confident man of acknowledged brilliance but of little popular magnetism, immediately set out upon a program of positive economic action. The Labour Party's long-range plans were frustrated, however, by a short-range economic crisis, the unusually large gap in the international balance of payments which it had inherited from the outgoing Conservative Government and which could only be countered by a temporary surcharge on all imports, a rise in interest rates, and a reliance upon the aid of the International Monetary Fund to stabilize the pound. The Government demonstrated its working-class sympathies by once again eliminating all charges on National Health Service prescriptions and by dismissing the cook in Number Ten Downing Street (Mrs. Wilson preferred to cook the Prime

Minister's dinners herself); its April 1965 Budget sharply curtailed tax-free business expense accounts and imposed the first capital gains tax in British history. By summer the country's continuing failure to balance her international accounts necessitated the imposition of curbs on new capital investments and tighter consumer credit controls.

In the meantime the Labour Government's narrow parliamentary majority, increasingly dependent upon Liberal support, came under growing attack from a swiftly recovering Conservative opposition which in July replaced the aristocratic Sir Alec Douglas-Home as leader with the aggressive and younger Edward Heath. Heath, the first Conservative leader to be chosen in open ballot by his parliamentary party colleagues (rather than by secret informal consultation within the party's inner circle), resembled Wilson in both background and temperament and promised to keep Britain's political pot bubbling brightly.

In the wake of this most recent economic crisis, as often before, there was much bewailing of Britain's decline. But the Cassandras of doom tended to forget that this one small island, 75th in size and 10th in population among the nations of the world, could still claim the world's largest active merchant fleet and still imported one fifth of the world's exports of food and raw materials and provided one sixth of the world's exports of manufactured goods. Britain was still the banker for the sterling area, the currency in which one third of the world's trade was conducted. While adhering to all manner of old traditions, this small island had spread the English language and English law and parliamentary institutions to all corners of the world (including even the United Nations), and it had maintained for almost three centuries an unrivaled national record of peaceful change without revolution. In the post-World War II world, its people and government had been beset with problems, but by the mid-1960s, they were materially better off than ever before.

In January 1965 the attention of the whole world turned once again to London, as Sir Winston Churchill grudgingly surrendered to death at the age of ninety. Sir Winston's funeral was attended by an ex-President of the United States and the President of France, by the Chancellor of Germany and the Deputy Premier of the Soviet Union, by the reigning monarchs of five European nations, by five Commonwealth Prime Ministers, and by countless dignitaries from every corner of the world. As the world mourned the death of a man acknowledged even by his enemies as one of the giants of our time, Britons recalled the words Tennyson wrote in 1852 on the death of another English titan, the Duke of Wellington:

> Lead out the pageant: sad and slow,
> As fits an universal woe,
> Let the long, long procession go,
> And let the sorrowing crowd about it grow,
> And let the mournful martial music blow;
> The last great Englishman is low.

The Iron Duke did not prove to be "the last great English-man" and Sir Winston Churchill is equally unlikely to hold that distinction for all time. His death, however, does mark the end of an era, for his country is a smaller place without him. The Victorian Britain into which he was born seems far removed from a world threatened by nuclear holocaust in which economically prosperous nations like Britain live side by side with underprivileged states demanding as their birthright the benefits of industrial technology and the miracles of modern science. Churchill the boy born within the ancestral halls of Blenheim Palace, Churchill the soldier who fought to win and hold the outposts of empire in Asia and Africa, and Churchill the statesman who refused to become Prime Minister only to preside over the dissolution of His Majesty's empire—such a Churchill now belongs to history.

But the end of a man and an era does not denote the end of a nation. The history of the England which Churchill preserved and led to victory in World War II has been filled with many brilliant chapters, medieval, Elizabethan, Augustan, Victorian, and Churchillian, and one may feel confident that many more chapters remain to be written.

APPENDIX

> ## Victoria as "Grandmother of Europe"
> *A Simplified Genealogy*

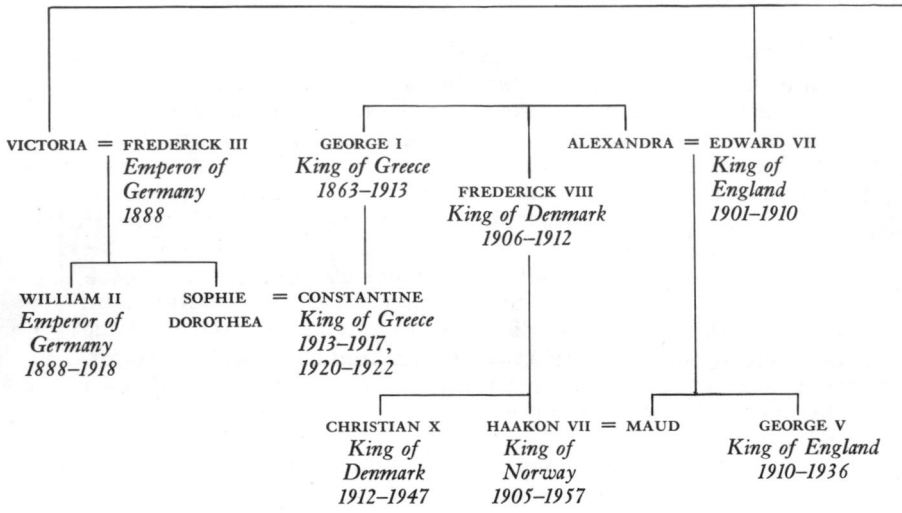

MINISTRIES SINCE 1830

FORMED	PARTY	PRIME MINISTER	CHANCELLOR OF THE EXCHEQUER
Jan 1828	Tory	Duke of Wellington	H. Goulburn
Nov 1830	Whig	Earl Grey	Viscount Althorp
Jul 1834	Whig	Viscount Melbourne	Viscount Althorp
Dec 1834	Tory	Sir Robert Peel	Sir Robert Peel
Apr 1835	Whig	Viscount Melbourne	T. Spring-Rice Sir F. T. Baring (1839)
Sep 1841	Tory	Sir Robert Peel	H. Goulburn
Jul 1846	Whig	Lord John Russell	Sir C. Wood
Feb 1852	Tory	Earl of Derby	Benjamin Disraeli
Dec 1852	Whig—Peelite	Earl of Aberdeen	W. E. Gladstone

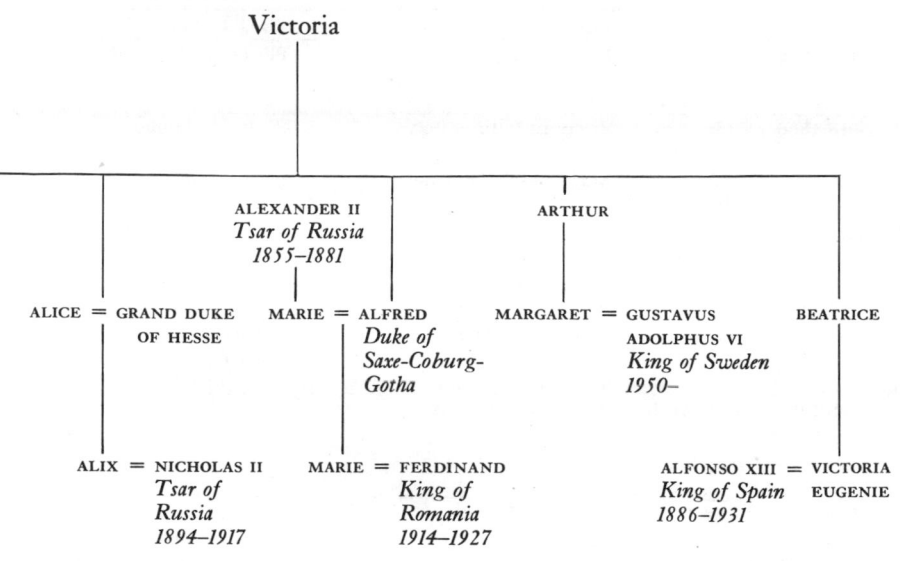

Victoria

	ALEXANDER II *Tsar of Russia 1855–1881*	**ARTHUR**	

| ALICE = GRAND DUKE OF HESSE | MARIE = ALFRED *Duke of Saxe-Coburg-Gotha* | MARGARET = GUSTAVUS ADOLPHUS VI *King of Sweden 1950–* | BEATRICE |

| ALIX = NICHOLAS II *Tsar of Russia 1894–1917* | MARIE = FERDINAND *King of Romania 1914–1927* | ALFONSO XIII = VICTORIA *King of Spain* EUGENIE *1886–1931* |

HOME SECRETARY	FOREIGN SECRETARY	OTHER MINISTERS
Robert Peel	Earl of Dudley Earl of Aberdeen (1828)	
Viscount Melbourne	Viscount Palmerston	Lord Durham (Lord Privy Seal)
Viscount Duncannon	Viscount Palmerston	
H. Goulburn	Duke of Wellington	
Lord John Russell Marquis of Normanby (1839)	Viscount Palmerston	T. B. Macaulay (Secretary at War, 1839)
Sir James Graham	Earl of Aberdeen	W. E. Gladstone (Board of Trade, 1843)
Sir G. Grey	Viscount Palmerston Earl Granville (1851)	
S. H. Walpole	Earl of Malmesbury	
Viscount Palmerston	Lord John Russell Earl of Clarendon (1853)	Sidney Herbert (War)

FORMED	PARTY	PRIME MINISTER	CHANCELLOR OF THE EXCHEQUER
Feb 1855	Whig	Viscount Palmerston	Sir G. C. Lewis
Feb 1858	Tory (Con- servative)	Earl of Derby	Benjamin Disraeli
Jun 1859	Whig (Liberal)	Viscount Palmerston	W. E. Gladstone
Oct 1865	Whig (Liberal)	Earl Russell (Formerly Lord John Russell)	W. E. Gladstone
Jun 1866	Tory (Con- servative)	Earl of Derby	Benjamin Disraeli
Feb 1868	Conservative	Benjamin Disraeli	G. Ward Hunt
Dec 1868	Liberal	W. E. Gladstone	Robert Lowe W. E. Gladstone (1873)
Feb 1874	Conservative	Benjamin Disraeli	Sir Stafford Northcote
Apr 1880	Liberal	W. E. Gladstone	W. E. Gladstone H. C. E. Childers (1882)
Jun 1885	Conservative	Marquis of Salisbury	Sir Michael Hicks-Beach
Feb 1886	Liberal	W. E. Gladstone	Sir William Harcourt
Aug 1886	Conservative	Marquis of Salisbury	Lord Randolph Churchill G. J. Goschen (1887)
Aug 1892	Liberal	W. E. Gladstone	Sir William Harcourt
Mar 1894	Liberal	Earl of Rosebery	Lord Tweedmouth
Jun 1895	Unionist (Con- servative)	Marquis of Salisbury	Sir Michael Hicks-Beach
Jul 1902	Unionist (Con- servative)	A. J. Balfour	C. T. Richie Austen Chamberlain (1903)
Dec 1905	Liberal	Sir Henry Campbell-Bannerman	H. H. Asquith
Apr 1908	Liberal	H. H. Asquith	David Lloyd George
May 1915	Coalition	H. H. Asquith	Reginald McKenna

HOME SECRETARY	FOREIGN SECRETARY	OTHER MINISTERS
Sir G. Grey	Earl of Clarendon	
S. H. Walpole T. H. Sotheron-Estcourt (1859)	Earl of Malmesbury	
Sir G. C. Lewis Sir G. Grey (1861)	Lord John Russell	Sidney Herbert (War)
Sir G. Grey	Earl of Clarendon	
S. H. Walpole Gathorne Hardy (1867)	Lord Stanley	
Gathorne Hardy	Lord Stanley	
H. A. Bruce Robert Lowe (1873)	Earl of Clarendon Earl of Granville (1870)	Edward Cardwell (War) John Bright (Board of Trade)
R. A. Cross	Earl of Derby (Son) (Formerly Lord Stanley) Marquis of Salisbury (1878)	Earl of Carnarvon (Colonial Secy.)
Sir William Harcourt	Earl Granville	Joseph Chamberlain (Board of Trade)
Sir R. A. Cross	Marquis of Salisbury	Lord Randolph Churchill (India)
H. C. E. Childers	Earl of Rosebery	John Morley (Chief Secy. for Ireland)
Henry Matthews	Earl of Iddleseigh (Formerly Sir Stafford Northcote) Marquis of Salisbury (1887)	A. J. Balfour (Chief Secretary for Ireland, 1887)
H. H. Asquith	Earl of Rosebery	
H. H. Asquith	Earl of Kimberley	
Sir Matthew Ridley C. T. Ritchie (1900)	Marquis of Salisbury Marquis of Lansdowne (1900)	Joseph Chamberlain (Colonial Secretary) A. J. Balfour (First Lord of the Treasury)
A. Akers-Douglas	Marquis of Lansdowne	Joseph Chamberlain (Colonial Secretary)
Herbert Gladstone	Sir Edward Grey	David Lloyd George (Board of Trade) John Morley (India) R. B. Haldane (War)
Herbert Gladstone Winston S. Churchill (1910) Reginald McKenna (1911)	Sir Edward Grey	Morley A. Haldane (As Above) Winston S. Churchill (Board of Trade, 1908, Admiralty, 1911) Earl Kitchener (War, 1914)
Sir John Simon	Sir Edward Grey (now Lord Grey)	David Lloyd George (Munitions)

FORMED	PARTY	PRIME MINISTER	CHANCELLOR OF THE EXCHEQUER
Dec 1916	Coalition	David Lloyd George	Andrew Bonar Law Austen Chamberlain (1918) Sir S. H. Horne (1921)
Oct 1922	Conservative	Andrew Bonar Law	Stanley Baldwin
May 1923	Conservative	Stanley Baldwin	Neville Chamberlain
Jan 1924	Labour	Ramsay MacDonald	Philip Snowden
Nov 1924	Conservative	Stanley Baldwin	Winston S. Churchill
Jun 1929	Labour	Ramsay MacDonald	Philip Snowden
Aug 1931	National (Mostly Conserva- tive)	Ramsay MacDonald	Philip Snowden Neville Chamberlain (1931)
Jun 1935	National (Mostly Conserva- tive)	Stanley Baldwin	Neville Chamberlain
May 1937	National (Mostly Conserva- tive)	Neville Chamberlain	Sir John Simon
May 1940	Coalition	Winston S. Churchill	Sir Kingsley Wood Sir John Anderson (1943)
May 1945	Conservative	Winston S. Churchill	Sir John Anderson
Jul 1945	Labour	Clement R. Attlee	Hugh Dalton Sir Stafford Cripps (1947) Hugh Gaitskell (1950)
Oct 1951	Conservative	Winston S. Churchill	Richard A. Butler
Apr 1955	Conservative	Sir Anthony Eden	Harold Macmillan
Jan 1957	Conservative	Harold Macmillan	Peter Thorneycroft D. Heathcote-Amory (1958) Selwyn Lloyd (1960) Reginald Maudling
Oct 1963	Conservative	Sir Alec Douglas-Home (Formerly Lord Home)	Reginald Maudling (1962)
Oct 1964	Labour	Harold Wilson	James Callaghan

HOME SECRETARY	FOREIGN SECRETARY	OTHER MINISTERS
Edward Shortt (1919)	A. J. Balfour Lord Curzon (1919)	Arthur Henderson Winston S. Churchill (Munitions, 1917; War & Air, 1918; Colonies, 1921) Stanley Baldwin (Board of Trade, 1921)
W. C. Bridgeman	Lord Curzon	
W. C. Bridgeman	Lord Curzon	
Arthur Henderson	Ramsay MacDonald	Lord (R. B.) Haldane (Lord Chancellor) Sidney Webb (Board of Trade)
Sir William Joynson-Hicks	Austen Chamberlain	Neville Chamberlain (Health)
J. R. Clynes	Arthur Henderson	
Sir Herbert Samuel Sir John Gilmour (1932)	Lord Reading Sir John Simon (1931)	Stanley Baldwin (Lord President of the Council)
Sir John Simon	Sir Samuel Hoare Anthony Eden (1935)	
Sir Samuel Hoare Sir John Anderson (1939)	Anthony Eden Lord Halifax (1938)	Winston S. Churchill (Admiralty, 1939)
Sir John Anderson Herbert Morrison (1940)	Lord Halifax Anthony Eden (1940)	Clement Attlee (Deputy P.M.) Lord Beaverbrook (Aircraft Production) Ernest Bevin (Labor)
Sir Donald Somervell	Anthony Eden	
Chuter Ede	Ernest Bevin Herbert Morrison (1951)	Sir Stafford Cripps (Bd. of Trade to 1947) Aneurin Bevan (Health) Herbert Morrison (Leader of Commons)
Sir David Maxwell Fyfe	Anthony Eden (Also Deputy P.M.)	
Gwilym Lloyd George	Selwyn Lloyd	Richard A. Butler (Leader of Commons) Marquis of Salisbury (Lord Pres. of Council)
Richard A. Butler Henry Brooke (1962)	Selwyn Lloyd Lord Home (1960)	Duncan Sandys (Defense) Richard A. Butler (Deputy P.M., 1962)
Henry Brooke	Richard A. Butler	Edward Heath (Board of Trade)
Sir Frank Soskice	Sir Patrick Gordon-Walker Michael Stewart (1965)	George Brown (Economic Affairs)

Monarchs Since 1830

WILLIAM IV	1830–1837
VICTORIA	1837–1901
EDWARD VII	1901–1910
GEORGE V	1910–1936
EDWARD VIII	1936
GEORGE VI	1936–1952
ELIZABETH II	1952–

Population in Thousands

	England & Wales	Scotland	Ireland	Total United Kingdom
1831	13,897	2,364	7,767	24,029
1841	15,914	2,620	8,197	26,731
1851	17,928	2,889	6,574	27,391
1861	20,066	3,062	5,799	28,927
1871	22,712	3,360	5,412	31,485
1881	25,974	3,736	5,175	34,885
1891	29,003	4,026	4,705	37,733
1901	32,528	4,472	4,459	41,459
1911	36,070	4,761	4,390	45,222
			Northern Ireland	
1921	37,887	4,882	1,257*	44,026
1931	39,952	4,843	1,280 **	46,075
1941	no census			
1951	43,758	5,096	1,371	50,225
1961	46,072	5,178	1,425	52,676

* 1926 Census   ** 1937 Census

Index

Baptists, 3, 80, 134, 199
Baring, Sir Evelyn (Lord Cromer), 166
Barrie, Sir James, 197, 212
"Battle of Britain" (1940), 315–16, 327
Beaconsfield, Earl of. *See* Disraeli, Benjamin
Beaverbrook, Baron (Sir Max Aitken), 244, 269, 283, 301, 316, 367
Beecham, Sir Thomas, 290
Beerbohm, Max, 85
Belgium: in 19th century, 62–63, 103–4, 141; in World War I, 234–39, 253, 258, 280; in World War II and after, 310–11, 313, 326, 354, 367
Belloc, Hilaire, 197
Bennett, Arnold, 197
Bentham, Jeremy, 48–49
Benthamites. *See* Utilitarians
Berchtesgarten Conference (1938), 304
Berlin: air-lift (1948–49), 346; Conference of (1884–85), 163; Congress and Treaty of (1878), 139, 223
Berlin-to-Bagdad Railway, 232
Bessemer, Henry, 73
Bevan, Aneurin, 331–32, 335, 349–50, 354, 356–57
Beveridge, (Sir) William (later Lord), 207, 318
Beveridge Reports, 318, 334
Bevin, Ernest, 299, 316, 331, 344, 347, 349
Birmingham: in early and mid-19th century, 2, 12, 34, 36, 85; in late 19th century, 131, 132, 186–87; in 20th century, 204–5, 320, 361
Birth control, 144, 180, 268
Birthrate, 19, 75, 180, 268
Bismarck, Prince Otto von, 95, 103, 137, 163, 173, 223–24
Blatchford, Robert, 185–86
Boer War, 174–77, 204. *See also* South Africa
Booth, Charles, 187
Booth, "General" William, 188
Botha, Louis, 203
Bowdler, Dr. Thomas, 79, 87
Bowen, Elizabeth, 340
Boycott, Captain, 151
Bradlaugh, Charles, 144
Bright, John, 39, 113, 115, 190
British Broadcasting Corporation (BBC), 290, 341, 365. *See also* Radio

British Expeditionary Force (B.E.F.), 235, 238, 244
British Medical Association, 335
British North America Act (1867), 109
Brooke, Rupert, 242
Budget: (1842), 40; (1861), 114, 209; (1894), 190–91; (1908), 206; (1909), 208–10; (1925), 276–77; (1931), 283–84; (1934), 291; (1965), 370; "Stop-Go," 363
Bulgaria, 138–39, 159, 346
Burma, 170, 323, 327, 343, 360
Burns, John, 202
Burt, Thomas, M. P., 134
Butler, Richard A., 352, 356
Butt, Isaac, 148

Cabinet, role of: in 19th century, 112–113; in World War I, 245, 262; in "National" Government, 285–86; post-World War II, 331
Cambridge University, 4, 48, 87, 121, 181, 348, 362
Campaign for Nuclear Disarmament (C.N.D.), 366
Campbell-Bannerman, Sir Henry, 177, 200–6
Campbell case, 274
Canada: and Anglo-U.S. relations, 64–65, 102, 148, 226; emigration to, 180; government of, 60, 109, 135, 139, 160, 167; trade with, 242; in World War I, 260, 262; in World War II, 308, 325; since World War II, 347, 356, 360, 362
Canals, 23, 26, 333
Canning, Charles John ("Clemency"), 108
Canning, George, 8–9, 62, 98, 141
Cape Colony. *See* South Africa
Cape-to-Cairo Railway, 171, 174
Cardwell, Edward, 120
Carlton Club, 132
Carlyle, Thomas, 34, 90, 364
Caroline affair, 64–65
Carson, Edward, 220–21, 242
Catholic Emancipation Act (1829), 9, 15, 31. *See also* Roman Catholics
"Caucus," 133
Cavour, Count Camilio, 101

Cecil, Lord Robert, 259
Ceylon, 166–67, 342
Chadwick, Sir Edwin, 28, 49–50, 52–53, 89, 186
Chamberlain, Austen, 276, 280–81
Chamberlain, Joseph: early political career of, 121, 133, 141, 143, 186–87; leaves Liberal Party, 154–56; as Colonial Secretary (1895–1903), 171–75, 191, 198, 224, 262, 286; splits Conservative Party, 200–1, 204–5, 209
Chamberlain, Neville: as Minister of Health, 276, 279; as Chancellor of the Exchequer, 286, 299, 300; as Prime Minister, 303–4, 306–7, 310, 311
"Chanak Affair," 269
Charity Commission, 54
Chartism, 30–37, 69, 113, 214
Chemical dye industry, 128
Chesterton, G. K., 83, 197
China: British influence in, 225; trade with, 104, 126, 225; in 20th century, 296, 360, 366, 368; war with (1839–42), 65–66
"Chinese Slavery," 202–3
"Christian Socialists," 90
Chronicle (London), 97
Church of England: and abdication of Edward VIII, 301; and biblical scholarship, 90–91, 182, and Conservative Party, 134; and contraception, 268; and disestablishment of Church in Ireland, 117, 119, in Wales, 216; and education, 56–57, 121, 136, 199; and the evangelical movement, 47–49; in the 1830's, 3, 9, 14, 32, 54–55; in the mid-20th century, 364–65; and missionary activities, 106, 163–64; and movements to disestablish the Church in England, 133–34, 155; and the Oxford Movement, 55–56, 80; and ritualism, 182
Churchill, Lord Randolph, 143, 152
Churchill, (Sir) Winston Spencer: early career of, 174, 311; as social reformer, 202, 207–8, 215; as First Lord of the Admiralty, 235, 241, 309; as Chancellor of the Exchequer, 276–77, 286; during 1930's, 301, 304–5; as Prime Minister (1940–45), 311–17, 320, 322–23, 325–27, 329–30, 346; as Leader of the Opposition (1945–51), 332, 337, 339, 347, 350; as Prime Minister (1951–55), 350, 352–54, 357; retirement and death of, 356, 370–71
Cinema, 267, 317, 339, 341, 362
Civil service system, in Britain, 77, 120, 181; in India, 77, 168–69
Classical economists, 45–46, 60, 76, 183. See also Laissez-Faire Economics
Clifford, Dr. John, 199
Clynes, J. H., 273–74
Coal industry, 20, 26, 73, 129, 194, 243, 259, 266, 277–79, 291, 317, 331, 337, 361; nationalization of, 333–34, 352
Cobbett, William, 32
Cobden, Richard, 38–39, 114
"Cold War," 327, 329, 337, 345–48, 350, 353–55, 366, 368
Cole, G. D. H., 334
Coleridge, Samuel Taylor, 46
Collins, Michael, 264
Colonial Office, 100, 109, 359
Combination Acts, 8, 45–46
Common Market (European Economic Community), 367–68
Commons, House of: in early and mid-19th century, 3–4, 11–13, 17, 112–13; in late 19th century, 130–32, 141, 144; in 20th century, 202, 213–14, 302, 320, 331, 348
Commonwealth of Nations: beginnings of, 174, 177, 263, 281, 286; in World War II, 306, 308, 322; since World War II, 342–43, 353, 359–61, 370. See also Empire, British
Communist Party (British), 274, 288–89, 307, 349
Congo, 162, 164
Congregationalists, 3, 80
Conrad, Joseph, 197
Conscription, military, 211, 230–31, 253, 316–17
Conservative Party: in 19th century, 122, 132–36, 143, 155, 171, 191, in early 20th century, 198–202, 204, 207, 209–13; in World War I, 236, 243–44; between World Wars, 256–57, 269–70, 272, 274–76, 281–85, 287, 299–300; during and after World War II, 316, 330, 348–50, 354,

204, 262, 297; independence for, 341–43; since independence, 360; investment in, 74, 109, 162; nationalist movement in, 169–70, 204, 262, 297–98, 309, 341; trade with, 60, 103, 126, 136; in World War II, 319, 323. *See also* Pakistan

"Industrial Revolution," 21, 28–29

Invergordon "Mutiny" (1931), 285

Investment, overseas, 74, 162, 172, 193, 327, 362

Iran (Persia), 228, 355

Ireland: civil war (1916–22) in, 263–65; disestablishment of Anglican Church in, 114, 117, 119, 149; emigration from, 26, 42, 150, 180, 262, 345; famine (1845–48) in, 41–43, 75, 148; government of, 6, 9, 117, 121, 156; as independent state (Eire), 344–45, 360; land reform in, 149–50; (treaty with, 1921), 265, 269; Ulster "revolt" in (1914), 220–21

Irish Land Acts: (1870), 149, 190; (1881), 151, 190

Irish Land League, 149–51

Irish Nationalist Party: in early and mid-19th century, 31, 34, 112; Home Rule (1872–1918), 135, 148–60, 202, 210–12, 220–21, 236, 242, 244, 257; Sinn Fein, 257, 263

Iron industry, 20, 26, 29, 73. *See also* Steel industry

Isherwood, Christopher, 289

Israel, 344, 355. *See also* Palestine

Italy: in early 19th century, 36, 103; unification of, 66, 101, 141; in late 19th century, 163, 173, 223; in World War I, 270, 280; before and during World War II, 295, 313, 317, 320, 322, 325, 345; since World War II, 346–47, 354, 367

Jameson Raid, 172–73, 224

Japan: alliance with, 225–26, 270; navy, 230; as trade rival, 242; after World War I, 270; before and during World War II, 295, 300, 322–23, 326–27, 345–46

Jellicoe, Admiral, 248

Jews, 61, 67, 117, 144, 180, 320, 343–44, 364

Johnston, Sir Harry, 170

Jowett, F. W., 273

Joyce, James, 290

Judicature Act (1873), 120

Judicial Committee of the Privy Council, 360

Justices of the peace, 4, 45, 50, 200

Jutland, Battle of (1916), 247–48

Kay, Dr. James, 56–57

Kellogg-Briand Pact (1928), 281, 294

Kennedy, John Fitzgerald, 312, 368

Kennedy, Joseph P., 337

Kenya, 359, 360. *See also* Africa

Keynes, John Maynard (later Lord), 287, 316, 318, 336

Khartoum, 145–46, 174

Khrushchev, Nikita, 353, 368

"Kilmainham Treaty" (1882), 151–52

Kingsley, Charles, 90, 184

Kipling, Rudyard, 164

Kitchener, Sir Herbert (later Lord), 174, 177, 237, 239, 242, 244

Korean War (1951–1953), 348, 350, 354

Kruger, Paul, 172–75, 204, 224

Labor, agricultural, 21, 33, 142, 250, 317

Labor, industrial: conditions: in 19th century, 27–29, 45–46, 75, 130, 187–88, in 20th century, 194–96, 207, 218–19, 245, 286–88, 316–19, 339, 348, 361–62; organization of: in 19th century, 32, 83–84, 136, 182, 188–90, in 20th century, 203, 218–19, 242–43, 246, 265–66, 277–79, 316–17, 331, 339, 363; regulation of: in 19th century, 50–52, 75, 136, 190–91, in 20th century, 205, 207–8, 216, 243, 245, 266, 279, 316–17, 333–34

Labouchere, Henry, M. P., 156

Labour Exchanges, 207

Labour Party: founding of, 190; in Parliament of 1906–14, 202–4, 210–12, 216, 218, 229; in World War I, 236, 244; 1919–39, 256–57, 269–76, 279, 281–85, 287, 289, 299–300, 306–7; in World War II, 311, 316–

17; since World War II, 329–32, 340–41, 347–50, 354–57, 366, 369

Labour Representation Committee, 189, 203, 331

"Laissez Faire" economics, 42–47, 88, 93, 151; decline of, 183–91, 198, 282. *See also* Classical economists

Lansbury, George, 285, 299

Lansdowne, Lord, 212, 227–28

Lausanne, Treaty of (1923), 269

Law, Andrew Bonar, 215, 221, 236, 243–44, 269, 271

Law, Courts of, 120

Law Reform, 8, 49, 85, 120

Lawrence, D. H., 290

Lawrence, Col. T. E., 254

League of Nations, 48, 159, 253, 258–60, 262–63, 269, 274, 280–81, 295–96, 298–99, 343, 359; mandates, 260

Left Book Club, 288

Lend-Lease Act (1941), 319–20, 336

Lenin, Nicolai, 161, 279

Liberal Party: and Ireland, 117, 153–56, 159, 211, 220–21; and social reform, 158, 190–91, 216–17; split over Boer War, 177, 198, 201, split over "Home Rule," 154–56; in the late 19th century, 117, 131–34, 142–43, 151; early 20th century revival of, 198–202; on eve of World War I, 210, 216–17; effects of World War I on, 245; between World Wars, 256–57, 269–70, 272, 274–76, 281–83, 285, 299; during and since World War II, 311, 316, 329–30, 349–50, 369–70. *See also* Whig Party

Liberal Unionist Party, 154–55, 158, 171, 198–99, 202, 213

Licensing Act (1904), 199–200, 202; Bill (1908), 205–6. *See also* Temperance movement

Liverpool, 5, 23, 25, 28, 53, 89, 118, 159, 219, 320

Liverpool, Lord, 8–9

Livingstone, David, 162, 164, 165

Lloyd George, David: and Boer War, 177; as President of the Board of Trade, 202, 205–6; as Chancellor of the Exchequer, 207–12, 215–17, 231, 234; as Minister of Munitions, 244–45; as Prime Minister (wartime), 245, 251–52, 262, 325, (peace-time), 256–59, 264, 268–71, 274, 278–79; and subsequent career, 272, 281, 285, 310

Local government: in 19th century, 4, 15, 181; in early 20th century, 218; after World War I, 279–80

Locarno, Treaty of (1925), 276, 280–81, 302

London: in early and mid-19th century, 2, 12, 14, 26, 34, 36, 75, 79, 85, 89, 116, 122; in late 19th century, 129, 180, 182, 184, 187, 189; in early 20th century, 195–96, 206, 224, 232, 235, 254; in World War II and after, 316, 317, 320, 326, 337, 340, 349, 361

London Conference: (1870), 104; (1913) 234

London School of Economics, 186

London, University of, 48, 198, 362

Lords, House of: as judicial body, 199, 203, 211; power of: pre-1832, 7, 11, post-1832, 15, 17, 50, 112, 114, post-1867, 120, 133, 142–43, 150, 155, 158, 199, in early 20th century, 203, 205, 209–13, post-1911, 213, 216, 268, 271, 320, 348, 369

Lovett, William, 34–35

Lusitania, 247

Lutyens, Sir Edwin, 204

Lyell, Sir Charles, 91

Lytton Report, 296

Macaulay, Thomas Babington, 35, 72, 88, 353

MacDonald, Alexander, M.P., 134, 143

MacDonald, Ramsay: as Labour Party leader, 203, 216, 236, 257; as Prime Minister (Labour), 272–75, 280, 282–84, (National), 284–85, 298–99, 331

McLeod, Iain, 369

Macmillan, Harold, 292, 356–57, 359, 361–62, 367, 368

Mafeking, Siege of (1899), 175

Maine boundary dispute, 64–65

Majuba Hill, Battle of (1881), 145

Malaya, 323, 327, 357, 359–60

Malaysia, 360

Malthus, Thomas, 45, 92

Manchester, 3, 5, 23, 25, 28, 34, 40, 53, 89, 103

Mann, Tom, 218
Manning, Henry Edward, Cardinal, 80, 187, 189
Maori Wars, 109
Marshall, General George, 323
Marshall Plan (European Recovery Program), 339, 347
Marx, Karl, 5, 184, 273
Maugham, Somerset, 197
Maurice, F. D., 90
Mayhew, David, 75
Mazzini, Giuseppe, 101, 169
Medical profession, 215
Mediterranean Agreements (1887), 173, 223
Melbourne, Viscount, 30–31, 41, 55, 60, 64, 83, 118
Menon, V. P., 342
Methodists, 3, 47, 80
"Midlothian Campaign" (1879–80), 140–41, 146
Migration, within United Kingdom, 20, 292
Mill, John Stuart, 49, 81, 88, 105, 113, 118, 181, 191
Milner, Sir Alfred (later Lord), 174–75
Mines Act (1842), 50
Mining industry, 50, 57, 194, 205, 216, 218–19, 243, 256, 266, 277–79, 283, 333–34
Mitchel, John, 42
Mohammed Ali, 63 64
Monarchy, power of: pre-1832, 7, 11; 1832–67, 15–17, 112; 1867–1901, 120, 121–22, 135, 137, 177; in 20th century, 213–14, 301–2, 311, 356
Montagu, Sir Edwin, 262
Montgomery, General Bernard (later Lord), 325
Morality, Victorian, 76–89, 159, 182
Morley, John (later Lord), 177, 190, 204
Morocco, 227–28, 231, 325
Morris, William, 184–85
Morrison, Herbert (later Lord), 299, 316, 331, 357
Mosley, Oswald, 283, 289
Mountbatten, Admiral, 342
Munich Conference (1938), 304–5
Municipal Corporation Act (1835), 15, 35
Murray, Gilbert, 212
Music, 78, 196–97, 290
Music halls, 85, 138, 242, 341

Mussolini, Benito, 298, 300, 302, 313, 326, 329

Napoleon III, Emperor of France, 72, 95–96, 100–1, 103
Nasser, Col. Abdul, 355
National Education League, 121, 133
"National Government," 284–87, 290–93
National Health Service (1948), 216, 334–35, 352, 369
National Insurance Acts: (1911), 215–16, 279; (1946) 334
Nationalization of industry, 194, 256, 332–34, 348–49, 352, 354
Naumann, Friedrich, 225
Naval Agreement with Germany (1935), 298
Navigation Acts, 46
Navy: in 19th century, 61, 64, 67, 103, 137–38, 167, 270; early 20th-century development and relocation, 208, 224, 226, 229–30; rivalry with Germany, 229–30, 232, 235; in World War I, 239–41, 246–48, 253; before and during World War II, 298, 304, 309–10, 313–14, 322–23, 327
Nehru, Jawaharlal, 342–43, 353
Netherlands, 62–63, 126, 311, 313, 354, 367
"Newcastle Programme" (1891), 158
New Delhi, 204
New Lanark, 32
Newman, John Henry, Cardinal, 55–56, 80
News of the World (London), 290
Newspapers: in early and mid-19th century, 5, 12, 26, 131; in late 19th century, 131, 165, 183; in 20th century, 244, 267–68, 278, 290, 301, 317, 339. See also specific titles
"New Towns" Act (1946), 361
New Zealand: emigration to, 60, 135, 180; government of, 60, 109, 160, 167; investment in, 162; in World War I, 241, 260; in World War II, 308; since World War II, 360, 362
Nicholas I, Czar, 64
Nicholas II, Czar, 232, 237
Nigeria, 174, 357–58
Nightingale, Florence, 100

Radicals (19th-century), 7, 11–13, 46, 112, 116, 117, 155. *See also* Utilitarians

Radio, use of, 193, 267, 278, 290. *See also* British Broadcasting Corporation

Railways: beginnings of, 23–27, 73–75, 78; nationalization of, 333, 337, 352–53; overseas, 172; before and during World War I, 219, 242, 245, 256, 266

Reconstruction, Ministry of (1917), 251, 265

Redmond, John, 220–21, 236, 242, 244, 257

Reform Bills: (1832), 8, 11–15, 32, 44, 111, 118, 159; (1867), 115–17, 131–32, 142, 190; (1884), 142–43, 146, 152, 190; (1918), 251; (1928), 280; (1948), 348

Reform Club, 132

Reform Union (1864), 113

Religion: in 1830's, 3, 9, 26–27, 38, 47–48, 54–57; in mid-19th century, 79–81, 90–94, 119; in late 19th century, 121, 144, 181–82, 188; in 20th century, 280, 364. *See also* specific denominations

Religious Census (1851), 80

Reparations Settlement (post-World War I), 259, 270–71, 273, 281–82

Representation of the People Act (1918), 251, (1948), 348

Republican movement, 121, 135

Rhodes, Cecil John, 170–72

Rhodesia, 171, 359

Rhonnda, Viscount, 246

Ricardo, David, 45, 339

Roads: 19th-century turnpikes, 23, 25–26; 20th-century, 361

Roberts, General, 175, 177

Rochdale cooperative, 33

Roman Catholics, 7, 9, 56, 80, 144, 364; in Ireland, 119, 147, 154

Romania, 97, 100, 139, 248, 253, 258, 305, 346

Roosevelt, Franklin D., 286, 319, 322, 329

Rosebery, Earl, 161, 171, 177

Rowntree, B. Seebohm, 187

Royal Air Force, 231, 315–16, 325–26

Rugby, 87

Ruskin, John, 90

Russell, Bertrand (later Earl), 212, 250, 366

Russell, Lord John (later Earl): and Reform Bill of 1832, 11; as Whig Party leader (1841–46), 40; as Prime Minister (1846–52), 42–43, 66, 68; as Foreign Secretary, 96, 101, 102; as Prime Minister (1865–67), 114, 115, 117, 118

Russia: under Communist rule (1918–39), 257–58, 270, 274, 288, 305, 307; and Crimean War (1854–56), 96–100, 104; diplomatic relations with: (1830–54), 58–59, 62–64, 67, 72, 74, 79, (late 19th century), 137–40, 163, 223–25; entente with (1907–14), 228–29, 241; trade with, 74, 125, 274; in World War I, 234–35, 241, 243, 248–51, 253; in World War II, 309–10, 320, 322, 323, 325, 327, 345; since World War II, 331, 341, 345–48, 351, 353–55, 356, 368

Russo-Japanese War (1904–5), 204, 225–26

Rutherford, Lord, 292

Sadler, Michael, 50

Sale of Food and Drugs Act (1875), 136

Salisbury, Marquess of: as Foreign Secretary (1878–80), 139; as Prime Minister (1885–86), 152–53, (1886–92), 155–58, 160, 173, (1895–1902), 161–63, 198, 226; also, 187, 191

Salisbury, Marquess of (grandson), 356

Salt Union, 129

Salvation Army, 188

Samuel, Herbert (later Lord), 277–79, 285

Sardinia, Kingdom of, 66, 98, 101. *See also* Italy

Saturday Review, 88

Schnadhorst, Francis, 133

Scotland: industrialization in, 32; and Liberal Party, 134, 158, 202, 288; political representation of, 6; population growth in, 19–20, 75; public health in, 318; religion in, 364; unemployment in, 291

Sebastopol, 97–100

Secret Ballot Act (1872), 120, 149

Thomas, Gilchrist, 127
Thomas, J. H., M.P., 273, 282
Three Emperors' League, 137, 139, 163
Tilak, B. G., 204
Times (London), 16, 53, 54, 65, 89, 131, 147, 307, 365
Tirpitz, Admiral Alfred von, 229–30
Tocqueville, Alexis de, 2–6, 82
"Tolpuddle Martyrs," 33
"Tory Democracy," 135, 143, 191
Tory Party: (pre-1832), 8–11; (1832–46), 39–40, 42–43, 46, 50, 57; (1846–74), 112, 113, 115–17. *See also* Conservative Party
Toynbee Hall, 188
Trade, overseas: in early and mid-19th century, 5, 37–39, 46, 59, 73–74; during late 19th and early 20th century, 125–26, 193–94, 232; in World War I and after, 242, 259, 277, 282, 286, 291; during World War II and after, 327, 336, 340, 362, 370
Trade Disputes Act (1927), 279
Trades Union Congress (T.U.C.), 83, 188–89, 219, 278, 339
Trade Union Act (1875), 136
Trade unions. *See* Labor, industrial organization
Transportation. *See* Canals, Railways, Roads, Shipping industry
Transvaal. *See* South Africa
Trent Affair, 102
Triple Alliance, 163, 173, 223–24, 228, 232, 248
Triple Alliance (trade union), 219
Triple Entente, 228–29, 232
Trollope, Anthony, 85, 110
Truman, Harry S., 329–30, 336, 347
Truman Doctrine (1947), 347
Turkey: in 19th century, 63, 74, 96–100, 137–39, 159, 224; in early 20th century, 231–32; in World War I and after, 241, 253, 258, 260, 269, 359

Ulster, 154, 220–21, 264, 345
Unemployment: in 19th century, 28, 116, 130, 178; in early 20th century, 207, 219, 245; (1919–39), 266, 277, 282, 287–88, 291, 349; insurance

against, 216, 267, 273, 284–85, 288, 318
Unitarians, 134
United Nations, 323, 327, 329, 344, 348, 356, 360, 370
United States: British attitude toward, 64, 102, 288; comparisons with, 2, 5, 37–38, 72, 73, 124, 127–30, 132–33, 159, 162–63, 194, 214, 225, 230, 282, 286, 292, 332, 362–63, 365; diplomatic relations with: in 19th century, 64–65, 95, 102–3, 170, 173, 224, in 20th century, 226–27, 258–59, 270–71, 281–82, 319–20, 322, 327, 341, since 1945, 345, 347–48, 350–51, 354–56, 367–68; emigration to, 60, 180, 362; influence on Britain, 115, 366; investment in, 64, 74, 162, 362; and Irish nationalism, 148, 150; trade with, 42, 70, 124; and World War I, 242, 244, 248, 251–53, 258–59, 282; and World War II, 319–20, 322–23, 325–27; post-World War II aid from, 336, 337, 339
Utilitarians, 48–50, 55–57, 77, 81

Vaughan Williams, Ralph, 196, 290
Venezuela, 173, 223–24, 226
Vereeniging, Peace of (1902), 177, 204
Versailles, Treaty of (1919), 259, 295, 298, 302–3, 306
Victoria, Queen: accession of, 31, and Disraeli, 137–38; domestic policy, 120; foreign policy, 67, 96, 101, 103, 227; and Gladstone, 121–22, 141–42, 177; as "Grandmother of Europe," 232–33, 237, *see also* Appendix; and the Great Exhibition, 72; and the Jubilees, 173, 224; last years of, 177; and Melbourne, 31, 40; and "morality," 82–83, 85, 182, 193; and Palmerston, 67, 96, 101; and Peel, 31, 40, 82; and women's rights, 181
Vienna, Congress of, 58–59, 62, 95, 139

Wales, and disestablishment of Anglican Church, 216; labor conditions in, 219, 243, 282, 288, 291, 317, 332;

12-302-